Man Bites Talking Dog

By Colin Dunne

Revel Barker
Publishing

First published by Revel Barker Publishing, April 2010
Copyright © Colin Dunne 2010

Other books by Colin Dunne:

The Landsbird
Retrieval
Ratcatcher
Hooligan
Black Ice
Frankenstein (New Library of Horror)
The Werewolf

Beyond the Poseidon, by Paul Gallico (editor)

Cover illustration by David Banks
www.bankscartoons.com

ISBN: 978-0-9563686-2-1

Revel Barker Publishing
66 Florence Road
Brighton BN2 6DJ
England

revelbarker@gmail.com

Dog bites man is not news; but man bites dog, that is news – Alfred Harmsworth, 1st Viscount Northcliffe (1865–1922) British newspaper proprietor.

Of all the money e'er I had,
I spent it in good company.
And all the harm I've ever done,
Alas! it was to none but me.
And all I've done for want of wit
To mem'ry now I can't recall
So fill to me the parting glass
Good night and joy be with you all
        –The Parting Glass (Traditional Irish folk song)

To Sarah, Becky, and Matt
(not forgetting the Wicked Steppie)

Standfirst

Five minutes before 9am one Monday in 1953, wearing my first-ever suit (Montague Burton's; change out of a tenner), I climbed the back stairs to the editorial room of a weekly newspaper in the Yorkshire Dales to start work as the new trainee reporter.

About this time, I'm prepared to bet, a slim Captain Robert Maxwell must have telephoned a wiry-haired Rupert Murdoch and said: 'What do you think, Rupe? Shall we move in on Fleet Street, stick it up the print unions and bring sanity to this lawless industry, while simultaneously improving the profit margins?'

And Murdoch almost certainly replied: 'Good thinking, Bob, but not just yet. Let's allow this skinny little bugger in that cheap suit up in Yorkshire to finish his career in journalism first.'

Laugh if you like, but it must've gone something like that. Because my time in newspapers exactly spanned what we cliché-collectors like to call the Golden Age of Fleet Street, and indeed of journalism generally.

At that time, every city had at least one morning newspaper of great distinction which all sold well into six figures, together with two or even three evening newspapers which often sold more; even small towns could support a local evening.

In London, where they also had three evening papers, the sales of the nationals climbed and climbed, well into the millions, the advertising poured in, and the hacks lived like millionaires, which indeed some of them were.

Almost four decades later, a fat Bob probably rang a balding Rupe and said: 'He's nearly finished now. Let's go get 'em.' And they did.

Look at that great industry now. The once mighty provincial press is reduced to a rabble of freebies and failure; London has one giveaway evening, and the nationals, deserted by readers and advertisers alike, watch their circulations drop like chain-smoking pensioners. The *Daily Express* (once The World's Greatest Newspaper) and the *Daily Mirror* (Largest Daily Sale on Earth) have less than a quarter of the circulation they enjoyed in the Good Old Days. Hacks who can't get a job on *The Big Issue* now sell it.

It didn't last for ever after all. And just because it all happened on my watch, I'm not prepared to take the blame. What I have done, however, is to write it all down, and, because my working life paralleled that of the newspapers, I may – quite unintentionally – have recorded a history of one of the silliest times in one of the silliest industries.

From the end of paper rationing, around 1950, to the birth of Wapping (mid 1980s), it was madcap stuff. Not that there was much off-to-hell wickedness. Naughtiness, deceit, dishonesty, idleness, cheating and vanity, of course. Not to mention daily drunkenness, financial fiddling, professional plagiarism and sporadic outbreaks of violence – mostly, thanks to the booze, ineffectual. Oddly, the epic boozing, in defiance of all the medical evidence, never for a moment slowed down the non-stop adultery. (A piece for *Lancet* there, surely?).

Outrageous? Of course. Disgraceful? Certainly. Although my account of all this can only be the viewpoint of a minor spear carrier – and a small, blunt spear at that – I think I speak for everyone when I say we'd all be ashamed of ourselves if it wasn't for one thing…

Gosh, it was fun and a half.

I like to think you will find all that in these pages. If it seems a little episodic, disjointed or even repetitive, that's because it was. I wrote it originally for a website which defines itself as The Last Pub in Fleet Street.

At *www.gentlemenranters.com*, as you step through the electronic tap-room door you can almost smell the untipped Senior Service, the tang of cheap wine, and the flat pints. Mine host is Revel Barker, an old mate and former colleague and now my publisher, who is himself a survivor of the glory days, and who witnessed it all from first pint to last punch. Each week I'd write a 2,000-word piece about my stumbling journey from Yorkshire weekly to EC4, recording the legends, the myths, the jokes and even the occasional snippet of truth (nobody's perfect) I encountered on the way. They're all in there, the ragtag remains of the most amusing bunch of scoundrels who ever forged a taxi bill.

Was it all true?

Amazingly, it was; a unique combination of soggy sentimentality and hard-eyed cynicism that soaked into every second and every sentence. Fleet Street boys would share the grief of a husband over his runaway wife even as they nicked the photo of her in a bikini off the mantelpiece.

Warm heart, cold blood: it works every time.

We took an absurd pride in our trivial trade. *Daily Mirror* managing editor Tony Delano once said that, like hookers and hit men, most hacks would happily do it all unpaid, which is exactly what we ended up doing on the *Ranters* website. *Sunday Times* writer Nick Tomalin defined the only essential qualifications for journalism as rat-like cunning, a plausible manner and a little literary ability. The last two, we always found, were optional.

Perhaps at this point I should mention that I'm rather under-selling my colleagues. The truth is that the people who made up the hack pack were the best. In the world.

Whenever they were required to perform they had to be quick, clever and get it right.

It was as personally tolerant as it was professionally unforgiving. Eccentricity was cherished. So the *Daily Express* reporter who, after some light social drinking with colleagues, crawled under the desk and bit the news editor savagely on the calf, was fired, of course, but he was reinstated the next day. Humour was never far away. A reporter who was criticised for having insufficient detail in his stories then went on to write: 'Thieves who broke into a Doncaster market stall last night stole an orange. It was a Jaffa.'

Was there really a reporter in Manchester who carried a crutch in the boot of his car because 'no-one can turn away a cripple'? Indeed there was. And did the *Sun*'s two top men, on being presented with airline credit cards, jump on the first flight to California and never come back? They did, they did. Was a reporter on the *Daily Mirror* instructed in an official editor's memo to wear his dentures at all times when on company business? He was, he was.

I always thought it was dealing with the frailties of human nature that made hacks unusually vulnerable to moral lapses. But we all admired the ingenuity of the feature writer who conducted an affair with the editor's secretary during the lunch hour. Until the editor came back early one day to find his desk covered in waving legs. Later he told her: 'Be sure to change that blotter, there's a dear.'

Some of those offices were hot beds of… well, hot beds.

Everything had to be contained in a headline. So the bride who fled a wedding reception in one of Glasgow's less dainty quarters after the guests began killing each other was dubbed The Virgin Bride. Suspended between wedding and honeymoon, clearly she must be a virgin. A reporter traced her to her uncle's house in Nottingham and, with the streets crawling with his rivals, opted to bring in some booze. Friendship blossomed. The next day, when he rang in and the news editor asked him

7

if he'd got the story, he replied: 'How about My Night of Sin with the Virgin Bride?'

There was a silence, then the reply: 'Don't even joke about it.'

What made it all happen was the nature of the hacks themselves. They were people who were temperamentally unsuited to proper jobs. If it hadn't been for newspapers, they would have been taking bets, pulling pints, dealing blackjack, or inviting trusting tourists to find the lady in Oxford Street. All that stopped them from being cowboys was a fear of horses.

In any office, you'd find a fake Old Etonian, East End jokers, Scottish toughies, the odd MPSIA ('Minor Public School, I'm Afraid'), Yorkshire grumpies, office boys on the way up, Oxbridge dilettantes on the way down, an editor's niece, a pissed poet, a failed priest and a couple of borderline psychotics. But drop any of them in the middle of China at lunchtime and they'd be on to copy by 5pm. As reporters, they were brilliant. They had to be.

At the memorial service of that fine writer Jon Akass, they had an Irish folk song with the words: '*And all the harm I've ever done, alas it was to none but me.*'

True, quite true. It's the perfect sentiment for any journalist's exit. But for all the wrecked livers and broken marriages, they did no more damage than fare dodgers and careless parkers, and a great deal less than social workers or government spokesmen.

It wasn't until months later, when I'd written the last piece, that I realised I'd caught a neatly contained slice of time and place. Now that distance has added charm, this could be the start of a book/play/film/musical fest. It was a world that had the shabby glamour of Runyan's Broadway, Isherwood's pre-war Berlin, or Wodehouse's Twenties, and they all responded well to showbiz treatment. Odd to think that our old workplace could become another of those mistily imperishable places, half fact, half fiction, a sort of Brigadoon with liver damage.

If Waterhouse was still with us, he could write it by lunchtime. Personally, I'd get Robert Harris or Lesley Thomas to do the book, David Nobbs the telly version, Michael Frayn for the stage. Then there's only the musical and I expect Herbie Kretzmer is humming the songs already. For the opening number, Herbie, I'd like to suggest: *The Mail's Got the Husband But We've Got the Wife.*

All gone now, of course. I knew it was over when an unsmiling executive showed me over one of the new Canary Wharf offices. It had all the atmosphere of a Swiss euthanasia clinic. What did I think?

'For a start,' I said, 'there should be several empty beer bottles, covered in dust, on the window sill. The floor should be covered in crumpled intros. There should be a reporter snoring on a damaged sofa, the sound of singing from the lift and weeping from the Ladies. At all times there should be a discarded bra in the paper bin.'

He was aghast.

'We've put a stop to all that,' he snapped.

Which is probably why nobody reads newspapers any more.

Part One:
The road to The Street

1

When I think of some of the boyfriends my sister had, I was lucky that the one who came into the Carla Beck Milk Bar that Wednesday morning was Bill. Tall, lanky, fair-haired, he swept in with his white riding mac flapping, newspaper stuck under arm, sat down and started regaling his chums with a story from the magistrates' court.

At the time I was desperately casting about for a job when I would leave school, which was only a few weeks away, and I had yet to see any form of work that looked faintly possible. Yet here was my sister's ex-boyfriend – amicably ex, I was grateful to recall – with a job that fed him wonderful conversation and allowed him to slop around in milk-bars in the middle of the morning.

All in all, I thought I could handle that.

What did he do? He was a reporter on the *Craven Herald and West Yorkshire Pioneer.* Suddenly a world of possibilities opened before me.

Now what's the element of luck involved in that? About 100 per cent, would you say? If it had been her current boy-friend who'd been my role model, I could have spent the rest of my life buttering teacakes. He owned a café opposite the church in the high street.

The more you enquire into how people of my generation came to be in newspapers, the more absurd it gets. I asked two friends: difficult to say which is the least likely. John Dodd got his chance thanks to the headmaster of the Churchers' College in Petersfield, and he wasn't even a pupil there. The editor of the local paper rang the school to ask if they had any promising youngsters who might fancy journalism.

Churchers was really only a grammar school with delusions of Eton, but the headmaster, aghast at the thought, averred (sorry: no other word for it) that no boy of his would ever enter journalism.

To hell with it, the editor thought, and rang the secondary modern school where John was a pupil, and where he'd just written a brilliant essay on how the English cricket team had won back the Ashes. 'I've got just the chap,' said his headmaster. John went on to write for everyone from the *Sun* to the *Spectator* and the *Observer*.

Chris Kenworthy longed to follow his father who was a distinguished journalist on the *Express*... only his father was determined that his son wouldn't be a journalist and packed him off to King's College to become a lawyer. So Chris joined the college newspaper, rapidly became editor, and after a year transferred himself to the *Surrey Comet*. From there to 30 years in Fleet Street and a shelf-full of novels.

You see? Happy accidents combined with a bit of opportunism. As any reporter knows, in today's terms, being lucky is worth about 270 GCSEs.

In my case, there had been earlier indications that I would never be able to do a proper job. I went to a school in Yorkshire where they prepared the scabby-kneed and snot-nosed sons of the Dales for a role in Empire, or the Skipton Building Society, whichever was nearer. It soon became clear to me that any science subjects were way beyond my reach. I realised this on the day that 'Titch' Cooper, the maths master, went mad. On the blackboard, he had written a mixture of letters and numbers. Now even I knew that numbers and letters couldn't be jumbled together like that. The man had clearly lost his mind. Yet he claimed it was something called 'algebra' and was allowed to continue his career.

A year or two later he awarded me seven per cent in the fourth-year exams. 'Seven per cent of what?' I asked, reasonably enough. He took me on one side. He'd had a long and disappointing career in teaching and felt, at this stage, he could do without me. What did I enjoy? The library and the art room, I said. In that case, he suggested, I should spend all my maths lessons there, which I did.

In biology, I never truly got over the only sex lesson we had, in which Mr Swainson, the sports master, glowed with embarrassment as he explained the reproductive system of the frog. I suppose I must have learnt something from it. Throughout my life I have had a weakness for girls with long legs, pop eyes and slightly greasy skin. Particularly if they jump a lot.

No, I never got the hang of the place, although I did get some advice on a possible career from the headmaster, M L Forster, the first time he caned me. I went into his study. He stood there, flexing the cane, pointing to the chair. So I sat down in it – I was always of an optimistic nature. 'I see you are some form of humorist, Dunne,' he said. 'Would you now like to bend over it?'

Now, here comes a confession. The truth is that, even before I saw Bill in the milk-bar, I had dipped my toe into the business of assembling words for pleasure and profit. And – let me get this in before someone denounces me – it is also true that I was the author of a critically-acclaimed work of fiction entitled *Tits*, which caused such a stir in the fifties. I'm sure you remember. No, sorry, I've got that title wrong. It was *TITS!*, because I felt that the lower-case letters may be too subtle for the market I was targeting. The market was Form 4B at the grammar school in Skipton: they were less discerning readers than you might imagine.

I was inspired in this by an author who was enormously popular at the time. Hank Janson. If you were a schoolboy with a fully functioning pulse then the name will touch all sorts of forgotten nerves. He wrote hard-boiled crime novels that relied heavily on half-naked blondes being tied up and thin silk being ripped from heaving breasts. In *Don't Dare Me Sugar, Gun Moll for Hire, Broads Don't Scare, Sweetie Hold Me Tight* and *Skirts Bring Me Sorrow,* the flesh was always creamy, voices were low and husky, nails seared across backs, everybody was panting uncontrollably, and nipples were permanently erect.

When you saw the illustration on the cover, no wonder they were erect. They were the only things holding the frocks up. And, take it from me, the uncontrollable panting was audible half-a-mile away from the teeming pit of tumescence that was Form 4B.

The problem was that we had only one copy of a Janson – hidden behind the radiator in the gym changing room (it's probably still there) – which, with 360 sweaty little paws tearing at it, was pretty ragged.

So I decided to write one myself. I avoided using Hank's vocabulary in the title because we didn't have much by way of Dames, Broads, Cuties, Guns, Death and Sorrow in 4B, although it may well have been quite different in 4C. On the other hand, we were just approaching an age where the bulging high-school gymslips aroused, among other things, our curiosity. So the title selected itself. It also presented no insuperable spelling problems.

Using a Swan fountain pen, it took me some time to write the book, which was why I thought it was called one-handed literature. My idea was to make several copies and sell them at twopence each. With 35 in the class, they could be a Murdochian money-spinner.

Sadly, after filling two pages of my English exercise book, the story came to an end. The trouble was one that has bothered writers over the centuries: lack of research. I knew nothing about the subject, in either lower-case or capitals, singly or in pairs. My steamy narrative ran out of... well, steam. And, with my Swan also rapidly running out of ink, I made only one copy.

When I say it was critically acclaimed, two members of the colts rugby second XV, the boy who came eighth in the junior cross-country, and the deputy paper monitor all expressed their approval. I sold it to Birtwistle for a penny. He ran off a dozen copies and sold them for twopence each. I believe he went on to become a successful literary agent.

Now the thing you should know about hero Hank is that he was an ace reporter on the *Chicago Chronicle*. I can't honestly say that sweeties ever held me tight, as they did him. On the other hand, skirts would certainly bring me sorrow, and many another hack too.

My first burst into actual print came the following year when I developed a passion for New Orleans jazz which has lasted to this very day. In the basement of Woods' record shop in Sheep Street, I spent all my money on Hot Fives, Hot Sevens, Jug Bands, Footwarmers, and Red Hot Peppers. Within three months I could whistle the clarinet break from *High Society* and sing all six verses of *Empty Bed Blues*. The neighbours must have been baffled to hear me lament that mah springs were gittin' rusty, sleepin' single like ah do. It's not often you hear the songs of Louisiana brothels sung in a Wharfedale accent. It must have been about as convincing as *On Ilkla Moor Bah't 'At* sung by Big Bill Broonzy.

Nobody was more surprised than I was when *Jazz Journal* used a piece I wrote. The editor appointed me a reviewer of records and sent me two 78s, *Bury My Body* and *Diggin' My Potatoes*, by Lonnie Donegan. Then the editor said he was going to promote me to review LPs, which was like going from lead to gold. Free records? My friends were practically vomiting with envy. I waited. And waited.

They never came. I never heard from the magazine again. Somebody had told them that their new writer was but lately out of short trousers, shaved once a fortnight, and was still wobbling between treble and tenor. I was rumbled. It was over.

My twin careers in porn and pop were behind me, and I feel better for having got this off my chest.

Where do you go when you're a 16-year-old semi-literate innumerate with a passion for jazz and soft porn? The Skipton Building Society didn't seem an option. Then I saw Bill in the milk-bar that morning and I began to wonder. I said to someone else who was there that it sounded a great job. Whoever it was said it was better than that: Bill had a key to the office.

To anyone who wasn't around in the fifties, this needs some explanation. At that time in Britain's history, as I mentioned earlier, 16-year-old boys were very interested in researching the contents of 16-year-old girls' blouses. Since none of us had a room, a flat or a car, and progress – mostly in Woolworth's doorway – was limited, access to an office was the fifties equivalent of a penthouse flat and an Aston Martin.

I went home and wrote my application letter.

Any hack would tell a similar tale, I'm sure. As a route for finding and pursuing your career, I have to admit it was all a touch random. Yet, years later, I remember seeing a minor public schoolboy, a northern droll, and an East End tough laughing together in the Stab In The Back, the Mirror pub, and I thought any system that can get three blokes like this to top jobs on the *Daily Mirror* has to be all right. But then, you can't imagine Richard Stott, Phil Mellor and Tom Merrin on a media studies course, can you?

What happened to Bill? Oh, Bill Freeman became northern news editor of the *Daily Mirror* (and later editor of the *Sunday Mirror*) in Manchester. He got me a job there too. Say what you like about my sister, she knew how to pick a boyfriend.

*

As soon as we heard the noise all five of us, in the reporters' room at the top of the *Craven Herald and West Yorkshire Pioneer* building, stopped work. Coming up the narrow back stairs was what sounded like a team of overweight removal men shifting several large pianos. There was an awful lot of puffing, cursing and bumping around.

Mr Waterhouse, the deputy editor and most other things too, looked at his watch. Ten to three. In the fifties, in our small market town, closing time was 2.30. Chapel-goer though he was, even Mr Waterhouse knew what that meant. Two-hour drive from Manchester. Two hours in the Hole-in-the-Wall back bar.

'That'll be the national lads,' he said.

A minute later they exploded into our room. The *Express*. The *Mail*. The *Mirror*. All the way from Manchester. My first glimpse of real reporters, right here in the offices of the *Craven Herald (and West Yorkshire Pioneer)*, over a shop in the Yorkshire Dales.

And what a head-spinning shock it was. Pink-faced from climbing the stairs, shiny-eyed from pints, swathed in sufficient sheepskin to stage *One Man and His Dog*, they rode in on a tidal wave of chat and charm. Perched on desk edges, flopped into bentwood chairs, they lit cigarettes, they joked, they swore, they laughed. If you had to find a collective noun, it would be a *swagger* of national lads.

14

For all his multi-tasking as deputy editor, chief sub, chief reporter, music and theatre critic, for all his 110wpm shorthand, Mr Waterhouse, in his darned cardigan, looked faded against their blazing glamour. They were fun on the hoof and, at 16, I knew, there and then, I wanted to be one of them.

What's more, it was my story that had brought them from exotic Manchester (a place I had heard talk of, without being sure where it was). A man who had sent his prize budgerigar to a show in Keighley had complained when British Rail failed to return it on time. So they'd put on a special train from Keighley to Skipton, just to bring his budgie back.

It got only three or four paragraphs in the *Craven Herald*, but the national lads had picked it up. Mr Waterhouse shook his head. He couldn't understand their interest. 'There's no story, lads,' he told them. 'Now if it was 20 or 30 *people* who'd been stranded, then yes – that'd be a story. But a budgie? Never in this world...'

They exchanged glances. With a shake of his head, Mr Waterhouse said they could take me over to the Carla Beck Milk Bar to talk about it.

Until then, I'd been pretty much satisfied with my career in journalism. To understand that you have to know what it was like working for the *Craven Herald* in the fifties. I cannot improve on the succinct definition provided by the editor, John Mitchell, when television's *Man Alive* team made a programme contrasting the *Herald* with a modern weekly in, I think, Bedford. It was not a kind comparison. Bedford had new technology. We had Charlie Ayrton, the printer, holding up a piece of ink-stained string to indicate 'copy required'. They had a photographer in a sports car. Our photographer, Fred, was also a printer who had to change out of his overalls before picking up his plate camera. Bedford had designers sketching out a front page. We had a front page full of adverts.

With a final piece of boot-inserting, they'd put it straight to John Mitchell in his office. Weren't we miles behind the times with ads on the front? John smiled benignly. 'Oh, that's what you're getting at,' he said, completely undisturbed. 'You see, you don't know what it's like round here. In Bedford they've got all their best news on the front page. Round here, we don't have news. Inside the paper, we confirm what people already know – who won the whist drive and the football. The only news is what's on at the Odeon next week, and that's on the front page.'

He was right. But it did mean that life for a young reporter was, well, something short of tearaway. I typed out wedding reports by the score (I still don't know what tulle is). I reported on the North Rib rugby team. I sat through hours of parish councils where they discussed the siting of litter-bins and the problem with dog mess. I scoured the yellowing files for items for *Fifty Years Ago Today*. For civilisation to endure, justice must be seen to be done, so I unfailingly recorded the fines on careless drivers, the most serious crimes we had on our patch.

My week peaked at around 4.30 on a Wednesday afternoon when Miss A. Walmsley (we only ever did initials) came in, hotfoot from the latest meeting of the Ladies' Happy Hour. She would dictate to me. It didn't vary a lot. Mrs L. Tupman (president) always presided. Miss A. Walmsley (secretary) would read the minutes. There would be a speaker (*In The Master's Footsteps: My Trip To Palestine*) or perhaps a competition for putting the most objects in a matchbox. A lovely warm-hearted woman, Miss Walmsley (doesn't look right without the A, does it?) took a motherly interest in me. So too, she assured me, did Mrs L. Tupman (president). 'Mrs Tupman thinks you'll go far.'

Well, it was more encouragement than I ever got off Kelvin MacKenzie.

Among the tea-ringed desks, the ripped lino, the curling files and the jammed Underwoods, the office style was a bit Baden-Powell: hard work, clean living. This came from Mr Waterhouse, who set clear moral standards. In our photographs of prize-winning bulls at agricultural shows, a little discreet trimming ensured they did not look too, well... bullish. That was sex taken care of. Drinking and swearing played no part in our office life, although Mr Waterhouse did offer his own vocabulary of near-swear words when provoked – 'we don't want any bally nonsense.' In real extremes, he could be driven to use the name of a local railway town. 'Well, I'll go to H–... *Hellifield Junction!*' he'd say. Then, triumphant, he'd beam around the room: 'You thought I was going to say it, didn't you?'

This, he told me many times, was the best journalistic training in the world. It was certainly the best training for working on the *Craven Herald*. They took on a trainee about every two years. Not so many before me had been indentured and unpaid, and before that they had themselves even paid for the honour, like articled clerks in a solicitor's office. Now, Mr Waterhouse said with some pride, they had moved with the times, and the junior reporter was paid.

It was true. At 16 I was paid five shillings a week. That's a quarter of a pound which I dare say is around 25 pence. At 17, it doubled to ten shillings a week, 50 new pence. After that, at 18, you moved on to the union rate which was slightly more than £2, and by the time you were 20, the company could no longer bear this staggering financial burden. You were encouraged to seek your fortune in the wider world down south.

Or Leeds, as we called it.

To my young eyes, the reporters from the *Express*, the *Mail* and the *Mirror* shone like diamonds in a dustbin. Bouncing with bonhomie, they whisked me straight past the Carla Beck Milk Bar and on to the Hole-in-the-Wall back bar where, they said, earlier research had suggested a look-in later on. 'This young feller's celebrating his 18th birthday,' said the *Mirror*. 'Give him a glass of mild.'

We sat down. I told them all about my budgie story. The *Express* gave me another half of mild. The *Mail* gave me a Senior Service, untipped. The *Mirror* told me a joke. They were rude, they were risqué, they were reckless – they were everything I'd ever dreamed of. Somewhere at the back of my mind I had always suspected that journalism must have a little more to offer than the Ladies' Happy Hour, and here it was. Perhaps this was the future Mrs Tupman had foreseen for me. If you can forgive the intemperate language, it was bally brilliant.

It was half-a-century ago, but I can still almost remember the three real reporters. The *Mail*, I'm pretty sure, was Don Turner who later opened their Dublin office. The *Mirror* – I think – was Alan Cooper who later ran a freelance agency in Huddersfield. The *Express* man is, I'm afraid, lost.

My budgie story made page leads all round. It confirmed all Mr Waterhouse's worst suspicions. 'These national lads,' he said, 'I don't think they're properly trained these days – they don't know a bally story when they see one.'

I agreed. He was absolutely right. Right that is for the *Craven Herald and West Yorkshire Pioneer*. But I had just had a glimpse of a world beyond.

*

What I'd forgotten, in that moment, many years later, was that there are two Claphams. So when Bill Mitchell told me that the traffic around Clapham was surprisingly heavy, I agreed with him without a second thought. I was just about to say that I used to live near Putney and I'd seen the way they poured round that London ring road, when he added a little bit of extra detail that confused me.

'Especially at milking time.'

Milking time? Now in the Clapham I know, they probably have an injecting time for all the druggies, and a mugging time for all the thugs, and quite possibly a condoming time for those single mums who don't wish to become double mums. But milking time? There are plenty of cows in South London but none, I think, of the Friesian or Hereford breeds.

Of course, the problem was that I'd been so long away from Yorkshire that I'd forgotten there was another Clapham up there. A scattering of grey cottages on the road that leads from the Dales into the Lakes. When the young newly-trained reporters from Skipton set out to scale the peaks of journalism, Bill went 15 miles up the road to the *Dalesman* magazine. Frankly, we thought that was a touch unadventurous.

This was the time – I'm sure you all remember it – when we had to move from our first job out into the wide world. What to do? Follow the sign that said: 'Cash! Exes! Girls! Power! Travel! Fun!' Or follow the one that simply says: 'Nice sensible life'.

Exactly. We all know which one I followed. And half-a-century later I'm beginning to see that I was wrong.

That first move was quite a jump. From the comfortable, familiar life on the local weekly or agency, you peep over the edge and wonder what happens next. It was a coming of age, a rite of passage, one of the most exciting and important decisions of your life; one that decided the direction you set off in, both geographical and professional.

On the *Craven Herald and West Yorkshire Pioneer*, in the news-free market town of Skipton in the Dales, it was a problem that had never concerned me. We didn't do forward-looking.

We stuck to good old monotype, about one century after everybody else embraced linotype. We printed on a press which, we were assured, had been bought from the *Yorkshire Post* in the twenties for £25. If you'd seen it you would've said nearer ten quid.

The editor, Mr Mitchell, sat in his huge office overlooking the High Street, wondering if it was too early to go for morning coffee or afternoon tea with his fellow Round Tablers at the Castle Café.

Mr Waterhouse, the chief reporter, sub-editor and general progress chaser, was waiting for Mr Mitchell to retire so he could become editor. He did... eventually. 'The time has come to give way to a younger man,' he said, at his farewell. Mr Mitchell was a master of irony. By then Mr Waterhouse was over 70.

So they weren't going anywhere, and nor were Charlie and Roy and Jack, the three seniors. But for the trainees, usually two of us, after four years of hammering reports on weddings and the Skipton LMS football team and Hellifield auction mart prices on Underwoods the size and weight of the *Scharnhorst*, the time would come when we would have to show the world what the *Craven Herald and West Yorkshire Pioneer* had taught us. 'You lads are getting the best training in the world,' Mr Waterhouse assured us.

We never questioned that, nor did we question the general understanding that Mr Mitchell was so well-connected in global communications that he only had to pick up the telephone to send his young fledglings off to romantic and lucrative posts. When the time came, of course.

It came, as it happened, as a bit of a shock. The time to move was governed not by our readiness to unleash our skills on the world's press so much as by the financial requirements of the paper. When a young reporter reached the age of 20, his salary rocketed to a wallet-packing wage of almost three quid, grievously worrying for the accountant who knew you could get a trainee from the grammar school for five bob-a-week. That was how Mr Mitchell came to call me down to his office for the fledgling-must-fly speech.

He was a lovely old chap, kindness itself, and he talked about the unconquered lands that lay awaiting my blazing talent and 80wpm shorthand. We didn't have oysters in the Dales, but what he was saying was that the world was my faggot and peas.

Eyes twinkling with pride (completely uninfluenced by the thought of a reduced wages bill), he shook me by the hand and sent me off to... wherever.

Did he have any suggestions where? Not really, he said, looking vague. Why didn't I have a look at the trade magazine? It was only then that I realised I wasn't flying the nest – I'd just been pushed, and my wings weren't working too well.

Long before *Press Gazette*, there was *WPN. World's Press News* was the trade mag with all the jobs at the back. I had often looked at them, savoured the magic of the names of these exotic journals, each one a challenge to the imagination. Was I ready for the *Smethwick Telephone*? Could I face the challenge of the *Falmouth Packet*? Hartlepool, Barrow, Totnes... a romantic roll-call of places that awaited me. Would I need sun cream? Would I be able to eat the food? Would the girls wear grass skirts?

A quick check in the office road-map book was something of a disappointment. The climate was unlikely to be radically different in Smethwick, there was every chance of a cheese sandwich in Totnes, and grass skirts in Hartlepool would be soggy from the sea-fret.

This isn't quite as silly as it sounds. Until then, I had no idea where these places were. They were certainly not within the circulation area of the *Craven Herald*, even though it extended from the steepling towers of Ilkley to the wilder shores of Barnoldswick.

At that time, my travelling was limited. True, I had been to Leeds once some years earlier, but not strictly on a news assignment. It was to see a panto with my mum. And I had climbed to the top of a double decker bus – the only one to reach Skipton – to go to my journalism class in Bradford every Friday, where a reporter from the *Telegraph and Argus* – Stanley Pearson, the smooth swine – had a trilby of his very own.

So, to me, even Hartlepool and Smethwick sounded pretty exciting.

And all my predecessors on the *Craven Herald* had jumped ship without drowning. Bill Freeman had gone off to the *Yorkshire Post* (or *Why Pee* as the old hands called it) and the *Sunday Express*. Ron Evans had prospered on the Bradford *Argus* (and possibly also had his own trilby). Don Mosey was in Manchester on the *Express*, and his brother Derek was editing – editing! – the Morecambe paper. There was a chap called Green who was said to be on the *Daily Telegraph* in London, which seemed rather hard to believe. Oh yes, and Bill Mitchell who was on the *Dalesman* in Clapham.

Off went my letter. Two days later the papers in Hartlepool and Barrow rang offering me jobs immediately. It was almost as if they knew I could do six wedding reports in an hour. Even so, I was suspicious. It wasn't until later that I learnt that, so desperate were the papers in Barrow and Hartlepool, they would offer a job to anyone who could spell the editor's name correctly. Maybe they still do.

But the letter from the *Northern Echo* in Darlington set my imagination ablaze. It had an embossed letter-head. It was a daily paper. A big daily paper. Darlington was almost certainly a sort of Venice of the north. This was all the stuff of dreams, and – this is what the letter said – if my interview was satisfactory, the starting pay would be £7 13s a week. Every week. More than seven and half pounds.

I remembered this 50 years later, when I was talking to Bill Mitchell about our working lives. Bill Freeman had gone on to edit the *Sunday Mirror* in Manchester. Ron Evans ended up running Harlech Television in Cardiff. Don Mosey was a radio star on *Test Match Special*. And Michael Green, I believe, ended up as news editor of the *Telegraph*.

I was saying that, whatever all their successes, Bill Mitchell had got it right. He'd spent his entire life living in the Dales, in a village overlooking the Ribble at Settle, driving a few miles up the road to his office. He was the editor, the chief writer, the heart and soul of the *Dalesman* which is – and here I must be careful not to exaggerate – the finest magazine in the history of publishing. You can't get much better than that, can you? And there I was slogging across London, cursing the traffic.

That was when he said it. That the traffic could get a bit heavy in Clapham around milking-time. By traffic I think he meant cows. And however you put it, it didn't sound quite as bad as Hyde Park Corner.

But that was all much later. Waiting for my interview with the *Northern Echo*, I could hardly sleep for excitement.

20

I mean, £7 13s a week. With an income like that, I could afford to buy Durex. And, in a sophisticated place like Darlington, I may well find out what they were for.

*

2

On those Friday mornings, I fairly skipped down the road past the castle. I couldn't get to the office fast enough. From the shop below, I would snatch up the magazine, clatter up the stairs, and seconds later have it spread out on the desk. All the world lay before me.

Almost literally. In the 1950s, the *World's Press News*, the journalists' own trade mag, was the market place for jobs on newspapers. I was combing its columns because I had become the first victim of the credit crunch. With their £2-plus-a-week investment in me threatening financial meltdown, the *Craven Herald and West Yorkshire Pioneer* had, in the nicest possible way, suggested that the world was now ready for my stupendous talent. In other words, move on.

Do you know, I'm not sure that this wasn't the most exciting time of my life. My first job was down to chance. But this time it was my choice, and there were dozens of jobs out there. And – as I saw it – I was good and ready. Oh those Friday mornings, scouring the ads, the fun and fear of leaving home, of getting away from parents, meeting new people, meeting new girls, finding a flat that would soon be the scene of multiple seductions…

All in all, the second job was the one that packed the most potential.

After more than three years in the front-line of weekly journalism in the Yorkshire Dales, I was battle-hardened and teak-tough. Wedding reports? I'd typed out thousands of 'em. Golden Wedding interviews? Hundreds. (Secret of 50 years of marriage? Give and take.) As for Addingham Parish Council, I liked to think that my rival from the *Ilkley Gazette* turned pale when I walked in with my rapier-sharp HB.

I was worldly too. Women? Don't talk to me about women. I'd removed Maureen Barrett's specs in the back row of the Plaza Cinema to make sure they didn't clash with mine. How many people could say that?

I was almost 20, I shaved most days, I had 80wpm shorthand, and I was all set to conquer the world's press.

Actually, maybe not the whole world. Not just yet. The truth was that although I may have beeen a living legend along the boulevards of Grassington and fashionable soirees of Giggleswick, I had never been south of Leeds. Or, for that matter, north of Sedbergh.

So the ads I saw before me were about as familiar as the mountains of the moon. The *Surrey Comet*? No thank you. That was the south, wasn't it? Where they couldn't play cricket, the beer was rubbish, and they know nowt. The *Bath Chronicle*? I'd need tuition before I could say Barth. Where the hell was Oban? Could Dudley possibly be as exciting as it sounded? I quickly realised that the Hartlepool and Barrow papers seemed to advertise every week which seemed to suggest that those who could read and write were leaving Hartlepool and Barrow in droves.

But what was this... the *Northern Echo* was looking for a young reporter.

Now bear with me here a moment, children. At that time England had a string of mighty regional dailies, publications of great distinction and importance, each one like a regional version of *The Times*. Birmingham and Liverpool and Yorkshire had their *Post*s, there was a *Press* in York and others in Norwich and Bristol, the North-East had its *Journal*, and just south of that, covering Durham and North Yorkshire, was the *Northern Echo*.

At that time – scarcely believable now – it had a six-figure circulation, which rather outgunned the *Craven Herald*'s 12,000. There was only one problem. 'Does anyone know where Darlington is?'

I found it. I even got there for the interview with Mr Reggie Gray, the editor. 'We are following,' he said, indicating a portrait on the wall, 'in the steps of the legendary W T Stead.' The only Stead I knew played scrum-half for Upper Wharfedale, so it seemed unlikely. However, rendered dumb with excitement, I got the job.

Two weeks later, feeling pretty superior, I left my pathetically old-fashioned weekly to join a mighty daily. Where I was going, I rather fancied that Charlie Ayrton the printer didn't clump upstairs with a piece of oily string to indicate how much space was left. Those days were behind me.

Even so, I found my eyes strangely moist as I took one last look around the old *Herald* office with its worn lino, shabby paintwork, typewriters the size and weight of agricultural machinery. I said my farewells to everyone, including Mr Waterhouse, Methodist chief reporter, who had taken personal responsibility for my virginity since I was 16. Every time I found a girl to go out with, he sent me to some distant parish council meeting.

'You don't have a personal life in this job, Colin,' he'd say, with immense satisfaction. It was code for 'you're not getting your leg over in this town'.

As I went down the creaking stairs, his voice followed me with one last piece of advice, a tip that I was to ignore for the next 50 years.

'Don't forget,' he shouted, 'allus check your copy.'

With my one suit (blue hopsack, Burton's, £8) in the back of the 1934 8hp motor (black and rust, Jowett, £15), I pointed north. A suit, a car, and soon I would have my own flat, a magnet for women crazed with desire for nine-stone Dalesmen. Then we'll see about a personal life, Mr Waterhouse.

My knees were knocking through the blue hopsack when I checked in to the reporters' room on that Monday morning. The other new reporter was Ian Irving, the tragic victim of a shoe-store accident. He came from Wimbledon. As I remember it, it was there that the front of a Freeman Hardy and Willis fell on him as he was walking past. One large stone landed on his foot, an injury that prevented him from swimming, sprinting and playing football for England. As he had never done any of these things, the loss was bearable, particularly since he also got enough money to buy a Triumph Mayflower and was exempted from National Service. After that, he always slowed down outside shoe shops in the hope it would happen again. I think that's how it happened. And I also think he ended up at PA, no doubt still limping.

In charge of the room was Dick Tarelli, who later bobbed up on the *Journal* in Newcastle. Andrew Grimes was there, whistling bits of Beethoven, and a chap called Colin Pratt, on his way to the *Express*. The immaculate dandy with the lapelled waistcoat and cuffed jacket reported football beneath the by-line of 'Robjay'. In later life, didn't he become Bob James, a biggish wheel in training journalists?

At first the reporters' routine there was a savage shock. For a start, there were only about ten of us which didn't seem many for a major newspaper. And there was no newsdesk or news editor – Dick Tarelli was chief reporter.

In the morning we'd go to the magistrates' court, write up all the cases, no matter how trivial, for the evening paper, the *Despatch*, and the bigger ones for the *Echo*. We'd take turns to run the hand-written copy back to the office.

They did have copytakers, of course. Two girls with earphones who took it all down in shorthand and then typed it up later.

We worked split shifts, so we had the afternoon off and then came back in the evening to cover for the *Echo*. If anything major blew up – and it really had to be a big one for this – the evening reporter had to go to

Maurice the night editor, explain the urgency of the story and, if Maurice judged it sufficiently important, he would authorise the use of the office Ford Popular.

It was the only paper I ever worked where you had to pin bus tickets to your expenses.

There was even shabby paintwork and more typewriters like Massey Fergusons.

That was how one of the biggest daily papers functioned. When was this? It was 1957, but it could easily have been 1857.

It seemed to be strangely like... well, like the place I'd just left. It wouldn't have surprised me to see Charlie Ayrton walk in with his piece of oily string.

Neither was my personal life developing as I had hoped. Because of a permanently flat battery, I was obliged to park my Jowett on a small hill so that I could start it in the morning. One night, a couple of Borstal escapees stole it.

At the first corner, they desperately spun the steering wheel but the car went straight on. They weren't accustomed to cars, stolen or otherwise, with ten inches of play in the steering.

I did have great hopes that I would be able to make progress with my treatise (*Young Ladies' Frontal Bumps: A Detailed Investigation and Comparative Report*) because I had found a small and cosy flat on the North Road in which to conduct my research. I moved in one dark November evening when the curtains were drawn. When I opened them the next morning I saw that I was about four feet away from a gas holder. Open the window, inhale, and it took you straight back to the trenches on the Somme.

No matter. From the Darlington teacher training college I had recruited Helen, a blonde so tiny that if teaching didn't work out there was always a career option with Bertram Mills. Poor little thing; I almost felt sorry for her smiling innocence as I smuggled her back into Gasworks View.

As I began my research, she gave a sudden and startling yelp. 'Eeeeee,' she went. All women in the north-east open every sentence with a mouse squeak. 'You've got desert disease, you have.'

'Really?' I yawned, with casual sophistication. 'And what might desert disease be, exactly?'

'Eeeeee,' she replied. 'Wandering palms, of course.'

Mr Waterhouse would've been proud of her.

Within six months I'd taken my wandering palms, my old Jowett, my blue suit, and my 80wpm shorthand off to the *Yorkshire Post* where they

24

were paying me a fiver more. 'Nearly £12 a week! Outrageous!' snorted Mr Gray. 'No wonder young men get into trouble.'

If only, I thought. As I left I found myself thinking that perhaps one day a dynamic young editor, ablaze with ambition and new ideas, would come to this old office in Priestgate, Darlington, and turn it into a bright, brilliant modern newspaper.

He'd probably be called something like Harry Evans.

*

3

Do you think it's possible that he's still out there somewhere? Theoretically it is. He'd be only in his mid-seventies by now. Okay, he'd lived quite a life, but look at Dresden: that was bombed a few times and it's still standing.

I'm talking about Peter Brooke. And if you are out there, Pete, I hope you're okay, and if you're having half as much fun as you used to, then you should be ashamed of yourself. Oh yes, any chance of that fifty quid?

Whoops, he's gone again.

It was my great good fortune to find Peter waiting for me in the *Yorkshire Post* Halifax office. This was my third job. In my first, on the *Craven Herald*, I had learnt how to write down names. Names of prize-winners at country shows, names of mourners at funerals, names of bridesmaids at weddings. In my second, the *Northern Echo*, it was pretty much the same, but without the *Herald* sense of urgency.

If it was going to be as dull as this, I might as well have been joined the SBS along with lots of my schoolmates.

By the way, that's not Special Boat Service. That's Skipton Building Society where life expectancy was 128, but seemed much longer.

Don't get me wrong, I was really enjoying journalism. But, as I reached 20, I somehow began to yearn for something a little more lively. Where was the excitement? Where was the danger?

Then I found them. In Halifax. In the late fifties. Honest.

It was a real reporters' town with plenty of real reporters. A whole building full of them at the *Halifax Courier*, a couple of blokes from the *Telegraph and Argus*, the famous freelances Stan Solomon and Max Jessop, with occasional appearances from Alan Cooper. There was even a man from the *News of the World*, Jack Nott, who once filed a story about a fire at a sewage works with the catch-line 'Shit-hot'.

All around were the local papers, *Examiners* from Huddersfield, *Echoes* from Brighouse, *Observers* from Morley.

It was a bustling town, buzzing with enough stories to keep us all busy. The *Yorkshire Post* was a distinguished paper of record. The *Evening Post*, with sales well over 300,000, was a slick, fast operation. Their standards were every bit as high as those of EC4.

And halfway down Horton Street in an upstairs room, the *Yorkshire Post* team. Tom Dickenson, who I think would have described himself as the doyen of Yorkshire journalism. Tweed jacket over woolly waistcoat, smelling strongly of the peppermints that had replaced his cigarettes 20 years earlier. In his desk he kept his very last packet of Senior Service, with 17 fags still there, alongside his emergency mint ration. His shoes always bore a high sheen. On his allotment they said he grew a mean parsnip. Sound, sensible, reliable.

A few weeks after I joined, in breezed Peter Brooke as Tom's deputy. He was certainly reliable in one respect: at any time of night or day, he always knew somewhere you could get a drink. But he'd need to borrow a tenner to buy one. That was Pete – charming, bright, one of life's cavaliers.

Newspapers attract rascals. I always liked them, and I've got the liver and the overdraft to prove it. We all remember them. They'd drift in, knock off a few good stories, quite a lot of booze, several women, and move on, leaving a trail of delight and dismay, about evenly balanced. For fun they were the best. For sobriety, morality and the work ethic, perhaps not.

Peter and Halifax provided me with my first sight of the reckless rackety side of journalism.

On that first Monday, as soon as Tom was distracted, Peter caught my eye. He raised his empty right hand to his mouth, tilted his wrist and nodded his head towards...

Towards the Royal Oak, around the corner. At opening time, he could give Marcel Marceau lessons in mime. And in the Royal Oak, I had my first sight of the cast of extraordinary characters that you find in and around newspapers. This was what I'd been hoping for.

Who was that fair-haired, blue-eyed teenage reporter who was caught doing horizontal jogging with a cinema usherette behind the grandstand of Halifax Town FC? Gilbert Holroyd, the *Courier* sports reporter, congratulated him – 'Tha's the only bugger to score at the Shay in years.' Many years later, I asked Roy Stockdill, a Halifax lad who joined the *News of the World*, if he could remember who it was. His scratched his fair

26

hair and blinked his blue eyes and said he couldn't remember either. Shame, that.

That same sports reporter, our Gilbert, used to write his match reports in a sort of parallel English that hadn't been used since the early days of Dixie Dean – phrases like 'The fearless custodian fisted the leather around the woodwork.' After writing that, Gilbert would no doubt enjoy a transparent utensil filled with a product of fermented malt – hell; he's got me doing it now.

This was a time when young men were returning from National Service. One of them, Ronnie, who worked for the Bradford *Telegraph and Argus*, was so overwhelmed by his spell in Hong Kong with the army that he could talk of nothing else. One lunchtime, after six pints of Webster's, he decided to write a book about it. At opening time that evening he returned with the first paragraph. I can remember every word of it.

> As the ancient Hercules circled, I looked down at the hundreds, nay thousands, of lights that lay below. So this was Hong Kong, which was to be my home. 'It looks brilliant, Ron,' said my pal Ginger, little knowing that whereas I would go mahogany brown in the sun, he would go pink and peel all over...

The second paragraph was never written. It's just as well. It would only have been a disappointment, after that opening.

Tom and Peter did the big stories; I was given the silly-frilly ones. Like the talking dog of Drighlington cross-roads. At the Spotted Cow pub (spotted cow, talking dog – it's not easy, is it?), the landlord teased his jolly little Corgi which would get excited and produce a growl which did sound uncannily like Corky, which happened to be the dog's name (Christ: Corky, Corgi – it's getting worse). Now maybe this wasn't talking in the conversation sense, I mean you wouldn't ask Corky's opinion on Boycott's cover-drive, but you could certainly recognise the one word. I wrote one of those light hanging-indent stories for the *YP*.

This was picked up by Neville Stack, news editor of the *People* in Manchester, who immediately, and quite reasonably, suspected it was a con by the landlord to publicise his boozer. He sent Max Jessop, the freelance, to unmask him. Neville had him marked down for a slot in the paper which was labelled Rat of the Week (oh no, not another animal). And Max asked me to go along with him.

I told him it was true, but Max wouldn't believe me. Corky the Corgi duly growled his name. Was the landlord a ventriloquist? Max asked him to leave the room while I played with the dog. It growled its name again. Max rang the *People* news desk and when Neville answered I got the dog to growl 'Corky' down the phone. 'Who was that?' asked Stack. 'That,' replied Max, 'is the dog that can't talk.'

'Get back to the office,' sighed a rat-less Stack.

Max was a wonderful character who became a brilliant tabloid journalist within about a fortnight of leaving his public school. He'd sung in the choir at Malvern College and occasionally this ruined boy soprano, ruined even more by several pints of Webster's, would attempt *The Ash Grove* and even *The Wings of a Dove*. Max is no longer with us. Perhaps it was this memory that inspired Stan Solomons, his fellow freelance, to take up choral singing some 40 years later. I've got his CD, *Songs My Mother Never Taught Me*. Very tuneful, Stan.

But among these colourful characters, Peter Brooke glowed iridescent. A slim, good-looking man, he carried with him an air of danger. Indeed, he was a martial arts expert and from time to time he'd do a shift as a nightclub bouncer to keep his hand in. One morning in the magistrates' court, a D-and-D with black eye and missing tooth pointed at the press bench and said: 'He's the bugger that done it.'

Peter gave a baffled but forgiving shake of his head.

'I hardly think so,' said the magistrate. 'That's the gentleman from the *Yorkshire Post*.'

Poor old Tom could never get the hang of him. One week, Peter failed to report in on the Monday. Tuesday, the same. Wednesday, at 11.30am he breezed in and took an electric razor out of his desk. 'Bloody hell, Peter,' Tom protested. 'You're not only two days late, but you're two hours late for today.'

'I know, Tom,' he grinned. 'And I haven't had a shave either.'

Women loved him. Whenever he was doing the night calls, he'd quite often take one into the office with him to help. Perhaps he was afraid of the dark. I'd never met women like them. They seemed untroubled by the Desert Disease. One night when I'd been to pick up one of Pete's girl-friends – a teacher with a laugh like a gurgling sewer – she read out an illuminated factory sign. 'Riley's Tool Works,' she said. 'So let's find bloody Riley, eh?' His girl-friends seemed to feel little need for ambiguity.

He also had a wife and two kids he'd brought back from New Zealand and whom he'd deposited in an old terraced house on a steep bank in the nearby village of Triangle. Since we were all either living at home or in lodgings, when the pubs closed we all headed back to Pete's. His tall, long-haired wife didn't seem to mind.

Those who stayed there overnight swore that the house was haunted. The Forgetful Ghost used to appear in the middle of the night, drifting dreamily among the sleeping half-drunk young men sprawled on cushions and sofas.

They called her Forgetful because, inexplicably, she always forgot to put on her nightie.

There was quite a cast of overnight guests – Roy, Max, Andrew Trimbee (later a *Daily Telegraph* sub), Jack Shaw, who went on to Spain via PA. They all stayed there and they all agreed not to mention the visits of the Forgetful Ghost to Pete, who was, we remembered, a martial arts expert. I only had their word for this, of course. By then, I was back in my lodgings swigging Ovaltine.

In the end, his wife and children went back to New Zealand, and when Peter left town, so too did a flame-haired assistant cinema manageress. That wasn't all that was missing. Tom's historic packet of 17 Seniors had also gone. At least he left the peppermints.

Over the years, I heard reports of him from Hereford and Hornsey, and later up on Tyneside. The only time he contacted me directly was when I was in London and he rang me from Paddington. He'd just arrived. He had nowhere to stay, no job, no money, and a young woman.

That's how I lost the fifty quid.

*

4

The first time I went to London, I landed lucky. Maybe I looked as though I'd jumped on the train after finishing the morning's milking. Maybe I gave off a faint whiff of sheep dip. I don't know what it was, but one way or another, the black-cab driver seemed to sense I wasn't a native-born Londoner.

When I asked him to take me to Fleet Street – and what a buzz that gave me – he slid back the glass window and said: 'Do you know, mate, for the life of me I can't fink where that is.'

Imagine – a cab-driver not knowing where Fleet Street was. No use asking me, I burbled. Never been here before. Never been in a black cab before. He was very good about it. Pointed out all the sights as we went along – Buckingham Palace, Harrods, Imperial War Museum, Hampstead Heath, before taking enough money to buy a new cab and saying: 'Good luck wiv the job, mate.'

Job? What job? Well, after just over a year in Halifax, I'd seen this ad for reporters wanted by the Press Association in London. That was really what I wanted to be – a real reporter – and I wasn't sure I was getting there.

29

Much as I loved Halifax, with its rich cast of remarkable characters, some of whom were occasionally sober, I never seemed to get near any big news stories. My older colleagues did those.

Ever since the Talking Dog at the Spotted Cow I'd been marked out for the nuttier end of the trade. All I got were chuckle stories. As soon as I heard either of the news editors – of the *Yorkshire Post* or the evening paper – chuckling down the telephone, I knew they'd found yet another quirky, funny, oddball story for me. 'You're going to love this one,' they'd say. I didn't love it. The way my career was going, I was to journalism what George Formby was to the dramatic arts.

That wasn't the plan. What I wanted to cover was the meaty stuff of which front pages were made: war, famine, pestilence and death – with the odd cricket match on a Saturday – but all I got were the chuckle stories.

So when I saw the ad for the major national news agency which was famous for employing hard, fast, accurate newsmen who never even smiled, let alone chuckled, I saw my chance. PA would make me into a hot-shot reporter.

And there it was. Fleet Street. St Paul's in the middle distance. The black vitrolite, glass and chrome of the *Express*, the architectural stately grey twirls of the *Telegraph*, the steamy windows of Mick's Caff, and there, at No 85, the stately stone monument that was PA. I stepped through the huge double doors into a reception area lofty enough to admit a giraffe. On stilts.

The interview panel of four department heads flicked through my cuttings and asked whether I'd ever done anything by way of serious crime, or strikes, or major industrial accidents. I shrugged. 'Ah,' said one of them, with that smile I'd come to dread. 'You got a good show with the talking dog, I see.'

After the other three had lost interest, a tubby chap on the end asked me a few serious questions. I didn't catch who he was, but he had strapped around his neck and resting on his chest what was either the western world' s first-ever hearing aid or a full-sized encyclopaedia.

Deflated, I headed back to Yorkshire. Three days later, the letter came, headed Press Association and signed by L C J McNae. He would like me to join his Special Reporting Service department. The pay, in 1959, was exactly £20 a week. My brother, a newly qualified solicitor, earned £14 a week in Yorkshire.

I'd hit the big time. And not just ordinary reporting. Oh no. This was Special Reporting. I was leaving behind those provincial news sheets like the *Yorkshire Post*, the *Northern Echo*, and the *Craven Herald*.

The second time I journeyed all the way down to London I had no problems at all. Everyone told me I would. I was going to share a bed-sitter with another Yorkshire lad who'd moved south a year earlier. He lived in Sussex Place, just off Sussex Gardens. Over the telephone he kept reciting directions. Everyone else asked me if I knew where it was. Had I got an *A-Z*?

Honestly. Why all this fuss? I'd been to Keighley. Alone. So London certainly held no terrors for me. With my new life in mind, I'd traded up from my £15 1935 Jowett, to a £20 1936 Morris Ten. At 50mph, it fairly gobbled up the miles on the old A1 (children: there was no M1 in those days), so that after six hours we were chugging into old London town.

Halfway down a narrow, crowded road, the gallant little Morris, like Dick Turpin's horse (only going in the opposite direction), died. From long experience of terminal cars, I swung two wheels up on the pavement and looked about me. This was the Edgware Road. Off to my right was Sussex Gardens. A three-minute walk and there was Sussex Place. So where was the problem?

The next day, I had a look around London. A trained observer, I could see it was bigger than Keighley. Perhaps there was a tiny trace of luck in my breakdown.

I also witnessed the dreadful poverty of the Londoners. In Yorkshire, we kept coal in cellars. Here they called them basements and put people in them. Cruel, but they know no better.

At 9am on Monday, I joined the Special Reporting Service. I bowled in, called out a cheery greeting, only to hear howls of laughter. 'Cor, it's bloody Wilfred Pickles,' they all called out. In the Dales, I had always thought of myself as a smooth talker: here I might as well have had my trousers full of ferrets. What was worse, they seemed unable to grasp that to my ears they all sounded like Eliza Doolittle before she met the professor.

I soon learnt what was so special about SRS. While the main newsroom got on with the national news, the SRS provided a specific service to individual publications. Like the *Yorkshire Post* and the *Northern Echo* and the *Craven Herald*. I had travelled rather a long way to end up where I started.

We did cover the Old Bailey, but only on behalf of the Essex papers. The only pleasure was in writing intros like: 'A Barking man was sent to prison today...' From the Restrictive Practices Court, we provided what was virtually a verbatim service for the *Financial Times*. A few days of that was the equivalent of being run over by a tram. Then there were the lists. Almost daily, it seemed, we took delivery of all those who had passed exams for barristers, solicitors, nurses, accountants, and very possibly trapeze artists: all we had to do was to type them up and distribute them throughout the nation. 'A Cleckheaton law student has passed the final exam…'

There were times when I yearned for an intelligent conversation with a corgi.

It was rather more like the civil service than a news operation. My colleagues, fine fellows all, couldn't wait to get home to Petts Wood or Pratts Bottom to walk the dog or clean the car, which was what passed for fast living in this office. None of them would have been a serious contender for the Fergus Cashin Trophy for Gracious Living.

But there were some good people there. I learnt much from Fred, the Cockney office-messenger who taught me that the human race could be divided into two types. There were the 'rat-faced bleeders', and the 'Jennelmen wiv a capital J'. I'm happy to say I was more Jennelman than bleeder. One of the really good guys was Jim Allen, who had a point to prove. As an evacuee during the war, he'd been taken off to a Somerset school where he announced to the teacher that he wanted to be a journalist. Hearing his strong London accent, the teacher – with some scorn – said it didn't seem very likely. Jim went on to become one of the *Telegraph*'s better reporters, and later news editor. Peter Pryke, I think, also went on to join the *Telegraph*, and Tom Corby became PA's Royal reporter.

You have almost certainly met L C J McNae, or at least seen his name on the cover of *Essential Law for Journalists*. He was a kindly man who struggled with his hearing problem. I can hardly believe that some of his young staff, when bored, would mouth silent conversations which could easily suggest to a deaf man that his hearing aid had failed. Poor old McNae would start banging away at it and fiddling furiously with the knobs.

Then I fell into conversation with one of the subs, a long, languid chap in his mid-twenties called Tony James. Like all the best people, he was a touch unusual. For one thing, he had worked on the *Daily Gleaner* in Jamaica, where he had covered the biggest story since independence – the opening of the first set of traffic lights on the island. He got it on the grounds that he'd seen a traffic light working in London. It was a good story too. Entranced by the novelty of flashing lights, in the first five minutes dozens of cars crashed into each other.

He was also a thinking man. He told me he was wrestling with a particularly difficult metaphysical question: where do women's breasts go when they lie down? I was unable to help him with this although, having seen his statuesque Australian girl-friend, I could tell him where they were when she stood up: three inches below her chin and two-feet out in front.

There were other reasons to admire Tony James. He was an enterprising chap. While working for PA he was also starting up an agency to supply features to provincial papers. To my great delight, he roped me in to help him. Under his direction, and with the aid of the PA's vast library, I put together a few series of features. Occasionally he'd let me take a turn with his regular columns. I was quite good as the Angry Vicar, although less convincing as the agony aunt. Either way, it was more fun than the Restrictive Practices Court.

Later he opened a features agency with Tony Sharrock from Central Press Features. They syndicated columns by people like the Queen's dressmaker Norman Hartnell, and ghosted pieces by sports stars such as Dennis Law, George Best, and Tony Jacklin. By the time they became Features International, they had ten staffers and dozens of freelances. They sold photo features to the Sundays. Tony's personal favourite was I Sold My Body for Lemsip.

In 1970, Tony moved down to Somerset taking some of his columns with him. He still does the occasional true crime, stories about the paranormal, and ghosted doctor columns, and writes enormously amusing books.

He married the Australian girl. But not for long. They had a row in church and on the way to the reception he leapt out of the car saying 20 minutes of marriage was enough for anybody.

For me, the good thing about the PA days was that I was the only single man in the office. Every evening I would pick up the invitations to all the various press receptions. One St Andrews' Night, I had dinner at the Grosvenor House, and went on for the same again at the Savoy. It made a change from bed-sitter baked beans.

I also picked up one or two Saturday shifts on the *Sunday Express* in Manchester, where Bill Freeman and Bernard Shrimsley ran the newsdesk. Then Arthur Brittenden, in the London office, said he'd give me an interview.

Was this going to be it? The real thing? At last? No, actually it wasn't. In a thoughtless moment, I happened to say two words in the wrong place at the wrong time. It's easily done, isn't it? The place was St Alkelda's Church in Giggleswick, in North Ribblesdale, the time was 11.30am, and the words were: 'I do.' On such slight errors are destinies decided.

Now you might think that someone born beside the Tems, which is what they call the beck in Giggleswick, would adapt easily to life beside the slighter wider Thames. Not a bit of it. Mrs Dunne, the first holder of the least coveted title in Britain, hated it. There was nothing for it. I had to leave London.

The Morris Ten, its health restored, pointed north. Hey ho.

*

5

It had taken me seven years to reach Fleet Street. Then I left, and it took me another seven years to get back there. In between, I did a sort of national tour, first the Midlands, then the North East, followed by the North West, and, my goodness, back to London again.

To the analytical mind, this could suggest a man who is incapable of forward-thinking beyond tomorrow lunchtime, and I certainly wouldn't quarrel with that. When it comes to a life-plan, I have always believed that the heads-or-tails system gives you all the precision you need. It saves all that painful thinking.

So when it became clear that the newly-appointed Mrs Dunne the First wasn't going to stay in London, I went straight back to the Friday morning flick... through the pages of *World's Press News* whose jobs page was a place of dreams. I loved doing this: every ad was a fresh place and a fresh start. I remember being tempted by a job in Oban on the grounds that Somerset had a good cricket team: someone pointed out it wasn't in Somerset. A district man in Diss sounded good until I realised it's so far east you'd need to speak Dutch. And Dudley? Did ever a place-name hold such promise?

But Leamington Spa was right bang in the middle and, what's more, I'd never been there. Two good reasons to chase up the ad for a chief reporter on the *Courier*.

When I look back on it, it does seem that the decision-making process was... well, a little lacking in detail. Tell me, dear reader, when you were making your way in life, did you follow a carefully researched route to the top? Or did you go just because it sounded like fun? I'd really like to know how others made their moves.

Now John C Algar knew exactly what he was doing. He was a sub on the *Yorkshire Post* who decided that he wasn't going to reach the top in daily journalism. He was right. He didn't have the showbiz-style flair, the outrageous personality, the indomitable drive, or the will to sacrifice his domestic life and liver to get to the top. He was too bright for that. He was an excellent journalist; he was steady, reliable and intelligent. So he very sensibly opted to be a big fish in a small pool and traded down to weekly newspapers.

In fact, I can think of only one mistake that Jack Algar made in his career. I'll come to that later.

By the time I joined him in Leamington he was producing a sophisticated paper with the highest standards in design and content – he won awards for it later – with a staff of a dozen or so journalists who were a match for anyone, anywhere. Jack Algar could certainly pick 'em.

My first day in the office – like all proper weeklies, it was above a shop in the main street – was also first day for a 16-year-old from the grammar school. In his flannels and sports jacket, Pete Fairley was a tubby little chap who walked like a penguin. Shy? Address one word to him and his face lit up like a traffic-light on Stop. His first job was to write a few pars on a health committee report on the reasons for lost dentures. He spotted that one unfortunate tooth-loser had sneezed his out of the car window.

'If you live in the Tachbrook Road,' he wrote, 'beware of flying snappers...'

It wasn't a bad start for a schoolboy. But Pete always had the magic light touch.

For me there was the great pleasure of seeing him grow through the colourful stages of late adolescence. There was the folk-singing phase when he and his pals – guitar-owners but, inexplicably, not guitar-players – would sing about shoals of herring with all the salty, sea-going authenticity that you find only in grammar school boys 100 miles from the coast. Next, the Oscar Wilde phase. For this he had a plum-coloured velvet jacket, a cigarette holder, and lots of witty things which never quite got said. Then there was the Marxist in denims which was a bit tedious. But he was a lovely chap.

Most mornings, Pete's first job was to go round to a flat in Rugby Road and throw stones at the window. Waking up Mike Stares, our ace reporter, was too much for a mere alarm clock. Mike was one of those wonderful reporters who regarded stories in much the same way as a Jack Russell with a rat: he'd never give up until he'd got it in his jaws.

The office smoothie was Tim Hurst, a lanky young man who had that indestructible charm and self-confidence that you get only from a first-class public school. When it came to reporting, Tim kept his nose well clear of the grindstone. He didn't do solid plod: what Tim did was brilliant moments, and they were always worth waiting for.

We also had a bright young trainee who'd had to drop out of university because of a fertility problem: his girlfriend got pregnant. Unlike most graduates, he was delighted to have the job and damned good at it.

Cheery and beery as you would expect of a landlord's son, Roger Draper wasn't the sports editor for nothing. When our scratch cricket team played a smart town side, big Roger wandered out in jeans, ragged sweater and one pad, and hit 50 in 30 minutes. He was in charge of office fun. Our slender girl reporter Hilary, who at a union meeting once shrieked: 'I'm getting the minimum!' was forever known as Thin Min.

Was Denis Morgan, Roger's trainee, known as Nod because he was a Mod? I'm not sure now. But in the early sixties, when Mod was in vogue, with his little pork pie hat and shortie coat, he was always up to the minute. Sometimes literally. One Friday, the shirt he'd bought at 4.55pm for a party that night, went out of fashion 15 minutes later. 'I'd've looked a right berk if I hadn't found out in time,' he said.

Now he was an interesting young man. Polio had left him with only one working arm, but his five good fingers could type faster than anyone I ever saw. It also made him unswervingly determined. When someone bet him he couldn't drink ten pints of beer, he did it – by making himself sick after each one.

The team Jack Algar pulled together produced some pretty good papers. Goodness knows, I had little enough to do with it. I enjoyed every minute of it, even though it taught me that I had no gift for leadership. The truth was that I wasn't fit to be in charge of a budgerigar let alone a room full of talented youngsters like these. As a boy on holiday, I had always been the one who stood on the edge, watching. I hadn't changed. I was still the outsider. I always was. At least I learnt that in Leamington.

Because he was totally focused on the paper, Jack Algar would have nothing to do with freelancing. His predecessor, Bob Knight, still a distinguished figure around the town, had been linage king, but he surrendered his title with retirement. Inevitably it came my way.

We had so many good stories that the national boys in Birmingham used to ring me on a Thursday so they could plan their visit the next day. I knew that Ray Hill (*Mirror*), Jack Hill (*Express*) and Keith Colling (*Mail*) would never jump the gun, until one day they did. The story, I think, was a woman councillor who'd got into trouble by posing naughtily in a bubble bath – 'Double trouble for Mrs Bubble' seems to ring a bell. I tipped them off just before Thursday lunch, and, to my great surprise and annoyance, the whole Birmingham pack was in town by mid-afternoon. Trevor, a freelance stand-in, simply said he didn't give a damn about me or the *Courier* and he was going to do the story that day. Rather shamefacedly, the rest of them followed. Fortunately, Jack Algar was his usual understanding self when he found our exclusive plastered all over the nationals the next day.

I had to wait 15 years, when the *Mirror* sent me on a PR stunt story to New York with the suggestion that I could do it or ignore it. The PR man in charge was the admirable Trevor. I was his only chance of national coverage. He paled when he saw me. 'Wasn't there a little misunderstanding when we last met, Colin?' he said feebly. 'No,' I replied, 'I understood it perfectly.'

I did do the story in the end, and it got a page lead. But I let him sweat for four days first.

In Leamington, I learnt again that hacks are rarely boring, and neither are their private lives. Long before the bunny-boiler, we had a bunny-drowner. A *Birmingham Post* district man – called Bill, I think – was a keen breeder of prize-winning rabbits who was having domestic problems. He came home late one night to find his wife had drowned his star rabbit and left it on the draining board.

And we had a West Country boy who tried to pick up every woman he met, even on the telephone. 'You sound noice,' he said, to one anonymous female. 'Oi'll bet you're one of them little blondes? No? Well you must be a lovely little redhead then? Wrong? In that case you've got to be a gorgeous little blackhead...' That was the one that got away.

On the town's tiny daily paper, the *Leamington Morning News*, there was a tall, skinny, pale young man who seemed too nervous to be a good reporter. But he became one of the *Sunday Times'* most celebrated investigative reporters... unless there are two Paul Eddys, that is.

What happened to them all? Mike Stares went on to work on the *Yorkshire Evening Post* with... Revel Barker. Then he started his highly successful freelance business in the Cotswolds. Before Leamington, Jack Algar had edited a weekly in Pudsey where he hired (writing for three-halfpence a line)... a kid still at school called Revel Barker: I told you he'd made one mistake. Later Jack Algar crowned a distinguished career by becoming editor-in-chief for the group. Tim Hurst, of course, prospered as a TV journalist. The unstoppable Dennis Morgan went to Canada and ended up on the *Toronto Star*. When Roger Draper, who became sports editor of the *Coventry Evening Telegraph*, died, the obits described him as a sports legend. Pete Fairley, the most talented of them all, followed me to Tyneside; sadly he had to hide his shyness in a bottle, and it did for him.

Years later, in the Stab, I mentioned that I'd worked in Leamington and knew Bob Knight. The man next to me burst into tears. It was John Knight. He was Bob's son.

And me? I did enjoy myself there. It was a great paper, smashing set of people, a good job. But to go on doing it for the next 40 years? Whatever that takes, I didn't have it. So, one Friday morning, I was looking down the jobs' column again…

*

6

Okay, I know I'm not unique. Bolder spirits than I must have experienced the same moment of shock when they first encountered the culture and customs of that odd corner of England, tucked away between the Yorkshire pudding and the haggis. Even so, it set me back, I can tell you.

Tyneside. First day. Visiting a council flat in Byker, which – I learnt later – is the heart of *Howway* country. Knock on door. Opened by chap wearing fashion statement of the time: shirt, collar-stud, but no collar. Big welcoming smile. No problem here. Opens mouth… what the hell was that?

It was a sound like a lorry loaded with pans crashing off a cliff, together with a few screeches from handbrake turns. It's him. He's talking. *'Way-man-han-dan-moon-doon-hyeer-canny-wheesh-divvant-workid-like…'*

Right behind me, Ivor Shale, the photographer, smiles. 'Have ye not heard Geordie before, Colin lad?' And Ivor, a perfectly normal human being until now, begins talking back to him in the smashed-pans language.

For many journalists of my era, Geordie-land was an essential stop on the way to Fleet Street. Half finishing-school and half borstal, this was the place where they knocked the last ounce of crap out of you, and quite possibly one or two teeth. There was a time in Fleet Street when, if you had stood up in any pub from the Stab to the Harrow and sung:

'Whisht lad, ha'ad yer gobs…'

At least half the drinkers would have responded:

'Ah'll tell ye aall an aawful story…'

They're probably all in retirement homes now, dribbling away as they sing snatches from *The Lambton Worm* and *Cushie Butterfield*.

I'd come upon Tyneside later than most. Via the *Craven Herald*, *Northern Echo*, and *Yorkshire Post*, I'd got to PA in Fleet Street, which wasn't quite what I'd imagined, then worked back through a weekly in Leamington, which didn't seem to take, and to the *Evening Chron* in Newcastle upon Tyne.

Why? Well, since the fast traffic of news reporting seemed to have swept past me, I thought perhaps I'd be happier in the gentler pastures of features. In Darlington, I'd always been singled out for advertising features (probably because I was the only one who didn't protest). And at PA, Tony James had roped me in to write features for his embryonic agency.

So when I found myself in Peter Stephens' office in the new *Chronicle* building in the Bigg Market, I was simultaneously tempted and daunted when he pointed at a page layout out on his desk and said 'Do you think you could fill that?' He was indicating about half-an-acre on the leader page, a space that would account for the entire output of the *Mirror* features department for a month.

Under the house name of Eldon, it had previously been written by an elderly gent who wrote charmingly about the visitors to his garden bird-table. What sort of column did the editor want?

Peter shrugged. 'Bright, busy, lively,' he said.

Like? He shrugged. He didn't know. I didn't know. But what I could see was that it would need one main feature a day, plus bits and pieces. Six days a week, that was more than 300 pieces a year. One every day, two on Fridays, copy before lunch please.

It was madness. So of course I said yes.

It launched me on the liveliest three years of my life. Three years of running everywhere, snatching ideas out of thin air, typing in my sleep, I lost a stone in weight (quite a lot when it's one-tenth of the total), and on a daily basis I experienced editorial despair. Each morning as I drove in, I'd be trying to think of something to write. When someone said the station clock had stopped, I rushed out to do a piece on the accuracy of Newcastle's public clocks: you can't get much more desperate than that.

'What is it to be today then?' asked Ian Jack, the deputy editor, with two hours to go.

'No idea,' I said. 'Any suggestions?'

He moved quickly for a big man.

The news room was run by John Brownlee, ex-naval petty officer, a mighty figure and a great news man. On one occasion he suggested a possible piece. 'Great,' I said. 'And what shall I do for the rest of the week?' He wasn't going to fall for that. 'I have every confidence in you,' he said, moving swiftly on.

Indeed on the day my daughter was born there was four foot of snow where I lived overlooking the Tyne valley. I rang John to say I couldn't get in as I was digging the midwife out of a snowdrift. 'I've no staff,' he said. 'Phone your copy in.'

The headline was The Blizzard and the Baby.

Somehow it always got done. As somebody said, it was mostly crap, but it was high-speed crap, and the spelling wasn't bad. It also taught me that you can write about nothing if nothing is all you've got.

It was my good fortune there to share an office with the man who introduced gamesmanship to journalism, the great Charles Fiske. To share an office with Charlie was to see a master craftsman at work. Small, with a bushy moustache, immaculate in his dark suit and Royal Artillery tie, he took on the system and beat it on a daily basis. He possessed invincible self-confidence. His job was to come in early and write the leader. This he interpreted as a senior executive position, and no-one quite had the nerve to contradict him.

He would assert his status by getting people to do things for him. Young reporters would find themselves running errands for him. 'Pop and get me a sandwich, there's a good chap,' he would say, and off they'd go.

When they opened an executive dining-room, Charles was the first in. 'Not bad,' he said, as he returned to his desk, 'but I've told the editor they'll have to improve the service.' No-one was quite sure whether he should have been in there or not.

His day's work over by mid-morning, he would spend the four hours that straddled lunch checking on the social side of commercial life on Tyneside. Not a bottle was opened twixt Tay and Tees that Charlie Fiske failed to hear the cork pop.

Every so often, an editor would try to rein him in. When Peter Stephens told him that once he'd done the leader he could lend a hand on the subs' desk, Charles put his own spin on it. He pulled up a chair beside the chief sub. 'Peter thinks standards have been slipping and he wants me to sort it out,' he said. He chucked copy and headlines back to subs telling them to try harder until he had to be withdrawn to prevent his own public lynching. 'Soon licked them into shape,' he said, as he came back to his own desk.

Only once did he try to recruit me to his personal staff of attendants. He handed me a plastic coffee cup and suggested I should water his indoor plants. I handed it back to him and said no. He looked astonished. 'But you have the pleasure of them,' he said. 'I hate plants,' I said. 'I hope they all die.'

He looked at me intently, and then a slow smile spread up his face. We were playing the same game.

He beat me in the end, of course. When I handed in my notice, Charles came back from the editor's office. 'Peter wants me to take over the column, Colin,' he said. 'Don't take it personally but he thinks it really needs a massive improvement.'

There were some great people in that office. Joe, the little Irish reporter who didn't like to be tied too tightly to the office, had his response prepared whenever John Brownlee pulled him up. The news desk was always desperate for overnights, news-feature pieces for the early pages. So whenever Brownlee called him over, Joe would whisper furtively: 'Will this help, John?' and slip out of his pocket a couple of overnights.

Bren Halligan, a *Journal* writer, was second or third generation Irish, but rapidly reverting. On the strength of my Irish father, he dragged me off to Clancy Brothers concerts to listen to those interminable come-all-yous songs (they start: 'Come all yous gallant Irish lads...'). In the end he went to work for the *Daily Mail* in Dublin, and ended up editing the *Limerick Leader*. You can't get much more Irish than that.

Tyneside exercised a powerful pull over those born there and over the casual visitors who still return regularly. Peter Fairley followed me up there from Leamington and stayed. He loved the place. Gordon Chester left to work for the *Birmingham Despatch* until it closed in 1963 ('not entirely my fault' he always claimed), when he set up a freelance agency in Worcester with Bill Newman and Vic Chappell. When they went off to Fleet Street Gordon, who could easily have done the same, came back to Tyneside.

While in the Midlands, he formed a close working relationship with Sally Moore. This was the Sally Moore of the long black hair, the almond eyes and the wiggle, who later worked in *Mirror* features. Perhaps Gordon thought he had experienced the best that life had to offer, and went home. Who could blame him?

The happy result was that he was there to help me with my research into liver damage in the Printers' Pie, the Post Office Buffet, and the Farmers' Club which I seem to remember was above a pork shop.

Probably the best writer on the Newcastle papers was Eric Forster, a man with a golden touch. He went to Canada where he quickly established a high reputation, but he made the fatal mistake of coming back for a holiday and popping into his old local in Stanley. He never went back to Canada. The lure of Geordieland was just too strong.

I would probably have been there still, if I hadn't bumped into Neville Stack on my one-and-only freebie.

Talking of which, the admirable Charles Fiske died on a freebie. We all agreed it was what he would've wanted.

Like many who left, I still carry a bit of Tyneside around with me. If provoked, and fed lots of Newcie Brown, I can still sing: *'theor was spice staalls 'n' monkey shows and aald wives sellin' ciders, 'n' a chep wiv a ha'penny roondiboot shootin' no me lads for riders.'*

*

Is there a pattern emerging here? No, I thought not. I'd become a victim to the Friday Flick, that is flicking through the jobs pages. 'Ooo, Basingstoke sounds nice...' and off we go. Not exactly scientific, was it? But I don't think I was alone: most of the hacks I knew approached their careers as they did their love lives: if you fancy it, have a go.

Look at the people in Thomson House on Tyneside with me at the end of the sixties. Talk about infinite variety – we'd got everything there. I mean, how did someone like Norman Baitey get to be an editor? Because there were no vacancies for guards at Auschwitz?

No, that's dreadful, and I withdraw it immediately. Mind you, he was a bit tasty. When he was editing the *Sunday Sun* he asked me if I would like to do shifts. Desperate though I was for money, I made some excuse. I knew it would only end with blood on the floor, and I didn't have any to spare. The man was notorious for his bullying rages. If he'd been in the boat, Capt Bligh would've jumped over the side.

Two years I spent hiding from him – under the desk kneehole, locked door in the gents. In the end, I was the only person who'd have a drink with him. What we wordsmiths call ironic. More, later.

As for the rest of them, you could divide them into the rapidly-flowering youngsters who'd soon be on their way to southern riches, and the blown roses who were headed for the compost heap. Why did the former never look at the latter and see their future? But we never do, do we?

Peter Stephens was not, I suspect, a Friday Flicker. His career looked carefully mapped out. From being a sub on the *Mirror* in Manchester, he stepped back into provincial papers to get his editorship (on the *Evening Chronicle*) and then moved up into Fleet Street. Clever chap.

I always thought there was an underground tunnel from Thomson House to the *Sun*. After Stephens, Tom Petrie, John Kay and Ian Hepburn followed the same route, and that lot would be in anybody's first team. Baitey went, too.

The delightful Maureen Knight reversed the process. An *Express* writer, she'd retreated from London after splitting with her husband, the *Mirror* sub Peter Rawlings, to take a job with *The Journal* where she produced wonderfully witty copy. She had a beautiful French au-pair who formed a European partnership with a Thomson House journo also called Peter. But which Peter? Answers on a postcard please. Later, Maureen went back to the *Express* in London, and her husband died a sudden and tragic death. I remember Maureen coming to the *Mirror* office to get the news from George Jenkins.

There were one or two sad sights around the Bigg Market office. There was an oldish Scots reporter with sandy hair, a droopy moustache to match, and pale blue eyes behind large specs. Jimmy Dollan was a quiet, kindly chap, but I noted he was always treated with great respect by John Brownlee: a sure indication of quality. Once, when told he had to cut his exes, he gave a sigh and murmured: 'I used to charge more than that for tram fares.' It was true. For years he was the *News Chronicle* man in the North East and after that worked for the *Sunday Express*.

Hack Town on Tyneside was a bit like Heathrow on a bank holiday, jostling crowds of journalists, some going a long way, some going nowhere, and many just going for a pint. Roy Smith arrived there as an investigative reporter and instantly fitted in. In the pub, he would quietly hover on the fringe with his half of Scotch (the beer), occasionally popping out to make a call or nip back to the office. What we didn't realise was that he was in three different rounds in three different pubs.

Yet he was a fine operator. When our motoring columnist, Gordon Chester, was unable to write his column after over-filling his tank with Exhibition Ale, Roy calmly sat down and trotted it out off the top of his head.

He was under some pressure at the time. He was keen to return to the Farmers' Club and Gordon was the man with the wallet. Even so, it wasn't bad for a man who didn't have a car and couldn't drive anyway. When he left, in his desk they found enough empties to recreate the Crystal Palace. Well, we all like to leave something to be remembered by.

Gordon formed a business partnership with Jack Amos, the man who reported on the working men's clubs, and a famous gambler who preferred to borrow money for his riskier speculations. The two of them hit upon a human weakness in young men... they always want to pretend they are bedding three women at night, one over breakfast, and a couple more at lunchtime. Young, stupid, and oversexed, they can never admit they aren't getting any. So Amos and Chester bulk-bought French letters and sold them to the young fantasists in large numbers. I hope their mums never found them: 25 packets of three could take a bit of explaining.

How on earth did Peter Hinchliffe wash up there? As Yorkshire as a clog-iron, he'd been chief re-write man and feature writer for the *Indianapolis Times*. When The Beatles performed at the State Fair in 1965, the fair's general manager rang Peter: 'Come along to my office, Limey.' He showed him a cheque for $110,000. 'This is what your countrymen are taking out of this town today.' Peter folded it and put it in his top pocket, but he never made the door. When he came back to England, he took his American wife Joyce into The Chancery pub in Wakefield with his old mate Derek Hudson, the *Yorkshire Post* reporter. Hudson handed her a pint and said: 'Get that down thee, lass.' She also considered the offer of the free tripe-in-vinegar from a bowl on the bar.

Not only did she not throw up, but she didn't go back on the next plane either.

He worked his way back to Huddersfield eventually, via Nairobi where he news-edited the *Daily Nation* and also filed to *The Guardian*. When he arrived at Kenyatta International Airport, the first thing he saw in the bookshop were remaindered copies of *The Covered Garden* by Ken Lemmon. Ken was the news editor of the *Yorkshire Evening Post* in Leeds.

Sometimes I could persuade Hunchloaf (as he liked to be called) to write my Eldon column for me. He had a lovely light touch. Among a party of graduate trainees was a tall, pale, rather wilting young man who hesitantly asked if I would overlook his impudence in asking if he could possibly attempt to write one, not that it would be any good... And so on. He wasn't exactly bursting with arrogance. But when he delivered the piece, it was perfect for length and style, and went straight in.

It was no surprise to me when Neville Hodgkinson became a distinguished medical correspondent for the *Sunday Times*. And loaned his name to Liz, author of *Ladies of The Street*, one of the *GentlemenRanters* books, and an inexhaustible freelance, and son Tom who owns and edits *The Idler* magazine and has a column in the *Telegraph*. And have we mentioned other son Will who's a pop journalist for almost everyone?

Makes you sick, doesn't it? One family filling up all those acres of newsprint. What is the Monopolies Commission doing about it, that's what I want to know.

Talk about all sorts and conditions of men – there was certainly one of everything in Thomson House. We had some rather lordly graduate trainees, and also the occasional office-boy who was upgraded. But the trainees weren't all graduates. After a few pints one evening one of the university lads confessed to me that he'd failed his degree (in those days, failure was a possibility). No-one had asked to see his bit of paper, so he just carried on. I still see his name around.

For a piece in the column, one of the promoted office-boys, the wonderfully enthusiastic Ernie, offered to demonstrate his mastery of the then new martial art karate. It all had to be done correctly. On the roof of the building, he set up a short block of wood between two bricks. Such was the power of karate that he could split this block with his bare hand. Dressed in the full pyjama outfit, he rushed at it, spun around, leapt in the air, and as his hand came down he uttered a spine-chilling shriek.

...Of, as it happened, pain. His hand was wrecked. The block of wood was unmarked.

It made a good piece. Once his hand recovered, Ernie, I believe, went off into local radio.

Because I wasn't doing news, I hardly knew the national reporters on Tyneside. But, like the Thomson House team, they too divided into the ones who were determined to stay in the north (Crickmer, Blenkinsop, Amory) and those who drifted south (Gay, Cable, Tyler, Barker).

And including the fierce Norman Baitey. While it was quite easy to cow the young innocents in Newcastle, he didn't have quite such an easy ride with the gnarled cynics of the *Sun*. It wasn't long before all the journos said if Baitey set foot on the editorial floor, they'd go to the pub. He was moved to another Murdoch paper in San Antone where the good ol' Texas boys had Norm for what they almost certainly call brunch.

He was a broken man when he came back. The only good thing that happened to him was that he married Annie Buchanan, who was a first-class journalist, a delightful woman, and a fully-qualified adopter of lame dogs. Norman was not only lame, he was legless.

On their rare visits to Fleet Street, she would call up all his old friends, but all of them would unfortunately be too busy to join him for a drink. So then she'd call me, and since she was an old friend, I'd go.

It was an odd scene. The lovely Annie and myself smiling and nodding in front of this pea-stick of a figure, smart suit hanging off his scarecrow frame, bolt upright, staring eyes, as he explained what he would use as the splash and what should be on the spread.

There's a lesson there somewhere. Wish I knew what it was...

That was Tyneside. I thought I was going to be a Crickmer and spend the rest of my life there. As it was, I ended up in London. Oh God, does that make me a Baitey?

*

You may be surprised to hear this (unless you've been paying attention from the start), but I came into journalism because I wanted to make a difference.

I wanted to join the staff of that distinguished journal, the *Craven Herald and West Yorkshire Pioneer*, in the Dales, so that I could say goodbye forever to school, homework and exams. That would be a definite improvement.

Next, and possibly more positively I wanted to hang around outside Staniforth's Celebrated Pork Pie Shop with my spiral-bound reporter's notebook, looking cool, just as the sixth-form girls came home from the

45

Skipton high school. This could, I hoped, lead to liaisons that would bring into play...

The office-key. A job on the *Craven Herald* came with a key – theoretically for late-night work – which I felt would enable me to pursue my research on an exciting project which concerned most 16-year-old boys at that time: how to disconnect a hook-and-eye fastening with one hand, blind, and behind the back of the wearer.

These days it's probably included in Citizenship classes for eight-year-olds.

Make a difference? Well, it certainly would've made a hell of a difference to my life. You've spotted the flaws in this, of course. The only difference I wished to make was more personal than global. Well, it's true. The only poverty I wished to make into history was my own.

But – I hope you're listening here – I did do one good deed. Just the one. And that was by accident, of course.

I was still in my early twenties and it was a good time to be on the *Evening Chronicle* in its new office in the Bigg Market. Even by newspaper standards, the *Chron* was staffed with an extraordinary assortment of characters, many of whom you would find only in a locked ward.

There was one reporter who was so keen that he ran everywhere: ran into the office, ran out on the job, ran back with his copy. He was terrific. Eventually he ran down to the *Sun* in London where he ended up running the news desk. Does anyone see Tom Petrie these days?

Any Fleet Street paper would have welcomed Gordon Chester, one of the few men to make grumpiness charming, but he chose to stay close to home where he discovered the secret to eternal joy: he married the barmaid. There was Doris Frankish, the feature writer, who said she was suing the golf club for restitution of conjugal rights, and Anthea Linacre who possessed the only two weapons a girl needs in this world – an influential dad and skirts so short as to be bordering on indecent, but thoroughly enjoyable, exposure. It caused such excitement that a senior, and highly susceptible, executive had to be sent to the Cardiff paper to cool down.

And who was that funny old guy at the bottom of the subs' table? A shabby, baggy figure, with NHS pebble-specs barely visible through an explosion of greying hair, bushy eyebrows and overgrown moustache, so he looked like a Morris Minor bursting through a hedge.

Grubby duffel coat, down-at-heel shoes, he cut a sorry sight, and surely he was too old still to be working. The story was that he'd lived abroad and had no pension rights, which was why the poor old guy was holding financial page proofs about an inch from his nose as he tried to read them.

He had a name like something out of a child's nursery rhyme.

Bunting. That's it... Basil Bunting.

And it was that name that saved him from a long sentence of slavery to the chinagraph pencil, and I claim a tiny hand in it too. Me and Allen Ginsberg.

Allen Ginsberg, the American beat poet, arrived in London. At that time he was quite a celebrity, and the cameras were there to greet him at Heathrow. What was he doing in Britain? He'd come to see the greatest living poet in the world. And who would that be? Basil Bunting.

This created some anxiety among the officer class of the *Chronicle*. Was it even remotely possible that this American chap could possibly be referring to the scruffy old sod on the subs' desk? Surely not? The next morning, the editor, Peter Stephens (later of the *Sun* and *NoW*) called me in. Would I like to make a few discreet enquiries? Because if it turned out that the scruffy old sod in question was rather more than he appeared, then this had the potential for embarrassment, an emotion newspaper executives were anxious to avoid.

I sat Basil down with a pint in the Printers' Pie and dragged the story out of him. And what a story it was.

A doctor's son from Scotswood-on-Tyne, he was educated at Quaker public schools. In the First World War, he was arrested and imprisoned in Wormwood Scrubs as a conscientious objector. Being a conshie wasn't much safer than being a soldier at that time, and several died in jail. But Basil believed the war was morally wrong and he stuck it out.

After the war, his life as a poet began. In Paris in the twenties, he worked with Ford Madox Ford on a literary magazine. The early thirties found him in Rapollo in Italy sharing a house with two other poets. Their names? W B Yeats and Ezra Pound.

He was something of an adventurer too. By the late thirties he was skippering a boat on the Chesapeake in America when rumblings of a new European war began. He wrote a letter offering his services to British Intelligence in the Middle East. His letter was written in classical Persian. He got the job and rose to squadron leader.

After the war, he served as a diplomat in the British embassy in Teheran and also as correspondent for *The Times*. In the early fifties, after a takeover by fundamental Muslims (which may ring a bell with today's journalists), Bunting was expelled and wound up back on his native Tyneside, living in a semi in Wylam, with a young family, no job, and decidedly dodgy eyesight. Hence the job on the *Chronicle*. This was not, he told me, the most fascinating or even the most rewarding time in his extraordinary career.

That's as I remember it now, and I'm pretty sure that's how he told it. Certainly I shot off to the library and it all checked out. It was all there. Ezra Pound, I saw, had described him as 'that stubborn Quaker poet'.

Determinedly single-minded, he was concerned that worries over money would distract him from the only work that mattered – his poetry. He had the acclaim of the literary world, including praise from Britain's foremost critic, Cyril Connolly, who described his poem *Briggflatts* as 'the finest long poem to have been published in England since T S Eliot's *Four Quartets*.' When I congratulated Basil, he shrugged. There were, he said, only two people in the world whose opinion he valued, and neither of them was Cyril Connolly.

This is the point where I have to confess that the story got away from me. My level of poetry appreciation peaks with dancing daffodils or highwaymen riding over purple moors. Basil, who also had a profound understanding of music, attempted to explain to me that the rhythmic patterns of his work were very similar to those of the composer Scarlatti. He even wrote out the musical notation to demonstrate this. That's what he said it was. It could have been Gregg shorthand for all I knew.

Without being in any way arrogant, he was completely confident about the quality of his work, which left him with one major concern... being well-published. By that he simply meant that he wanted to see his verse in strong, well-made books so that his poetry would be there for generations to come. That was the most important thing – that his lifetime's work should not vanish.

That was the story. Although we hadn't noticed, we had on the staff one of the truly great modernist poets of the 20th century.

I bore this story back to Peter Stephens with some glee. It wasn't often I had the chance to cause a flutter of nerves in the higher echelons of newspaper management, although I did get better at it in later years. For one thing, what if somebody else did the story first? So the *Chronicle* ran it, along with the Scarlatti-style music. *The Guardian* immediately followed it up, then the rest, with the final accolade of a full-blown piece in the *Sunday Times* colour magazine. Television wasn't far behind.

What on earth were they going to do with him? This was the next problem as poor old Basil still came trudging into the office in his old duffel-coat, blinking through his wire-rimmed specs. The senior management couldn't work out how to respond to having a cultural celebrity on the staff. Meeting him in the corridor, one of the directors stopped and gave him a nervous smile. 'How's the poetry going, Mr Bunting?' he squawked fatuously. Bunting mooched past, head down.

You could see their predicament. What do you do when you discover you are employing one of the world's most gifted poets in a job that could be mastered by a well-trained Labrador in half a day? Should they ask him to write a verse for the company Christmas card? It's a wonder they didn't.

So the management were as relieved as anyone when he was awarded an Arts Council bursary, fellowships at the universities of Durham and Newcastle, and suddenly there was a vacancy on the subs' table ('Only famous poets need apply').

Although my part in this was purely fortuitous, he was kind enough to write me a letter of thanks, and we did meet for the occasional pint.

There was an amusing post-script to this. Delighted to find the real thing in their midst, a group of local poets adopted Basil. One of them asked for his opinion on a poem so long that it filled an entire exercise book. Basil said he'd be pleased to do so. However, it would have to be a completely candid opinion because no serious poet would want meaningless flattery. That's right, replied the young poet, with a flicker of uncertainty.

A fortnight later, Basil returned the exercise book. In it, he had underlined half-a-line, five words. 'If you work on that,' he said, 'you might have something.' The young poet was most upset. 'That took me nearly a fortnight to write,' he said.

'My last poem took me eight years,' said Basil.

The lesson for the young journalist here is quite clear. If you concentrate all your energies on selfish pleasures, brassiere fastenings, greed and fun, you may still – by accident – do some good. Worrying, isn't it? I can tell you, I was always most careful to ensure that it never happened again.

*

Harold Wilson got me my first job on a national. If he'd taken his holidays in Bermuda or the Bahamas, I doubt if I would ever have made it. As it was, he holidayed on the Isles of Scilly, and that got me home and dry.

Yes, I see what you mean: it does call for some explanation. Right...

As a reward for my efforts to fill pages of the *Evening Chronicle*, I was offered a freebie with a pack of Manchester journalists to go to Luxembourg. There were eight of us, mostly honest Other Ranks, apart from two of our party. One was Neville Stack, news editor of the old broadsheet *Sun* in Manchester, a job that probably rates as an NCO. Later, I seem to remember, he edited the *Leicester Mercury* before flying off to all manner of journalistic triumphs from Trinidad to Singapore. He's retired in Ireland these days.

But that's by the way. All you need to know here is that Neville is one of the funniest men in our trade which, in this barmy business, is saying quite a lot. When Murdoch made Ken Tucker the head of his Manchester operation on the new *Sun*, it was Neville who came up with the theory that Murdoch was sitting banging the desk and shouting: 'I want my tucker...' and someone misunderstood him. Well, that's the story.

The officer-class chap in our party was the northern editor of the *Daily Mail*.

Sorry, I mean Northern Editor. He was very much a capital letters sort of chap. Northern Editors are, as you will know, far superior to mere Fleet Street editors. In London, where the streets are thronged with the rich and powerful, a mere editor rates somewhere between a street entertainer and a mini-cab driver. In Manchester, the complete VIP list at that time was Bernard Manning and George Best, so the Northern Editors were pretty swanky people.

Naturally, during our trip, this particular NE found it necessary to remind us of this.

Occasionally, this edge between editors boiled over. Wasn't there a *Mirror* story about one afternoon in the Douglas when Derek Dodd introduced Bob Edwards as 'my London editor'? If that really happened, it would be no surprise that Bob responded: 'No, Derek, I am the editor. You are the northern editor. For the time being.' I don't think Bob saw northern editor as being a capital letter sort of job.

But our man in Luxembourg did, and his moment came on the last night. We were escorted around Luxembourg by that country's Director of Tourism. Silkily suited, crisply collared and cuffed, with his silver-winged hair and elegant charm, he looked a million dollars, which, at a guess, was his weekly salary.

So it came as something of a shock when the NE, our self-appointed leader, suggested we should give him a present. It would've been like slipping the Queen a quid and saying: 'Get yerself a pint on me.' Or that's what I said, and I'm afraid the NE took some offence. 'Not just any present,' he said testily. 'I was thinking of giving him my cuff-links.'

Hysteria welled up. Stack's face, I noticed, was distorted with suppressed laughter. Although I came to know him much better later, this was the first time that I realised he was a man with a wonderful sense of humour (which means, of course, the same as mine). We avoided each other's eyes. It was our only hope.

The Editor, becoming more pompous by the minute, insisted that the Director of Tourism would be delighted to receive these cuff-links once he realised that 'they had been purchased in the Scilly Isles where Harold Wilson, the British Prime Minister, took his holidays' and where, indeed, the Editor took his.

Clearly I was dreaming all this, or thought I was until, at the farewell dinner that evening, he rose to his feet and solemnly stripped himself of his cuff links. He handed them over after a speech in which the PM and the Scillies featured strongly. The Director of Tourism looked down at them in his hand without a trace of comprehension.

When you get a Spike Milligan moment like that, there's no saying how it's going to affect you. In my case, quite simply, I lost my mind.

Lurching to my feet, exploding with laughter, I began to unfasten my tie which, I said, I would like to present to the Director because it had been bought in a Yorkshire market town where Fred Trueman had once had lunch. Or possibly a sandwich. I think Neville offered a lighter that had ignited the cigarettes of several fully qualified sub-editors, or something like that, and in no time we were all at it. Ties, shoes, combs... they were all being offered.

Without a doubt, it was totally disgraceful and later, when the laughter had subsided, Stack and I sat down over a beer. He said he thought I'd enjoy working for a national. I went down to Manchester for interviews and, thanks to a general leg-up from Neville, was given a job on the *Mirror*... by Bill Freeman.

Now it's just as well that I didn't want to write City analysis for the financial pages because, for one reason or another, I was only ever offered really silly stories to do. Or perhaps I should say Scilly stories. Certainly if Harold Wilson had holidayed in Rhyl it would never happened.

Destiny? You can't fight it.

*

Round about the middle of the sixties, did anyone see me pushing a bed to the tip on Tyneside? Was I observed selling off pairs of pyjamas (one owner, hardly used)? I ask because at that time I must have entirely given up sleep. It's the only explanation I can think of for the insane burst of activity that came over me.

Firstly there was my daily column for the *Evening Chronicle*: six times a week, to be delivered by 2pm. That left the afternoons free so I began writing op-ed pieces for the *Journal*, allegedly humorous, perhaps twice a week. After that, there was always the danger that I might find myself with time on my hands, so I would then whizz off a quick four-minute talk for the BBC's *Voice of the North* radio programme, which was anchored by John Craven, long before he even owned a pair of wellies. All I had to do then was to race up to the BBC studio and record it.

After that, my time was my own. Why I didn't take on a milk round to stave off boredom, I'll never know.

51

But I did recall all this years later when I worked – whoops, take that back – when I occupied a desk in the *Mirror* features fourth-floor room in London, the one that was known as the Mink-lined Coffin. There the average was one feature every three months. And I distinctly remember our NUJ man saying that we should have our four-day week reduced to three because of the stresses of the job.

Oddly enough, writing eight or even 10 pieces a week is easier than writing one every three months. It came as a surprise to a fully qualified Idle Sod like me to discover that too little work was much more exhausting than too much. I really enjoyed buzzing around Newcastle like a supercharged mosquito.

I can only think that it was the dizzying spectacle of all this activity that led Peter Stephens, the editor, to give me my first freebie: that four-day trip to Luxembourg. If I hadn't gone there, I would never have met Neville Stack, who asked me if I would be interested in a move to Manchester. At the time I was unable to reply on account of the heavy linen napkin I had stuffed into my mouth. I had put it there to muffle my laughter.

I had just met what may have been the last of that endangered species, The Appalling Yorkshireman. They were endangered, I expect, because they were so bloody irritating, and I speak as one born, bred and escaped. I know whereof I speak. I tell you, if Geoff Boycott and Fred Trueman had ever had a lovechild – for the moment, I'm assuming they didn't – Eric would have been him.

It was at a state banquet in Luxemburg and their tourist department really threw the lot at us: a high-vaulted palace, lashings of gold-leaf, vast chandeliers, heavy silver cutlery, crystal goblets, and waiters dressed in the style of light-opera emperors serving food fit for the gods, and only executive gods at that. It was certainly a step-up from my usual banquet at Pumphrey's Tea Rooms in the Cloth Market.

If I was impressed, and I was, then Eric, sitting opposite me, was decidedly not. Carefully he scraped the exquisite sauce off the piece of beef in front of him. 'I knew it,' he said, triumphantly. 'Red raw. They wouldn't have to cover it up with this muck if it were fit to eat. You wouldn't catch me eating that rubbish.'

My heart lifted. I hadn't heard a griping tyke in years. Considering this was the sixties, he appeared stuck somewhere round about 1947. Brylcremed hair parted as though with an axe, best dark-blue suit as worn on Sundays, birthdays, and wedding anniversaries, and paisley-patterned tie, as worn every single day of the week. He worked for a smallish evening paper in south Yorkshire.

As he pushed the plate away, and with it the glass of red wine, Eric sighed: 'What I wouldn't give for a pint of Sam Smith's.'

Surely they'd bring him a beer? He wouldn't want them to bring him a beer. The beer here would be German beer which was, personal experience had proved, no more than gassy maiden's water. You wouldn't catch him supping owt German, thank you very much. And the wine? French, he said, with some scorn. We had all seen what the French were made of during the war. You wouldn't catch him drinking owt French.

He said this as though there was some sort of secret government inspectorate that was constantly trying to catch him eating and drinking foreign food. And failing, clearly.

It turned out he didn't think much of Luxemburg, which I thought was a very grand little duchy indeed. Two strides, he said, and you'd passed it. The rest of Europe fell into much the same bracket. Belgium, Holland, all these places, were all jumbled up because, he believed, they were all the bloody same. He personally wouldn't give you tuppence for the bloody lot of them.

I say he was the perfect Yorkshireman because, when it came to geographical loyalty, he was not much given to self-doubt. He didn't rave on about the wonders of his home county, but rather preferred to point out the deficiencies of non-Yorkshire places. I'd been brought up with dozens like him. From cradle to grave, they never set foot outside Yorkshire because where else could possibly be better? Exactly.

By this time, we'd covered most of Europe and he was working his way through other places he wouldn't give you tuppence for. London for one, the south of England, even the Midlands. Speaking personally, he couldn't get back to Yorkshire soon enough.

With an apologetic cough, I said I was from Yorkshire.

'Aye, so you say' he said, sounding far from convinced. Eric fixed his dark-brown eyes unwaveringly on mine. I had the feeling I was about to be tested. 'So where are you from then?'

I told him. The Dales. He waved away the next course and sipped at a glass of water while he formulated his reply. That wasn't really Yorkshire. As far as he was concerned, people from The Dales were no better than Geordies and Geordies, as he was sure I would know, were no better than Scotsmen with their brains kicked out. What wouldn't he give you for them? Tuppence – that's what he wouldn't give. He lay down his napkin. His final verdict.

So what was he doing here, avoiding disgusting food and drink in countries he hated with such worthless people? Ah. He had to come because he'd just been promoted to a new and important job. Which was? A look of quiet pride flickered across his face. 'Travel editor.'

Beside me, Neville Stack whispered that he had to admire the man's sense of humour. 'Eric?' I asked, in some surprise. 'No,' he said; 'the man who gave him the job.'

It was a true tragedy. The man who loathed abroad, and everything that dwelt therein, was doomed to roam the earth, dreaming of Sam Smith's. That was when I had to put the napkin in my mouth.

I liked Neville Stack from the moment I met him. He'd been on the *Daily Mirror* in Manchester in the early sixties, with Roly Watkins, Brian Park, Stanley Vaughan and Alan Staniforth. When I met him, he was then news editor of the old broadsheet *Sun* in Manchester, where, with endless ingenuity, he somehow matched – and often beat – newspapers with three or four times the staff and money. More important, for all that he was an astute operator; at heart he saw journalism as paid fun. Earlier, when he was news editor of the *People* in the north, he found both he and the London office were working on the same story, somewhere in the Midlands. It was about a man who collected unwanted dogs. 'Saviour of the Strays' was how London wrote it. Neville's team discovered he was selling them for vivisection and the Saviour became Rat of the Week.

He went on to edit a major weekly and then an evening paper before travelling the world instructing others on how to produce newspapers. Taking his journalists out for a drink one night in Trinidad, he noticed that the deputy news editor, Romeo, was nowhere to be seen. It was a chance not to be missed. 'Romeo, Romeo, wherefore art thou Romeo?' he cried out. 'He done gone to de gents, Mister Stack,' said one of the others, to which Neville replied: 'If William Shakespeare had known about that, it could have changed the course of English literature.'

Hard not to like such a man.

Indeed, I think it was Neville who first detected what could possibly be a pattern in my career path – so far, Skipton, Darlington, Halifax, London, Leamington and Tyneside. Since my first daughter was born in Radford Semele (Leamington) and my second in Heddon-on-the-Wall (Tyneside), was I perhaps just looking for villages with silly names in which to father children? In which case, had I thought about Chapel-en-le-Frith, down the road from his home?

So persuasive was this argument that a few days later I found myself doing a reel around Manchester pubs, talking to news and feature editors. In a pub called the Swan with Two Necks, I again met Bill Freeman, whose carefree lifestyle on the *Craven Herald (and West Yorkshire Pioneer)* first lured me into this industry. He'd gone from the *Yorkshire*

Post and the *Sunday Express* to be news editor of the Manchester *Mirror*. I'd like the *Mirror*, he said. Well, I liked Bill Freeman, and since I seemed to have been following him for most of the past ten years, it seemed only logical to follow him into Withy Grove.

And a month later, I handed my house over to Peter Hinchliffe (then on the *Chronicle* news desk), my column to Charlie Fiske, packed up my Morris Minor Traveller, a half-timbered Tudor car – we had moved on from pre-war ten-quid models – and set off for Manchester. We headed first of all for the southern suburbs where you could find an NUJ quorum in most pubs. You know the places: the grove of Hazel, the hulme of Cheadle, the hall of Bram. Once I learnt, however, that in that area there was a better than even chance of bumping into Denzil Sullivan, I moved just over the Derbyshire border. Working for Bill Freeman, with Neville Stack for my neighbour, and Chapel-en-le-Frith just down the road. It had worked out perfectly.

Except for one thing. At the back of my mind there was one tiny concern. In my ten years in journalism, I had yet to cover a proper news story.

Oh dear.

*

7

You know how people say they can remember the exact where and when of a significant moment in their lives? Well, I can. It was halfway up a Pennine, on a cold clear Sunday afternoon. The man responsible was a dapper little chap in a shortie car-coat, perched on a limestone rock.

That was the point at which all my dreams of becoming a hotshot international reporter perished. He'd done it. And I never even thanked him.

Although, to be quite honest, my dreams had begun to look a bit wobbly before then.

I had never actually covered a big news story. Or even a medium-sized one. Whenever a big story came in, the news editor's eyes would pass blankly over my eager little face and find someone else. I would get the story about the talking corgi.

Over the years I've had more conversation with corgis than I have with news editors, which must prove something. Certainly more intelligent conversation.

So, by the time I arrived at the *Daily Mirror* in Manchester, I knew roughly as much about news reporting as I did after two weeks on the *Craven Herald*. As Bill Freeman carefully explained, everybody had to work as a reporter for at least a year before attempting to get a place in features. As I took my seat in the lines of desks in the Withy Grove office, I had a nervous feeling that I was about to get found out.

And of course I was. But not immediately.

At that time the *Mirror* had enough reporters to use people as specialists, and I found myself cast as the Daft Story man. Before they had nipples on Page Three, they used to have a daft story, and that was my role. They could have had my nipples too but nobody asked. It never occurred to me at the time, but I suspect the desk-men who handed out the stories knew my limitations rather better than I did. I was – thank god – being protected. Britain's worst singer... the bloodhound that got lost... the traffic wardens' strike... they all came my way, to the great relief, no doubt, of real reporters.

But it couldn't go on for ever. I had a near miss one evening when I was about to go on a multiple motorway crash (without the faintest idea of what to do about it) when Maurice Wigglesworth, night news editor, called me back and sent Tony Gubba instead. I have had to learn to live with the thought that I was second-choice to a chap who ended up reporting footie for the telly. You can't get much lower than that.

Another night, when all my protectors were looking the other way, I found myself in Bradford on a murder. I followed the others from police station to door knocking, then the pub. 'Okay,' said the Bradford freelance, 'it's a Mystery Shotgun Blast, agreed?'

'Mystery?' I chipped in. 'No, it was the husband who shot her.'

Silence fell as they all turned and stared at me. The freelance moved me quietly to one side and said: 'You don't know how to do this, do you?' I agreed there was something in what he said. Like the truth. He wrote it for me. I don't know what happened to John Dale but, oddly enough, I see his namesake did terribly well editing *Take a Break*.

One or two of the more experienced reporters also seemed to sense they had a bumbling amateur in their midst. For a competitive trade, people were surprisingly helpful, and not always the people you would expect. Quite often, Terry Stringer went out of his way to make sure I was okay. Harry King or John Flint would wander over if I appeared to be struggling.

Stringer was famously known as Kid Vinegar, for the merciless stab of his wit. He'd take on all-comers and he could draw blood. But I was there to witness his only recorded defeat, to, amazingly, Tom Hopkinson. It was Kid Vinegar versus the Farmer's Boy.

Terry was a razor-sharp little bloke, mentally and physically nimble. Tom Hopkinson, a freelance who lived up the Dales at Buckden (which is like living on Dartmoor if you work in Fleet Street), was a large, red-faced lad who spoke in a slow Yorkshire accent, sometimes thought to indicate slowness of wit. The people who thought that had plenty of time for regrets.

He looked as though he'd just come in from doing the milking when he ambled into the office one morning wearing a huge, heavy tweed suit.

'Mornin' Tom,' Terry winked at the rest of us. 'Wife knitted you a new suit, then?'

'Aye,' said Tom, with a long slow blink of his brown eyes. 'Shall I get her to knit thee one? She does 'em for dwarves.'

In the sixties, the *Daily Mirror* in Manchester was a great place to be. Every once in a while London would send up a new editor, either to sober up or to go on the piss, which they did. Either way, it made surprisingly little difference. With several editions, there was always space for good stuff so, unlike London, Withy Grove didn't need a surrounding infrastructure of wine-bars and pubs to accommodate its workless. And although the professional standards were every bit as high as Fleet Street, the atmosphere was much more provincial. Most hacks lived within half-an-hour of the office. Many of them knew each other and socialised outside work. When I finally settled down just over the Derbyshire border, I had two news editors, one night editor, one columnist, and several reporters and subs within a few hundred yards. Go in any pub and you'd find people speaking fluent Pitman's. Whereas in London, when I lived near Tunbridge Wells, the only hacks I ever saw were Bob Rodrigo, a golf writer, and John Taylor, from the *Tailor and Cutter*.

Again unlike London, wives in Manchester were allowed to make public appearances in the pub and even the office, which kept the adultery rate at much the same level as the *Craven Herald*. Imagine the strain of attempting to conduct an affair with a secretary behind the filing cabinets in Martin Keats' room in the lunch-hour, when your wife could pop in with the shopping at any moment. Exactly. It never happened.

Not that it was without merriment. There was always a good chance that Mike Gagie, a born leader of men if they happened to be heading towards the pub, would insist that everybody drink champagne cocktails in the Swan with Two Necks. It usually ended with Mike leading the entire staff round the building in a conga line, waving bottles of champagne, and singing 'Lily the Pink'. Life there was full of pleasurable possibilities. Out on the road, there was the possibility of being trapped in a phone box with Pam Smart and Those Two. The bruises would last for weeks.

Years later, in the King and Keys in Fleet Street, the peerless Ken Donlan, news editor of the *Mail* and the *Sun*, told me that he rated the *Mirror* Manchester set-up – meaning Bill Freeman and Leo White on news and Alan Price in features – as the best, excluding of course his own.

Now I'm not qualified to issue a judgment on this. Those of you who understand this stuff, discuss and report back.

The challenges were not always restricted to journalism. The new reporter, on nights for the first time, had the fearful responsibility of being in charge of the catering for Maurice Wigglesworth and George Harrop. If there is anyone left who doesn't know of this *Mirror* late-night double act, Maurice was the night news editor, a man not much more than five-foot high, but quite a bit more than 20 stone in weight. Imagine a Michelin man dangerously over-inflated. You wouldn't want to put a sharp implement too near Maurice. His friend George was the night picture editor, his empurpled jowls flapping like a turkey's on Christmas Eve.

Half-an-hour before closing time, Maurice called me over and suggested I should go down to the Swan and, to avoid a last-minute rush, get in my round of three pints. Perhaps, as he pressed money into my hand, I would also get in his round. 'And mine,' said George, also passing over the cash.

Nine pints looked a lot: they almost covered the table top. In bustled Maurice and George, with Maurice anxiously looking at the clock. 'Best get another round in, lad,' he said. 'And mine while you're at it.' And off we went again.

By the time we got back, they were ready for food. 'Make a note,' said Maurice. 'I'm sure I can remember it,' I said. 'Best make a note,' Maurice repeated. 'Bacon and egg…'

I began to write.

'And a couple of sausages, and black pudding. Have you got that?'

Yes, I'd got that.

'Tomatoes, mushrooms I think. And a nice slice of fried bread. Have you got the fried bread?'

Fried bread is quite easy in Pitman's.

'And a few chips.'

I set off for the canteen. As I reached the door, Maurice called out. 'Twice,' he said.

'All of it – twice?'

'Aye, I'm feeling peckish.'

There was no reason why the pothole disaster should have been a problem. The story broke early on a Sunday morning, giving me plenty of time to get there. What's more, it was Alum Pot, which was near Selside, not far from Horton-in-Ribblesdale, an area I knew quite well. I even knew one or two of the potholers. And, since I was in my mid-twenties and quite fit, I fairly zipped up the hillside on foot.

At the top, it was mayhem. Police, potholers, rescue teams of cavers, ambulance men, were washing about, and I darted here and there, not sure who to talk to or what to ask. By the time Stanley Vaughan sauntered up the hill, I was in panic.

Stanley was the *Mirror* man in Sheffield. A dapper little figure in his car coat, neat moustache and even neater hair, he didn't look like a hard-case newsman who'd kick a door down to get at the truth. He didn't need to. He'd got the whole story.

Names of the missing potholers, the situation underground in feet and inches, the difficulties facing the rescuers, and the chances of success, bags of quotes, enough information for the art desk to produce illustrations, and addresses for pick-up pix and back-up interviews.

Calmly in control of events, without a trace of fluster, he perched on top of a chunk of limestone and invited me to join him. 'I think we've cracked it between us,' he said, rather more than generously. 'Now do you want to write it, young man, or shall I start it off?' If he knew I was lost, he was far too kind to mention it. As I scribbled, he dictated the splash and the spread and a couple of sidebars. 'You're the writer,' he said, on no evidence whatsoever, 'why don't you do a colour piece?'

At least there was one contribution I could make. Since my legs were 20 years younger than his, at least I could run down the hill to phone it over.

As we had a beer at the Crown in Horton that evening, he explained how he'd got it wrapped up so quickly. Before you went up the fellside, you had to get some information from the police in Skipton, some from the police in Settle, and some from the Cave Rescue guys at Clapham. They'd tell you who to talk to at the scene. What you sought to avoid was isolating yourself halfway up a Pennine with no information 30 years before the invention of the mobile phone.

It was experience. Quietly, modestly, he listed all the major stories he'd done – something like a couple of hundred disasters, both land and sea, a score or so of air crashes, several international wars and insurrections, hundreds of murders, and scores of pothole calamities. I may possibly be exaggerating the numbers here, but they were enough to depress me. By now, he sort of knew what he was doing.

I didn't. I looked at him as he raised his half-pint. The realisation slowly dawned inside me that if I lived to be 100 I would never be able to do what Stanley Vaughan had just accomplished. He was the real reporter. I was nowhere near.

'I hear you're keen on features,' he said.

'Yes,' I replied, making my mind up at high speed. 'I've been thinking I might try to do more on that side.'

'Good idea,' he said, with an encouraging smile. It was the best careers advice I ever had.

*

Don't blame them, for heaven's sake. It wasn't their fault that in the late sixties the *Mail*'s Edwards, the *Sun*'s Akass, and all the rest of the international brigade found themselves chasing the Kennedy and King shootings, Biafran wars, the Prague Spring, and Vietnam. At the time, these probably seemed to be the big, big stories.

What they didn't know at the time, of course, was that this meant that they missed the lawnmower racing, the dispute over the oldest brass band in Derbyshire, the pig-smuggling scandal, and the lady molecatcher.

I'll bet they're still kicking themselves.

If they'd all followed me into the *Daily Mirror* features department in Manchester, all these jewels of journalism would have been theirs. Wrong place, wrong time: simple as that, I'm afraid.

If that sounds as though being a feature writer in the north did not invariably put you in the orchestra stalls for the great drama of history in the making, then I wouldn't quarrel with that. It wasn't so much the last helicopter out of Saigon for me, as the last bus out of Stockport, which in some ways was even more frightening.

But, don't get me wrong, I'm certainly not complaining. Thanks to Stanley Vaughan's demonstration of how to be a real reporter, at a pothole disaster, I had been obliged to face the fact that I wasn't one. Or likely to become one. On the other hand, during my time on the *Evening Chron* in Newcastle, I had written about half-a-million features. On the basis that you should always do what you're best at, I asked Bill Freeman (news editor) if he'd let me go to features, and Alan Price (features editor) if he'd accept me.

Since most reporters wanted to be like Edwards and Akass, I had only one rival – a district man in the North-East. He had a wonderfully light touch, damn him. Once I remember finding Alan Price sitting chuckling over a piece he'd written. It's probably just as well I didn't have my lighter with me, or I might've set fire to it.

Two men, one job. A classic confrontation. But I had my secret weapon.

This chap was not only a highly-regarded district man, a hard-news reporter of some reputation, but he was also making a name as an investigative reporter.

My secret weapon was that I couldn't do anything else. And since I could really only do truly trivial stories, I was that equestrian rarity, a half-trick pony.

Faced with the prospect of losing one of their best guys, or being stuck with me cluttering up the reporters' benches for the rest of the century, the news desk decided to let me go.

What became of my rival? He went on to become a Fleet Street executive and one of Maxwell's high command and later retired to a small island near Malta. I always tell people that he invented Gozo journalism, which was later stolen by Hunter S Thompson who couldn't even spell it correctly. I mean, 'Gonzo', for heaven's sake.

Since he was also about eight-foot-six, the guy could well have pursued an alternative career as a lighthouse. Actually, I never knew whether he wanted the job in features: but I did know he was the only other candidate.

At that time, Manchester had everything. Or, more accurately, it had one of everything. One decent hotel, one restaurant worth eating at, one quality department store, one television studio, and one celebrity. People came from miles around in the hope of a glimpse of George Best. So did Manchester United's manager, because at this time George was forever getting lost.

Round about Thursday every week, he would go missing. Where's Georgie? Will he play on Saturday? The city was in a fever. Each week, without fail, came the Great George Chase. It wasn't usually that much of a mystery. By the time the hacks found him, the usual pic was George in a dressing-gown at the half-open door of a Chelsea flat, with the owner, invariably a blonde actress, standing just behind him. In her nightie.

There was a definite pattern to his disappearances. For the reporters, this meant a couple of days chasing around pubs and night-clubs in London, on expenses. Their complaints were less than audible. I know reporters who built extensions on their houses called the George Best Wing.

The sad thing about the golden times in our lives is that we never realise it at the time: that was one of mine. At that time, the *Mirror* had a great appetite for frivolous features, and, as a man trained on conversations with corgis, most of them came my way.

By this time, I had begun to realise that I was temperamentally – if not actually genetically – destined to be a features creature. Good newsmen liked being in the limelight. Loud of voice, strong of limb, they were assertive, definite sort of chaps, who'd elbow their way to the front of a crowd. They'd grab people. They'd demand answers. Newsmen had no nerves.

Whereas we weedy features people were much happier on the edge and in the shadows, lurking and skulking. When the hard news guy was asking the police chief if they'd arrested anyone, the feature writer would be noting the colour of his socks. Reporters ran in packs. Writers sneaked about on their own.

As a natural lurker, skulker and sneaker, I was much happier away from the mainstream.

And what a joy those stories were. The New Mills Prize Brass Band, which claimed to be the oldest, boasted a tuba player – a famously macho breed – who had simultaneously put two women in Stockport maternity ward. For the 1914 war, the entire band marched off blowing bravely to enlist together, and before long one of them paid the supreme sacrifice. He was knocked down by a despatch rider in Buxton. With their uniforms amateurishly modified for women and children – anyone who could blow was in – they were said to look like the Light Brigade.

On the way back.

The Yorkshire Freedom Fighters, another of my major exclusives, had a coat-of-arms of a nude Fred Trueman holding a Yorkshire pudding in one hand and white rose in the other. Their motto was *Demos Eboraci Semper* – the House of York Forever, and their policy was based on a twin platform: to push Lancashire into the sea and to export Pontefract cakes in large quantities.

Then there were the inventors with the plastic pillow to bring comfort to curlered heads (this was the north, after all), a magnetic tea-caddy spoon, and a pram alarm to frighten off baby-snatchers. The man who put a Perspex panel in an umbrella handle with name, address and telephone number was ejected into the street by the manufacturers: 'We like people losing umbrellas,' they said.

Even the ones that went wrong were funny. Somebody sent me out on the streets to attempt to give away the new £50 note. The theory was that people would be so suspicious nobody would accept them. After about 30 seconds, in which time I'd got rid of five of them and had a queue halfway up the street, the story was called off. I mentioned this years later to Bill Greaves, ex-*Mail* man, who had been asked to do the same thing with fivers. He couldn't get rid of one. Obviously, I pointed out to him, I have a more trustworthy face.

A similar disaster loomed when I was sent to interview a man called Bill Shankly. I phrase it like that because I knew nothing about him. I also knew nothing about football, as I believe the game is called. He was, or so I understood at the time, the boss of some team or other. The theory was that he would be so charmed by my innocent ignorance that he would reveal secrets he would never share with his sporting chums.

I realised the flaw in this theory within about a minute of arriving in his office. The only thing in his life was football. He only ever talked about football. He hated people who couldn't talk about football. The only journalists he ever spoke to were football reporters, and he certainly had no wish to be interviewed by a feature writer. I think he believed feature writers to be men who conducted most of their social lives in public lavatories. My hair, curled poetically over my collar at the time, my yellow suede jacket and purple loon pants did nothing to contradict this belief.

He proceeded to give me a 30-minute non-interview. To every question he said it was a team game, and the man who cleaned the boots was as important as he was, and so on, and so on. Even my tape-recorder was yawning. Somehow I wasn't touching his soul. In my research, I had noted that they had one young player (Steve Heighway? Does that sound right?) who'd been to university. Did that, I asked him, raise the level of the conversation among the knuckle-scrapers in the changing room?

For a minute, I thought he was going to hit me.

To be quite frank, I had thought he looked a bit finely balanced, and at this point he went crackers. In a burst of high-speed sporran talk, the little Glaswegian was off like a machine-gun. Fu'ba' was nae aboot brains. In fu'ba', you had yer brains in yer boots. Sorry, I can't keep up this dialect stuff any longer. What it amounted to was that if they wanted intellectuals the managers would all be queuing outside Oxford and Cambridge, but they don't, because fu'ba' came from the back streets...

And so it went on, ranting and raving. It was marvellous stuff, and I got out, with my tape, before he decided to spill my brains with his brain-filled boots. As I was leaving, I heard him say: 'Who was that fuckin' cowboy?'

I had made a complete fool of myself. On the other hand, it wasn't a bad spread.

And, do you know, I'm still not sure who he was.

There were then, as I'm sure there are now, several men who'd like to hit me. I'm surprised Allan Staniforth didn't, for one. He was the *Daily Mirror* man in Leeds. For years he'd been building and driving racing cars. One Sunday, his great day of triumph, he broke three world and six British records.

On the same day, I won a lawnmower race. Who got top billing? Talk about no justice.

It was a cricket club near Sale that staged the world's first lawnmower racing championships, and Alan Price, my boss, told me to enter with a view to writing a few mildly comical pars. Beforehand, just to make it interesting, I went to Atco's lawnmower factory at Preston where the mechanics were sick to death with slowing their machines down for old ladies. Could they speed one up? They thought they could.

Was I cheating? Well, nowhere near so much as Jimmy Savile, who had come to record his own athletic triumph for his radio programme. Never mind my little Atco; he'd got a cricket lawnmower the size of a grand piano with four forward gears.

After four half-mile heats, I finished the final by opening up the accelerator and letting my magnificent flying machine drag me round one last time. Sad if unsurprising to report, Mr Savile was not a gracious loser.

But Allan Staniforth, good chap that he was, didn't mind sharing the front-page plug with me.

At least by then I knew that lurking and skulking was the life for me. Not that we didn't get our share of the big foreign jobs in Withy Grove features. Oh yes, occasionally I had to dig out my much-stamped passport to jet off and bring back world-shaking stories to a hungry public. Edwards and Akass and Co weren't the only ones to witness war, pestilence, famine and death... and that lesser-known fifth horseman of the apocalypse, nudity.

I was sent to Sweden to report – exclusively, you may care to note – on the world's first naked beauty contest.

It was a wintry night so I wasn't all that surprised when the winner shivered and said: 'Your notebook is so cold.' Well, I had to rest it somewhere.

Unlike Saigon, there was no rush for the helicopters to escape.

*

Did you ever see it? I never did. But somewhere in the sixties, in the north of England, there must have appeared an advert along these lines: 'Wanted, character for a living museum of eccentrics. Must have peculiar appearance, personality and habits. Some journalistic experience useful but not essential.'

How else could you explain the features department of the *Daily Mirror* in Manchester? Looking at the people in it, you'd swear that they had been invented by Charles Dickens one night when he'd OD'd on the laudanum.

There was one sub who was slowly dying of a combination of despair and gravity, and it was a toss-up which would get him first. He lived in a smile-free zone. Newcomers, the only ones foolish enough to enquire about his permanent depression, would soon regret it. 'Because my much-loved Uncle Jack has just endured a terribly painful death,' he would say. Someone close to him had always just died. And always in great pain – his family didn't do merciful release. What it did to house prices in his neighbourhood, I never liked to ask.

As for gravity, he seemed to be slowly sinking into the earth. His face, his shoulders, his clothes, every part of him was gradually sinking, even the heavily-loaded carrier bags that he always bore, one in each hand. Nobody knew what was in them. I suspected dead budgerigars.

Amazingly, his telephone manner must have transmitted his personality with complete accuracy. On his only visit to the London office, as he stepped through the door, John Garton and the features subs, who had never set eyes on him before, turned as one and pointed and shouted out his name. Now that's fame.

Then there was Alf Gibbon, who tended towards the more serious side of feature writing, but with a lovely touch. When he wrote about a railway signalman who was a moderately successful inventor, his intro – I remember it well – was: Did you hear about the railwayman who got ideas above his station?

Alf and another features creature, Neil Bentley, were both well over six-foot and weighed, in stones, in the late teens. When they went for lunch, if they enjoyed the meal, they'd have the same again. I once went for a drink with Bentley to Sam's Chop House. The drink turned out to be six huge schooners of sweet sherry. How I got back to the office I'll never know. I believe he may have put me in his pocket. I never went with him again.

For the most part, it was a quiet office, disturbed only occasionally by Ken Tossell, a telly reporter, with a chronic identity crisis. A delightful man, Ken was also something of a worrier. He worried that people would confuse him with a sports reporter called Bob Russell, or that they may think he was from the *Daily Mail*. Both names, he thought, were easily confused. Rather like Ken himself.

So when he rang someone up he would always introduce himself at top volume and break up the words into distinct and carefully enunciated syllables. 'My name is KEN-NETH TOSS-ELL of the DAIL-EE MIRR-ROAR'. He left a trail of perforated eardrums behind him.

Sometimes he was so concerned about establishing his identity that he would jump into an interview a little too quickly. After spending an entire day tracking down Gracie Fields for a quote on a news story, he eventually got her to a telephone in Capri. Once he had established that he was not Bob Russell and not from the *Daily Mail*, he went straight for the jugular. 'How old are you these days, Gracie?' A look of bewilderment spread over his face. 'I do believe she's rung off,' he said.

After lunch one day he returned to the office with a box featuring an illustration of a large mouse and the label Scram. Ken, a Londoner with a

Livingstonian accent, pronounced it Scrame. He explained that he had been having trouble with mice at his home in Glossop and Scrame, a mouse poison, would soon see them off. I picked it up and pretended to read it. You've made a terrible mistake, Ken, I told him. This wasn't mouse poison. It was mouse food. He was appalled.

He snatched it up and hurried back to the shop. It is one of the major regrets of my life that I was not there to hear Ken protest to the manager that they had sold him the wrong product. With this, he insisted, he'd be offering the mice a free meal. Mice would be coming from miles around to eat at Ken's Rodent Restaurant. Eventually, by careful reading of the instructions they did convince him it was poison, but he was very forgiving. 'Don't worry, Col. It was a mistake anyone could make.'

Come to think of it, all the television staff were… well, interesting. As sometimes happens with specialists, Mike Kerrigan had been overcome by the Stockholm Syndrome. He had been subsumed by television – rather in the way that crime reporters become more like policemen. Or criminals.

He spent most of his time drifting around asking for ideas for a title for a new sit-com he was writing. We never came up with a title. Whether he ever came up with the sit-com I'm not in a position to say.

He was trying to follow the example of one hack who did make the leap from paper to screen. John Stevenson, the *Mail*'s telly man in Manchester, became a scriptwriter for Coronation Street at a time when it was distinguished by a wonderful thread of humour. His wonderful thread of humour. There weren't many funnier writers around than Stevenson.

Visitors to the Granada studio were shown, among other things, a scene of Coronation Street at its very best. You must remember this: the Ogdens house, Stan is going to the pub, but because it's her birthday Hilda demands a kiss before he goes. He stoops to kiss her. A puzzled look crosses his face.

'What's that funny taste, Hilda?'

Hilda gives a smile of immense satisfaction. 'Woman, Stanley. Woman.'

I always thought that had to be a Stevenson line. I was wrong. He didn't write it. But he could've done if he'd wanted to.

Our other TV reporter, Bill Keenan, a man of deep religious faith, was particularly fervent when it came to abortion – or, as he called it, 'murdering tiny babies'. I can't say that Dennis Hussey, Brian Wood or myself were all that sympathetic: in our order of priorities, abortion was some way behind exchanging blank bills, office gossip, Maggie McCoy's mini-skirt, and Man United. All three of us banned Keenan from mentioning the subject again. Ever. Occasionally he outflanked us.

One Monday morning Keenan, a breezy soul, came bouncing in. He'd just had a marvellous weekend in the country. Perfect weather, beautiful surroundings. So far so good, we thought.

From where he was staying, you could look out over north Lancashire and there was nothing but beautiful countryside all the way to the Lake District, he said.

Nothing to fear here.

And then, he went on, there was the wonderful empty vista of the Lakes and the Scottish borders, all the way up to Glasgow.

Fascinating, we yawned, unaware that we were drifting nearer the danger.

'Hardly a house or a person all the way,' he said. 'And yet they say this country's overcrowded so they can slaughter tiny innocent babies.' How we never slaughtered a tiny innocent TV writer has never been adequately explained.

Mike Irish, the deputy features editor, followed Kerrigan to Florida and the *National Enquirer*, a mass-selling (in shopping malls) weekly paper of dubious repute but generous salaries. I even tarried there temporarily myself.

Kerrigan suggested a weekend in New York on a cheap deal he'd found that involved sharing a room. Mike Irish seemed uncertain about this. In the hotel reception, as they were signing in, Irish started jigging about, tucking his chin into his chest and firing short punches and hooks with his fists. 'Any good gyms round here?' he asked the baffled woman on reception. 'Gotta put in some work on the heavy bag.' Then he jigged some more and blasted off a tearing uppercut. This was a surprise as Mike Irish had some difficulty in lifting a prawn out of a cocktail. As they headed for the lift, Kerrigan asked him what the hell he was doing. 'I don't want them to think we're gay,' he said. He never became welterweight champion of the world, although he did become an estate agent. And achieved a degree of fame from letting accommodation to Middle Eastern pilots with an ambition to fly into skyscrapers in New York City.

In Manchester at that time, there were quite a few people who were either planning to join the two Mikes in the Florida sunshine or who just sat waiting for Bernard's Call. Bernard Shrimsley, ex-news editor, had gone off to show them how it should be done in London. His friends in Manchester didn't like to stray too far from a telephone in case he needed them urgently. 'Two Lunches Bentley' was in the waiting room. Otherwise he was mainly employed on organising events and competitions, because his high-octane charm was wonderfully effective with mayors and middle-ranking police officers. His main function was as unpaid, self appointed office chaplain, with a special interest in the morals and manners of the staff. If anyone was misbehaving – an unlikely concept, I know – with a crook of the finger, Neil would summon them down to the Swan with Two Necks and give them some corrective instruction. It was known as Neil's Ten-bob Sermon. Oddly enough, when he eventually got to London he found himself in need of one, but don't let's go into that.

He certainly preached one to Brian Wood, who was probably the only member of the features staff who could make any claim to being normal. Handy writer, keen sportsman, semi-professional guitarist, amusing company and a useful man with a pint, Brian – like most people in our dangerous trade – found himself suffering from a seriously fractured marriage. Shortly before Christmas, when he was living with girlfriend (whom he adored) and apart from wife-and-family, he was overwhelmed by guilt and confusion.

Covered in shame, he announced he was returning to his wife, and left girlfriend in tears. On the way home, as a sign of intent, he put on his old wedding-ring. It wasn't easy. He'd been so happy with girlfriend that he'd put on a little weight and even his ring finger had fattened up. By the time he got to the marital home, it was really quite painfully swollen.

No sooner had he got through the door than he realised this was a terrible mistake. His marriage was completely beyond repair. His wife didn't want him, he didn't want her. He left. Then it struck him what he'd done. He could hardly go back to his girlfriend after treating her so shabbily. The only place where they would let him in was… his mother's, which is not what you want when you're thirtyish. By then, his finger was like a fat black sausage. Mums know about these things, of course. The only thing to do, she said, was to bring the swelling down with ice, then remove the ring. She had no ice. But she did have another idea.

As Brian put it to me the next morning, he had seldom been so depressed as he was that night. Sitting in the kitchen of his mum's council flat, having upset the love of his life, with the third finger of his left hand stuffed up the anus of a Buxted frozen chicken.

'A great pic,' said Dennis Hussey.

The story, however, had a happy ending. He and the girlfriend were married. It is not true that the wedding breakfast consisted of frozen chickens.

Extraordinary, wasn't it? All from one room in Withy Grove. And it was there in that room that one man pretty much doubled the pay of journalists throughout Britain. There ought to be a plaque up for Mike Gagie.

The exact opposite of me, big and burly, constantly bursting out of his shirt collar, Gagie, who sat across the desk from me, was a rough tough hard news man.

Whenever I was in need of some real reporting, he would quietly give me a steer. Whenever he wanted a piece jessying up, he'd slip it over the desk. 'Top and tail it,' he'd say. Strap the two of us together, you might've had one decent all-round journalist.

Even when at peace with the world, Mike was a definite sort of chap. Angry, he was bloody terrifying. And this day he had reached hurricane force. He was also FoC, and he'd just learnt – in the Swan, of course – that Sogat had negotiated a house agreement with the *Mirror* for nearly twice the journalists' rate.

When he came back from the pub the only reason he failed to defenestrate the senior management was because they were later in coming back from lunch than he was. He had steam coming from his ears and other less obvious orifices. It was rumoured that when they opened the windows in the upper reaches of the Holborn skyscraper, they could hear a roaring so terrible that it froze the blood. It was a peeved Gagie. He called a strike. No-one argued.

Elsewhere, everyone, our own union and even our colleagues in London refused to support a claim for pay parity with the messengers. They all thought it was madness and doomed to fail. They didn't know Gagie.

Watching from the sidelines, or from the other side of his desk, I believe that he carried his totally unofficial strike forward by the sheer force of his own personality. The management capitulated. We were granted our own house agreement which almost doubled our income. Journalists on all the other nationals demanded and immediately got the same. Plus, of course, a higher differential rate under the guise of 'London weighting' in Fleet Street. No questions asked. No industrial action required.

A plaque? We should have declared a National Gagie Day.

Everyone was happy, even Percy Roberts, the MD, who made off with Paula, one of the secretaries.

When, a few days later, editorial manager Peter Moorhead, who handled the company's long-term strategic thinking, pinned up a notice in the newsroom warning of the dangers of discarded food encouraging rodents, Terry Stringer inquired if this was the new Mouse Agreement.

Looking back, do you think it's possible that Stringer might've set up this entire series of events just so he could crack that joke? Dafter things have happened.

*

Exactly why an outwardly friendly features sub made such a determined effort to murder me I have never entirely understood. Was it something I wrote?

It was when I'd moved to the *Daily Mirror* in Manchester and finally settled just over the Derbyshire border. After Mike Gagie doubled the wages of all national newspaper journalists with his strike, I bought an Enterprise dinghy at a sailing club just outside Whaley Bridge.

I was so desperate to sail it that I couldn't wait until the first weekend. So I was delighted when a friend, near-neighbour and subbing colleague in features offered to come with me one evening after work. We got there about eight o'clock.

At this point, there were one or two fairly obvious reasons why we should perhaps have hesitated. For a start, it was beginning to get dark. Secondly, there was a near-hurricane blowing. Thirdly, we were the only ones there so there was no safety back-up. And fourthly, I had omitted to tell my crew, who had never been in a racing dinghy, that I had served only about 20 minutes before the mast myself: and that was with Neville Stack, the *Sun* news editor, in a boat too small to hold the washing-up, on a placid Sunday afternoon.

There was also another reason which we didn't know about. I still wake at night screaming when I think of it.

There we were, at the waterside, rushing to get it on the water. The sub leapt in; I pushed off, as the wind whipped into the sails and sent it hissing through the waves at a startling speed, I reached behind me for the tiller. My fingers grasped only flying spray.

Suddenly, and with complete clarity, I knew where the tiller was. It was in the boot of my car where I had left it.

Did my crew warn me of this? No he did not. And if that isn't attempted murder, I'd like to know what is.

It was a voyage distinguished by brevity and terror. Those of you who have driven a car with the accelerator jammed down and no steering wheel will know what it's like to sail a boat without a tiller in a high wind. Round and round we spun, faster and faster, before we hit land at such speed that we shot up the beach and were halfway to Buxton before we stopped.

I was given an official reprimand by the club for dangerous practice. I didn't press charges against my colleague. Even so, he never offered to crew for me again.

Ask him where he lives now? Whaley Bridge. Talk about returning to the scene of the crime…

Outbreaks of attempted homicide aside, working as a hack in Manchester around 1970 was a delightful conflation of two worlds: the journalistic standards of a top national tabloid with a lifestyle that was both provincial and homely. The Gagie-led editorial uprising that doubled our pay meant I could afford a four-bedroomed Edwardian house, handsomely set on a Peak District hillside, cost £3,000.

To celebrate the birth of my son, I also bought an old MG TD which could comfortably accommodate me, one passenger, and a packet of Bensons. It would have to be a packet of 10 – the 20 pack would be too big. This was described by my son's mother as a typically unselfish gesture for a father of three. She had a point.

It was a good life. By train or by car, I could be in Withy Grove in 45 minutes. Finishing work at 6pm, I could have a pint in the Swan with Two Necks and still be home in plenty of time for the Archers.

It was all delightfully small-scale so that work and home overlapped. My friend the sub lived just over the hill from me. His neighbours were Charlie Wilson (with whom he later had a small difference, I believe) and his wife Annie Robinson, who at that time was still taking a social drink with friends. When I dropped off my daughter Becky at Miss Latham's nursery school in Disley, Annie would be there with her daughter Emma.

Neville lived across the field at the back, Chris Clark – the *Mail* backbench whizz – was 50 yards away, and *Sun* reporters Gerry Brown and Clive Bolton lived on the new estate. Peter Fairley, who I'd known in Leamington and on Tyneside came down to work on the *Sun*, and also lived there. Sad to say, his move ended in failure. Peter could write high-class colour, which is why Neville hired him. But time after time, Peter turned in a straight news piece. 'I'm not good enough to do that stuff,' he protested. Poor chap, he was strangled by his own modesty.

When the Wilson government introduced an astonishing deal which meant anyone made jobless would receive half his last salary until a suitable job came up, Peter became contentedly unemployed. Some would argue that the distinction between being a journalist and being unemployed is too small for the human eye to detect, but he was, officially, on the dole. He was quietly confident that a small Derbyshire town would never be able to find a job appropriate to his skills. And so it was for several months until the manager called him in.

'It has to be a suitable job,' Peter warned him. The manager nodded. Then the interview started.

Was Peter used to dealing with the general public? He had to agree that he was. Was he used to asking them questions? Again, there was only one answer. Was he used to writing up reports of these interviews? Yes, dammit, he was – but what was this job?

'Working here in the job centre,' said the manager, triumphantly.

Defeated, Peter went back to his old job on the *Chronicle* on Tyneside.

To be honest, I didn't achieve this consummate work-life balance the moment I arrived in Manchester. (Incidentally, they only started calling it a work-life balance when I had none of the former and very little of the latter). At first I rented a bungalow in Hazel Grove. It was a mistake. I'm not a bungalow sort of person. Without a staircase, I get sort of moody and pace a lot. And the whole of Hazel Grove is at ground level: even standing on a chair isn't allowed. It wasn't the place for me, as I soon discovered.

As the Pickfords van pulled away, I sprang into my car to go to the local shop. Left arm over the passenger seat, right hand on top of the steering wheel, head turned for full rear view, I zipped down my drive and on to the narrow estate road. So far so good, but I still can't quite explain what happened next.

I stayed with left arm over passenger seat, right hand on top of wheel, head turned, as I reversed briskly straight across the estate road and down the drive of the bungalow opposite. I couldn't seem to stop, and indeed kept on going down the side of the house. I came to a halt only when I hit the front of a car that was parked in the garage.

Drive back on to road, knock on front door, warm greeting from resident. 'Ah, our new neighbour, welcome to Hazel Grove.' I said I was sorry to tell him I had just crashed into his car. 'Not mine,' he replied, cheerfully, 'mine's in the garage.' As he looked round the side, he saw his car with steam coming out of the radiator and some bits hanging off the front. No, he did not regard it as a contributing factor that he had left his garage doors open.

Between the bungalow and the boat, settling in to Manchester was not without its problems. The *Mirror*, however, was a joy. In fact, I think that Manchester journalism had got it more or less right. The amount of work we had to do was nicely poised between that of Bertie Wooster and a galley slave – possibly a little nearer the Wooster end of the scale.

The Withy Grove office had a pleasantly benign atmosphere. In the Holborn office, you could hear the whisperings of vicious plots, characters being assassinated and careers in flames, as soon as you turned up Fetter Lane. The *Mirror* in Manchester – and I suspect most of the other nationals there – was pretty much a malice-free zone. When – on Cudlipp's instructions – they had to fire a reporter, no-one knew how to do it. They had to give night news editor Maurice Wigglesworth a day-shift so he could show them how. Fortunately the old master hadn't lost his touch.

The Wigglesworth technique was simple. Go through the spike until you find a completely unreportable story – something like a man in court for having sexual intercourse with a goat (unknown in Yorkshire, but surprisingly common in Lancashire). Send the reporter to the man's house to get a full interview with both man and goat. When he rings in with several teeth missing, you say: 'Try again and if you can't do it, go straight home. Your cards will be in the post.'

Certainly the feature writing in the north was as good as anything coming out of London. When he wasn't doing straight reporting, or writing his fishing column, Alan Bennett on the *Express* could conjure up a piece like spinning thistledown: light, funny, clever. And I never saw anyone who could put together a piece with such grace and intelligence as Shelley Rohde on the *Daily Mail*. Sent to provide the colour on a brewery strike, Bennett's first line was: 'Warrington was spitting feathers last night...' When Shelley interviewed a man who'd lost his memory, she came up with the best last line I think I've ever seen. To cheer him up, she told him that he could be in for a pleasant surprise – maybe he was George Best.

'George who?' he said.

If you went on a job and saw either of those two, the wisest course was to ring in sick. It worked for me.

Between the stuff for the northern feature pages and for the Irish edition, we were busy enough. Then, of course, there was London.

Could you hear the sigh implicit in that sentence? The trouble was that the London office really did see themselves as the Champagne Set, sophisticated poets, doomed to deal with the roughnecks of the Northern Beer Boys. I well remember the cheers of delight from the subs when they received a complaint from some London exec about a page layout – 'in future, please be good enough to omit your absurd provincial curlicues'.

And we thought curlicues were only found in Ena Sharples' hair.

We always enjoyed the Four-bottle-Four-thirty Inspiration Call. That was the time it came, when the London office began to fumble their way back to their desks, and the four bottles of wine were the inspiration. This so freed up their creative thinking that they would sometimes invert the whole editorial process. The first thing was to come up with a headline that was both original and hilarious – easy-peasy after four bottles. Then they'd design a page or a spread around it. Almost as an afterthought, when they realised they had no copy, they'd ring Manchester and ask them to oblige.

They were the dreamers of dreams: we were the poor bloody movers and shakers who had to make it happen.

Oddly enough, this upside-down journalism sometimes came off.

A week after *Oh! Calcutta!* had opened in London, over lunch they came up with the headline *Oh! Accrington!* It was, they all agreed, wonderfully clever. Then they asked Manchester features in general – and me in particular – to write it.

This piece was described by a local reporter as plaiting fog. He was spot-on. In the complete absence of any facts, I find that fog is a useful substitute. And it looks good on a passport.

Occupation: fog-plaiter.

AT the end of a week in which 'Oh! Calcutta!' pushed human entertainment into a brand new dimension, the Mirror looks, for one night only, at the other end of the show business spectrum...

OH! ACCRINGTON!
By Colin Dunne

Accrington, Friday. – He pauses outside Isobel's 'From Cot to Schoolroom', and exchanges fixed grins with the little plaster boy in the window.

Solemnly, he loosens his tie, holds in his spangled jacket and vomits unhurriedly into a grid.

Then the young man stands back to assess his accuracy. Nods to the little plaster boy. And lurches, unsteady but fulfilled, up the hill.

Accrington was winding up another night of hell-fire fun.

I mislead you, perhaps. It isn't like this every night. Some nights, it's fairly quiet, and there are those who believe that Sodom and Gomorrah will hold on to their title.

But this is Wakes Week. And those who are deprived of that once-a-year pleasure of being on Blackpool's sands like to do it it here instead.

In London 'Oh! Calcutta!' finishes its first week, and a new epoch of entertainment opens. Accrington, in its own small way, is pushing back the frontiers of human experience too.

Young men who ten years ago would have been happy with ten pints and a mill girl now want nothing less than twelve and a shorthand-typist. Progress they call it.

Rolling down to Ackie at 8.30pm you know that down there somewhere it's all happening, the minute you pass the ragged-edged sign which proclaims

BOROUG

ACCRIN

WELCOM

Accrington is taking out its curlers ready for the night. What is it to be? *Chitty Chitty Bang Bang* at the Classic? High stakes at the Sunspot

74

arcade? Rice and chips and HP sauce at the Happy Garden Chinese restaurant?

'Nay, they're nowt a pound,' said the young man who sports possibly the last Tony Curtis in Britain, in the Commercial Hotel. 'Get yersel down to t'disco or t'folk club – finish off at t'Con club.'

He spits with deep relish past a shoe as sharp as a needle.

Up steep steps, 'Rockers were here' carved on the side, into a room pulsating with blue and red lights. Black-walled. Like a carnival night in a coffin.

Eyes penetrate the dusk and see... nobody. The disco is empty. A girl in a green sweater emerges from the brightness of the kitchen. 'Nowt toneet' says our hostess blankly.

Over the cobbles to t'folk club. The club is there. But no folk.

'Nowt toneet' says the man in the Working Men's Club downstairs.

So – t'Con club. A tired light shines wearily outside three storeys of black bulk. There's the Windsor room, the billiards room, and at the top of the stairs which leaves the steward wheezing, the Majestic Ballroom.

All empty. In darkness. Downstairs in the back bar, four old men play cards. It is the sort of game where you lose three points if you blink. On Saturdays they say, the ballroom is packed with four-shilling-a-head Socialists, Liberals and Don't-Knows, quick-stepping with apolitical fury.

Tonight just four men playing cards. 'Tories,' they mutter. 'We're all Tories in this bar.'

Suddenly an old Tory hand impetuously puts a card down. Excitement flares. Accrington's night life is rising off the launch pad at last.

In clubs glistening with teak and leatherette, men refrain from playing snooker in their working attire, as requested. Gaunt Accrington faces light up slowly as the Danny Browns, Big Bens, and Old Dans sink down the glasses. Everywhere there is the clack of dominoes, the snick of snooker. Middle-aged ladies sit stiffly over their glasses, beneath a sea of frozen perms.

Two young men survey the Blackpool postcards pinned on the wall, and lean forward to examine...

On the wall, young ladies of impossible dimension sport through the Blackpool surf. A young man squints at one of them. 'By God, tha doesn't get many o' them in a pound.'

Ten-thirty. Careless people lose their fingers as bar-grills snap down. Screwmen, rake hands and roller drivers, shoddy rustlers and cone-and-hank winders, waddle, sway, lurch and totter home.

Outside the Market Hall, the smallest skinhead in the world stands in his boots like an under-nourished begonia in an oversized pot. 'Yer want any bovver?' he inquires, weakly. He doesn't look as though he could bovver Jimmy Clitheroe.

Beside the Commercial Hotel, a man tells his wife that he feels as rough as a badger's bum.

In the Sunspot arcade the lights shine but the doors are closed. A little old lady clasps an unlit, wet cigarette between mean gums as she peers through the window of a fruit machine and mutters dejectedly: 'Two soddin' lemons.'

In the bus station two burly lads, chatty with beer, say yes, this is it, the night's over. 'Unless,' with a leer, 'tha's going up Whinny Hill.'

Up Whinny Hill, Accrington's homespun evening ends in the traditional way. Here, the young ones of Ackie preserve the Northern way of life by entertaining themselves.

Shadows lock and sway in the gloom. And through the silence of a town once again back in its curlers, a shrill voice giggles: 'Gi' up, 'arry, you great daft devil.'

Oh! Accrington!

*

Okay, let's get this straight before we start: I've got no experience of reporting wars or terrorism or any of that military mayhem. But I can tell you this – I know a petrol bomb when I see one. And I was looking at scores of them.

I could see the bottles of sinister pale yellow liquid packed into the half-open cardboard box behind me in the Ford estate. The box must have held a couple of dozen bottles. Since there were 20 or more boxes that meant there must be...

Enough petrol bombs to damage my eyelashes, and quite possibly my fringe, which was always a worry for us dainty features folk.

Since this was Northern Ireland when the fashion for blowing people up was at its height, and since my driver was almost certainly fully-qualified in such matters, it wasn't looking good. For a start, he was driving at high speed and the bottles kept jiggling against each other as we slid round corners. I mean, how much jiggling can a petrol bomb take before it starts to simmer, or whatever it is petrol bombs do?

What made it worse was that each bottle was labelled, with black irony, Crisp 'n' Dry Cooking Oil. Crisp 'n' Dry, presumably, because that was how the onlookers were left after the big bang.

'No,' said my driver with a sharp laugh, 'they really are bottles of cooking oil. We took the rep's car and we haven't had time to unload it.'

So – Edwards and McQueen and the rest of you war boys can laugh – it seems I don't know a petrol bomb when I see one. In fact what on earth I

76

was doing in Londonderry behind enemy lines, I'm not sure to this day. It wasn't supposed to be like that.

'London,' said Alan Price, with the weary sigh that accompanied his every mention of that city, 'have a good idea for you.' At that time, the IRA had set up no-go areas where they held supreme authority: no soldier, no policeman, dare set foot in the place. Alan, features boss on the *Daily Mirror* in Manchester, explained that the London office wanted me to go into the no-go areas. His briefing was slightly different. 'The whole idea's too silly for words. Stay for a couple of days, have a drink or whatever it is you reporters do, then come back.'

That sounded more within my range. Even so, I thought a gesture towards doing the story would help.

I booked into the City Hotel in Londonderry, just down the road from the Bogside and Creggan, 'Free Derry' as they called it, where the uninvited would have the life expectancy of a belch. Announce what you had in mind in the bar of the hotel, I was told, and word would reach the IRA. So I mused aloud about how I would like a conducted tour of the area. That was that. Job done. Unless the IRA was setting up in the travel business, that's the last I would hear. I settled down to my pint and the paper.

Twenty minutes later I was called to the phone. Explain what you want, a voice said. I did. 'Be on the corner of Williams Street at 11am tomorrow,' the voice said.

Oh my god. I was in serious danger of getting a real story, which in my case was pretty much unprecedented.

That was how the next day I came to be taken on Terrorists' Tours in a rep's car loaded with cooking oil by my guide, Harry McCourt, a Sinn Fein politician.

Look, he said he was called Harry McCourt. He said he was a politician. If he'd said he was the Wizard of Oz I wouldn't have argued. He was a chatty chap with a downturned Mexican moustache about ten years after the fashion had gone. What he was like as a terrorist I don't know, but he was a first-rate PR man.

By way of superficial bonding, once he knew I was from Manchester he said he used to like the city when he worked there. As a Mister Softee ice-cream man.

The only reason I'd got in was that my phone call had coincided with a decision by the political branch of the IRA – the ones with the brains, however small – to show the world how well they were running their empire. He pointed out how they'd replaced the shattered street lamps and organised taxis to replace the buses. By way of law and order, they were obliged to do a little tarring here and a bit of feathering there – he even introduced me to one young man who'd had the double treatment for joy-riding. 'I deserved it all right,' he said, just as if he'd practised saying it all day. Then he went off-script: 'Actually they'd run out of feathers so they had to do me with straw.' I wasn't at all sure that an organisation that ran out of feathers was equipped to run a country, but what would I know? For more serious offences, there was a bullet: in either the knee-cap or the head, depending. Apparently running out of bullets wasn't a problem.

'A snack?' Harry suggested. He took me into a council house where we had tea and buttered scones (delicious, by the way) while two young men watched Laurel and Hardy on television. Apart from the carbines across their knees, it was all quite decorous.

By the time I got back to the hotel it was early evening and there was a slight panic in the air. Nobody had ever thought I'd get in; then they thought I'd never get out. They'd been giving Catholic taxi-drivers large wodges of cash to drive round looking for my remains.

After I filed the piece Tony Miles, the editor, came on, all the way from London. It was fine, he said, but my descriptions of the daffodils in the neat gardens and the litterless streets made the Creggan sound like a desirable residential area. I had to point out that it was. Although the rest of Londonderry was shot to hell, the terrorists didn't burn down their own buildings or blow up their own houses.

To an outsider it was inexplicable that 'the enemy' were right here. Everybody knew the Provos' HQ was halfway down the Falls Road opposite Casement Park. This seemed to me a bit like the German SS having a press office in Kensington High Street in 1942. A reporter who was there when the British Army surrounded it said they all paled when they heard a hideous screeching noise outside. Blood on the pavements? Not quite. One of the armoured cars had parked on a set of bagpipes.

For a visiting hack, this was all very confusing. Until then, as far as the British press were concerned, there was only one Ireland: it was a land populated by loveable, whimsical, twinkly-eyed rascals who believed in the little people and liked a drop o' poteen. All their sentences began with the words: 'Would you ever...'

Mostly my trips to Ireland were pure joy: a day or two at the Gresham, a pint or two with the excellent Liam Kelly, and a trip down the country for a comical story about mouse-racing or pig-smuggling or moonshine-making. I used an awful lot of begorrahs in quotes, I remember. The Irish, a shrewd lot who knew the comical Mick image was good for tourism, were always happy to go along with it. Hence all the tea-towels wittily inscribed 'May ye be in heaven half an hour before the divil knows you're dead.'

I remember once saying this to a professional chap – a solicitor, I think – who was sitting at a table at a race meeting in Kerry, reading his paper, as American tourists swarmed around. He knew immediately what I meant.

'Ah, it's a bit of the ould paddy-whackery you're wanting, is it?' he said. He may even have said Begorrah. He sprang up, tilted his hat over his eyes, tucked his rolled-up paper under his arm, and began to jig to and fro as he sang :'With a shillelagh under me arm, and a twinkle in me eye, I'll be in Tipperary in the morning.'

They could turn it on like a tap, and very enjoyable it was too. So naturally when I was doing a piece on the introduction of the breathalyser, it wasn't about drink, it wasn't about road safety, it was about paddy-whackery. The joke in this case was that the conviction rate was low. 'Jaysus,' said one well-briefed official, 'you'd have to be sick in the bag to fail.' For feature writers, Ireland was the land of smiles.

Yet here was this other Ireland, where the residents had abandoned whimsy in favour of mutual destruction. So it was a bit of a leap to find myself getting out of a taxi at 'a mean abode down the Shankill Road', as one of their lovelier poems says. So proud to be British were they that they'd painted the kerbs red, white and blue, which encouraged me to think that they'd welcome a fellow monarchist from over the water. Not a bit of it. They were even more unpleasant than the other lot. So much for a shared heritage.

I was there to see a man called Tommy Herron, who was a top man in one of the Protestant 'defence' groups. Three young men were blocking the doorway. I said who I was, and attempted to slide discreetly through, when one of them produced something from his pocket.

I'm not saying it was a gun. It looked like a gun, it clicked like a gun, and I had a nasty feeling it would make a hole like a gun. But for all I know it could have been a water-pistol which would, in any case, have been quite enough to frighten me. It didn't matter because a voice from inside said I was expected, which meant that I wasn't obliged to take the young men's advice. To feck off.

As far as I remember, Tommy Herron didn't say anything to push back the frontiers of international understanding or to threaten Oscar Wilde's reputation as a drawing-room wit. The only thing I do remember is that one of his bodyguards was reading a copy of *The Beano*.

As you will perhaps have gathered, personally I was quite at home with the mouse-racers and moonshine-brewers. When The Troubles revived, at first, the natural instinct of the journalists, as perpetual outsiders, was to sympathise with anyone who claimed the title of rebels. If we were confused, imagine what effect this had on the Irish. I shall never forget the

79

look on Liam Kelly's face one night in the Stab when a packed room of English hacks demanded a rebel song, and cheered uproariously as he sang about a couple o' sticks of gelig-a-nite and me ould alarum clock. Even Liam was a touch surprised to find himself feted for singing about IRA bombers in a London pub.

He was about as baffled then as I was when a reporter in McGlade's bar told me that Coleraine was 'a naice wee Proddestan tine.' I wasn't accustomed to hearing any version of Christian faith used to describe a municipality. I mean, was Skipton a nice wee Methodist town?

After a visit to Belfast, I was glad to get down to see an old friend in Cork. He wanted to know how I found it in the North. Didn't I think that the Prods were disgustingly bigoted? Nervously, I said they seemed much the same as anyone else.

That, he protested, was rubbish. 'Why,' he said, 'I can even recognise a Prod in the street. With their nasty little pale feckin' faces and mean little feckin' mouths, won't put a hand in the pocket for fear of spendin' a feckin' penny, Jaysus their feckin' teeth'd fall out if they gave you a smile...'

And did he find them bigoted, I asked. Yes, he said. Without a doubt.

For all that *me da was a culchie* (ask Google for a translation), this was all beyond me. I wasn't even all that surprised when I got two threatening phone calls after the pieces on Free Derry and Tommy Herron appeared. Was it because I had called them murderous, heartless bastards who loved to gun down women and children?

No. They quite liked that.

The IRA were enraged because I'd reported that Harry was a former Mister Softee, which had apparently led to a certain amount of teasing – good-humoured, no doubt – from his bloodstained chums.

And what had upset the Loyalists was not that I'd mentioned the thug reading *The Beano*. But surely I didn't have to say that his lips moved, did I? I removed myself before my knee-caps became a matter for discussion.

I should've known better. You can't be too careful when dealing with such sensitive souls.

*

'Right then,' said Tom Hopkinson, the Bradford freelance. 'Here's your choice. The 15-minute tabloid news reporters' talk-through, the feature writers' two hour tour, or the colour-supplement half-day job.'

What was it about his response that made me think I wasn't the first?

As long ago as 1968, Lumb Lane, Bradford 8, was becoming famous as a home-from-home for Asians. Tom, never a man to miss a story, had evolved a range of crash courses for visiting hacks who were eager to see what was probably the first instance of reverse colonisation. With his tweedy jackets and country-tanned moon-face, he looked as though he'd just come in from a long night's lambing. Since he knew everybody in Lumb Lane, he made an excellent white hunter.

The response from the Yorkshire locals to this new community was amused curiosity. In a pub just outside Ilkley, I was ordering a pint when a car-load of young Asians came through the door. 'Hang on a minute,' the landlord said, 'I'll just serve these Bradford lads first.' Smiles all round, including the new arrivals.

Fearlessly, I followed Hopkinson-sahib on his hacks' safari into the uncharted territory of the street that was known to locals, with cheerful innocence, as The Khyber Pass. Here you could have a meal, drink a pint, watch a film, visit the bank, book a holiday and get a taxi without seeing a white face.

Reactions all round seem laughable today. Some young white boys boasted to me that they had entered an Indian restaurant and had a sort of spicy stew called curry. 'Not si bad either,' said one, 'if tha's had a few pints.' An elderly Indian woman told me she wept with pride when she saw Lumb Lane. 'At last I have seen Paradise before I die.' A young Sikh, an accountant, said he was brought up to believe that all Englishmen were like the one they knew best at home. When he arrived in Bradford – unluckily, closing-time on a Saturday night – it wasn't easy to spot any resemblance to Lord Louis Mountbatten. In fact, it wasn't easy finding anybody who could stand up.

With just a trace of embarrassment, I have to tell you that the cutting before me records that I described these newcomers as coloureds and remarked with some pride that there had been no 'nigger hunting'. I must've been reading too much James Baldwin.

Why am I reviving this old story? Well, if we'd only had eyes to see, what we were witnessing then was the start of the world around us today. But neither I nor Tom nor any of the *Daily Mirror* readers realised that within a few years scores of towns and cities would have their own Lumb Lanes. Only nobody calls them Paradise any more.

This all came about when Cudlipp launched one of his rare forays into the north, which he knew rather less well than Tom knew Asian Bradford. While in Manchester, he launched 'Voice of the North', a series of features that was going to tell the world about all the exciting things happening in the north. Why? Well, whenever he ventured north of Holborn Viaduct, he felt obliged to launch something: we were lucky it wasn't a battleship.

Laser eyes combing a room of shivering executives, Cudlipp spotted Alan Price, who was sticking to his usual policy of trying to hide behind a pillar. He was also eating an ice-cream. That was a mistake.

'Hey, you, Mr Vanilla,' called Cudlipp. 'What do you think?'

Alan turned pink, gave one of his theatrical shrugs and, with ill-concealed insincerity, replied: 'Marvellous'.

So he was given the job of coming up with a list of features that would bring some sort of sense of this barmy venture. Alan, who viewed popular newspapers, those who wrote them and those who read them, with contempt, was also astonishingly good at things tabloid. Before Cudlipp fell off the train at Euston, awash with claret, he'd come up with the list.

It caused some alarm in London. Malcolm Keogh, originally from Liverpool, was told to oversee it. A fine journalist, he knew immediately what he must do first. He made a few phone calls to ensure that his exes would be put through open-handed London, rather than miserly Manchester. Things like that mark out the real pro.

Pilger, the big gun we'd been promised, came up and did a couple of pieces. We didn't see much of him after that. And since London soon abandoned the whole idea, we were left explaining all the wonder of the north to... the people who lived in the north.

Somehow that didn't seem to have the same missionary purpose as telling the world.

Oddly enough, the Voice of the North turned out to be curiously prophetic.

There was 'redeployment', under which coal-miners were helped to find jobs above ground. I talked to a 43-year-old pitman who at 14 had followed his father down the pit at Crook, in County Durham, for 17s 3d a week; now he was working in a light-industry factory. He had only two regrets. One was that he could no longer pick a live coal out of the fire to light his cigarette because his hands, once calloused and leathery, were now pink and soft. The other was the coal bill.

Long before Scargill and Mrs Thatcher turned the coal industry into a battleground, the pits were beginning to shut down.

The same was true of the cotton and woollen mills. In a hill-top village called Shore in Lancashire, I found a woman who for 20 years had been a spinner in Clegg's Mill. She still worked there but now she was assembling shaving cream and deodorant sticks.

All over the north, pits and mills, shipyards and furnaces, were closing, and with Voice of the North we told our readers. Although, with half-a-million people losing their jobs, it's possible they had noticed this already.

Then there was the story about 'reclamation' – odd how vocabulary is just as vulnerable to fashion as skirt-lengths. The aim of this was to restore land made derelict by the vanishing industries.

Work was just starting on The Wigan Alps, three massive pit-heaps, to turn them into a playground for ski-ing and sailing, riding and rambling. Maggie Hurst, who lived across the road, told me she used to pick bluebells there. 'I've seen 'em go up, and I'll see 'em come down.'

I wonder if she did. I've never been back (look: there's quite enough disappointment in my life), but I haven't heard too many reports from the Wigan ski slopes.

This was one of those stories where the editor comes back with a silly question. Why don't we have a couple of paragraphs of statistics to show the whole picture? We didn't because there weren't any. Just a few lines then? Okay. So I wrote a couple of pars – something along the lines of 'Every week, a team of 50,000 men with 2,000 bulldozers, shift half-a-million tons of muck in clearing 5,000 acres a day...'

You know the sort of thing. It was hailed as a triumph of investigative journalism. For a couple of years afterwards, I used to see those figures repeated everywhere from the *Guardian* to *Panorama*. And very fine figures they were: I had crafted them myself.

Then there were pieces on the steady demolition of the rows of terraces that were at the heart of northern life. As the houses came down, the life there was recorded by television's Coronation Street. – mostly written by newspaper escapees, like John Stevenson.

The cult of celebrity flickered into life. In the Yorkshire Dales, Clapham (the one near Ingleton, not the one near Wandsworth) had Alan Bennett, occasionally at least. Dent had Mike Harding and his rhinestones, and later Janet Street-Porter, the well-known elocution teacher, and in Giggleswick where I had a cottage, we acquired Russell Harty, who lived with his boyfriend at Rose Cottage.

Not all our northern villagers were ready for this influx of metropolitan sophistication. One evening, when Russell Harty's young man friend had just left the bar of the Black Horse near to the church, I asked a pal of mine, a farm worker, what he thought of it all. 'What? Harty and that feller?' He pondered for a moment. 'Well, if it were down to me, I'd line 'em all up agin yon wall, and I'd mow 'em down wi' a machine-gun.' He paused to take a sip out of his pint. 'Other than that, I've no strong feelings.'

I digress; I digress.

These were good days for journalism in the north. Sales were good. For us, there was lots of hiring, very little firing. We lived well. One lunchtime in the *Mirror* pub, I remember Mike Gagie, tough news deskman, remonstrating with Ted Macaulay, stylish reporter-writer, over a blue suede coat that made him look like the best-dressed highwayman in Farnsworth. 'It's easy for you. If you're feeling a bit down,' Gagie went on, 'that's all you need – a new suit or a coat to cheer you up. I have to have a new Jag.' These were our choices and problems. They could've been worse.

None of us realised what was staring us in the face. We were not only witnessing, but we were also recording, and some of us living, the beginning of the end.

Mills, mines, factories, all the heavy industries – this was where *Daily Mirror* readers worked. Behind those polished front door-knobs, that was where they lived. Piece by piece, the *Mirror* readership was being dismantled. The traditional working-class, now laughably old-fashioned, were hard-working, thoroughly respectable, law-abiding, good-hearted people who were not afraid to want to improve themselves. To do so, they joined book clubs and went to WEA classes and tried to ensure their kids got a decent education.

The *Daily Mirror*, with its clever mix of fun and information, was exactly what they wanted.

They voted Labour, but *Mirror* readers were by nature conservative. Wrenched out of my Sunday leisure, I once had to dash up to a Working Men's Club at Walker-on-Tyne. I was wearing pink cord trousers. No tie. Longish hair. They had to have a committee meeting before agreeing to let me in... reluctantly. I heard two lads at the bar talking. One of them said: 'He's from the *Mirror*, he's called Dunne.' The other replied: 'He looks more like bloody Marje Proops to me.'

Then, even the young guys were traditionalists. But that world was slipping away, vanishing before our eyes, and I for one never saw it.

Even my old weekly, the *Craven Herald* (don't forget *And West Yorkshire Pioneer*) reported, somewhat baffled, that the editor's wife, Molly Mitchell, who was also on the local council, had demanded that she be addressed not as Mr Chairman, or even Mrs Chairwoman, but as Madam Chair.

The idea of it. Calling someone after a piece of furniture. How ridiculous could you get?

At that time, of course, we hadn't heard of Ms Harriet Harman.

Someone had seen it coming. Rupert Murdoch. Cudlipp handed him the *Sun*. He created a new paper for the new readers – readers with tattoos, six-packs, shaved heads, who didn't frequent the WEA: their idea of self-advancement was to rob a bank.

A couple of years later, with the *Sun* sales rocketing and the *Mirror* (and the *Express* too for that matter) limping, poor old Cudlipp still couldn't face up to it. Glass of claret in hand, silver quaff in place, blinded by his own vanity, he strolled around his penthouse reassuring his executives. 'This Ned Kelly, this antipodean bandit, he's nothing. It's the old enemy, the *Express*, that's the one to watch.'

He was the last man in Britain to know.

*

About half a lifetime ago I was living in a Chelsea street two doors away from Bob Geldof. Sharing the street with him was interesting. First, we were always worried that down-and-outs would follow him home in the belief that he must be heading for a hostel. Secondly, his wife was given to crashing her car into others in the street (including mine) when she was over-excited.

Then there was the embarrassment over their daughter. Paula announced that her new-born child was being named after the fruit or vegetable she most resembled. For years we called her Turnip. She didn't look much like a peach to us.

But the one good thing about having him there was that from time to time, usually when pots and pans began flying, I'd open the door and find a friendly pack of hacks and snappers on the pavement. This meant, naturally, that, since freelancing from home was a lonely business, I felt obliged to take them down to the Coopers Arms for a restorative.

Until then I hadn't had much contact with the younger hacks, and this lot were mostly in their early twenties. They were always curious to know about life B3M (that's Before the three Ms – Murdoch, Maxwell and Montgomery') and I was happy to tell them. Was there, one of them asked, any writer-reporter from that time who was outstanding? Only one answer, of course. I told them, and looked at their blank faces. 'Who's Vincent Mulchrone?'

I was astonished. In my half-century of this nutty industry, I had never previously had to explain to anyone who Mulchrone was. The surname was quite enough. Everybody knew. Everybody knew because we all wished we were Vincent Mulchrone.

Typing out the parking fines from the morning court, standing outside the church at a funeral collecting names, asking golden wedding couples the secret of happiness, every young trainee dreamed of being Mulchrone. I once tried to graft his style on to my report of Addingham Parish Council: it wasn't altogether a success.

Incredibly, he died over 30 years ago. And for well over 20 years before that, at a time when newspapers were awash with talent, he was regarded as the best. Given that we were all working with the same 26 letters of the alphabet, I could never understand how what he wrote was so totally different – and inarguably superior – to the others. Reading some people was like wading through congealed porridge; with Mulchrone it was like ski-ing downhill. Some writers made you yawn; he made you smile. Some pieces just lay on the page, dead and dull. His glowed. All with the same 26 letters – I never understood it then, and I don't understand it now.

Let me get this straight immediately – I met him only a handful of times, and I certainly didn't know him well. But I have to correct a wicked lie he once wrote about me.

What I can also certainly do is to speak for the effect he had on that generation – my generation – immediately behind his. We studied his pieces as we had never studied for O-levels, trying to work out what he'd got and how we could get it. Even now I can quote several of his more famous intros. 'Two rivers run silently through London tonight and one is made of people…' for the queue to see Churchill's lying-in-state.

And 'If the Germans beat us at our national game today, we can always console ourselves with the fact that we have twice beaten them at theirs,' on the morning of the 1966 World Cup final. That's hardly a boast on my part. Any journalist over 50 could do the same. That's the measure of his influence.

At the Friday morning journalism class in Bradford Tech, we used to read this stuff, sigh, and get on with our shorthand. It seemed a world away.

A few years later, as new boy in features in the *Mirror* in Manchester, I was off on my first foreign job. Albert Hirst, a butcher from Barnsley, was competing at the International Black Pudding Festival in a little town in Normandy, and I was taking him. What we hot-shot reporters called an exclusive, I think you'll find.

As we flew down to Heathrow, he said he'd had a call from somebody on the *Daily Mail* who also wanted to be there. 'Someone called Mulchrone,' he said.

My heart leapt and sank simultaneously. It was rather like being invited to bowl at Len Hutton. I was overjoyed at the thought of meeting my hero. I was also terrified at the prospect of having to write the same piece.

He was waiting at the airside bar at 9am with a small row of bottles in front of him. He explained the line-up: Fernet Branca for his hangover, iced water to remove the taste of the Fernet Branca, and a half-bottle of champagne to get going. 'You can't start the engine without the diesel,' he said. 'Would you like a drink yourselves?'

I was half-hoping that he'd be supercilious and patronising. Instead, he was charming and self-deprecating, and Albert Hirst and myself were utterly disarmed. And we hadn't even had a drink.

As we drove up into Normandy with me at the wheel, at Mulchrone's suggestion we stopped here and there, and there and here, to sample a local product – Calvados. Every establishment made its own and it was necessary, he said, to try them out. It soon became clear that he was one of those charismatic men who could light up a room. He chattered and chuckled and charmed (in fluent French, of course, the swine), and in every bar they almost wept when he left.

When we got to Mortagne-au-Perche, the market town was packed with black pud makers and black pud aficionados. As we fought our way to the bar of the one small hotel, Albert was hanging on to a plastic bag inscribed 'Albert Hirst, High-Class Family Butcher' which he'd carefully carried all the way there. He asked Mulchrone for some whispered advice before plonking it on the bar and opening it to reveal the biggest pork pie in the history of such things. *'Ern petty caddo from Barnsley, England,'* he rumbled in his Yorkshire baritone. It went down a storm, as indeed did his pork pie.

The next morning we strolled through the huge tents with tables laden with puddings both black and white, and quite possibly striped. They'd come in from all over France, but from Belgium, Germany and Italy too. There were hundreds and hundreds of them. So thrilled were they with this British invasion (it was a long time ago) that they made Mulchrone and me judges for one table of 25 black puddings. To clear our palate after each one, we were given a glass of Muscadet.

We emerged from the tent not knowing much about black puddings, but as very fine judges of Muscadet. Or, at least, that's what Mulchrone wrote in his piece. After all this time, I think I can safely nick it.

That night we had a stroll around town and several more glasses of Muscadet and Calvados. Towards midnight, I remember we were comparing our favourite intros. He said he had a weakness for Police With Tracker Dogs. I said I preferred Schoolchildren Turned Detective For a Day. He countered with Angry Housewives Yesterday. Yes, I think I can safely say he passed on to me the secrets of his trade.

The next morning we retired to our respective rooms to write. It didn't so much flow as coagulate. How can you write anything when the man who is the best is doing the same thing yards away? I had managed to scrape a few paragraphs together when there was a tap at the door.

It was Mulchrone. He was holding out his copy. 'I've finished,' he said. 'Would it help you to have a look at it?' I thought of trying to explain that not only did I not want to see it, but I didn't want to be in the same hotel as him when he was writing, or indeed in the same country. So I just said no thanks.

The two pieces appeared. His was... well, Mulchrone. Mine wasn't. That's all you need to know.

To my personal delight and professional dismay, he kept on popping up after that. And he was always great fun. In the Grand Hotel in Parknasilla, Co Kerry, where scores of pressmen had flocked to see the newly-retired General de Gaulle, Mulchrone was doing the colour piece. At nine one morning, I saw him pick up the telephone in the bar and call Donald Seaman, the *Express* writer, who was of same vintage.

'Get down here, Don,' he snapped, with some urgency. 'There's something pretty dramatic happening.' A minute later, Seaman tumbled down the staircase still fastening his shirt and demanding to know what was happening. Mulchrone indicated an open bottle of champagne in an ice-bucket on the bar, with two glasses. 'That's pretty dramatic, isn't it?'

When Hereford's football team did well in the FA Cup, I went to do a colour piece, only to find that he'd been there the day before. I'd just got as far as 'Happiness is a town called Hereford today...' when I realised what it was and hurled it away.

There weren't many who could do that light-as-thistledown writing. The *Mirror* sent one of their more mature ladies, who was more foot-in-the-door than Scott Fitzgerald, to do a story about a brothel in Aberdeen. To everyone's astonishment she filed the most delightful piece, and graciously accepted all our congratulations. It wasn't until I opened the *Mail* and saw Mulchrone's piece that I realised where all the graceful phrases and clever insights had come from. I remembered that time in France when he'd offered his copy to me.

That's not to say no-one else could turn in a good light piece. John Edwards could do a colour piece on a jumble sale just as well as on the end of the world. Liz Gill (then married to Danny McGrory) was wonderfully funny when she did the basement piece on *The Times* feature page. The sons of Mulchrone bobbed up all over the place. Alan Bennett, on the *Express*, had a lovely touch, and there was a man on the *Guardian* – Michael Parkin – who did their hanging-indent pieces, and did them beautifully. You won't believe this but there was a young *Mirror* reporter in Newcastle who used to trot out sweetly crafted funny pieces that were up there with the best. He should've stayed with it; Revel Barker would be a great by-line for a comic writer.

One year, when I took my kids down to West Cork for a holiday, I was driving slowly around the quay at a place called Crookhaven when a man jumped out waving in front of me. It was Mulchrone. He had a cottage there. He also had his supporters' club. In the bar of the Crookhaven Inn sat Ken Donlan, Terry O'Connor, and Peter Donnelly, the *Mail*'s news editor, rugby writer and star sub. If David English had made it, we could've had a chapel meeting. Oh yes, and Vincent's son Patrick was behind the bar. When we got up to his cottage, his wife Louie had already opened the champagne.

So what about the wicked lie? Right. A couple of days after our French trip I got a typed letter on *Daily Mail* headed paper. He said what fun it had been and thanked me for doing the driving. Beneath, in his handwriting, was a PS: 'How dare you write a better piece than me!'

Sadly, not even I could believe it. And believe me, I tried.

So let's raise a glass to the master of them all. First of all, the Fernet Branca, then the water...

*

Imagine Cameron Diaz when she was 19. And Charleze Theron. Then perhaps Scarlett Johansson at the same age. Got that? Now try – this won't be easy – to picture an island where almost all the women look like this, except for the unlucky ones who look like Sienna Miller.

You should also know that this was an island where going to bed alone was pretty much against the law. Going to bed sober certainly was.

I had to spend a month or so there. It was hell.

For all their ingenuity, the tabloids have rarely succeeded in fitting chess into their view of the world. They've never shown much interest in Iceland either. It's up there somewhere, just north of the *Daily Record*, isn't it?

So when the two coincided – a chess game in Reykjavik – most editors were fairly yawning with excitement. In 1972, with Watergate, the miners' strike, and air-crash survivors in the Andes eating each other, they weren't exactly scraping around for stories. Since Iceland was Up North, it was a Manchester job. 'Two days in and out,' said Alan Price. 'Take your thermals.'

Both bits of advice were wrong. Iceland doesn't have ice: it's damp, wet, cold, and miserable, with the sort of dim half-light that you might get from a 40-watt bulb. Not unlike Manchester in fact. And the story that was worth no more than a quick colour-piece miraculously exploded all over the world's front pages.

There was I, steaming like a sponge pudding in my all-over thermals, the *Mirror* man-on-the-spot for a story that got bigger and funnier with every passing day. Let me remind you that I was the reporter whose experience of major news stories had peaked with, but never risen above, the Talking Corgi of Drighlington Crossroads.

Quickly, the story began to fall into shape. Since the two contestants were Russian and American, it was immediately seen as a war without bullets on the roof of the world. What made it even better was that one of the players – a genius, without a doubt – would have been more at home wearing a jacket with tie-around sleeves and a room with cushions for wallpaper. Bobby Fischer was, to use a psychiatric term, nuts.

He was a touch unpredictable. At the last minute, with the whole world waiting, he cancelled his flight from New York. 'He's so sure he's the best,' said one expert, 'that he sees no point in coming.'

Fischer didn't think much of the location when he got there. 'Where we gonna play – the back of a whale?' Told it was a modern 3,000-seat stadium, he didn't like the lighting, he didn't like the heating, he'd need a Merc on call (an automatic, naturally) in a place that had only about 80 miles of decent roads. And could he be sure to get his favourite apple juice?

He didn't think much of the money either. It was only when a British financier doubled the prize money to £100,000 – not bad in 1972 – that he got on that plane. When the first game started, three days late, Fischer was even late for the kick-off.

It was wonderful stuff. A ditchwater-dull story about a game for school swots had revved up into a blazing extravaganza that combined high drama with pure panto. Hacks from all over the world poured in. Ian Wooldridge did the first piece for the *Mail*, then handed over to John Edwards. Clement Freud, then a journalist, was covering it for the *FT*.

A cuddly little Irish girl called Mary Kenny was there for the *Standard*. Keith Hatfield was there for ITN.

The *Express* sent a political chap who'd brought his wife for a break; every day he filed one par, adding a phrase I have personally never dared to employ: 'Take in agency'. The *Telegraph*'s Maurice Weaver had to get his wife to rush to the airport with the passport he'd left at home. Tim Jones for *The Times* gave us the occasional recital of Welsh misery music.

In all, 200 pressmen flooded the four hotels and the little tin town of Reykjavik. These days, with international tourism and whale-watching, it's become much like anywhere else. Then it was like only one other place: Dodge City. Fishing had made Iceland highly prosperous. But what do you do with wallets fat with krona when you're stranded on a hot volcanic rock out in the middle of a freezing ocean? You go mad, that's what you do.

For a start, they abandoned any moral standards (much as we did 30 years later). If the only alternative was reading those bloody sagas, then no wonder sex was a popular pursuit. There was only one television channel: it was evenings-only and didn't operate at all on Wednesdays.

On an island where drink was almost unobtainable, you had to admire the population's response to the challenge by getting smashed every night. There were, I think, only four bars and they were in the hotels. They didn't open officially until 7pm. One day a week they didn't open at all. The beer was almost alcohol-free. A gin-and-tonic then was about a fiver.

On my first day, when I arranged to meet our stringer from the local paper, I suggested the hotel bar at seven. 'Are you sure?' he said, sounding thoroughly doubtful. I saw why when I went through the door. It looked like Glasgow on New Year's Eve. There were people slumped against the walls, people attempting to fight but mostly missing, and people asleep on the floor.

To work around the limited opening hours and horrific prices, they topped up with home-made hooch at home before launching themselves on an evening of Reykjavikian sophistication.

Why anyone would want to be permanently legless in a country with the most beautiful women in the world is one for the psychiatrists. It was the first thing you noticed. In every bus queue you'd see three or four Miss World finalists.

Cameron, Charleze and Scarlett would have been lucky to get a date.

All around, journalistic jaws dropped at the sight of shop-girls and waitresses with blue-grey eyes, soft fair hair, and a perfect white slash of a smile. In Britain, we were accustomed to the same old choice: it was either a splendid chest – which always came with a huge bum, or the slim-hips-no-tits model. In Iceland, you could have slim and voluptuous in one person. Our boys had never seen that before. Frankly, our boys liked it.

What's more, their traditional Icelandic welcome seemed to involve a lot of leg-waving.

The problem wasn't Icelandic women. The problem was Icelandic men. I have never seen so many men get so drunk so quickly every day of the week, and I speak as a man who's been to the photographers' Christmas party. They were big fellers too: powerful from all that net-hauling, I suppose.

Big, strong, ugly, drunk and usually looking to end the evening with a traditional attempted murder. They liked battered cod, true, but they preferred battered Brits.

We were the guys who had attempted to steal their fish.

On our first night out, our tidy little British team of half-a-dozen hacks edged into the dance-hall adjoining the hotel to see what looked like open night in the infernal regions. From the mass of brutish brawling emerged, incredibly, a bride still in her bridal gown. She was stunningly lovely. She was also stunningly drunk. 'You English?' she said. We nodded. With a sweet smile, she added: 'I am Icelandic and I like the sex.'

You see what they were up against. Before getting close enough to these women to discuss a little mutual harpooning, our gallant hacks had to negotiate a way around bands of murderous men.

I brush away a tear of pride here as I record that one or two of our brethren made it through what was in many ways an early video game: daring death to win the hand, or some other part, of the fair maidens.

One of the smaller members of our group – now what was his name? – somehow smuggled a vast Valkyrie up to his room. At 2am, the rest of the corridor was awakened by a glass-shattering soprano shriek: 'Give me a son!' It was an odd time of night to start being gender-specific. Unless, of course, she'd actually been shouting 'Give me the *Sun*.'

Another chap called – oh my memory, there it goes again – found himself engaged in a pelvic clash with a blonde, several floors up in what appeared to be a council tower block, when he heard a noise behind him. He looked over his shoulder to see a tattooed tower of a trawlerman in the doorway. 'It is my husband,' piped up a voice beneath him. 'He does not care.'

Somehow, this reassurance failed. He left. A trained observer, he had made note of a telephone box outside the flats, so he knew he would not be stranded. Even as he flicked open the directory, he realised he was in one of the few countries in the world where the local word for taxi isn't taxi. He got back to the hotel just in time for breakfast.

Even for a band of travelling hacks, this was bad behaviour of the highest order, and – feminists will rejoice to hear – it was on an equal-rights basis. Where was that slim blonde girl from? It will come to me. It certainly came to her. One morning she burst into breakfast to announce that she had just screwed a grandmaster from Prague.

'Ah,' I quipped, 'that would have been a Czech mate.'

Actually, I lie. Like all the best lines, it only came to me nearly 40 years later, about ten minutes ago.

With so many journalists there, one of the problems, obvious to all the practised foreign reporters, was getting copy back. The handful of young women on the switchboard were under heavy pressure. Some said a few folded notes helped speed it up. But I saw one of the girls almost melt when a famous international reporter laid his hand on her shoulder. He had clearly laid his hand elsewhere. 'Sometimes,' he confided in me later, 'you need to make a personal connection.'

Meanwhile, the story just went on getting sillier and sillier, and therefore better and better. Bobby wanted the seats in the hall moving. Bobby didn't like the television cameras.

Bobby thought the Russians were trying to hypnotise him. He threw games away by simply not turning up.

What made it even more fascinating was that somewhere the two chess players seemed to have swapped identities. The American was behaving like a crazed and ignorant Russian madman.

With his well-cut sports jackets, his friendly charm and good looks, his morning games of tennis, Boris Spassky, who chose to live in Paris rather than Moscow, was giving a passable impersonation of the young David Niven. Fischer was alone, but teams of Russian grandmasters worked out all the possibilities for Spassky while he rested.

It wasn't enough. The Russian smoothie might be winning the PR, but the ungainly clodhopping Fischer wielded a mean pawn. Even though he persistently threw away games, Fischer was too strong for this pleasant young Russian. One evening when the game was suspended until the following day, Fischer had to write down his next move and place it in a secure envelope. The next morning, he wasn't there when the game resumed. The referee opened the envelope and made the move for him. Spassky instantly resigned.

In a couple of minutes, Fischer had worked out the one move that made his victory inevitable. It had taken the Russian team of experts all night to come to the same conclusion.

As they all left, the Russians and the officials and the spectators, I stayed in my seat in the auditorium to write up my copy. As I sat there, I saw a tall figure step out from the wings and come to look at the board. He was giggling. It was Fischer.

How was this accomplished non-newsman managing? To be honest, I'm not at all sure, although Dan Ferrari, the London news editor, seemed happy enough. But as the days turned into weeks, the place became claustrophobic. You can go and look at hot springs only so often. All the food – even the one Chinese takeaway – tasted vaguely of seal. We were getting stir crazy. David English rewarded John Edwards with a break at Charles Forte's fishing lodge on the Nordura river, one of the most expensive salmon beats in the world. He caught nothing. Were we sorry for him? No.

93

Finally, Fischer won. It was over. The more imaginative among us had bills written out in Old Norse, a language not usually understood in most accounts departments.

I was packing my case when the news desk rang. 'It looks as though the Cod War is starting up again, old chap. Do you fancy staying on to cover it?'

My studies of chess had not been wasted. I employed the King's Sicilian Defence and buggered off to the airport.

*

THE CHESSBOARD JUNGLE
By Colin Dunne

Iceland, Wednesday. – About 100 years ago, I saw this chap rise before an international VIP gathering to proclaim that chess was every bit as good as table tennis for cementing universal good-will. People clapped, too.

Come to think of it, that was only 11 days ago; But we've packed a century's experience in meanwhile, and the same comment now would raise a multi-lingual hoot of laughter.

Chess, I now know, ranks roughly alongside the hydrogen bomb as a builder of bridges between nations.

The world's Chess Championship here has also taught me two other priceless lessons. First, keep chess out of politics - it's far too tricky for mere diplomats.

And second, never trust a whaler's wife.

Until now I've always thought that chess finals were usually played between two unpronounceable Russians in unspellable places, watched by a cheering throng of three professors and a dog.

Winners were generally prepared to settle for a chiming clock as a prize - inscribed, of course.

Obviously not true. Or, at least, the summit meeting between Russia's Boris Spassky and America's Bobby Fischer has changed it all.

Fischer, like the good capitalist he is, immediately got the prize money doubled to £100,000, with 30pc of everything, including - I wouldn't be surprised - the latest cod catch.

Spassky, a cunnng Russian propagandist, bowled around kissing babies and signing autographs like a Westminster-bound Tory, scoring brilliantly on international goodwill.

One is the champion for five-year plans, a profitless society and lady street cleaners. The other, in there pitching for Mom's apple pie, Old Glory, and the hamburger.

I managed to follow the duel in the midnight sun as far as that.

But if you get a political propaganda battle fought by men whose IQ figures sound like the latest premium bond winner, Einstein himself would have trouble keeping pace.

Reporters from the 200-strong international press corps paled before a fusillade of charge and counter-charge, dashing frantically from press conference to press conference, praying to be sent somewhere quiet and simple. Like Belfast. Or Vietnam.

Honestly, it's been hell out here. You don't know where the next hand-out is coming from.

'Greedy Yanks,' grunted the Russians. 'Scared Reds,' snarled the Americans, while the Icelanders, nervous matchmakers in this coy courtship, had their 10-piece string orchestra diplomatically sawing out every national anthem short of 'Ilkley Moor Baht'at.'

The Americans said Spassky had a back-up team of grandmasters to help him. 'Our boy's playing ten goddam Russkies.'

The Russians hinted that the Americans had a hot line to a New York computer.

To keep the stars entertained away from the board, the Icelanders desperately offered Fischer a bowling alley and Spassky a tennis court. This way they hoped to preserve their fragile neutrality, and doubtless wished they'd stuck to something easy like wall-of-death riding.

All this would perhaps be more or less comprehensible in Wisconsin or Minsk. But the Icelandic setting - a sort of refrigerated Ruritania - only increases unreality.

How do you adjust to a place where opening time is 7pm, the beer is non-alcoholic, the bars all close on Wednesday, but the inhabitants drink till their teeth fall out?

Night-time Reykjavik is like Dodge City: you don't know whether to step over the bodies or duck under the fists. Every night is like Glasgow on New Year's Eve.

And where the girls - every one of them looks like Britt Ekland, only more so - stride up to total strangers in bars and say: 'I am Icelandic and I like the sex.'

We have seen a few casualties. There is one grey-haired grandmaster here that I know of who will shortly be carried home on a stretcher. His King's Sicilian defence failed before the world's first chess groupie.

Somewhere in this town, they say, there are two men pushing political pawns around while the White House pales and the Kremlin trembles.

For them it may mean a ticker-tape welcome in New York or a quick transfer to a sub-post office in Siberia.

Let them worry. I am listening to a band playing 'Roll Me Over in the Clover' in improbable Icelandic, enjoying the cold war comedy in a cool climate and prepared to surrender my sanity to the first decent offer.

The whaler's wife? Wait till I get back and I'll show you. It's a very odd place to have a harpoon scar.

95

Come back ping-pong, all is forgiven.

*

If you could dig them out of retirement – or, possibly, out of the ground – you'd probably find at least a handful of *Mirror* writers who, wiping away a nostalgic tear, would swear that their careers peaked gloriously with *Mirrorscope*. Count me among them – and I never wrote a word for it. But it gave me my happiest year in newspapers, enough money to build an extension on my house ('Dublin' we called it), and introduced me to the funniest double-act in journalism…

Kelly and Kenealy. Kenealy and Kelly. How on earth did it happen that they came to be locked away in loveless union high in the skyscraper overlooking the Liffey? It was almost like love, in that they couldn't leave each other alone: I always thought it was a sort of passionate hatred combined with mutual fascination. One of them couldn't leave the room without the other whispering: 'Did he say anything about me?'

When I come to think about it, maybe it actually was love.

But, first of all, where does *Mirrorscope* come into all this? For those who weren't there at the time, *Mirrorscope* was one of those brave and brilliant ideas (almost certainly by Cudlipp, out of Molloy) that come to those who have achieved massive popularity then want to Do Good. So the five million *Mirror* buyers (14.2million readers), no doubt to their astonishment, found themselves with a pull-out section packed with intelligent backgrounders, elegant profiles and scholastic analysis – and often not a single picture. All those *Mirror* readers with doctorates and IQs over 150 found it most rewarding: the rest turned to Quizword before returning to the coalface.

To produce this, the paper recruited writers of high reputation… Matt Coady, Richard Sear, Don Gomery. Not me, needless to say. I was trainee assistant junior feature writer in Manchester, only recently promoted from pencil-sharpening.

The only reason I came to be involved in this was because of the Irish Edition, a revolutionary production method that provided Ireland with a colour version in the mid-sixties. Before then, the odd stringer was more than enough to cover Ireland, but now Dublin needed something much grander. And for this, naturally, the *Mirror* had to have the finest reporter in the land: Jack Kenealy, of the *Express*. He didn't come cheap, but he came.

The story goes that as he was leaving the interview he asked about his deputy. Deputy? Who'd said anything about a deputy? Kenealy pointed out he didn't work seven days a week and he'd heard Liam Kelly of the

Herald was a good man. But he'd cost. He did cost. But he too was hauled on board.

Then there was the matter of holidays. If Jack was away for a couple of weeks you could hardly expect Liam to work 14 days non-stop... A third reporter (Bernard Falk, then Chris Buckland) was sent over from Manchester. So was a photographer (Kevin Fitzpatrick, then Bill Kennedy), and they had to have someone to do the sport (Tom Keogh) and who was going to work the tape machine? Doris, as it happened.

And that's how the Dublin empire started. At least, that's the way I heard it and, as always, we must prefer the legend to the truth. Since it was a high-prestige operation, they needed offices in Ireland's only skyscraper, Liberty Hall, on the banks of the Liffey.

Where it got tricky was that *Mirrorscope*, being whatever the phrase was then for cutting-edge, would insist on covering such subjects as birth control, condoms, homosexuality, orgasms and lots of other rudenesses that simply didn't happen in Holy Ireland. The censors kept banning the paper to prevent it making perverts of Ireland's saints and scholars. And quite right too.

That was where I came in. London, fed up with the paper being banned because of their super new pull-out, told Manchester to find someone to fill the gap. Manchester found Alan Price, the features editor, who found his newest and least prized feature writer, me, and recited the sweetest sentence I ever heard in my life...

Would I please go to Ireland, stay as long as I wanted, spend as much as I liked, but come back every week with four pages on any subject I fancied? Oh yes, and would I take Dennis Hussey, the best photographer in the north and all-round good guy, with me?

I nodded. It lasted longer than a year in which we stayed at every multi-starred hotel and ate at every big-name restaurant in the country. What did we write about? Whatever we fancied. We used to decide that on the plane over.

How about a pull-out on Sixties Women? Fine. We assembled one ardent feminist, one Rose of Tralee, the head of the Irish equivalent of the Women's Institute, a career woman, and a woman who had a market stall and 23 children ('two in heaven, the rest down here'). Quick chats, quick snaps, one pull-out. As you can imagine, it wasn't difficult. We worked the same formula again and again – chefs, business tycoons, sportsmen... we even once did Racing in Ireland simply because Dennis loved a bet and wanted a few tips.

Naturally, we based ourselves in the Liberty Hall office of the dynamic, thrusting new Dublin team. Kelly and Kenealy. Kenealy and Kelly.

97

Luckily for me, the first time I set foot in the office, only Liam was there. Now Liam was – and I'm sure still is – one of the funniest and nicest men you could wish to meet, and he was also very helpful to visitors. What I didn't know was that because I had spoken to him first, I had then signed on with Liam for life. Jack would be civil, but that was all. I was on Kelly's team. Any help, ask Kelly. 'Liam, your pal's here,' he would call out. He never said don't ask me, but it was there in the small print.

They were both terrific reporters, both great company, and both widely liked and respected on either side of the Irish Sea. Individually, that is. But together? Together produced an electric tension that induced quivering nerves in English visitors.

Kenealy was sophisticated, urbane, darkly sardonic. When Kenealy picked up the latest visiting Manchester editor at the airport at 8.30am, the editor asked him what he thought of someone on the Irish desk. 'Feckin' eejit,' said Jack. 'That's rather a nasty thing to say,' spluttered the editor. Kenealy looked at his watch. 'Nasty feckin' hour,' he said.

One day in the office he strolled over to the window and looked out over Dublin. Misquoting a popular television programme of the time, he announced: 'There are eight million stories in this city, and I haven't got a feckin' one of them.'

On the other hand, Kelly was lively and cheeky and much given to wicked gossip. It was said that an Irish journalist once burst into a bar where Kelly was sitting on a stool, and sent him flying with a vicious punch.

As Liam sat up rubbing his jaw, his attacker said: 'Jaysus, it's the wrong man.' Everyone agreed that he may have been the wrong man on this particular occasion; any other time it could well have been right.

One morning, Liam picked me up at Jury's hotel after a night of Dublin hospitality that had left me semi-derelict. As we walked to the office, an old tramp – ragged, smelly, toothless with red-rimmed eyes – held out his hand. 'Give him a few bob, Colin,' said Liam. 'He's a feature writer from Manchester who came over eight years ago and missed the plane back.'

It was Liam who introduced me to Sean, the phantom car hirer. Long ago, his firm of undertakers had hired out cars, and he still had the paperwork. He couldn't provide a car, but he could provide a receipt for a car – much more important. First of all we had to go through a procedure that was conducted in a sober and proper fashion, with much use of the subjunctive and conditional. We would shake hands, then he would ask me where I would have gone, if I'd had a car. I said Galway. He expressed the opinion that such a long journey would necessitate a car of large engine capacity. I agreed. He suggested a two-litre model. I agreed. He then pointed out that there would be a very high mileage charge. I agreed. He would then write the whole thing out, sign it, and appear not to see the note that I slipped into his hand as he gave it to me. That's how I got the extension on my house.

In the office, Kelly and Kenealy conducted their personal warfare beneath a cover of civilised manners. Visitors like myself sat quietly watching, heads nervously swivelling like Wimbledon spectators. 'I'm off to the Curragh army camp for lunch, Jack,' said Liam.

'They'll do you proud up there, Liam,' said Jack.

'If you want me, I'm in the officers' mess.'

'Enjoy yourself, Liam. Don't worry about getting back, have a few jars.'

As the door closed, Kenealy, his foot drumming away at the carpet as it always did, gave a bark of laughter. Putting on a mock-posh accent, he said: 'Aim off to the officers' mess, says Kelly. Him, in the officers' mess. He didn't wear feckin' shoes until he was ten years old, and I hope to God he gets the knife and fork in the right hands...'

He went on in this vein for a minute or two, until the door burst open and a red-faced Kelly leapt back into the room.

'I heard that, Kenealy,' he shouted. 'What sort of a man would talk behind a colleague's back like that? What sort of a man would stab someone in the back like that? What sort of a man would sneer at a colleague like that?'

Calmly, Kenealy dabbed the ash off his cigarette. 'And what sort of a man listens at feckin' keyholes, Kelly?'

By this time I was under the desk.

For a relationship as compellingly tempestuous, you'd have to go back to Rhett and Scarlett. You'd think, with Jack Kenealy demanding all his attention, that Liam wouldn't have room in life for any more romance. But he did. A beautiful and charming young woman called Ann, to whom he had been engaged (is this possible, do you think?) for 13 years. While Ann had lived a life beyond reproach, Liam had... well, now and again sort of enjoyed himself. When they decided to get married, it took Liam some time to find a priest who would accept him, and it was said his confession took three days.

With, I think, his audience in mind, the priest took a tabloid line. First, he quoted from a pop song of the day. 'Liam can't guarantee Ann happiness. Today he is saying to her: I beg your pardon; I never promised you a rose garden.' Then, emphasising that this was a spiritual rather than a social event, he described the congregation as 'these so-called friends.' As Liam left, he murmured that the priest had clearly spotted Jack in the church.

Even then, it wasn't over. As the couple bent to get in the bridal car to go off on honeymoon, the voice of Mrs Kenealy floated over the crowd: 'Now don't you be going at it like an expert tonight, Liam, or she'll kno-o-o-w.'

It all had to end, of course. The IRA blew up the Belfast colour plant, although there were vicious rumours suggesting a senior London executive had been seen dancing in the flames. Certainly when Percy Roberts, the chairman, came to make his farewell speech, one of journos sang: 'He's got the key of the door, never blown up a plant before...'

And the whole thing, the new colour printing, the Irish edition, the Liberty Hall office, the assembly of all the talents, the phantom car hirer, all gone. Kelly and Kenealy carried on freelancing for a while before the inevitable divorce.

I was rather sad when I heard. And what's the betting that they were, too.

*

Excuse me, this won't take a minute. It's a question for anyone who was in Manchester around the sixties and into the seventies. Okay? Now was there at that time a man called Arthur Brooks?

Worked on the *Mirror* news desk, About 40, I think. Had a sort of a cowboy look about him, whippet-slim, low-slung trousers, narrow tie, and very, very cool. Had a bent-kneed stance, possibly caused by the weight of his black hair which swept back in a thick well-oiled sheath.

He was never without a half-smile that betokened unassailable self-confidence. This was a man who was untroubled by doubt.

If my memory is right, if he really did exist, he was a man of dazzling accomplishments. Key desk man – in status I'd place him slightly below Don Smith and somewhere above the hat-rack. Legendary reporter. Sports writer who reputedly filed even when his life was in danger from heavy fire. Author of a string of sports books. And certainly the only journalist I ever knew who returned to the office after filing to find executives begging him to autograph his copy for them to keep. Nobody ever asked me to do that, I can tell you.

That's why I'm asking if anyone else remembers him. I mean, talk about multi-talented, it's scarcely believable. He was a sort of C B Fry of Withy Grove.

I first became aware of his name when colleagues told me a story that seemed incredible even in a newspaper office. A major revolution had broken out in – I think – Beirut. No reporters were being allowed in. Airports were sealed. Flights cancelled. But the *Mirror* already had its own

100

man in there – Arthur, right up on the front line, on his way to Australia to report a tour by the English Rugby League team.

He was the only journalist at the centre of the world's most important story, but no calls were getting through.

London was waiting. Manchester was waiting. The tension was mounting. We couldn't get a call in. But could Arthur get a call out? They needn't have worried – this was Arthur they were talking about. Yes, he did get a call through and he was on to copy. Feverishly the night editor – Peter Thomas, I think – snatched up the copy…

'Wily Wigan scrum-half Willie Smith was nursing a sprained ankle last night…'

You see? Even though he was in the middle of a war, he was staying with the sports story. What a man. Peter cut in to talk to him. Arthur didn't seem able to understand. 'Can't hear you,' he said, against a background of thunderous bangs and crashes. 'There's bloody guns and bombs and all sorts going off here. You wouldn't believe it…'

That was Arthur. Imperturbable even when his life was in danger.

But wait…

I've been telling that story for almost half-a-century now, and over the years it must have brought pleasure to millions. So it came as something of a shock when it was first published on the *Ranters* website and several old Mirrormen pointed out that it wasn't Arthur at all: it was Joe Humphreys, the Rugby League writer. They're right, no doubt about that. All I can say is that Joe must have been taking tuition from the Great Arturo, because that (everybody agrees) is exactly what the Sage of Saddleworth (see how contagious it is?) would have done himself.

My best excuse is that readers don't expect accuracy (hard though we strive for it) from feature writers. Reporters are expected to get facts right. We're too busy juggling adjectives.

You see what I mean, though, about the stories about Arthur being unbelievable.

I wasn't there for one of his major successes. In the Swan With Two Necks, whenever a reporter was being feted for some triumph or rocketed for some disaster, whatever the story it always reminded Arthur of the Pennypot Lane murder. I think I've got that right. I'm not sure, because, to be honest, I'd never heard of Pennypot Lane, I didn't even know where it was, and what's more I had no knowledge of any crimes that may or may not have taken place there. But it must have been a classic, because whatever was being discussed, Arthur always chipped in: 'Reminds me of the time I was doing the Pennypot…'

It served as a sort of all-purpose primer for trainee journalists. A whole generation learnt their trade from this one example. There are probably reporters in rat-holes in Afghanistan even today who run over Arthur's coverage of Pennypot Lane before picking up their sat-phones.

However, I was lucky enough to be around when Arthur decided to cover a natural disaster, the Small Snowfall of Saddleworth, some time in the late sixties. He lived there. Like most people who lived in the foothills of the Pennines he was inclined to scorn the limp-wristed softies who cowered in the lusher pastures of Cheadle and Bramhall. Saddleworth, or so he and the other residents liked to imply, shared its weather system with Alaska. Real men lived in Saddleworth.

Then the day came when he was proved right. Mother Nature, in all her raw rage, sent a smallish snowfall that scattered several centimetres over the land. An icicle was seen in Oldham. People openly wore scarves. Even Arthur, not a man easily cowed, couldn't get into the office. He tried… and failed.

What did he do next? He did what James Cameron or Ann Leslie would've done. He filed, baby, he filed.

About how he fought his way out to the garage. About the way his MG-B (he liked people to know about his sports car) 'coughed' into life. About the spinning wheels in the snow. About the blinding blizzard. Until he came up with the immortal line: 'so this is the White Hell that they call Saddleworth.'

Indeed it was. Fortunately, the sun came out around noon, the white hell melted to no more than running gutters, his MG coughed into life again, and Arthur was able to get into the office. When he did, Peter Thomas, a man who knew when he held history in his hand, was holding Arthur's copy. Would Arthur please be kind enough to autograph it for him? 'No trouble at all, my friend,' said Arthur, with a deft swirl of the ballpoint. Talk about grace under pressure.

Indeed his manners were always beyond reproach. Once, one of the young reporters – Ted Macauley, I think – rang in from a story somewhere. When Arthur answered the news desk phone, this young chap asked: 'Who's that?'

'Arthur Brooks,' he replied.

'In that case,' said Ted, 'can I please speak to somebody sensible, Arthur?'

A lesser man might have sensed an unintended slight here, or even arrogantly insisted on dealing with the call himself. Not Arthur. It took more than that to disturb his composure.

Without a pause, he replied: 'Certainly, my friend. I'm putting you on to Leo.'

What really set Arthur apart were his books. He'd written several, mostly about northern sports stars, that were notable for his astonishing mastery of literary devices and for their titles. The life story of Roy Gilchrist, the West Indian fast bowler, was entitled *Hit Me For Six*. Good, eh? And he completely excelled himself with the biography of a Liverpool footballer. *Boom at the Kop*. How could you better that? I'll tell you.

The footballer, apparently, came from the east coast of Scotland and had worked in a slaughterhouse before joining Liverpool, a few simple facts which, for his opening sentence, Arthur converted to pure poetry: 'From the abattoirs of Aberdeen to the arc-lights of Anfield, this is my story.'

An admirable assembly of astonishingly artful alliteration, I think you'll agree.

He actually co-wrote this one with Malcolm Keogh, a stylish writer who'd been seconded from the London office to work in Manchester for a while. He wasn't particularly interested in the book, but he needed some cash and Arthur had offered to split the fee. When it was completed, Arthur came to Malcolm's desk in the features room and said the publishers needed to know about the billing: on the cover, was it to say written by Arthur Brooks and Malcolm Keogh or, and Arthur gulped slightly at this point, by Malcolm Keogh and Arthur Brooks. Whose name was to come first? And who was to be second? There was clearly a lot at stake.

Malcolm shrugged. He said he didn't mind. He wasn't bothered which name came first. Or second. He really didn't care as long as he got the money.

Now Arthur was a scrupulously fair man and this wasn't good enough for him. Malcolm had done half the work, so he insisted that Malcolm should have an equal chance of this honour. Arthur knew how to solve this sensitive problem. He would toss a coin. He did so. Malcolm called tails. It fell to the ground. Arthur looked at it. Tails. He looked questioningly at Malcolm.

'In that case,' said his slightly exasperated co-writer, 'I've won and it's my name first.'

Arthur picked up the coin and left, a troubled look on his face. He was back five minutes later with his half-smile back in place. 'I've spoken to the publishers, my friend, and they insist we make it alphabetical.'

In alphabetical terms, Arthur Brooks takes some beating, unless you happen to be called Arthur Askey.

Now here I really must plead poor memory. In the Swan one evening, Arthur was telling us that he was just completing the life story of Albert Pierrepoint, the famous hangman. He was looking for a title, but it would have to be something that captured the unique nature of the man himself yet also lived up to the subtle wordplay for which Arthur was noted. In no time at all, the air was thick with suggestions. *Just Hanging About... A Swinging Time... No Noose is Good Noose... Rope and Glory*. He liked them all, but I'm damned if I can remember which one he decided to go with.

The sad truth is that Arthur's particular genius was not always recognised in the way it might have been. I think it was in one of his columns that Michael Parkinson spent some time analysing Arthur's sports books; his conclusion, oddly, was less than generous. The problem for people like Arthur was that from time to time they did come up against... well, I guess you have to call it professional jealousy.

As you might expect, Arthur was quite upset about this. He went to see a solicitor. The solicitor said this sort of stuff was beyond him, and took it to a London barrister who specialised in this kind of work. The barrister said he would have to read the books before he could reach an opinion. After several days, he responded. Having read the books, he advised against any action. Indeed, read in a certain way, it seemed to suggest that he thought Arthur had got off lightly. What nonsense.

That's if it happened, of course. That's if there really was this extraordinary man called Arthur Brooks in Manchester. No, it hardly seems possible. Pennypot Lane, *Boom at the Kop*, the White Hell of Saddleworth... no one man could be responsible for such splendour.

I expect I dreamed the whole thing. No more cheese before bedtime for me, my friend.

*

What must have happened, I suppose, is that someone in Cudlipp's office would put a call in to the Manchester editor. At the morning conference, the editor would make the important (not to mention terrifying) announcement to the heads of department. They would then spread the word back to the troops.

It always took the same simple form of words... 'They're coming up from London.'

You wouldn't believe how this basic sentence set nerves tingling, hopes glowing and terror trembling.

Why were they coming? To thank us? To punish us? To see what we got up to? To check our exes? Was it true that Cudlipp always made a point of firing at least one person when he went walkabout like this? Was it also true that he liked to pick out an unknown and make him a star? Or – as Pam Smart liked to say – make *her* a star?

The mighty could be struck down, the lowly could be raised... didn't bear thinking about. Those who wanted a quiet life – corned beef sandwiches at the desk, the 6.22 back to Cheadle – wondered about a short burst of coward's flu to avoid the great man's eye. The ambitious schemed and plotted so that they could catch the great man's eye.

London – by which we meant the Holborn Circus office and all the power and glamour resident therein – rarely came on a northern expedition. But when they did, fear and hope bubbled all around.

It couldn't happen now, because there wouldn't be much point in mounting an expedition to inspect two men, one laptop and a mobile in the back of a café in Oldham. But in the dear dead days we all remember, Withy Grove was a thriving newspaper centre with, if you include all the district offices, around 150 hacks (more, some hasbeen-counter would claim later, than the Murdoch *Sun* had worldwide) and enough editions to keep most of them beavering away every day.

It was a national paper, of course, yet the office remained essentially provincial and domestic. Lunch was a pork pie. With home only half-an-hour away, wives popped in to leave the shopping. Really, it wasn't all that different from the Bradford *Argus* or the Ilkley *Gazette*, whence we sprang.

Manchester only ever had one celebrity, and George Best went and moved to Chelsea and became a smooth southern bastard.

Manchester and London co-existed amiably enough, with suspicion from one and granite indifference from the other. Manchester secretly thought that London knew nowt about newspapers, had never met a *Mirror* reader in their lives, and were locked into a work-free lifestyle dominated by dray whate wane, name dropping and compulsory in-house adultery.

This was best exemplified by a splash about a transport strike when London used a blob par about the weather. 'It's going to rain, so remember to take your brolly.' Thousands of boilermakers, furnacemen and miners rushed to get their gamps.

London seldom thought about Manchester at all. London, truth be known, didn't know where Manchester was or who worked there. And why would it matter when it was too far to go for lunch and there were worrying rumours that you couldn't get wine by the glass. Anyway, wasn't it all a bit humdrum?

Oddly, they were both right.

So when the two mingled, there was a certain frisson in the air.

Cudlipp, of course, was the top-of-the-bill act. I always had the impression that he used these occasions to amuse himself as he staved off the boredom. Hunched in his chair, his snake eyes swivelling, he'd lob out a question that would be either tricky or plain impossible. Then he'd point to some poor sod: 'starting with you'...

You could be cautious. Or you could be bold. One senior exec, whose entire career had been built on never delivering a judgement of any sort, decided to show himself as a daring decision-maker. Cudlipp pointed to a picture on the back-page of the old broadsheet *Sun*, taken from a television documentary, showing a woman giving birth. 'Is that good journalism or bad taste?' he asked, then pointed at him.

He took a deep breath. 'It's brilliant,' he enthused, in a slightly shaky voice: he'd never done daring before. 'We're not bloody Victorians. Women give birth to children every day – why shouldn't we show it in the paper?'

There was a long silence. Snake-eyes speared him to his chair. 'People go for a shit every day,' said Cudlipp. 'Should we have pictures of that?'

As it happens he was a stout party. And yes, he did collapse.

Occasionally, Cudlipp was mischievous, which presented a different problem. How do you tell the boss-of-bosses that he's taking the piss? You don't. Although Neville Stack, news editor of the *Sun* and something of a mischief-maker himself, came dangerously close to the edge when Cudlipp insisted he was going to cover the front-page of the *Sun* in adverts. 'Why not?' he asked, daring Stack to disagree.

Neville said he thought it wouldn't work because you should have at least one big story on the front page.

'Okay,' Cudlipp replied. 'I'll have a panel among the ads for that.'

Stack shook his head. 'It wouldn't work. China On Fire, See Page Five...'

Cudlipp's laughter came as a great relief.

There was always the feeling that there was much to lose, and possibly to gain too. We'd all heard the story – I wasn't there, so this is hearsay – of how Terry Stringer took the most appalling risk, and lived.

Cudlipp assembled the *Mirror* editorial staff and demanded suggestions to improve the paper. One or two toadies attempted to offer praise and admiration and were slapped down. He wanted to know where it was going wrong. Was there anyone foolish enough to attempt to field this one?

Now Terry Stringer was a terrific reporter, had a sharp wit and was more or less fearless. Ask him what's wrong, and he'd tell you. Editors, deputies and assistants shrank down behind their desks rather than watch a suicide.

This was some years ago when the *Mirror* ran a gossip column by Rex North. The same Rex North was thought to be a personal friend of Cudlipp. And it was his page that Stringer said was a waste of space, had outlived its time and should be kicked out. *Mirror* readers, fresh from a day down the mines, didn't care too much about who was drinking champagne with whom at Knightsbridge parties, or what the Duchesses were doing for their birthdays.

Hearts shrivelled. Everyone waited for the bolt of lightning. It didn't come. Cudlipp stared at him, then nodded. Terry Stringer didn't meet an abrupt and bloody end. But the Rex North column did.

Well, that was legend. Did anyone fancy trying the same thing? No.

Sometimes, I felt, our response wasn't always as sophisticated as it could have been. Once, when Mike Molloy was in the raiding party, he suggested popping out for a drink in the afternoon. At that time, the only place you could get an out-of-hours drink was a club over the road which was mostly supported by minor criminals and ladies who earned a living examining ceilings. Mike got his drink and turned to a young woman sitting on a stool at the bar, with a large medallion dangling round her neck.

'And what did you win that splendid medal for, m'dear?' he asked, charming as ever.

The best sub in Britain couldn't have tightened up her reply. 'For bein't best fuck i' Manchester.'

Inevitably, these visits brought about a scurrying around as people tried to make an impression, and not always getting it right. One departmental head thought he'd scored handsomely by sending Cudlipp champagne on the train home. One of the London party – a tall man who held the job because he was good at getting taxis – was quite scornful. 'Hugh drinks only claret,' he said.

Charles Dickens was probably thinking of the *Mirror* Manchester-London relationship when he wrote *Great Expectations*. We in the north were poor Pip, scruffy urchins forever trying to impress the beautiful but haughty girl. London, of course, was Estelle, ignoring us with a toss of curls.

Whenever a new northern editor was about to be appointed, Manchester waited anxiously to see who would be honoured with this distinction. In London, they wondered which poor sod was going to be stuck with it. We thought it was a reward. They saw it as a punishment. When he was told he'd got the job, one London senior exec – a tough journalist hardened in the cynical world of Fleet-street – burst into tears and pleaded for mercy.

What's more, we never quite knew what they were sending us. Wasn't it Jane McLoughlin who rushed in through the front door of Withy Grove one Monday, late, panicky and cross? I think it was Jane. Anyway, the lift doors were closing and although she jabbed at the open-door button several times, they went on closing. She gave vent to her feelings, which involved shrieking several words derived from the acts of procreation and bowel evacuation. (Odd how you never get any obscenities from gardening or knitting, isn't it?). Miraculously, the doors quivered, stopped, and began to open. Standing at the front was the new editor, up from London, on his first day. He simply fixed a glassy stare over her head towards Warrington. Jane did her best to climb into her handbag.

When the lift arrived at the third floor, the doors clanked open. The new editor extended one courteous hand to invite her to leave. 'Ladies first,' he said.

Actually, it really was a glassy stare and the new man, Mike Terry, was not the sort of chap to be upset by colourful language, as we later found out when he dropped his glass eye into a pint before singing raucous old blues songs.

Occasionally, London would make a show of being fair to their northern colleagues. Once, when they were looking for a reporter for the New York office, they said there were two in the frame. A reporter from London. And me. Me. I could get quite excited about just going to York, without the New. Bill Freeman, Alan Price, everyone wished me luck as I hopped on the train.

In London I was ushered into a room where Ralph Champion, the New York bureau chief and imminently my new boss, was talking on the phone. He put it down and looked at me with raised eyebrows.

I said who I was. He looked baffled. I mentioned Manchester. He still looked baffled. I mentioned I was there for an interview for the New York job. With him.

'Ah yes,' he said, looking around him for a suitable question for a person from Manchester. Then he came out with it. 'Are you pretty good with a menu?' I was so surprised I asked why. Well, he explained, they often had to do a lot of entertaining, Hugh was a regular visitor, and he wanted someone who was at home with knives and forks. I said I thought I was. He said jolly good and that was the end of that.

I had a quick drink in the Stab before catching my train back north. There was a lot of revelry in there. Apparently one of the reporters had just landed the dream job.

I didn't ask where.

*

Look, my excuse is that it had been a long, dull day. In Manchester on February 15, 1971, when Britain went decimal, we were all braced to sniff out the cheats. The *Mirror* had its Decimal Diddlers (or possibly Dodgers) Desk and the *Sun* its Decimal Dodgers (or Diddlers) Desk – at this distance, I can't remember who was dodging and who was diddling. Anyway, what we were both pledged to do was expose cheats who used this currency adjustment to jack up their prices, as we knew they would.

I was one of the team, and by late afternoon we were all yawning and sprawling after a hard day's failing to detect the flimsiest signs of dodgers and/or diddlers. Not a soul had rung in. Dodgeless and diddleless, we had no complaints and had no stories. And it was still over an hour before the Swan With Two Necks would open.

So why not, I thought, brighten the day for our fellow sufferers at the *Sun* with a story that would gladden their hearts?

I gave them a call. I said I was a war-hero who had been wickedly victimised by decimalisation. My wartime heroics had tragically left me with a condition that required the regular purchase of a certain item of equipment from the Stockport Medical Supplies shop. Last week it was 7s 6d and now suddenly it was more than £17. Was this, or was this not, a clear case of decimal diddling?

The *Sun* reporter said he thought it certainly was. Trying to conceal his delight – they'd obviously had the same sort of day we'd had – he enquired after the exact nature of this item. I said it was embarrassing. His voice oozed sympathy. He would understand.

So I told him my sad story. At the Normandy Landings, as I was leaving the landing craft with a view to driving Jerry out of France, I chanced to *pull* myself (know what I mean?) Even so, I landed and fought my way not only up the beach but all the way to Berlin.

Limping every inch of the way.

Ever since, I had worn a truss as a matter of medical necessity, the price I'd had to pay for defending freedom for a bunch of ungrateful Froggies.

In a trice the reporter had my name and address and was on his way. Actually what he had was *A* name and address.

We all had a good chuckle and made our way to the pub. An hour later in came a chum from the *Sun*: 'I've just missed a belting story… Misheard an address…'

I slipped out the back door.

After all this time, I'm more than happy to offer my apology to the chap. I'm truly sorry. I shouldn't have done it. Reporters shouldn't play tricks on other reporters.

While the public may see us as leather-skinned cynics, distrustful and sceptical, we know it isn't true. Since our stock-in-trade is the absurd, the ridiculous and the highly unlikely, we are desperately willing to believe anything and anybody – even the impossible. Particularly the impossible. Otherwise, how would we ever get a story? There are those who say you shouldn't believe what you read in the papers, but we do, because we wrote it. So it's unfair to trade on the credulous nature of our colleagues.

It's fun, though, isn't it?

To be quite honest, it's not the only time. I have a bit of previous here, I'm ashamed to say. There was the matter of the Midhurst-to-Petersfield Hopathon.

When my son Matt was training on the *Haslemere Messenger*, a cheerful little giveaway, he worked with a girl who he claimed would believe anything. To test this, I rang in with a news item from the Sussex Unipeds Assocation. I asked her if she knew what the Unipeds were. She replied: 'Not as such,' which I thought was a trifle guarded. So I explained that we were a group of one-legged people who got together to help each other. For example, a man with a missing right leg could be matched with someone with a missing left leg for joint shoe purchasing (assuming similar foot-size and taste, of course). 'What a good idea,' she said. My son was obviously right.

I went on to explain that we unipeds were staging an outing from Midhurst to Petersfield to raise money. Those who had twice our number of legs would call it a sponsored walk; for us, inevitably, it was a Hopathon.

'Brilliant,' she murmured. Without so much as a chortle, she said it would make an interesting paragraph for the *Messenger*.

And indeed so it would if Matt hadn't intercepted it at the proof stage. Now Matt was a touch scornful over someone so easily deceived, which, with a father like his, was asking for trouble...

All you need to know for the next bit is that my son's first love, when he was about 11, had been a girl called Monique Hayes.

I rang back the next day with a silly voice and a fake name and address and spoke to Matt. I asked him if he would be interested in my singing dog. It sang, I explained, over his half-stifled giggles, that old Elvis favourite, *Are You Lonesome Tonight?* and, rather more obviously, *How Much is that Doggie in the Window?* By this time he was choking.

What sort of dog was it, he spluttered. A French water dog, a rare breed which was called a Hayes terrier. And because it was French, my good lady wife had given it the name Monique. Slowly, I repeated, 'Monique... Hayes...terrier.'

There was a long silence. In a dreamy voice, almost talking to himself, he said: 'Hey, I used to have a girlfriend called that.'

At that point, I anticipated a *Sun* headline of years later. That's right... 'Gotcha!'

He is speaking to me again now, you'll be glad to know.

Juvenile, wasn't it? Totally childish. But not quite as juvenile as the occasion when Chris Kenworthy, of the *Sun*, was on a phone-in radio debate. It was a mildly absurd discussion in which he was supposed to argue that men were more intelligent than women and some woman journalist was doing the reverse. Radio phone-ins are God's gift to hoaxers because they never have enough people calling in, and the ones who do are deadly boring. A call from somebody a little, shall we say, different, and arms are taken off at the shoulder.

In a voice that could equally have been a feminine male or a masculine female, I claimed to the researcher that I had personal experience which proved men were more intelligent. When I was a man, I explained, I could do *The Times* crossword in 20 minutes and now I was a woman it took more than an hour.

Chris told me later that on the screen in the studio there flashed an urgent message about a call from a sex-change loon which had been jumped to the front of the queue. They simply couldn't get me on fast enough. Chris knew immediately who it was. He couldn't say: it would have wrecked the programme.

Rather warily, he accepted my gushing support. 'Aren't you a fabulously successful author?' I asked. He was attempting to deny this when I said I'd love to go on a date with him.

The rest of the programme went into a sort of mist. My telephone rang the minute it ended. It is my belief that Mrs Kenworthy would never believe her husband knew such language.

At one time I was a regular caller to a morning phone-in on LBC. I starred in a number of roles, each more preposterous than the last, and the more outrageous the more they loved it. Fox-hunters should be fed to their hounds. Chain-gangs for single mothers. All over the country listeners were dropping like shot rabbits. The radio producers loved it.

Then I hit on a splendid device for livening up a debate. This was to attribute the most disgraceful views to the radio presenter himself. 'Yeah, you was right what you said abaht that Neil Kinnock being a pooftah'... 'Like you was saying, mate, these coppers want a bloody good kicking...' Presenters get very agitated when they're accused of opinions that would make Satan quail.

111

One of them, an Australian I suppose, who liked to think he was a hard-nosed toughie, fell for one after another. Even the lonely Tynesider – 'Geordie' of course – who rang in to say how unfriendly people were in London. In an accent that made Ant and Dec sound like Brian Sewell, I said my southern work colleagues were very unfriendly. 'Every neet like, when we're gannin' off home, I axe if neebody fancies a pint like, but they nivvor do.'

'Strange,' said the presenter. 'What exactly is your job, Geordie?'

'Why man, Ah'm a ballet dancer, me.'

He could barely splurt out: 'Next caller please.'

I did once meet this presenter. Naturally I asked him if he ever had fake callers. 'I can spot 'em a mile off,' he said. 'They never get past me.' I thought of asking him if he had any doubts about the Geordie ballet dancer, but decided against it.

Disgraceful, isn't it? And I'm the first to say how ashamed I am. I think the most shameful of all of them was the call to a 'personal problems' phone-in they had on Capital Radio, with an agony aunt, a doctor and a presenter to handle the calls. What they hoped for, of course, was for emotional cripples to call in to confess their tragic failures, preferably of an embarrassingly sexual nature.

Who was I to let them down?

The Woman Whom I Honoured With My Name used to listen to this programme in the bath. At first, she didn't recognise my weepy voice as I said, sobbing, that my wife didn't fancy me any more. The trio of vultures fell upon me, coaxing out every last salacious detail, which was, after all, the point of the programme. I wept as I told how she slept with her back to me, how she would never let me touch her, and how I suffered with sexual frustration. They couldn't get enough of it. Had I asked the agony aunt, in honeyed tones, tried to discuss it with her?

'Dozens of times,' I said. 'But Anita won't even talk about it…'

From the bathroom came a loud shriek, shortly followed by louder shrieks as a wet wife naked but for a swiftly snatched towel came hurtling down the stairs.

'I'll have to go,' I said to my radio audience. 'I think my luck's turned…'

I burn with shame just to think of it now.

The trouble is that once you know half the voices on the telephone are fake, it does tend to make one distrustful, sometimes needlessly. At the height of my phone-in fame, I took a call at home from a woman with a suspiciously upmarket accent. She'd just moved into the village – or so she claimed – and was inviting me to a drinks party. The name, she said, was

Parker. As a long-practised spoofer, I spotted her immediately. 'That wouldn't be Mrs Nosey Parker, would it?' I said, giggling with delight.

There was a pause in which ice wouldn't melt. 'No. Mrs Veronica Parker actually. And the invitation is withdrawn.'

That was when I realised it was getting too dangerous. I retired. And with me went all my new friends – the truss-wearing war hero returned to Hernia Bay, the ballet-dancer minced home to Tyneside, the singing dog went back to Battersea, and the uniped hopped it to Midhurst. All of them, gone. I still miss them.

*

There comes a time when even hacks have to start thinking about the terrifying process of growing up. Since most of us go into journalism with the specific intention of remaining in perpetual childhood, it's not easy. If you doubt that, ask any hack's wife. We're like Peter Pan's Lost Boys with Pitmans.

By the time I returned from Iceland, still reeling from the putrid puffin diet, I heard people whispering the word 'thirty.' Was it Maurice Wigglesworth's waist size? Or a sports writer's IQ? Sadly, no. It was my age.

One looming stroke of midnight would suddenly make me older than Ted Macauley and Bob Russell in Manchester, and every woman journalist in the *Mirror* London office. Including Marje Proops.

It was nearly 15 years since Mr Waterhouse, chief reporter of the *Craven Herald*, and a cautious man even with other people's money, had handed me my first pencil and notebook with the warning to make them last: 'They don't grow on trees, you know.' As ever, he was wrong on both counts.

In a blur of delight, the *Northern Echo*, the *Yorkshire Post*, the PA Special Reporting in London, the *Leamington Spa Courier*, and the *Evening Chronicle* on Tyneside had sped past.

And here I was on the *Daily Mirror* in Manchester, three decades under my belt which practically made me a pensioner. I had to face it: all that was left was a straight run to the grave.

What had I achieved during all this time in what Bill Deedes so wonderfully called the mackintosh trade? One thing was certain. Whenever there was a story so trivial, so superficial, so plain silly that no proper reporter would look at it... I was your man. I had no complaints about that. We Fancy Dans must take our pleasures where we can.

And after Iceland I was soon back on the comedy journalism. Eddie Braben got the job as scriptwriter for Morecambe and Wise at (hang on to your hats here) £20,000 a year – 'Don't tell the wife,' he said, 'she'll want a new pair of wellies.' A gay club opened in Burnley where one of the protesting locals told me: 'They're not proper homosexuals – I saw one of them kissing a girl.' An Italian priest who was trying to dissuade people from swearing suggested that, when provoked, we should all use the phrase 'Orca Lorca.' It meant duck. At least, I think he said duck.

Occasionally a little sadness crept in. At the school for strippers in Sunderland, one woman disrobed in a dispirited fashion and said: 'I'm sorry.' Five children, gallons of Newcie Broon and several tons of stottie cake had not helped her. 'Don't worry,' said the teacher. 'We'll use you on a Sunday lunchtime when they can't see straight.'

And I'd been sent to Hereford to do a piece on their football team doing well in the FA Cup, only to be greeted with the news that Vincent Mulchrone had been there yesterday. If there is a more depressing sentence in the English language, I've yet to hear it.

I completed my day of triumph in that town when, in the evening, I was presented with the sort of exclusive proper reporters savour in their dreams. Howard Booth and I took a local reporter for a drink in The Green Man. Howard, the sports reporter who was there to do the real work, was a gent. Blazer, silver hair, thin silver 'tache, he was doing Leslie Phillips before Leslie Phillips. He was a bit of a charmer too, so he was as pleased as I to meet the local reporter who was, as it happens, tall, slim as an eel, long black hair shining over her shoulders. Veronica, known as Ronnie.

Then she began to talk about her ex-husband, and we realised we were in the presence of a high-grade nutter.

She scattered photographs in front of us of what she claimed was her husband disguised as an Arab, holding a camel. She also had pictures of him posing with guns and goodness knows what. He belonged, she said, to a secret British Army unit that was trained in disguise, survival, silent killing and deadly warfare. No-one in the world knew that there were hundreds of them in the barracks just down the road.

Shame, I thought, that such a lovely looking young woman should have lost her mind. Years later, when I first began to read about the SAS, I remembered Ronnie.

It wasn't often that I stumbled across a real gold-plated exclusive. And when I did I kicked it into the gutter and walked blithely on.

I damned near stopped smoking too. Frightening, that was. Granada TV had persuaded almost everyone in the Staffordshire village of Longnor to give up its fags for a *World in Action* programme. They had all sorts of back-up to help them, including an aged stage hypnotist who bore a marked resemblance to Mr Pastry. He offered to stop me smoking. For a laugh I agreed.

In the packed bar of the pub he wiggled his fingers in front of my eyes, counted up to ten, muttered some rubbish about feeling sleepy, and then went behind me. 'Keep your heels together and fall backwards,' he said. I did. Just for a laugh, of course. He caught me.

What he said next I remember, word for word, today. As I lay on the floor, he described me smoking a cigarette in each hand, over a bowl of water. All the ash falls into the water. In go the cigarette stubs. Stir it with your fingers. Then more cigarettes, more ash, until the bowl is full of a black, sticky glue. I pick it up and drink it. Every poisonous drop. Every cigarette I smoked, he said, would taste like that.

What was that heels-together business all about? To make sure I was properly hypnotised, he said. If I was faking, I wouldn't be able to stop one heel moving backwards – a pure reflex.

All nonsense of course.

As he left, I picked out a delicious Benson and lit it. Christ, it tasted foul. He was right. I tried three more and had to throw them all away. The next day, I tried again, and it wasn't until lunchtime that I could manage to smoke a whole cigarette. I didn't really enjoy one until three days later.

Years later I paid a double-barrelled doctor in Harley Street £150 to hypnotise me to stop smoking. The minute I left I lit a cigarette. It tasted wonderful.

The *Mirror* office had its moments too. They'd taken on a young woman reporter – Emma, I think – who, after only four or five weeks, rang Leo White on the news desk and said she was resigning. She had fallen in love. Head over heels. She was going to Scotland for a new life with her new man.

What had happened was that in that pub near Granada she had noticed a bearded man staring at her intently. He pushed through the crowd to her. 'You are mine,' he whispered in her ear. 'The minute I saw you I knew this was it.' She almost swooned with delight.

Of course they had to go off to her flat where she went head over heels again, rather more literally. Between bouts, she rang Leo White and handed in her notice. The bearded suitor then took her up to his farm in Scotland where they would live happily ever after, or at least for five minutes. Because, as she went through the door, she noticed a broken-down woman washing up at the sink and several snot-nosed brats brawling and mewling. Who were these people? The wife and kids, he said, casually.

Before she came back to Manchester, she rang to ask if her job was still open. Tragically it had gone.

In the early seventies, Manchester was a great newspaper city. With people like Leo White, Bill Freeman, and Alan Price running it, the *Daily Mirror* was a great newspaper. I've seen regimes that were brutal but efficient; I've seen regimes that were kindly but useless. Just for a while there, the Manchester *Mirror* effected that miraculous combination of competence and contentment. It was good fun, and it worked. It seemed then as if it would go on for ever.

Personally, life was good too. In the evening, I would escape to my home in the Derbyshire hills. There was still this business of being 30. It was time for me to attempt the feat that so few hacks ever achieve – growing up. The signs weren't good. I had these three children, who seemed to keep coming, and delightful they were. But, if we are to be honest about this, fatherhood is pretty boring. I mean, you can only say 'Look at dat big red bus' so many times before losing interest.

There were moments, of course. One summer afternoon, when two-year-old Matt was struggling up the hill in his tiny swimmers, the heat and the friction – or god knows what else – had a curious effect on him which caused a noticeable physical change. The next-door doctor, weeding his flower-bed, looked up and said: 'I've got patients who would pay £100 to be able to do that.' I felt strangely proud of him.

As for my two daughters, I felt I had little to offer by way of small-talk on the life of Barbie and her friends. Instead, I made a point of telling them preposterous but interesting lies. WHAM – a band or group or whatever they were called at the time – got their name, I told them, because it stood for We Hate Awful Music. And did they realise that David Bowie only got his name because of a misprint on a poster. His real name was David Bowtie, but they missed the T out and he stayed with it.

As they expressed open-mouthed amazement at this stuff, I pointed out that I was a journalist with a great national newspaper, so naturally I knew about these things. Off they went to school where they enjoyed massive popularity because of the insight they offered into the world of the pop-stars.

Just north of Buxton, there may well be several middle-aged people who still tell their children Dave Bowie's real name.

You may think this was cruel, but I can assure you it served them well in later life. It taught them the crucial lesson that most people are lying half the time and journalists are lying all the time. Some years later, when they were around 17 and 18, in the pub on the green in the village of Groombridge on the Kent-Sussex border, they were sipping their orange juice when a dashing chap with blonde curls, blue eyes, a dazzling smile and an expensive sun-tan swept in. He'd just flown in from LA, he said. Been interviewing all the top stars. Knew them all personally. He was a big-name showbiz writer in Fleet Street. Would they like a drink? Maybe go on to a club somewhere? Make a night of it? All around him, women were melting, watching enviously as these two teenage girls were swept off their feet by this handsome charmer.

'Do you know our dad?' asked the Dunne girls.

Kit Miller, international prize-winning bull-shitter and an all-round good chap, gulped, finished his white wine and suddenly remembered an appointment he had a long, long way away. So that early training hadn't been wasted.

But back to Manchester and my attempt at maturity. First there was the old MG sports car which the First Mrs Dunne described as a typically unselfish gesture for a father-of-three. She was right. Time to grow up. With a deep breath and a damp eye, I sold it.

Perhaps the answer was a change of job. Much as I was enjoying the *Mirror*, maybe I should look for a job that would give full rein to my more serious, philosophical and intellectual qualities. Was it time to put interviews with talking corgis behind me?

This time the *Press Gazette*, which had filled so many happy Friday mornings in my younger years, was no use. There was no point in dreaming about the joys of being a district man for the *Smethwick Telephone* or the *Falmouth Packet*. Once you're on a national, sadly, those days are left behind. Then it's down to the wretched business of who you know, and the only man I knew who could help in these circumstances was my chum and mentor, Neville Stack.

'There is one bloke you could talk to,' he said, immediately. 'He likes your stuff too.'

Likes your stuff? Isn't that what we all long to hear? Things were looking up. I was so delighted I went out to treat myself. I bought a Morgan sports car.

*

8

It's a question that we've all asked in our time, and I really don't know why. Whether it's Paxman or the lad from the *Craven Herald* doing the asking, they all get the same answer. Politicians, captains of industry, lollipop ladies, footballers, diamond wedding couples – when they come to resign or retire or reflect on their lives, asked what they would do if they had to do it all again, they all chirp: 'I wouldn't change a thing.'

Is that right? Well, I would like it to be understood that if I am offered a replay, there will be changes. Quite a number of them. Of course, out of the 100 or so major life-changing decisions I have made, it would be plain silly to say I got them all wrong. Three of them were probably right. Possibly four. The rest of them I'd like to reverse and do again.

For example, I should never have opted for general science O-level. I should never have let Judy Nettleship slip away like that. I should never have worn those purple loon trousers. Most of all, I should never have let Harry Whewell down. That was my biggest mistake of all, and I speak as a man who has made some howlers in his time.

Harry was the man Neville Stack had in mind when he said he knew someone who might be worth talking to. Neville was news editor of the broadsheet *Sun* in Manchester (and also my friend and guru), Harry was the news editor of the *Guardian*. He was also a fine newspaperman, which is not a description you would apply widely to the *Guardian* staff. He was married to Esther Rose, *Daily Express* and later *Coronation Street* writer, who was the daughter of Henry Rose, famous sportswriter.

Now here's a piece of information that I suggest you file under Fascinating But Useless. Harry volunteered for circumcision when he converted to Judaism to marry Esther. Greater love... and all that. Certainly you could not comfortably eat baby squid rings in his presence.

All by the by, of course. The minute I met Harry, I liked him. He was a chipmunkish sort of chap who in his battered sports jacket and worn cords looked as though he might have just come in from doing the garden. He was also as sharp as a tack.

He gave me the best interview I've ever had.

Which university had I attended, he asked gloomily. None. Did I have a view on the liberation of women? No. What did I think of Yankee imperialism? I didn't think of it.

All these wrong answers cheered him enormously. 'They come in here from university, put their bloody suede shoes on my desk and sound off about world issues,' he moaned. 'You wouldn't happen to do a bit of shorthand too, would you?' Indeed I did, and he was so excited by it that he offered me a job there and then. He was encouraged – and so was I – by one precedent a few years earlier. Arthur Hopcraft had moved from the *Mirror* to the *Guardian* and it had been a great success. Indeed Arthur went on to become a highly-acclaimed television playwright. He was also famous at the *Mirror* for writing the weather-based splash one winter, the one headlined BRRRR!

On that occasion, instead of just listing all the incidents sent in by corrs and agencies, as you were supposed to do, he simply made up one that read: 'Gamekeepers in Northumberland were pulling frozen rabbits from their burrows yesterday.' In newspaper terms, that's probably the equivalent of writing Hamlet. What's more, no-one ever complained, not even a gamekeeper. Nor any letters in from Watership Down.

Harry wanted me to write their hanging-indent pieces. Younger readers will find this impossible to imagine, but at that time the *Guardian* had a highly-developed sense of humour, and these quirky pieces were very much a part of the paper's character. It sounded like a lot of fun.

I bounced back to the office and typed out my resignation, which brought well-wishing responses from Len Woodliffe, the northern editor, and Bill Hagerty, the features editor in London. I was on my way. A couple of weeks later, at around 4.30pm (note that time), I took a call from Bill. 'You're not leaving,' he said. 'Do I have to come up there to sort it out or will you come down here?' He always was a forceful sort of chap.

I went to London, of course. His machine-gun rattle going at full belt, he offered me money, a car, all the best jobs, and a title – Chief Home Feature Writer. The only thing about this title was that I must never refer to it: that would be sure to piss off the other feature writers. It was a bit like having a million-pound note: it cheered you up to think about it but you couldn't actually use it. To top it off, he took me out to dinner to a carefully-selected restaurant with a carefully-selected companion.

The restaurant was one in which he thought I would feel at home. It served authentic northern fish-and-chips at the authentic southern price of about twenty-five quid. And they didn't even wrap it in paper. His other guest was a woman who – as I thought at the time – wrote the captions to photos of females in silly dresses for the *Sunday Mirror*. I later learnt Eve Pollard was known as fashion editor. When she leaned forward, I was so overwhelmed by vertigo that I was unable to concentrate on my northern soul food for fear of over-balancing and falling in. Mountain rescue teams and tracker dogs would have struggled to get me out of there.

They were both hospitable and welcoming and charming. So mightily flattered was I by all this attention that of course I said yes. It wasn't until I got to London that I saw the catch.

Many years later, I was able to return Eve's kindness. When I was working for the *Sun*, I was on a nostalgia raid to the Stab one evening when the door was flung open and there was Eve. Her huge eyes alighted on me.

She had, she said, recently met the most marvellous man. He worked for the *Sun*. He was called Nick Lloyd. 'You work for the *Sun*,' she said. 'Do you know where Nick is right now?' As it happened, I did. He was in the upstairs bar of the Tip. She stormed off into the night to find him. It was my own small part in the creation of the love story that shook EC4. Nick never even thanked me.

Now where were we? Ah, yes, back in Manchester I had to call Harry and tell him I wouldn't be joining him. He was cross. I was ashamed. I still am.

It was even trickier breaking the news to the First Mrs Dunne. Older readers who were here at the outset of my journalistic jobs journey around Britain will remember I had to leave London in the first place because she hated it.

Here I was seven years later going back. She managed to conceal her delight. She would return to the south only if she could live a long way from London. Which was how I came to buy half a rambling Victorian villa complete with swimming-pool in the basement (or flooding, as it was known in the north) in a village just outside Tunbridge Wells. To get there took about two hours in the morning. I rarely managed the return journey in the evening so I couldn't tell you how long that took.

Here's a useful tip for young marrieds: if you wish to stay married, don't try to combine a job that involves a high fluid intake with a home life more than 50 miles away. They are – as you soon will be – incompatible.

At first, however, I moved into the Ryan Hotel in Farringdon Road on the Sunday. I was so excited that I couldn't wait for the morning – I sauntered down to the *Mirror* pub, the Stab, just off Holborn Circus.

I tucked myself up on a stool in a corner of the bar and savoured every second.

My first and last move to London seven years before ended when I found myself working for a section of PA that supplied stories to provincial papers, pretty much like the ones I'd left to get to London, where everyone went home at 6pm. This was different. Here I was surrounded by a heaving mob of genuine Fleet Street stars. They didn't look as though they had homes at all. Perhaps at night they just threw dust-sheets over them and woke them up in the morning.

Was that chief features sub Des Lyons playing jazz on the piano? That was certainly a wild-haired Bill Marshall who barged up to the bar and shouted: 'Flood this place with wine and friendship.' Oh yes, this was the real thing, and I was a part of it at last. And as soon as they found out I'd come to join them, they would welcome me on board. There was sure to be a gap for a chap with my experience in interviewing talking dogs.

At that point, as I was musing on the glory that awaited me, the door opened and in swept two women. The scrum of beer-swilling and beer-spilling men suddenly parted for the taller and the wider of the two, a woman in her middle years, who brandished a cigarette like Barbirolli with his baton. Swathed in ankle-length skirt and black velvet, she had a commanding presence. Behind her, smaller, slighter, younger and even more impressive was a woman with glowing copper-coloured hair and eyes like brown suede. She was somewhere between pretty and beautiful – not a bad place to be.

They stopped by the bar. The older woman's haughty gaze hit on me. She waved her cigarette with an operatic flourish.

'Colin Dunne?' she said.

'That's me.' Recognised already. I was delighted.

'So you're the boy who's coming down from Manchester to show us how it's done.'

The younger woman stepped forward. 'Don't be so mean, Paula. He looks perfectly sweet to me.'

Ouch. I had just experienced a London welcome. From Paula James and Jill Evans. Also known as the Kray Sisters.

The next day, a little nervously, I walked down to Holborn. Even then, just before ten o'clock, it was buzzing. Telephones were ringing. Typewriters rattling. Jackets over chair-backs. Ties undone. Cigarettes in ash-trays. Coffee machine firing out plastic cups. A major national newspaper was swinging into gear. Wow.

That was the news room on the third floor. In the features room on the fourth floor, it was... well, a little quieter. I sat at a spare desk in the corner. One by one the writers came in, each one picking up a paper and sinking invisibly behind it. Certainly they had woken up, got up, and got to the office, but otherwise this was sleep-walking. Here, no phones rang and no typewriters rattled to disturb the silence. They looked as though they had been silent for years. Miss Havisham would have liked it. In time, the cobwebs and scampering mice would follow. It was *Great Expectations*, only without the expectations.

Someone muttered something about making a reservation for lunch. Someone else suggested a raiding party to get an advance.

A thin-faced man with large glasses and longish hair that gave him an academic air wandered over to shake hands. Matt Coady had been bought in years ago to write his elegant and witty profiles for *Mirrorscope*, but *Mirrorscope* had somehow dried up. So had its writers.

'All you need to know,' sighed Matt Coady, as he slumped back behind his paper, 'is that in newspapers, nothing ever lasts.'

Dimly I began to see the catch. This was a retirement home for writers who were never required to write.

So why had I been recruited to this army of ghosts? I think it was Sid Williams, or some similar well-wisher, who told me the story. My new job at the *Guardian* had been mentioned at a high-spirited lunch, round about that time when the wine-waiter's wrist is beginning to ache. Somebody (the name Waterhouse was mentioned) had bet somebody else (possibly Hagerty or Molloy) that they couldn't talk me out of it. Hence the timing of the phone-call – 4 30pm.

Now this isn't a retrospective gripe. Not at all. I shouldn't have let Harry Whewell down like that, but even so, I can't think of a more appropriate way to resolve the careers of ragamuffin hacks than a bet over a wine-washed lunch. And it was nobody's fault that they already had dozens of writers stacked above Holborn Circus like planes (that were never going to land) over Heathrow. Clearly what I must do now was to go with the flow.

'How about lunch?' I said.

Paula paused as she adjusted her eye-shadow. 'I thought you northern boys called it dinner.'

I thought about telling her that I was the Chief Home Feature Writer. Then I thought of not telling her. Make no mistake about it, I was in Injun territory.

###

Part Two:
The Boulevard of Broken Dreams

1

My new colleagues in the *Daily Mirror* features room in Holborn Circus assured me that I would be given a handsome reward for moving down from Manchester.

As she worked away on her mascara, peering into the mirror on her desk, Paula James could hardly believe it hadn't already been arranged. 'What? They haven't given you a lovely trip yet? They'll have to give you something for being such a good boy.'

All you could see of Sid Williams was his polished shoes on the desk, the wide opened *Daily Telegraph*, and the curl of cigarette smoke above the paper. 'Don't worry, old man. They always reward their favourites.'

Call me a sensitive little flower if you like, but it wasn't gushing goodwill I sensed in these remarks – more simmering resentment. I had the feeling that they weren't congratulating me on imminent good news so much as bracing themselves for – for them – bad news. In a room where writers waited months, even years, for an assignment, someone else's good fortune was not always an occasion for popping champagne corks. There was also this suspicion that somebody had posted a sign on the door. It would say: Not Required On Voyage.

At first it was tricky trying to adjust to the atmosphere of the London feature writers' room. Dozing torpor shot through with occasional shafts of dazzling malice, just about covers it. But then, what else would you expect if you recruited some of the finest writers in journalism and then banned them from writing? Did this bring out their finest qualities? No, it didn't, and they were a pretty rum lot to start with.

Our hero was the legendary Eric Wainwright, who had simply given up attending the office at all. We'll celebrate Eric later. At that time, Bill

Marshall had adopted the same tactic. When a new features editor, Roy Harris, rang to enquire whether he was coming into the office, Bill asked if they had any work for him. Not at the moment, said Roy. 'Ring me when you have,' Bill retorted, and banged the telephone down.

Richard Sear, ex-military, straight of back, crisp of manner, appeared not to have noticed that the department was effectively closed. He was the man who, when one marriage ended, produced a new potential wife within weeks. 'Just the same as being thrown off a horse,' he said. 'You've got to get back in the saddle before you lose your nerve.'

Richard worried. One evening, about 5pm, there were stories that Cudlipp was patrolling our floor. Richard had his jacket on. 'Cudlipp will think you're leaving early if he sees you dressed like that,' said Don Walker. Richard thanked him and hurriedly hung it over the back of his chair, revealing his handsome scarlet braces.

'You wearing those for a joke, old man?' asked Sid Williams. He explained that Cudlipp would assume that Richard was mocking Lee Howard, the editor, who always wore red braces – and would be sure to tell him. 'Thank god you told me' said a seriously ruffled Sear, as he swiftly put his jacket on again.

'Now he'll think you're ready to go,' said Don.

And so it went on. Creativity stifled, imaginations blocked, the writers of the fourth floor devised all manner of ingenious means to pass the time. Two of them were locked in a feud that went on for months. Since neither of them was up to physical confrontation, the battle was conducted in the office garage. They took turns to sneak down and rip off a wing mirror or scratch a door. 'You'll never guess what that loony has gone and done now,' they both said. Shame they never married really.

Paula James and Matt Coady had drummed up a sort of sketch in which he was the manager of an old-fashioned department store and she was an assistant.

'I'd like to see you in haberdashery today, Mrs James,' he'd say. 'Oh I was thinking I should spend a little time in men's hosiery,' she'd reply.

Matt had been compelled to give up the booze because, as he himself said, after a few whiskies his sharp wit became so wounding that there was a real possibility somebody would kill him. It was a shame, because this was the way that most of the fourth floor responded to their predicament: self-pity was swiftly doused in the pub. Paula, who was herself of statuesque build, brought men literally down to size with her cunning use of the diminutive. Walker was always Little Donny, I was Little Col (not, thank god, and I speak as a dog-lover here, Little Collie). Even the new editor was always referred to as 'Little Mickey Molloy,' which made him sound like a cartoon strip.

As proud as I am of having helped Eve Pollard find Nick Lloyd, I was even more proud of having introduced the terrifying Paula to Frank Howitt, the wild man of the *Express*. They got married, a match made not so much in heaven as in Vagabonds (an adjacent drinking club) at closing-time, and the fight went the full 15, with – as we all expected – Paula winning on points.

The lovely, gentle Don Gomery could judge his intake of nicotine and alcohol so finely that he kept himself amiably anaesthetised for years. Although I don't think anybody actually tried it, I believe you could have removed his tonsils without pain. On the one occasion when some fool accidentally gave him a piece to write, Don Walker, whose self-medication was nothing more dangerous than guitar practice, wrote it for him.

The only ones with any regular work were George Thaw, Freddie Wills, and Peter Senn, who was just across the corridor. George was literary editor, which meant he took delivery of all the new books which some people – not George, obviously, because he was Scottish – sold to the local bookshops for half-price; with dozens of titles each week, that provided what our readers would have called a living wage. For this he was obliged to write half-a-dozen or so paragraphs each week. If he'd failed, someone may even have noticed.

Freddie was the diplomatic correspondent which carried its own demanding responsibilities: every day he had to float around London's embassies taking a drink at each one. With Peter Senn, the arts correspondent, his particular art was to be at the bar of El Vino by twelve-thirty. He rarely failed.

With the flamboyant Paul Hughes, we always thought we were dealing with a mad genius of a Welsh poet who liked to fire himself up on what he called 'the red enrager'. It came as a shock when we later learnt that in fact he came from Torquay. Even so, he was known as Crazy Horse, and not without reason. A keen eye on the main chance, he spotted fortunes to be made in the b-and-b business and, looking to please visiting Americans, he ended up with half of Devizes Castle and a title – he found the latter in the small-ads, I think. Sadly, soaring interest rates brought the b-and-b castle to an end. I don't know about the title.

There were one or two leftovers from another era. Audrey Whiting, a six-foot-plus royal writer who was married to a long-gone editor (an occasion Cudlipp called The Night of the Long Wives) popped in from time to time. And there was a slightly faded blonde who had been the girlfriend of another forgotten editor. This brought some comfort to the various mistresses, girlfriends and bits-on-the-side, to know there was long-term care in place if their particular executive fell off the perch.

It was an odd department all right, poised somewhere between a waiting room for the journalists' home in Dorking and an informal psychiatric unit.

The queen of this ramshackle world was, without doubt, Jill Evans. She came from South Wales and had been married to David Francis, later a sub on the *Mail on Sunday*. She was probably the most glamorous woman in Fleet Street, where her principal gift, and indeed function, seemed to be to enchant men. At this she had no equal. Copper-haired, small and slim, she'd been a dancer and an actress as well as a reporter. She could play outrageous Welsh tart (''ere, you starin' at my massive knockers?') or sophisticated Belgravia lady ('I always think the *Looking Glass* sounds so much smarter than the *Mirror*, don't you?').

It was just as well there was so little work. Every time Jill walked past she left men sitting at their desks dazed and dreaming in a sort of sexual shell-shock.

They all tried. One very Senior Executive indeed called her into his office where she was surprised – although I can't think why – to find him red-faced, panting, and trousers agape. 'It is a very nice one,' she said, gently, 'but I'm afraid I've just had luncheon.'

Another, in drunken despair, climbed up to her fifth-floor mansion flat in Highgate to present her with an engagement ring at midnight when she was already involved in an altogether more personal engagement in her bedroom.

When he arrived on the *Mirror* Paul Callan, who spent a lifetime combating celibacy wherever he found it, slunk up to her in the Stab and said: 'They tell me I'm wasting my time trying to catch you.' She patted him on the hand. 'Don't worry,' she said, 'there are lots of others who won't be so difficult.'

They were all a little daunted by the Rolls-Royce that parked outside the office to pick her up after work. Bryan Morrison, sometime pop-group manager zillionaire who started his own polo club in Berkshire, wanted to marry her. But then, so did most people.

Occasionally they would unleash her on showbiz stars where she had exactly the same effect. After she'd been to interview Burt Reynolds, he rang her at the office about 20 times a day. I took one of the calls. 'Tell her Burt Reynolds rang again,' he said.

'Okay,' I said. 'That's B-E-R-T...'

'No no, for Chrissakes, I'm Burt Reynolds.'

'I'm afraid you're going to have to spell that, Mr Reynolds.' And, bless him, he did. I couldn't tell you what pleasure that gave me.

126

Then we had a couple of days of Michael Crawford desperately ringing for her. And a football referee who she'd met at lunchtime followed her back to the office and offered to desert his wife and family there and then if it would improve his chances.

As she said afterwards, if he'd been a rugby referee it might've been different. She was, after all, Welsh.

Her flat in Highgate, as well as being the target for drunken nocturnal suitors, provided a temporary home for all manner of Fleet Street's waifs and strays. Jeff Bernard turned up there at one time. So did Mike Taylor. Shelley Rohde, ex-*Mail*, ex-*Express*, then Granada producer, lived there for a few weeks. When she arrived in London as a freelance, Wendy Henry and her black dress ended up there too.

Jill's last job for the *Mirror* was in Los Angeles where she had an art deco apartment – one that was used in the Cary Grant films – which looked out on to the Hollywood sign on the hillside. She'd come home.

For me, this was all a long leap from the homely offices of Manchester, where people brought sandwiches in for lunch and wives popped in with their shopping. As Sid Williams pointed out, sandwich shops didn't do blank bills. And wives and husbands, if they existed at all, were all at the other end of a long train ride.

I was still uneasily trying to adjust to all this when I was summoned down to the features editor's office. This was it. My first job as the Secret Chief Home Feature Writer. My reward, if my new companions were right.

They were. It was a trip to the Seychelles to see the shooting of the Pirelli calendar. Fifteen of the world's top models, an ace Swiss photographer, sunshine, white beaches, blue skies. My new colleagues, naturally, rejoiced at my good fortune.

'How nice for you,' said Paula, sweetly. 'It will remind you of Yorkshire.'

*

No way am I going to start this piece with any words other than those two – No Way.

Remember? There was a time in the seventies when it was deeply unfashionable to begin a sentence in any other way. It was a great test of ingenuity. Are you going for a pint? No way am I going to miss having a pint. Have you done your exes? No way have I failed to do my exes…

If you couldn't find a way to make No Way your answer to every question, you'd have been well-advised to have your lips stitched up.

Like all the true adornments to our lives, this expression came in from America – California, I should think – and the first person I ever heard employ it was Ian Woolridge. As an international sportswriter he travelled the world and was thus in a position to import the up-and-coming phrase fresh off the production line. He smuggled No Way through customs and unleashed it in the streets of London where it infected the entire population.

In no time at all, we were all No-Waying like mad.

I was trying to write a piece on this new addition to our national speech when Terry O'Neill came into the features room of the Mirror Holborn office. At that time, snapper O'Neill was based in Los Angeles where he mingled freely with, and was occasionally married to, glittery starry ladies. He was just the man I wanted.

He knew all about No Way. In America, it had practically run its course and was beginning to look suspiciously last-yearish (a phrase I am thinking of marketing myself). So what should we be saying, we apostles of the zeitgeist? What was winging its way across the Atlantic now?

He told me. It was two words, usually hyphenated, and it meant sort of cool and relaxed. We fairly howled with laughter. He'd obviously got it wrong. No-one would ever use such an expression. We simply couldn't imagine a time when grown men would use a phrase like...

Laid-back.

That, you could say, was the spirit of the times when I moved down from Manchester.

And although I may have moaned about the writer-story ratio in Fleet Street at that time – and griping is not only the right but also the god-given duty of every freeborn newspaper person – the odd gem did occasionally come my way. There was, as I mentioned before, the trip to the Seychelles to see the shooting of the Pirelli calendar that was my reward for transferring to the London staff.

That too caught the spirit of the times. The art director simply hired 15 of the world's most beautiful models and a photographer so famous and so sought-after that they had to tempt him out of retirement in Africa with vast bundles of dosh. They thought they should go somewhere where the light was good, for the snaps. So they all upped and went to the Seychelles.

Our happy little party had their own dramas. One of the models seemed to claim much of the photographer's attention, particularly at night. Suspecting favouritism, the other girls were upset. Three became human sacrifices by laying in the sun until they burnt. Two others set about demonstrating that girls can enjoy themselves in all sorts of ways, even man-free. I think they'd mistaken the island for Lesbos.

The snapper took 3,000 shots from which he thought he could find a dozen for the calendar. Our photographer, Doreen Spooner, thought even Kent Gavin wouldn't have needed as many as that. I wasn't so sure.

Being trapped on a tropical island with women who kept on removing their clothes had its dangers for me too. One day, lying on the beach watching chaps as brown and slim as liquorice sticks run up the coconut trees, I had a sudden thought. If they could do it then I, with half-a-dozen O-levels, could surely do the same.

Barefoot, I shot up a tree that angled out at 45 degrees over the white beach. It was easy. That's to say it was easy until I looked down, wobbled and fell off. On the way down I grabbed the trunk of the tree which was rather like that of a crocodile's back. Arm ripped open, hence highly original receipt for exes: 'Medical treatment following fall from coconut tree: 50 dollars.'

And, would you believe, nobody even queried it. Sometimes I think features editors just don't care.

By this time, it was firmly established that I was not to be let near anything that bore any resemblance to a real story.

I was cast as the candy-floss writer who would have a shot at any old rubbish, which was a fair summary of my talents. Sometimes it got me into trouble.

The story was that in America people were adopting rocks as pets. Somebody on the desk tentatively suggested to Ron Ricketts that he might like to try a day with a pet rock. Now Ron was a man of principle, in fact a man of many principles, almost too many you might say, and one of them was that he should not be required to dabble in the trivial. He exploded. Didn't they know he was a journalist of some authority? Didn't they realise it was this crappy journalism that got the press a bad name? And so on.

Not that I knew any of this. So, when they passed it on to me, I thought it sounded like a good laugh. With Charlie Ley, one of the jollier photographers, I got a brick from a building site and marched it around London on a leash. We did lots of fake pet stuff – brick tilted against a tree, and so on – before eventually deciding to put it down by hurling it off Westminster Bridge.

Was this the same sort of breakthrough journalism that led to Watergate? Possibly not. But it made the spread, which caused Ron to burst into flames. He told me I was a disgrace, but since Ron invariably identified at least three disgraces before breakfast most days, I wasn't too worried.

When they needed someone to dress up like a prat and go to Ascot, they didn't ask Ron. Nor did they ask John Pilger, or Keith Waterhouse, nor, for that matter, even the Old Codgers. I got Moss Bros to deck me out in the latest racing finery and presented myself at the gates.

A middle-aged woman accosted me in the street. Heavily decorated with veils and flower-loaded hat, her face an inch deep in make-up, she looked a bit too tarty to be a real tart. Imagine Tom Merrin if he'd ever tried transgender – that's it.

'You look splendid, sir,' she whooped. 'Can I interview you? I'm Jean Rook from the *Daily Express*.'

'Of course you can,' I replied. 'But only if you promise to distort what I say. I'm Colin Dunne from the *Daily Mirror*.'

Would you believe it, she didn't even use my quote. I used hers though.

I had a rather happier meeting with a fellow distorter, the wonderful Annie Buchanan, when she celebrated her 50th birthday at the City Golf Club. With her non-stop ciggies and handbag filled with betting slips Annie, who was then on the *Sun*, was the very best of that armour-plated breed, the Fleet Street Ladies. What have you learnt, I asked her, in your five decades, that will act as my lodestar in life? She didn't hesitate for a second. 'Never waste your time with bores, darling.' It took me another 20 years to discover she was right.

For a summer series Mike Molloy sent me, photographer Doreen again, and cartoonist Keith Waite around Britain's seasides to illustrate and write about... well, anything. I always liked a brief that wasn't too prescriptive. We found our way to Trecco Bay, the biggest caravan site in Europe, where whole mining villages moved street-by-street into the caravans, so that you took your neighbours with you. The miners called it 'Hi-but Week' because you were always saying Hi to people you knew.

'People have died here,' said the manager, delighted to have recognition at last. 'People have been born here. And many have been conceived here. When I told a couple I wasn't licensed to marry them, they asked me if I'd mind just saying a few words to see them over the weekend.'

As something of a change, we went to Eastbourne, where – then as now – the buttered scone still held sway over the hot-dog, and the piers were glassed in to prevent the more frail from being blown away.

In Teignmouth, we found an end-of-the-pier concert party that had a soprano ('Popular Return') who sang *When I Get Too Old to Dream*, an Al Jolson impersonator from Bradford who even blacked up for his own wedding (like to see him try that today), a Delightful Dance Duo, a Popular Singing Accordionist who once toured with Carmen Miranda, and, best of all, Billy Burden.

With his smock, straw, and bulging belly, The Happy Yokel had a great line in rustic humour: 'Doctor says Oi thinks you want some castor oil. Oi says: T'ain't castor oil I want. It's a bloomin' ferret.'

Oh, how we laughed.

Finally, the *Mirror* recognised my weakness: dealing with any form of reality. They asked me to interview the one celebrity I could confidently handle – Mrs Florence Capp, wife of Andrew Capp, unemployed, of Tyneside.

But isn't she a figment...?

Look, it's not for us to debate what's real and what isn't. I found my interview with Flo where you usually find such things, at the bottom of a glass of red wine. I interviewed her. She was entirely co-operative. And she gave me some revelatory stuff about her husband. Like he never voted Labour because they kept promising full employment, and it frightened him.

Well, at least she never complained of being misquoted.

The woman behind Andy Capp (but only in case he falls down...)
By Colin Dunne

Forget Greta Garbo. Forget Howard Hughes. At last the Mirror brings you an exclusive interview with the most elusive personality of our time. Since 1956, Andy Capp has acquired a readership of more than 250,000,000 fans. And now, for the first time, answering questions about their life together and the major issues of the day – MRS FLORENCE CAPP.

The front door slammed. Into the distance faded the tramp of boots, the whistling, and the companionable clink of a carrier bag full of empties.

The back door opened. 'You can come in now, pet – he's gone.'

Inside, the debris left in the wake of the great man himself. Three empty bottles of stout. A plate recently stripped of steak and kidney pie. A redundant betting slip.

The trappings of greatness.

And here also, in the back kitchen of that famous terraced-house, somewhere in North-East England, in full ceremonial regalia of full-length pinny and curlered hair in turban – Mrs Florence Capp, wife of Andy.

'Yes, pet,' she says. 'You're right. I am the Woman Behind Andy Capp... But only in case he falls down.'

International fame has not touched their integrity. Flo and Andy live on exactly as before.

For him, the club, the pub, the betting-shop, the snooker hall.

131

For her, cups of tea with her neighbour Ruby, the bingo, and the full-time job of supporting her husband in his demanding role as the last of the male chauvinist pigs.

How does she feel about topical subjects of the day?

Tell me, Mrs Capp, what do you think about the president scandal?

'I knew you'd ask that, hinny, but it were nowt to do with our Andy. He never goes in the President normally – he says you get a better pint down the Trades Club.

'Anyway, the day he were in there, when he goes off to the netty, he marks his beer level in his pint with his billiard chalk as usual.

'When he comes back, it's down two inches. He came home with one tooth missing, but he had three of someone else's in his toe-cap.'

Hmmm. Ye-e-es. We do seem to live in a violent world, Mrs Capp?

'You're right there. Our Andy's dead against it. At the match the other day, there was a feller who got right violent every time our Andy hit him.

'He's still pulling boot-studs out of his backside. Andy says you've got to stamp out violence.'

Quite so, quite so. And how does the famous man feel about politics?

'He's Labour, but he never votes. Every time he's going to, they promise full employment and it fair puts him off his pint.'

Well, we all know Mr Capp is thought to be a layabout. Has he ever actually worked?

Mrs Capp pointed to a clock on the mantelpiece.

'See that? For 25 years with the same firm. They had a whip-round down the dole and gave it to him on the anniversary.

'He's like that, Andy. When he starts something he sticks to it.'

Another topical question. How does Mrs Capp herself feel about Women's Lib?

'Are them the lasses what don't wear brassieres? Well, I don't wear one meself either. Not since 1953.

'Andy used it once to carry the empties back to the pub and I never saw it again. I was always a C-cup you see.

'But my friend Ruby wouldn't be without hers. Says she's nowhere else to put her purse for bingo.

'Andy's a good husband in many ways. He does his little jobs. Always opens his own bottles. Always collects his dole himself.'

You can sense the deep trust that lies between them. Mrs Capp says she doesn't even lock her handbag any more. Not since Andy took it down the club and raffled it.

Doesn't she feel, though, that she's treated as a sex object?

She frowned. 'Sex? Object? Well, I wouldn't object meself, speaking personally, but Andy's got his snooker to think of and anything like that makes bridge tremble.'

That is not the reason, however, why the Capps have remained childless.

132

Andy, says his wife, refused to have children until the family allowance was raised to at least £15 a child.

'He says he won't subsidise no government,' she adds. 'A canny lad like that, Andy.'

How ever did they meet, this amazing couple?

'Years and years ago, pet, when his cap were quite stiff and clean and new – what you might call his peak.

'It were a quiet wedding Well, until they tried to close the bar.

'And it was what they call a touring honeymoon – the Fleece, the White Horse, the Trades. I thought we were never coming home.'

Mrs Capp, surprisingly, agrees that he is a wife-beater. She says that is fair enough, since she is also a husband-beater.

And the balance of power in the Capp household has shifted slowly over the years.

She sighs a little as she explains: 'He's not as fit as he was. He always says he was winning on points for the first ten years but that I'll drop him in the end.'

There is really only one question left. Has Mrs Capp ever seen...

'...Andy without his cap. Never, pet, never. No-one has. He says he was born with it on.

'I says gerraway. But he says yes; it had to be a Caesarean, otherwise he might have had it knocked off. That's Andy – full of tricks.'

From down the street, there sounds a distant burp and the slur of approaching boots.

Flo smiles and puts out on the table the Band-Aid and the TCP ready for his two-fisted nightcap.

Thank you, Mrs Capp. And try to pull your punches, won't you?

Every day, soon after six, we'd go over the road to the Stab where there'd be considerable griping and moaning, followed by more moaning and griping. If you didn't do both, I don't think you'd get served in a newspaper pub – they'd assume you were an impostor. About this time a new figure arrived in the Stab. Wendy Henry had also moved down from Manchester. I knew her as the freelance who could always find exactly what you wanted, and with unnerving speed.

'Wendy, can you find us a nun who used to be a stripper and who supports Halifax Town...?' Pause. 'Will tomorrow be okay?'

A plump young woman with a lisp, she presented herself as an endearing innocent lost among the big-time boys of Fleet Street. 'Fanthy a daft girl from Manchethter like me with all you thlick operatorth...'

Some of us big-time boys from Fleet Street were stupid enough to believe it. She asked me if I could introduce her to the handsome fellow with the moustache standing at the bar. That, I explained with some

133

patience, was Mike Molloy who would be the next editor of the *Daily Mirror*, which of course meant he was far too important to be pestered even by me, and certainly by itinerant freelances like her. 'Hold thith,' she said, pressing a half of beer into my hand. A minute later she was talking to him. Twenty minutes later she came back to claim her drink. 'Nithe guy, Mike. We're having lunch next week.'

All you need to know is that Wendy became an editor. Three times (two top-selling tabloids in Fleet Street, one in America). I became an itinerant freelance.

This was my second assault on London. Seven years earlier, I'd done the weekly paper, provincial daily, route to Fleet Street, only to retreat when the first Mrs Dunne became unhappy. The second time I'd done weekly, daily, and northern national, and here I was in London again. This time it seemed to be working, with the Dunne family settled in a village just outside Tunbridge Wells. Sometimes, however, our rough northern ways were too much for our gentler southern cousins.

For his first day at school, I had advised young Matt, who was the tiniest and thinnest boy in the village (something of a family tradition), that he must never allow himself to be bullied. On that first day I was summoned to his school from the *Mirror*. When I got there, the headmaster was practically weeping. If the Kray twins had been enrolled as his pupils, he couldn't have been more alarmed. My son was terrorising the entire school. He had punched two of his classmates on the nose, one was bleeding and the other was being consoled by his mother who was threatening to sue.

'Were they bullying you, Matt?' I asked, gently.

'No,' he said, thoughtfully. 'But they looked as though they might.' In Yorkshire, the pre-emptive strike was a popular weapon: not, apparently, in the soft south.

I was still a little surprised by the complete separation of work and home, unlike the north where they overlapped. On the Kent-Sussex border, I met only one other journalist, a man whose golden career should be held up as an exemplar on all the media courses. Bob Rodrigo – by-lined more familiarly as Bob Rodney – was the *Mirror* golf correspondent, which meant he was compelled to spend his life touring the warmest and most beautiful places in the world, where bands of sleek PR girls would feed him whatever facts – and whatever drinks – his heart desired.

When this ended, he teamed up with Noel Whitcomb, Cudlipp's favourite reporter, who came up with the idea of the Punters' Club. The two of them organised holidays at the most exciting and glamorous racetracks in the world, sold the tickets through the *Mirror* – oh, and a couple of seats for Noel and Bob please.

He knew he'd retired only when he realised there was no room service. Bob was a fine fellow and anybody that clever deserves everything he gets. I just wished I'd met him when I was 16.

There was, however, a germ of doubt about the First Mrs Dunne's enthusiasm for the state of matrimony. On New Year's Eve she asked me, with a slightly acid tone, if I had any resolutions in mind. I said yes: next year I was going to try to put myself first instead of thinking of other people all the time. I was going to try, at whatever cost, to be more selfish.

She gave me a smack over the ear. After Ron Ricketts and Wendy Henry, I was now being humiliated at home.

*

Personally, I always wanted to be a toady. Oh yes, I know most reporters dreamed of a foreign posting or craved the glamour of a column or the power of the back bench, but toadying was the job I fancied.

Toadies got the lot: the best jobs, the best exes, and a seat at the most important lunch and dinner tables. All you had to do was to laugh at the editor's jokes, marvel at his (or her) wisdom, ensure her (or his) glass never emptied, and be able to whistle up a taxi in a minute. Best of all, it was a no-talent appointment. Surely I could handle that?

Actually, no. As it turned out, I was hopelessly unqualified for the job. In the first place, I couldn't drink. You've heard of the Churchill Gene, which enables you to drink all day, non-stop, without a single hiccup, just like Winston? Most evenings there were enough Churchill Genes in the Stab to fight them on the beaches.

Unfortunately I had the Attlee Gene, which meant that after three drinks I was speaking perfect Pitman's. You didn't know Pitman's is a language? It isn't. I was the only *Mirror* employee who could be having his first drink in the Stab at 6pm, and be home in time for Coronation Street, totally smashed, having spent only £3. That rather cut out the courtier's late-night attendance duty.

On top of that, for some reason I never entirely grasped, my sense of humour seemed to jar. I laughed in wrong places. My own cheery jokes never seemed to hit the right note. Like the time I asked an assistant editor if people of his rank were allowed to choose their own mistresses or were allocated them from the secretarial pool. I thought that demonstrated shrewd observation and cavalier wit. He nearly bit a piece out of his glass. It wasn't my fault if he got the one with the squint, was it? In those days, the seventies, no-one got fired, but I got closer than most.

The truth was that, for me, socialising with my superiors was far too dangerous. I worked out my own Disaster Ratio: 10 minutes with an executive equalled career setback of 10 years.

My only chance of survival was to keep my head down and steer a wide course around anyone with a carpet in his office. And it worked fairly well until the day I returned to the fourth-floor features room in Holborn (yes, the one day in the month I'd been out on a job) to find my colleagues grinning with a glee that had a suspiciously malicious glint.

Hugh Cudlipp had invited everyone who'd worked on a special Shock Issue up to his ninth-floor palace for congratulatory drinks. This was deeply worrying. For a start, nobody was more important than Hugh Cudlipp – he wasn't God, that's true, but he had given God a couple of subbing shifts on *The People*. What's more, office legend insisted that on these meet-the-lads occasions, somebody always caught Cudlipp's eye, and that somebody was soon emptying his desk. What caught his eye was anything out of the usual which was why my colleagues were grinning.

They'd received their invitations as soon as they'd arrived in the morning so they'd had all day to ensure that they presented a picture of bland conformity... Sensible haircuts, dark suits, smart shirts, silk ties, shining shoes. Similarly, the men were immaculately coiffed and sober suited. You simply couldn't fault them.

On the other hand...

This was in my ageing hippy period. Certainly I was an arresting sight. My hair at that time touched my shoulder-blades. My suit was a sort of electric blue colour, with wide lapels and flared trousers. It was velvet. No tie, but a huge collar that flopped like bunny's ears. Dark glasses completed the look which was of Little Lord Fauntleroy posing as a drug dealer.

'Well, old man,' said Sid Williams, in his kindliest tone. 'Cudlipp likes to have a victim – good of you to volunteer.' Sid often suspected there was a conspiracy afoot from which he was excluded. It was clear on this occasion that if there was a conspiracy here, he was on the inside and I was on the outside. This appeared to be causing him no distress.

Paula James, another soft-hearted sweetie, looked at her watch. 'Got to go,' she snapped. 'We mustn't be a minute late. You know what darling little Hughie is like – we don't want to attract attention, do we?'

Williams, James, Evans, Hughes, Gomery, Sear, Hellicar, Walker, the whole damn lot of them swept me up and headed for the lift. I'd done human interest, but this was the first time I'd done human sacrifice.

There wasn't a lot of cover on the ninth-floor but I did the best I could, retreating between a tallish filing cabinet and a tropical plant, as far as I could from our noble leader. Cudlipp had a lovely time delivering one of his bitter-witty speeches, taking the mickey out of Murdoch ('this amateur Ned Kelly') and the *Express* ('a burnt-out case'), and praising to the skies this assembly of astonishing talent. The pix, the layout, the writing, the headlines, all in the finest traditions of the *Mirror* at its best.

Boy, was he proud of us all. With people like this, the *Mirror* had nothing to fear. Not a damn thing. Then – oh God – he began to move around among his talented, and in one case terrified, team. He stopped here and there. A word with Walker. A bit of a lech with Evans. Coming nearer and nearer. I was just wondering what jobs were open to a man with the Attlee gene when I looked up and there he was, right in front of me. I tried to slide further behind the filing cabinet. Too late. He'd spotted me. What was worse, he'd spotted the suit.

His hand came out and touched it. He took the lapel between finger and thumb. 'Velvet?' he enquired, his sharp eyes driving into mine and quite possibly six inches out of the back of my head. 'Mmmmm,' I gulped, trying to avoid confirmation or denial. Was there time, I wondered, to sink two g-and-t's quickly and reply to him in fluent Pitman's? Could I have three and die of alcoholic poisoning before he fired me?

He stepped back. 'Blue velvet...' It was barely audible. It didn't need to be. He was talking to himself. He was talking to himself to see if he liked what he was saying.

'Blue velvet...' he repeated, slightly more loudly. 'Yes, I rather like that.' He cocked his head on one side. What he really liked was the sound of himself saying it. 'Yes, I think that's good. No, it's great. No it isn't, it's absolutely bloody marvellous.' The more he said it, the more he liked it. He wasn't some old stick-in-the-mud afraid of new styles and fashions. Not a bit of it. Scared of change? Not me, sunshine.

Then he turned to address his editorial team. He did so at a volume pitch that would have been sufficient to address the entire British Army assembled on Salisbury Plain. 'That's what newspapers need,' he thundered, in his rasping voice. 'A bit of fun, a bit of colour, a bit of bloody daring – that's what newspapers are all about.'

He ran his eyes over the astonished throng. With contempt he looked at the neat partings and the blade-sharp creases in the trousers. 'What we don't want,' he said, dropping his voice to a low growl, 'is little grey men in their little grey suits... with their little grey minds.'

The little grey men shifted about uncertainly and wondered what to do. Start a fist-fight perhaps? Unzip their trousers? It was too late. Bloody daring had passed them by.

'People who're like that – people who wouldn't know excitement if it bit them on the leg – shouldn't be in journalism. I don't want them on my newspapers. I want to see them behind the counter in the bloody bank where they belong. What I want is people with guts and courage who don't give a damn what anyone thinks. That's what we need in Fleet Street.'

He turned back to me. 'Tell my secretary where you got it. I want two.'

It was quiet ride down in the lift. I couldn't seem to catch anybody's eyes. They were all looking down, closely examining their brilliantly polished toes.

I did tell Cudlipp's secretary. She wrote it down too. 'Lord John, Carnaby Street,' she repeated. Then I reverted to my heads-down policy, and avoided speaking to anybody who was more important than myself. This eliminated nine-tenths of the people in the building.

I saw him occasionally over the next few years. Not once was he wearing flyaway lapels and flares. And this stunning bit of luck didn't advance my career one jot.

Cudlipp was never once heard to shout: 'Bring me my man in blue velvet.' Not once.

But it did earn me the respect of Sid Williams. It proved that he was right all along. Clearly there was a conspiracy afoot, and equally clearly I was in on it. 'Just one thing, old man,' he used to whisper to me, when we met in the corridor. 'Who told you that he liked velvet? You can trust me.'

*

Goodness knows, my 30-odd years in Fleet Street produced very little by way of achievement, fame or trophies. All I've got to show for it are a few divorce court appearances, arteries as congested as Shoe Lane, and a collection of anecdotes that can never be told. Why not? Because normal people would never believe them.

But I do have one claim to distinction of which I'm seriously proud, and it's one that very few old *Mirror* men can make…

For I knew Eric Wainwright.

Oh yes, there are plenty who are familiar with the legend of Invisible Eric, the ghost of the fourth floor features. But I doubt if any of them ever actually set eyes upon him. And fewer still who heard, first-hand, his explanation of why he found it necessary to wear his St James's Street hat while seated upon the lavatory.

But I did. I knew him quite well. And his hat. And I'm glad I caught his show while it was still – just – in town.

It happened at a time when I found myself working in the fourth-floor features room on Sunday mornings.

I always had it to myself. Until one morning when in bowled this dapper chap. Although clearly startled at having to share the room, he gave a jovial wave and sat down at a typewriter. The telephone rang. 'No,' he said, with complete conviction, 'there's no-one here called Dunne.'

At this point I thought it wise to introduce myself. He apologised for not knowing me. In fact, he didn't seem to know anyone. 'Who's the features editor now?' I said it was Bill Hagerty. 'Is he a little blonde chap with a moustache?' I said no, he was a tallish dark chap with a clean upper lip. He nodded. 'Bit out of touch these days,' he said. 'I try to keep out of the way.'

At that he was triumphantly successful. His contact with the office was his monthly visit, on a Sunday morning when the place was deserted, to do four weeks' expenses. A little cautiously, I said that I hadn't seen his by-line recently. 'No, old boy, haven't had a piece in for six years.' I murmured something about how upsetting it must be to have all that copy spiked. He looked at me as though I was insane. 'Lord no; haven't written anything for six years.'

At this point, we need a little history. In the mid-seventies, the *Daily Mirror* features department had reached its zenith with a splendid one-way employment policy: new writers were shipped in, but no old writers went out. One idle day (there were about 342 a year) I counted the number of feature writers and gave up when I passed 40. They were a mixed bunch. Former girl-friends of long-gone editors, executives who'd forgotten what they were executing, columnists who'd misplaced their columns, foreign correspondents returned home, and some people who I think just came in for the warmth. There were even one or two who wrote features. This wasn't encouraged.

Passing the time could be a problem. Some took to the drink. Some took to adultery. Some took to both, and not always in the right order. Don Walker set up a music stand and taught himself classical guitar. Paula James made restaurant reservations. George Thaw was Scottish all over the place. Don Gomery sighed a lot. Occasionally we'd move the desks and have a badminton tournament.

Several of the writers, like Eric, became no-shows. His sports jacket – Daks, of course – was left over his chair, so that if anybody asked for him we could say he'd popped out to the bank and we would ring the number he'd left. The number, somebody said, was for a drinking club in Soho in which he was a partner. We never rang it. Nobody ever asked for him.

Years slipped by, and he became a sort of invisible yet indestructible folk hero. Once he put in a memo asking to be made Pub Correspondent. Tony Miles, the editor, asked somebody to check with accounts to see if he was still on the staff. He was. 'What the hell does he do?' Somebody said he spent most of his time in pubs. 'In that case,' said Miles, 'he might as well have the title.' So he achieved his ambition, and, true to the last, he never wrote a story.

Mike Molloy once called a conference which was a must-attend for all writers. Bars and bedrooms all over London emptied and by the time he'd begun, the room was packed. At that point in walked this distinguished figure with his rolled umbrella and perched himself at the front. Mike was saying the new policy was to attract young readers when Eric spoke. 'Delightful little boozer just outside Guildford,' he said. 'Lots of young people in there. Shall I pop down and have a look?' A minute later he'd gone. It remained one of the great unwritten stories of our time.

Over the months, I got to know him well. With his slick of silver hair, florid face and drawing-room accent, he was of a type that even then was rapidly running out of fashion. He was – there's no other word for it – a gent: British warm overcoat, yellow chamois gloves and tightly-furled umbrella with a whangee handle, he was clearly an ex-officer from some smart regiment. Only he wasn't.

The story was that he was a Canadian who'd come over here with the Canadian air force and stayed on. There were rumours of military heroics. At one time he'd made a living as a cartoonist (some of his cartoons were on the walls of the office pub, The Stab In The Back). Even more incredibly, he'd dressed up as a huge half-wit woman called Cynthia who was the silent stage stooge for a northern comedienne called Hylda Baker. 'She knows, y'know', Hylda would say, elbowing Eric in the ribs.

It was the sort of CV that could end only one way – in the *Mirror* features department. Long before those Sunday morning meetings, he'd built up quite a name for doing first-person pieces under the by-line Danger Man. He was terrific. He rode a motor-bike through a hoop of fire. He went into a cage full of lions armed only with a chair. He even went to the photographers' Christmas party... no, no, that was a joke, he wasn't that crazy.

He was what he himself would have called a genial sort of cove. Full of good spirits, full of good stories. Around noon, he would slip over to the Stab, and return a couple of hours later, even fuller of good spirits. He would slump down in his chair and ring all his friends around the world. Occasionally, the odd snippet would drift over to me, and what collectors' items they were...

'Yerrs, still got the same old place out in Bucks. Thatched roof, y'know. Trouble is, bloody squirrels in the thatch. Gnawed through the bloody water pipe. Drips through the ceiling. Bloody nuisance. Have to wear a hat when I'm on the lav.'

With the writer's true eye for detail, Eric knew this required further definition. 'Y'know,' he said, 'the one I got at Lock's of St James.'

There were stories that in his younger days he was an accomplished pub fighter. Someone who once saw him in action said he used the pub furniture like they do in cowboy films. To me he was never anything other than charming, apart from the day Roy Harris upset him. Roy, who was, I think, deputy features editor, sat in on a Sunday, and when Eric presented his expenses, he ventured a mildly casual enquiry about one item.

Eric was furious. He went immediately to the Stab. He stayed longer than usual. When he came back he was purple with, among other things, rage. He asked my advice. What was the silliest story I'd ever done? A talking dog, I said. Where was the furthest point from the office? Land's End. With finger-jabbing anger, he typed away, took it downstairs and slammed it down in front of Roy. It was for a trip to Land's End to interview a talking dog. It involved well over a thousand miles' travel, several overnights, lots of entertaining and taxis. All with no bills. The final, some might have said contemptuous, item was the one that caught Roy's eye. 'Bone for dog – £10.'

Roy, who was not a big man, shivered in the shadow of the figure looming over him. 'Must have been a big bone,' he whispered weakly.

Eric slammed his hand on the desk and roared: 'It was a fucking big dog.'

Roy's signature fairly skidded across the paper.

Somebody somewhere must have let me back in, because my Sunday mornings in the office came to an end. I missed them. I missed Eric. With him, I felt as though I was catching the last act of a wonderful long-running comedy.

About a year after I left the *Mirror*, Don Walker rang me up. I knew it was some sort of spoof because he was trying not to laugh. Eric was leaving, he said. They were having a farewell party for him. And would I go along because I was the only person who knew what he looked like.

Just me.

Sadly, Eric isn't around any more. Any more? What am I saying?

*

He was always one shave behind the rest of the world, and, I suspect, one drink ahead. With his crumpled linen suit, dark glasses, and fat French cigarette, Stanley Bonnet was always too exotic a figure for the *Daily Mirror* office and the Stab. He needed a bigger stage.

141

He was the real thing. He'd been an agency man in Africa, I think he'd worked around the Middle East, he was even said to have been an MI5 man, and to have run a bar in Beirut at one time. I was never quite sure whether he'd taken his character from Graham Greene, or whether Graham Greene had used him as an inspiration. Either way it would've worked.

So I was delighted, if a little overawed, to find myself in the same Hamburg hotel as Stan one Friday in the seventies. But I was quite upset when I saw the look of grave distaste on his face: I'd said the wrong thing.

'You're doing what?' he asked, eyebrows rising. I explained again that I was going to take an evening coach tour of the city to see all the fascinating sights and I asked, rather timidly, if Stan would like to do the same.

His face creased into a smile of ineffable weariness. 'I don't do coach trips,' he murmured, stubbing his fag out in an overcrowded ashtray. 'But I'm sure you'll enjoy it.'

Now he didn't know how that coach trip was going to turn out, and neither did I, of course. I wish now I'd never told him. It almost broke his heart.

It was sheer coincidence that we ended up in the same hotel – that one opposite the station. We'd both been on missions for the *Mirror*. His was proper journalism – something about the political line-up in Europe. Mine was the saucy lightweight crap to which I was dedicating my entire career.

This one was interviewing a girl who worked at an Eros Centre, which was what they called municipal brothels in Germany. Luckily, I'd found one who spoke excellent English, with a marked upper-class accent. She'd learnt it, she told me, when she worked as an au-pair in Finchley and had a smart surgeon boy-friend. Was her new life very different from England? 'Wherever you are the sex is the same. But here the money is far better.'

This was all a bit of a shock to me. I'd not long left the Yorkshire Dales where sex and money were much the same: unavailable. The excuse-me quickstep with Antoinette Thompson at the Wharfedale Young Farmers' Ball in Grassington Town Hall, music by the Craven Players, was about as racy as it got. So it's no surprise that by the time I'd finished the Eros interview my biro was quite moist.

I found Stanley in the bar. We were both due to pull out the next day, so we were discussing what we would do with our last night in Hamburg. Stan, the old hand, had just had another £100 wired through. I had about £15 left and daren't ask for any more. That's why I was proposing to go on the coach tour. 'It only costs a tenner and includes a free glass of champagne at a leading night-club,' I pointed out, in the hope of catching his interest.

It failed. He sipped his whisky, and said maybe he'd jump on a flight that night. 'Have a good night with the grannies,' he said. As I climbed on to the coach, he waved from the back of a taxi.

Stanley was exactly what an international reporter should be. I'm pretty certain that I heard him refer to James Cameron as 'Jimmy'. Fifty-ish, short, thinning hair, he looked as though he was planning a revolution. You couldn't look at him without somehow hearing the whirr of cicadas and the croak of frogs. A high humidity man, he belonged beneath slowly stirring fans in a steamy Congo bar, possibly in the company of something with impossibly long legs, dabbing tears from her eyes. He'd done decadence, without a doubt.

What few facts I know about him are remarkable enough. Unlikely as it seems, he began on the *Slough Observer*, but it was when he was on the *Daily Mail* that his talent for the unpredictable had surfaced. He was sent to cover an American glamour girl – was she called Jane Baldesare? – who was attempting to swim the Channel, underwater...

I know, I know. The early sixties were desperate days.

Astonishingly, this attempt failed – after about 20 yards, I should think. Stan not only covered the story, he married it. He and Jane dashed off to open a bar in Beirut, which went the way of the underwater swimming bid. After that, he was a stringer in the Middle East hot-spots like Aden where he slept with a gun under his pillow.

We hadn't seen anything like him on the *Craven Herald and West Yorkshire Pioneer*, that was for sure. I was so thrilled to find myself in his company, and so disappointed that he wasn't interested in my night out.

Hey-ho, off we go, on to the coach, and he was right about the grannies. There were four or five at the back, two couples from southern Germany, a thirty-ish textile salesman called Trevor from Baildon in Yorkshire, and a pale young man with a spotty complexion. The three of us, as the youngest males, sat together. As we went round, Trevor said he was worried because he'd been unable to telephone his wife, Brenda. Brenda was worried about Trevor meeting exotic continental girls which, looking at Trevor, seemed a bit of a long-shot. And the pale young man held out a limp hand and said: 'I am Hamid. I am from Dubai.' He said it as though it explained everything. He was right: it did.

Our guide was a middle-aged man called, oddly, Winston. I mean, do they have London guides called Adolf? Anyway, Winston showed us elegant streets and smart shops, vast yachts on an inland lake, several fascinating ball-bearing factories, a couple of old churches that had somehow survived the RAF's scene-shifting, more bridges and canals than Venice, and marzipan shops. People in Hamburg eat marzipan by the ton.

No doubt people in Marzipan do the same with hamburgers. Finally, he took us to the nightclub, with an emphatic warning to stick to our free glass of champagne and not to order any more drink. 'Very, very expensive,' he said.

Next to me, Hamid, who'd been telling me he was educated at Eastbourne College, again announced: 'I am from Dubai.' Good, we said, and went into the night-club. It was a sort of Talk of the Town affair, plumed and towering showgirls on stage, a smooth big band in light-blue jackets, lots of glitter and flashing lights, and all pretty harmless.

Trevor wondered if there was a telephone where he could ring Brenda. I thought it was perhaps as well Stan hadn't come: no cicadas, no frogs, no revolutions. Hamid called a waiter over and ordered champagne. Instantly, Winston appeared and said no, no, no, it was far too expensive for mere tourists. Hamid again came back with his simple statement: 'I am from Dubai.'

Slowly, we began to see what he meant.

Winston told him the price which, as Trevor said, would have bought a beer for every man in Baildon, and for one or two in Shipley. Hamid gave a shy smile. The price, no problem. As we toasted Hamid, Winston vanished to make enquiries, then returned. Did Hamid really want to spend serious money? If so, Winston knew a place that was more... well, a little more geared towards the Dubai trade. But, these places didn't come cheap. Instantly, Trevor and I ruled ourselves out.

But Hamid put his arms round us, we were his new friends, he wanted us to go with him or it wouldn't be fun. He would pay. He was from Dubai.

At first sight, the Pelican Club looked like a fantasy in Habitat. A long, low-ceilinged room, with sofas and baggy armchairs scattered around glass-topped tables. The colours were all pale creams and browns. I didn't pick up much more detail because it was then I saw the staff. The waitresses were all around 19, they were all stunning, and they seemed surprisingly unconcerned about their uniform: one smallish silver star and a pair of high silver stilettos. The star was placed exactly where you would place a star if that was all you had to wear. The shoes were on their feet.

In Grassington Town Hall, the girls sat down one side and the boys down the other. In the Pelican, the system was different. The men – only seven or eight in total – sat on the sofas and the girls swarmed all over them like smooth-skinned bees. I could not compare them with Antoinette Thompson because I had never seen her wearing a star. Trevor said the same of his Brenda, and looked anxiously at his watch.

Hamid mentioned his home town, and once again the charming staff bore in more bottles of champagne. It was beginning to occur to me that 'I am from Dubai' was some sort of international code meaning 'Please help me get rid of lots of cash.' Well, the club certainly kept their side of the bargain. Trays came round bearing delicious titbits (not a word you could easily use in that setting). Champagne followed more champagne. Trevor told me all about 'the textile game', as he liked to call it and, like good young Yorkies, we discussed the poetry of Boycott's cover drive. It wasn't easy through a tangle of scented and wriggling limbs, but we men of Yorkshire are not easily deterred.

A hand tapped me on the shoulder. It was a man in a suit with a bill on a silver tray. It had now reached £500, an astronomical sum in those days, and he would like an interim payment. Where was our friend from Dubai?

A good question. Where was our friend from Dubai? He'd vanished. I didn't think that bill would sit too happily on my exes. We whizzed around, calling out his name, until we heard a strangled cry from a side-room. There, lying on a bed beneath a sort of living duvet of human flesh, was Hamid. They kept pouring champagne over his head to keep him awake. They even.... Oh you don't want to go into all that. Let's just say that they had developed ingenious means of helping clients fend off sleep. When he was asleep, he wasn't spending. One hand came out from beneath the flesh duvet, holding – thank God – an Amex card.

I don't know what time it was when we left. Trevor and I more or less carried Hamid back to the hotel. 'You can have a good sleep now,' I told him. He shook his head. 'Tonight I go to Copenhagen,' he whimpered. It's not easy, being the Man from Dubai

Somehow, I got my flight back. I didn't see Stanley until noon on Monday, in the Stab. He dabbed his cigarette into another overflowing ashtray and gave me a pitying smile. 'How was the coach trip?' So I told him.

As I did, he ground his cigarette out with some ferocity. He called up another large Scotch and asked me to go on. His eyes, which had seen into the darker corners of the world, filled with moisture. His fingers took my wrist in a tight grip. 'You're not making this up, are you?' I assured him I wasn't.

Graham Greene could have described the effect my story had on Stanley. He had the countenance of a man who felt he had been betrayed by everything that, until that very moment, he had believed he understood.

Unfortunately, Mr Greene was not present in the Stab that day.

'All my life...' Stanley began. 'All my life...' He never finished the sentence. He waved me aside. A little hurt, I went back to the office. If I was writing this for the paper I'd have added that, as I left, I could've sworn I heard a sob.

You never read Bill Marshall's finest and funniest interview. I didn't either. In fact, nobody did because Bill never wrote it. And all because a Frenchman was touchy about the size of his todger. Honestly, some people...

However, I was there at the time, and I still have the tape of that totally unforgettable interview. For days afterwards, as word spread, a queue formed beside my desk: editors, department heads, and half of Fleet Street lined up to listen to it. Without doubt, it is a classic.

For those of you who weren't around, this was the time when the *Mirror* had rather more feature writers than there were words in the paper, including full-stops. This meant that the Holborn office was a sort of national museum of neglected talent, bruised egos and certifiable eccentrics, and Bill Marshall scored top marks on all three. There was nobody quite like Bill. Actually, that's not true: there were quite a few like Bill, but he was better at it than they were: he'd had more practice.

Bill was better at most things. He was a wonderful writer of the pyrotechnic school – all whiz-bangs and wallop – marvellous stuff. He was the man who described Sinatra as being a little old man wearing somebody else's hair. It was Richard Stott's stroke of genius, as assistant editor (features) to get Bill doing show-biz interviews. When it comes to talking to people with nothing to say (which is usually any actor without a script), who better than a writer who was at his very best when writing about nothing?

Give Bill too many facts – like three – and he became confused. His best pieces were constructed entirely between his ears, with as little outside interference as possible.

With celebrities, his technique was to ask questions that had never been asked before. By anyone. Of anyone. His questions were completely unpredictable and mostly irrelevant. It worked like a dream. He once wrote an excellent piece on Ronnie Corbett who he provoked by asking how often he cleaned his shoes. Corbett probably thought he was from Jimmy Choo's house magazine, but it did make a brilliant read. He lifted show-biz crap into the realms of the surreal.

In life as in his copy, he was over-the-top. So far over the top that he was across No Man's Land and drinking schnapps in the enemy trenches – a metaphor almost worthy of the man himself. From his wispy wizard's hair to the trainers he always wore, he was a one-off. He spoke in a unique amalgam of Scouse and Los Angeles with lots of hippy slang, through a sort of forced whisper. To Bill, everybody was Baby.

There are many Bill stories but a couple will help to capture the style of the man. When he was a district man in Liverpool, he was an assiduous supporter of the city's Press Club. He'd even lived there, for a while. Under the snooker table. He'd be surrounded by food and books brought in to him by friends. He was, it was matter-of-factly explained to visitors, practising to become a hermit.

On the day he got married (or rather on one of the days he got married), his guests waved him off in the morning. In the evening, alone, he strolled into the Press Club. 'Where's your wife?' a bemused customer asked. Bill looked at him with some disdain. 'Don't you know? They don't serve women in here.'

Move on a few years to that half-forgotten time just before the Maxwell Terror when a one-legged man called Clive from the Abbey National Building Society was put in charge of the Mirror Group with a view to importing some sanity into the building. He didn't do too well and, to be frank, I doubt whether he would have done any better if he had ten legs. He never really got the hang of the place.

This may have been because of an experience soon after he arrived. Wandering down a corridor, he heard sounds of revelry by day. He opened a door to reveal a scene of exuberant joy – Bill entertaining friends and secretaries with an open case of champagne. Bill recognised Clive immediately, sprang to his feet, flung his free arm around him and burst into Mersey-California: 'Come on in, Clive, baby – welcome to the *Mirror*! Now grab a glass!'

In all his years at the Abbey, Thornton could never have encountered such a scene. He pointed at the champagne. 'Where did that come from?'

Bill exploded into laughter. 'That's why you're gonna love it here, baby. You just pick up the phone and it keeps coming!' All the Bill stories – true or not – were like that.

For a while, Bill and I used to share interviews. If he had a good one set up for the *Mirror* he would include me, and I did the same with interviews I did for magazines. I'd set one up with Roger Vadim and Bill said he was keen to come along.

Now Vadim was the French film producer and director who'd created *And God Created Woman*. He'd had almost as many women as John Penrose, but of a slightly superior quality. He had been close to Brigitte Bardot and Jane Fonda. Close, that is, in the sense of being on the inside. While he was of little interest in himself, if he would say anything about these two famous ex-wives then we had a piece.

So there we are, Willie and myself, sharing a taxi on our way to the St James' Club. Bill is getting excited, indicated by a sort of demonic cackle.

147

'I got some great stuff to throw at this guy,' he says, chuckling away. 'I'm gonna wrong-foot him, see what comes out.'

A little nervous, I ask what he has in mind. Bill thinks it would spoil the moment if he tells me. 'Just watch the fun,' he says. I am not reassured.

At the club, we are greeted by a young lady who is doing some PR between Benenden sixth-form and her first city banker husband. A stint, I imagine, of about three weeks. In a high, fluting voice that would be well-suited to singing *O For the Wings of a Dove* she lists all the things we cannot talk about. Covering, as it does, his past life, his future life and any opinions he might hold, it leaves only the book whose publisher she represents.

Naturally, we promise to observe these minor restrictions. And in comes the man, early sixties, a little bit chubby around the middle, exquisitely dressed in what appears to be exclusively cashmere. He has the face of a sensitive, intelligent and strikingly handsome artist, flanked by silver wings of hair. Beside him, Roman emperors would have looked a bit common.

Careful handling would seem to be the approach. The PR fluting lady introduces us. We sit on the two sofas on either side of a glass-topped coffee table. He murmurs greetings and shakes hands. Bill wants to get this on a more matey basis. 'Hiya, Rodge!' he says.

Rodge winces. This is not a good start.

I lob in all the harmless stuff about what time did he get in to London and how does he like his hotel when Bill interrupts. 'Hey Rodge, you've known some great chicks, y'know, Bardot and Fonda...?'

This is not an unexpected line, so Monsieur Vadim gives a gentle nod and says yes, it 'as indeed been his good fortune to know some exceptional women.

The next question causes some mystification. 'Is it, y'know, 'cos you're kinda blessed...?'

Blessed? The interviewee does not follow. Nor does the PR Flute. Nor do I, although I do experience a slight sense of foreboding.

'Per'aps you would explain zis question?' says M'sieur Vadim.

Bill leans forward, eyes sparkling with excitement. He reaches his hand out over the coffee table and points – unbelievably, so it seems – at the man's crotch.

'Blessed – y'know, Rodge-baby... kinda lucky down there.'

We all follow the direction of his pointing finger. We know what he means. There is no doubt where Down There is. 'With these chicks, you gotta be well-hung, right?'

Bill sits back on the sofa and smiles with satisfaction. He's pretty pleased with the effect, but not for long. Slowly, the well-hung (or not) Roger Vadim rises to his feet. He keeps his eyes fixed on Bill as though he expects him to make a murderous leap at his throat. 'Zis man,' he says to me, eyes still on Bill, 'Zis man is asking me about ze size of my preek.'

This is followed by the sort of silence that I'm told follows an atomic bomb. Then all the noise erupts at once. PR Flute springs forward, her pearls fairly clicking with outrage. She has never heard such an offensive question in her life; it's a disgrace, she would never have agreed... Luckily at this point her voice reaches such a pitch that it is audible only to dogs.

Had there been a fan in the room, it would have been coated in waste materials. Muttering to himself, Roger Vadim begins to make for the door. PR Flute is still shrieking and pointing at Bill. I rush round the sofa, grab the Frenchman by his sleeve and begin gabbling that it's all a misunderstanding and that Bill doesn't mean what they think he means, although my French is not sufficiently inventive to offer another translation of well-hung.

PR Flute comes down to about budgie level, Monsieur Vadim is persuaded to return to his seat. There's no way of retrieving it, of course. Almost any question now sounds like pure porn. He offers a few trite quotes while Bill sits in silence staring at the carpet, like a bloodhound whose bone has been stolen. After a few more minutes, we break up.

Bill doesn't speak again until we're in the taxi on the way back. 'You loused that up for me, Col,' he grunts. Loused it up? I attempt to explain my efforts to save the situation but he's not listening. 'I didn't get a chance to get my killer question in, baby.'

His killer question? There was another one we hadn't heard?

'Yeah,' Bill leans forward, invigorated once again. 'Next, I was gonna say to him, Look Rodge, you're 63 – can you still raise a gallop?'

As I say, Bill never did write the story. Nor did I. By the time you took the shrieking out of it, there wasn't much left to write. And, without discussing it at all, we never did any more joint interviews.

Days later they were still coming up to me asking me to play the tape. I'm often tempted to replay it after reading some lack-lustre 'celeb' interview by one of today's colourless and formulaic amateurs. Maybe I'll have it made into a CD and flog it to a Media School.

Looking back on it, as I frequently do, there's one thought that always springs to mind. Ronnie Corbett got off damned light.

*

149

All these years later, it still makes me laugh now when I think about it. There's a *Daily Record* minor executive peacefully sleeping at home. Two in the morning. Telephone rings. Dozily he picks it up. A voice which at that time had instant recognition across several continents bellows in his ear.

'Why are you giving away my fucking money, mister?'

It's not difficult to imagine the rest. Did he fall out of bed? Probably. Did he experience several near-fatal heart attacks? Almost certainly. The addition of 'mister' at the end of such a sentence was always particularly ominous. Dithering and quaking simultaneously, he comes up with a rhetorical question. 'Is that… er, is that Mr Maxwell?'

At this stage in his career, Cap'n Bob doesn't think it necessary to produce proof of identity. This time his voice rises to a roar. 'WHY ARE YOU GIVING MY FUCKING MONEY AWAY?' No 'mister', this time: doubly dangerous.

What had happened was that while the world and Scots execs were restoring themselves with dreamless sleep, Robert Maxwell, finding a moment to spare in the middle of the night, was flicking through some old expense sheets. Much the same as you would yourself, I suppose. One of them, from a Glasgow photographer (Ian Torrance, I think), includes £5 for coming seventh or thereabouts in a photographic competition. He'd claimed the same on his exes because there was a tradition then – not any more, I'd bet – that the company would match any prize money. This he attempts to explain.

Unfortunately, Mr Maxwell is not a keen adherent of Scottish traditions. It is, he says, his fiver (can we take the f-word as read, now?). He wants it back. By return. Or exec and photographer will both be fired. End of conversation.

When we all first stepped into the wonderful world of free money – or expenses, as it was called – we didn't know it was going to end with nocturnal telephone calls that would imperil both job and sanity. Even so, we sort of knew the gravy train would hit the buffers one day.

You'll have to excuse me for a moment while I explain something to that sub on the *Indie* who, at any mention of old-style Fleet Street, e-mails me about dishonesty and false pretences. Now my first thought is always to wonder how anyone without at least a brushing acquaintance with dishonesty and false pretences could hope to make a living in newspapers. Are all the monasteries full? My next thought is that somebody should explain to these young puritans that the expenses system involved neither.

So here goes. Sit down, sonny, hang your halo on that hook, and I'll explain it very slowly. This was how the management chose to enhance our salaries during what was called a Pay Freeze. No-one was deceived. There was no fraud, as such. Every journalist knew roughly what he was allowed to charge. It suited the management because they could change our income by the week, if they so wished. We were probably foolish in going along with it, because this part of our income didn't figure in holiday pay or pensions: great for them, not so great for us. But journalists, simple folk at heart, liked the idea of collecting cash from a sliding window on the tenth floor and going to the pub. It was fun, it seemed slightly dodgy, and it could be creatively challenging – all things that our raffish lot loved.

Now we've cleared that up, can we carry on?

We've all got our favourite exes story, but let me go first, okay? My first expenses scam was one I inherited from Bernard Ingham. As a district man for the *Yorkshire Post* in Halifax, he had – so it was said – introduced 'the Calder Valley calls', a 40-mile trip each day that added up to a large chunk of mileage by the end of the week. The best thing about the Calder Valley calls was that you did them on the telephone, which made it even more profitable. When I took the job, a few years after Bernard, I was looking forward to this weekly bonus. It never came. The news editor cancelled the calls in the first week. By then Bernard was probably making daily calls to Washington and Moscow – bet you anything he rarely went.

If you'd spent the week in the office, it required some ingenuity to make it look convincing. Once I remember finding a really good story on somebody else's expense sheet. It was Peter Stubbs, the Manchester photographer, who'd left them in the typewriter and it was a headline he'd lifted from the *Accrington Observer* about a woman who confiscated some kids' football after it landed in her garden. He deleted it from his exes and substituted another one I'd found for him – about a beauty contest in Rhyl, I remember – and the football story developed from an exes item into a Page Three lead.

There was a tradition that quickly established its own classics. Everybody claims at some time or other to have paid for a mooring for a boat or for being towed out of a bog ('money for old rope: £5'), some of which may even be true, and all the show-biz writers in London were always delighted to see their Scottish counterpart, Billy Sloane...

'Entertaining Mr Sloane – £30'.

Small triumphs like that were very satisfying.

And there was the story of the photographer (said to have been Tommy Lyons) who, just before Christmas, charged: 'One year's reversing mileage – 187 miles.' Asked to explain it, he said: 'You know when you're looking for a house and you drive a bit past... then you have to back

151

up to it. Or when you drive into a cul-de-sac and have to reverse out. It doesn't show on the milometer, but I did 187 miles like that, this year.'

We all have our personal favourites. Mine was typing out that simple, unadorned sentence: 'Medical treatment following fall from coconut tree: £50, see bill attached.'

Certain skills were required. I think it was Paul Hughes who showed me how a line of firmly-struck full-stops on a typewriter (yes: we still used typewriters) enabled you to tear off a potentially embarrassing letterhead so that it looked as though it had been ripped off a waiter's pad. Thus a bill for a shirt from the Savoy Taylors Guild could in seconds become a receipt for entertaining unidentified 'Scotland Yard contacts'.

If you were lucky enough to have bills from some distant country, preferably in early Sanskrit, you didn't even need to do that. After six weeks in Iceland (chess and fishing wars), the first thing I did was to ring the accounts department and ask whether any of their staff spoke Old Norse. None did. Whoopee.

Sadly, I never truly mastered the language of accounts departments that was the key to it all. After a serious clamp-down on advance expenses, which threatened massive unemployment in the restaurant trade around Holborn Circus, it was said that Keith Waterhouse had cracked the code. He simply wrote 'Cash Adjustment: £50' and the cashiers, who recognised their own tongue, were more than happy to hand over the money.

There was a similar device used by freelances when – as happened very occasionally – they were paid twice for the same piece. Feebly, I used to hang on to it in the hope that nobody would notice. They always did, and I always had to return it. But those who were smarter than me would send a note saying: 'I regret we have no machinery for effecting this repayment', and it was never queried after that.

One of the saddest sights I ever saw was when I shared a room with Jim Lewthwaite on the *Sun*. He was sitting typing out some exes, cursing foully with every key-stroke. It was enough to break any hack's heart. Ken Donlan had presented Jim, John Hiscock and Dougie Thompson with air travel cards so they could whiz off on major international stories. After a few drinks in the top bar of the Tip, John and Doug decided to try them out. They went to Heathrow, took a flight to Los Angeles, and never came back. While they sat in the Californian sun, Jim was left to complete all their back expenses in Bouverie Street. By the way he spoke, you'd never have known they were all good friends.

Years later, after a month at the Hacks' Holiday Home, otherwise known as the *National Enquirer* in Florida, I sat down to do my four weeks' expenses. 'Those are no good,' one of their staffmen said, pointing to my pile of bills, 'they're all blank.'

From my pocket I produced a set of multi-coloured pens and pencils. I thought of all those great creative artists who'd gone before me... Penrose, Jackson, Hagerty, Williams, men whose creative genius did for the expense sheet what Sam Beckett did for literature. How fortunate for me that I should be the lucky one chosen to take this ancient wisdom out to our innocent colonial cousins. 'Let me introduce you to an old Fleet Street tradition...'

Now, like the lamplighter and the candle-maker, the Old Exes Forger of yore is no more. One day, I'd like to think he will appear in those illustrations of the Street Cries of Old London Town. A hack crouched over his typewriter calling out: 'Any blank bills? Any blank bills?'

*

Susan should never have been working in Fleet Street. Susan should have been at home in Braintree, making chutney, walking Fritz the dachshund, taking her turn on the church flower rota, and popping in to the library to get her weekly Mills and Boon.

Instead, here she was sitting straight-backed on her stool in the... was it the Stab, or the Bell, or Peter Evans? I forget now. Anyway, there she was, at the age of 45 a full-time secretary and part-time mistress who got her weekly romance from a senior editorial person on the... was it the *Express*? Or the *Mail*? Or the *Mirror*? My damned memory...

When she'd been married, she'd always thought Axminster was an easy lay. Then the husband had cleared off with The Other Woman. In her middle years she'd had to resume her long-abandoned career as a secretary and washed up in Fleet Street. There, to her surprise, she became another Other Woman and as easy a lay as Axminster, although not, sadly for her, foam-backed.

Having been a model of suburban sanity, she had some problem adapting to her newer and more racy persona. But she did possess the one quality that we hacks admired above all in a mistress: she was gloriously indiscreet. Jill Evans and Paula James used to trek along Fleet Street to seek her out for the latest bulletin on her personal life.

The Kray Sisters got quickly to the point. Was the sex good? Oh yes, she nodded, as though they'd asked her if she was enjoying the latest Dick Francis. Quite enjoyable, she thought. Did they go in for oral sex, the Sisters wanted to know. Ye-e-e-s. This time the answer sounded a little less certain. They pounced. Didn't she enjoy oral sex? 'Well, it's not bad,' she said, 'but it does make your arm ache.'

On one occasion she was back at her lover's flat when Mrs Lover came in. 'What on earth are you doing here?' the wife wanted to know. Now Susan could truthfully have said she had no idea. Equally truthfully, she could have said that she should be at home baking scones or catching up on the ironing but, sensing this was not what her new role required, she just grabbed her knickers (rather large, apparently) and ran for it.

No-one quite knew how she came to be there, including Susan herself. But, for all that, she was a mature and sensible woman; she had been swept away in the non-stop Fleet Street party that ran from the Embankment up to Gray's Inn Road.

If Susan wasn't really cut out for the arm-aching life, others were. They approached the pubs where journalists slouched against bars much as kids approach Woolies' pick'n'mix counter. To these women the tough guys of The Street, who thought they'd been around and seen a thing or two, were about as menacing as a handful of jelly babies or a quarter of allsorts. Not only did they pick and mix, but they swapped notes later, and many were the men who couldn't understand why all the women in the office giggled as they walked past. You just had to hope they weren't going to hold up a little finger, bent over.

Lesley Hall was refreshingly open about it. I loved Lesley – we all did – sadly, in my case, only in the way of friendship. She was never terribly impressed with the quality of lover to be found on newspapers, and when in need of cheer she would pop down to El Vino and grab a takeaway barrister. At one time, John Mortimer, the author and playwright, asked her if she was trying to recruit a cricket team. 'Rugby,' she replied, since 15 seemed a rounder number.

We can tell these stories because Lesley told them all herself, usually the morning after, with full match reports on them all and scores out of ten. She set pretty demanding standards. The only guy she ever gave the full ten was a departmental head called... Jim? John? Jack? Tony? Oh damn, name's gone. Anyway, I'm sure he'll know; he went off and married somebody in show-biz.

Okay, I must admit she did slow down a bit as the years passed and her health became a little wobbly. Even so, to celebrate her 50th birthday, she returned to her old haunt of El Vino, found herself a handsome young barrister who was indeed a burly Rugby player. He was a boisterous boy apparently. In her report the next day, she did confess that at one point she'd had to call out: 'Hey, be careful, I've got brittle bones.'

Outrageous is the only word for the lot of them. Lesley's friend – Susan, I think she was called, since that's the name we're settling for – was having a tumultuous affair with a chap who had thoughtlessly been to the altar with someone else. They do that, don't they? Not that it bothered Susan, who was a feature writer on the *Mail*. Or maybe it wasn't the *Mail*, I forget. It'll come back. She was due to fly away for a week's illicit holiday in the sun with the Errant Husband when he rang to cancel at the last moment. His wife had become suspicious. She was bringing him to the airport; if she saw Susan there, she'd know. Poor chap was in a breathless panic. When Susan told him not to worry, she'd get there somehow, his pulse rate went off the clock.   .

At Heathrow the next morning, he was shaking with nerves as he cast about for any sign of Susan. He didn't even glance at the nun who swept past. Neither did his wife, which was just as well. On the plane, with a sigh of relief, he sank into his seat next to the nun. When she squeezed his upper thigh (very upper thigh, actually) with a surprisingly well-practised grip, he almost knocked himself out on the overhead locker.

The only problem they had was after Susan had been to the lavatory to change into her normal clothes. The pilot announced that the crew were most concerned that a nun who had certainly boarded the aircraft seemed to have vanished. Susan had to confess to the crew. They gave her a round of thoroughly well-deserved applause.

That was the trouble with borrowing husbands: a worried and fearful chap is not always a sure guarantee of sexual ecstasy, and indeed can sometimes lead to complications you don't necessarily want when you're in your baby-dolls. Another friend of Lesley's (shall we call her Susan?) from one of the posh Sundays rang her one night to say that she had a tricky disposal problem. She had borrowed a husband – they talked about them rather as others talked of library books – and the history of long lunches, cigarettes, alcohol, deputy editor's stress, and finally pelvic gymnastics had proved too much.

He'd dropped dead. In her bed.

This is when you find out who your friends are. Lesley shot round there. The two of them dragged the re-trousered corpse into a car, and took him home to Sevenoaks. There, they propped him in a seated position against the door, and gave the bell a quick jab as they left. As Lesley said, at least they had returned him to his legal owner, complete in all respects, if a little colder. I think one of her other friends engineered the story into a novel.

You must all remember… what was her name now? Felicity? Phyllis? Oh, it'll come back. She was a freelance who tried out every form of cosmetic and sexual enhancement and wrote about it. Breast implants, colonic irrigation, bum lifts – she'd done everything, including having rings dangling where no ring had ever dangled before. Get one of those caught up in your specs and you'd need the fire brigade to set you free. On the train from Charing Cross, she met a sub – was he a friend of John Garton's? – who was on his way home to Orpington, where his wife was holding a party for the neighbours. I should say that at this time Garton's friend did not know the lady freelance had a sex life which these days would be called inclusive. Inclusive, all-embracing and highly experimental.

He took her home. At midnight, the wives were sitting in the kitchen nursing cups of tea and trying to ignore the shrieks of ecstasy, mostly male, coming from upstairs. Some of the wives were weeping. In the next few months there were several divorces in Orpington, including Garton's friend. What really annoyed him was he was the only man who didn't.

Fleet Street ladies and neighbours were never an easy mix. Sid Williams, the *Mirror* feature writer known as Sinister Sid, once invited Jill Evans to his Ealing home for a Saturday night dinner party. It was one of those affairs where the place mats featured hunting scenes cheerfully captioned 'Tally-Ho!' Around the table were members of the Rotary Club, the odd estate agent, the deputy headmaster of a small primary, a Nat West manager, and Jaeger wives coiffed within an inch of their lives. For three hours she listened as they talked about school reports, the new Ford Fiesta, the price of holidays in the Algarve, and the use of rosemary when roasting lamb. She nodded and said 'Oh really?' all night. She was quiet, polite, attentive, and bored almost to the point of screaming.

The next day she thanked Sid. He said, frankly, he was very disappointed by the way she'd behaved.

'But I behaved impeccably,' she protested.

'I know,' he said. 'That's why. I only invited you because I hoped you'd say Fuck.'

*

2

It was obvious really. If you were looking for a ghost, where better to start than the less frequented corridors of the Fleet Street offices. Open a door down there in the seventies and you'd find hacks from history: everybody thought they were by now tucked away beneath an appropriate gravestone but no, here they were, in a sort of living museum for writers.

In the old Mirror building at Holborn, writers who'd become unwanted, unused, unfashionable or simply unconscious were shunted upwards.

Anything above the third floor was a graveyard for the undead. I was one of them and I tell you, some days it was difficult to raise a mist on a mirror no matter how hard you breathed. For some of us, only a substantial cash advance from upstairs could convince us that we were still alive and employed.

Employed, that is, in the looser sense of the word. I was brought down from Manchester, given a fattish salary, handsome expenses, a company car, a desk with typewriter and a telephone. But no work.

Some work, I heard it said, was done on the third floor, but any higher than that, forget it. There were people up there who hadn't written a piece since the *News Chron* closed down. No phones rang. Spiders established homes and families in typewriters. When a lost messenger once opened the door on the fourth floor features room and inquired: 'Back numbers?', 34 voices said: 'Yes.' No execs set foot up there, for fear of weeping writers snivelling at their feet, pleading to write – 'just a few words, guv, a paragraph would do me...'

It was terrible to see what befell them. Some took to drink. Some took to women. Some – may God help them – even stayed home and painted the spare room. It's frightening what despair can do.

No-one was to blame. The truth was there were well over 40 feature writers – I counted them one day: that was another 15 minutes gone – and if you shared the features space between them, that would be about three lines each. A week.

So I felt well-qualified when David Niven asked me to help him out with a bit of writing. It happened like this. I'd done a piece on the shooting of the Pirelli Calendar. He'd been asked to write an introduction to a book of Pirelli calendars and he'd seen my piece in the cuttings. As he explained to me over lunch in La Capanina in Soho, he was happy telling stories and polishing anecdotes, but he couldn't do what all hacks do – what we used to call a think piece.

He hosed me down with charm and when I was suitably sedated, sent me to see George Greenfield, who was the agent for Niven and almost everybody who mattered. He offered me £200 for around 2,500 words. I ripped it from his wallet before he could say 'Only kidding.'

Big mistake. A couple of years later, I met George again. He told me I should have asked for a percentage, however small. The book was in the best-sellers' list for months. 'But we all know that you journalists will always take cash in hand,' he said. He was right. Still, it was a nice lunch.

Now if you ghost a piece, the deal is that you don't talk about it. Since it was a long time ago, and since neither of these gentlemen is around any more, I think I can say that my denials are getting feebler.

Whereas, if you were to ask me if I had a hand in writing Paul Gallico's *Beyond the Poseidon* – a sequel to the book and film *The Poseidon Adventure* – I shall profess astonished indignation, or something like it.

That happened when the life of a fourth-floor ghost was beginning to pall. Without the stamina for drink and adultery, and no gift at all for DIY, I didn't know what to do with myself.

I complained to Mike Molloy that when I came to the Occupation box on official forms, I couldn't remember what to write. He pointed out that of all the massed battalions of feature writers only one had more pieces in the paper than I did. John Pilger had six pieces in. I had five.

That was about 10 days' work.

The truth was that the *Mirror* didn't want anything I wrote. So I left. In doing so, I made about a thousand enemies because most Mirrormen regarded walking out as an act of supreme folly and ingratitude. They were probably right.

Around this time, Paul Gallico had hit a problem. He'd been contracted to deliver his *Poseidon* sequel in ten weeks' time. But it was incomplete. And he was unlikely to finish it. He'd died. Would I like to help ensure that the required 90,000 words were delivered on time?

This would mean going to live in a flat behind the Gallico's five-storey family house overlooking the bay in Antibes. Well, it certainly wasn't my idea of fun, but I'd nothing else to do, I was unemployed, and winter was on its way. I went.

Few people remember Gallico now, but for about 40 years he'd been one of the big international authors. An American who lived in Devon, he'd made his name with *The Snow Goose*, a wonderfully semi-poetic book based around the Dunkirk retreat. At that time people believed he was the man to write the Great American Novel. It never happened, although for year after year he produced books that were mostly best-sellers. Books about lovable cats, books about a wise old Cockney charwoman called Mrs Harris (or, forgive me, Mrs 'Arris), and huge-eyed little Spanish boys with their pet donkeys. Many of them were made into films. He was the super-pro. Whatever the market wanted, he could do it. So when disaster movies came in, Gallico was there with *Poseidon*, and this was the sequel. He was well over 80 when he died.

Shall we have a few journo-links here? Gallico was a famous sports writer before moving into books. He'd once sparred with – and been knocked out by – Jack Dempsey, the world heavyweight champion, to get a story. Ian Woolridge interviewed him for his *Mail* column. The intro, I think, was Gallico sitting down with Ian, placing a bottle on the table and saying: 'Mr Paul Gallico and Mr Bush Mills are at your service.' His step-daughter Ludmilla – he named a novel after her – was an actress who at one time stepped out with Jonathon Kenworthy, a celebrated English sculptor who was also brother to Chris Kenworthy, one of the better television writers (*TV Times, Sun*, freelance).

He may have failed to write the Great American Novel, but he had sort of scraped by. Apart from the huge house on the headland in Antibes, and the flat behind, he and his wife Virginia had a flat in Monaco (for visiting their close friends, the Rainiers), a flat in New York, a mews house in Chelsea, a house and a few acres including the source of the Liffey in Ireland, and a country house in Sussex. Any way you look at it, that's a lot of council tax.

Time was a problem. The sequel was due in ten weeks to Hollywood producer Irwin Allen.

As I was climbing the stairs to the flat at the back of the house in Antibes, the telephone was ringing. The voice was American and female. She was the wife of Robert Littel, a former *Time* magazine journalist who was making a big reputation as a writer of spy novels. She'd heard I'd just got in and since tonight was Hallowe'en would I like to go to a fancy-dress party? Well, yes, I bumbled, but what as?

'How about Gallico's ghost?' she said.

Except of course I wasn't his ghost. Absolutely not. I must make that clear. I was employed to 'edit and collate' the book. For ten weeks, I sat there every day, editing and collating like mad, although it did sometimes seem like bashing keys on a typewriter.

Every evening, I took my edited and collated words over to his widow, Virginia. And every day I had lunch with her. Once we were joined by her friend from Monaco. As I crossed to the main house, I saw a pair of pink knickers outside the front door. It was the friend's daughter, Princess Stephanie, doing handstands. I may be the only man alive who's seen Stephanie's knickers... or maybe not.

When I referred to her friend as Gracie-baby, Virginia was most upset. 'When she's here,' she scolded me, 'you must call her Your Serene Highness.' I thought this was a bit over-the-top for a piece of Hollywood totty, although, with her title, she had certainly become terribly grand. Compared to her, the Windsor family was a touch common.

By all accounts, Gallico was a lovely chap. Everybody said so, including Barbara Johnson, the woman who had been his secretary for years. A New Yorker, she'd stayed on in Antibes after his death. Because of arthritis in his hands, he used to dictate his books to her. He tried to adapt his writing to whatever was the fashion of the time, and when books began to be increasingly sexy – Harold Robbins was a neighbour – he became

159

concerned for Barbara. If he wrote some hot sex, would she be embarrassed?

Barbara, who was in her thirties and I think an unlikely candidate for a nunnery, said she thought she'd be okay. Privately she wondered whether Gallico's memory could deliver on this particular subject.

He dictated the scene where the man and woman fell (I think) into a haystack. Then they began to kiss. Then embrace. 'Now we're coming to sex, Barbara,' he warned her. 'Are you okay with this?' She said she was fine. He took a deep breath and declared: 'She adjusted her clothing to receive him.' That was it. Amazingly, Barbara survived the shock.

With 90,000 words to be edited, not to mention collated, I didn't have much time for a social life and, in any case, however ingeniously I moved around my seven words of French, remembered from school, it didn't allow for a lot of deep conversation. When the milk kept going off in my fridge I knew I had to get some Longlife milk. But what was it in French? Walking up to Maison Robert supermarket, I tried to work it out. Firstly, I had to say something pleasant to the girl on the till, because I was forever asking her advice. Then I had to find a way of asking for Longlife. In the end, I managed it.

'You are the girl with the kind face who will help me find the milk which endures for three days,' I said. To be honest, I don't think the Yorkshire accent helped the French.

But the girl smiled. *'Ah, oui,'* she said. *'Vous voudrez le Longlife.'*

The 90,000 words – every one of them written by Paul Gallico, and scrupulously edited and collated by me – were delivered on time. I have copies of it here on my bookshelf, in German, French, Japanese even. And there on Page 79 is the strangest coincidence. One of the characters is remembering people from his American childhood – Mr Delano and old Marcus Dowdney. And who were the *Mirror* men in America at that time? Tony Delano and Mark Dowdney. Now isn't that amazing?

Obviously Paul Gallico must have met the boys from the New York office.

*

Around the mid-seventies in Fleet Street – and here I mean the state-of-mind as well as the geographical location – there was one question that was on everybody's lips. 'So what are you then?'

After the briefest of initial courtesies, this was the first question to put to a stranger. When I moved down to London, it happened to me, and I was lost for an answer. I tried several.

'Yorkshire' I tried, to smirks of pity. 'A reporter' raised only mutters of 'That's your opinion.' And when I tried a fuller response – 'A passable off-spin bowler and useful middle-order batsman' – it was clear to everyone, even me, that whatever this language was, I didn't speak it.

The correct answer was Capricorn, or Libra, or Pisces, or any of those other star signs. I don't know what it was like among normal people because at that time I didn't know any normal people but among the fringe fashion of media folk, astrology took up about 90 per cent of their conversation.

Journalists who were fully qualified cynics and sceptics, people who had been known to question the existence of Rupert Murdoch, let alone God, subscribed unwaveringly to this weird new religion. Anyone with an eye for irony would appreciate a situation where hacks who actually tried quite hard – well, hardish – to resist the temptation to jazz up the quotes and spruce up the facts actually chose to believe the only section of the paper that was total prefabricated bunkum.

I say everyone, but that isn't quite true. All the women journalists believed it, of course, but their grip on reality was always a bit shaky. Designers, sipping their *cab sauvignon*, certainly did. Gays kept their astrology charts alongside the picture of Judy Garland in their bags. Anybody connected with any form of show-business, from pop to Corrie, could tell you the star signs of every member of the Grateful Dead or Albert Tatlock (who soon afterwards joined the Dead: whether he was grateful or not, I couldn't say). And for anybody else who wished to be seen as in touch with the mood of the moment, it was pretty much imperative.

That left only about half-a-dozen unreconstituted old newsmen, many of them openly heterosexual (or at least up to the fourth pint), forming a sullen knot in the corner of the Stab to talk about the eternal verities: football and women with big tits. They spoke in the raw accents of Tyneside and Belfast and Glasgow long before it had become fashionable: these days they'd be television presenters.

At six o'clock, when the hacks had sufficiently recovered from lunch, they flowed from their offices and into the bars, where they would breathlessly compare their astrological characters. 'Oh, you're a typical Libra, you're a real tart...' Or 'Normally I don't get on with Aquarians but somehow you're different.'

It was a pain in the Aries, I can tell you.

And if Patric Walker, the *Mirror* astrologist, should choose to come and move among us, as he sometimes did, then it was like a visit from the gods. He had only to walk into a room packed with Ebbetts and Hopkirks and Fawkes to have them begging for his advice. 'I've been so depressed, darling, is it because Juno's in the ascendant?'

Women loved him. He loved them (although, you understand, not in that way), and would fearlessly advise them on the type of eye-liner he personally favoured. He was a clever chap. One night in Angelo's – we had to go fairly early while we could still pronounce Albemarle Street – someone cunningly placed me, a known unbeliever, across the table from Patric so I would get the full blast of his considerable charm.

He immediately established common ground. He was from Yorkshire too. Whitby. At the age of 16, he'd declared to his GP that he was homosexual. Still making notes from the last patient, and without even looking up, the doctor replied: 'You can't be – it's against the law.' It was Yorkshire for heaven's sake – what other sort of response did he expect? But, no matter, it was enough to persuade Patric to move to London. In the course of the journey, the K fell off the end of his name, thus preparing him for the world of glamour. Indeed, he shared an apartment with an ancient but distinguished theatrical couple, Jack Hulbert and Cicely Courtneidge in Mayfair.

At one time he was stepping out with a young American actor. 'Richard Chamberlain – and whatever became of him, darlings?' Patric would demand. Everyone knew that Chamberlain later became television's Dr Kildare. One evening he came to the Stab with a young Russian ballet dancer he had chanced upon. Against all the odds, the man was straight. He pushed him through the door straight into the middle of Paula James, Jill Evans and Lesley Ebbets. 'One for you girls,' he said, trying gamely to mask his disappointment.

This evening in Angelo's could end only one way. 'So,' he asked, as he faced me across the table, 'what are you?'

With some diplomacy, I told him that much as I admired the way he had made a highly successful career out of astrology, and while I did not for one moment question his qualifications or his sincerity, and although I could see that half of London society hung on his every horoscopic word, without wishing to cause any offence, and with all respect, I would rather not answer his question because I knew it was, without exception, a load of old tosh.

He smiled. Patted my hand. Sipped his wine. And said: 'Oh I know, I know. You see, you're just like me. We Scorpios are such dreadful sceptics, aren't we?'

For a moment there, I felt like a Stradivarius – one that had just been played by a maestro. My dropped jaw may have given me away. Afterwards, talking to the woman writer who'd invited me, I was obliged to concede that since my birthday did fall mid-November, he was certainly a very good guesser. 'Guess?' she said. 'He rang me last night to ask when your birthday was. He always does.'

He knew everybody, was wonderfully amusing company, and a pretty nifty businessman. He became astrologer to the world, or something very similar, made lots of dosh from his astrological tosh, and went to live on Mykonos. He did not go there, so far as I know, to support the local rugby team.

There were quite a number of flamboyant gays in newspapers. Jack Tinker, the *Daily Mail* theatre critic, could assemble an audience of fans within seconds. Gays brought wit and glitter to Fleet Street bars that were not always overstocked with either.

Two of the nicest blokes in Fleet Street were gays who insisted on posing as straight. If they happened to meet in the same bar, they'd stand at opposite ends. They lived near each other, but no matter how scarce taxis were, they never shared. We never knew why they were so nervous about it. Surely they can't have worried what we thought. The general level of morality was about that of Gomorrah on pay-day, and most hacks couldn't care if you had sexual intercourse with field voles. Several probably did.

Every day was party day, and there were plenty of heterosexuals who still practised their strange antique skills to join in.

We moved around in tribes. In the early evening, the *Mirror* decanted into the Stab, the *Express* into the Bell, the *Telegraph* into the King and Keys, the *Sun* into the Tipperary, and the *Mail* into the Witness Box and the Harrow. Round about 7 30pm, raiding parties would be formed which would then conduct forays into enemy territory. There were few more unnerving sights than a team of *Sun* commandos, led by fearless Fergus Cashin, bursting into the *Mail* pub, or Jim Allen spearheading a *Telegraph* attack on the Bell.

When the *Mirror*'s John Penrose made a daring one-man incursion into the King and Keys, he toppled while entangled in the footrest and broke his leg. Did he fall or was he pushed? Only Tony Conyers would know.

It was a moveable feast. By the time you got to clubs like Vagabonds or Scribes, the swirling eddies of hacks had mingled and merged, invariably ending with one of life's two most significant collisions: a fight or sex, and sometimes it wasn't easy to tell the difference. Even then, gender equality was firmly established. For every Scottish sports writer looking for a fight, there was also a lady hack scouring the bars for a take-away night-mate. Who was that statuesque blonde who used to reward her pick-ups with a steak supper? And some didn't even insist on a bed. There was a tall, moonie-eyed young hackette in the Stab who only required an escort as far as the office garage and a back-seat. At least you could be back in the bar before your beer had gone flat.

Party time meant party tricks. Don Walker, *Mirror* feature writer, could recite a cheeky-chappie rhyme called *It's a Funny Old World That We live In – But the World's Not Entirely to Blame* that he'd stolen from Roy Harris, and John Garton, features sub, could dampen his own eyes, if nobody else's, with: *I Live in Trafalgar Square – Four Lions to Guard Me.* The most popular performance was Jill Evans who would stand up, fingers locked, swaying like a little girl at the school concert party, and sing in a terrible cracked soprano voice...

> Vio-late me in the vio-let time
>
> In the vilest possible way.
>
> Rape me and ravish me, cruelly savage me,
>
> I will never say Nay.
>
> Though I may scream for mercy, ignore every breath.
>
> All I require is a fate worse than death.
>
> So violate me in the violet time
>
> In the vilest way that you know.

Where she got the song, we did not know. Some said it was an old Beatrice Lilly number. It certainly wasn't from Robert Louis Stevenson's *Child's Garden of Verses.*

All in all, it was a seductive way of life in every sense of the word. Days slipped by. Then weeks, months, years, and with them dozens of careers, not to mention livers and marriages.

Just a little more work, say one job a month, and I might have stayed. But I had neither the stamina nor the conscience for a full-time career in hedonism. I suppose my grousing and grumbling must have reached such a pitch that it was detected on the higher floors of Holborn, and Sydney Jacobson, a director who later became lordly, called me in. A good-hearted man, he was genuinely concerned. He'd heard I was unhappy. He'd spoken to Bob Edwards on the *Sunday Mirror.* Would I be happy on a smaller team perhaps?

Well, I would, except for one thing. The *Sunday Mirror* already had a Colin. And Colin Wills was one of those journalists who could do anything from hard news to funny features and do them brilliantly. So no thanks.

In the downstairs restaurant of the Peter Evans bar, over an Arnold Bennett Omelette (or was it an H. G. Wells hot-dog?), a slim, dark-eyed lovely with long hair propositioned me.

Anthea Disney, features editor of the *Daily Mail*, offered me a job there. I was sorely tempted because the *Mail*, then as now, was a writers' paper.

But, as she explained it, it wouldn't be so very different. On the *Mirror*, you wrote very little, and some of it was used. On the *Mail*, you wrote lots and lots, and very little of it was used.

It didn't seem much of an improvement.

I could always leave. Walk out on the *Mirror*? The idea was beyond imagination. Lots of money, no work, fun galore, why would anybody clamour to escape from paradise? At that time I knew only one man who had voluntarily done so. Don Coolican had walked out of paradise, but then walked straight into heaven, or, as it was more formally known, the *Daily Express*.

Even so, I knew that I couldn't carry on doing nothing for the rest of my life, which, at this rate, would be about a fortnight.

I went over to the Stab. I drank three pints of bitter. I went to see Mike Molloy, the editor. I told him I was leaving. 'I'll believe it when I see it in writing,' he said, in a way that suggested he'd had this conversation before.

It took some writing, that letter. Not so much because my resolve was wavering... more because it was so long since I'd written anything I couldn't remember where I'd put my quill.

The popular view was that I had lost my mind. Why on earth would anybody wish to slip away from the warm embrace of Big Momma *Mirror*? It made me enemies too. Somehow my leaving was taken as a criticism of those who stayed, which was not the intention at all. Molloy was miffed, for which I was sorry, because he was a fine editor and a good bloke.

Of course, it made not the slightest difference to the *Mirror*. My place on the ramparts was taken by Bryan Rimmer who, without a second's hesitation, took on all my many responsibilities and duties, with complete success. Thanks to Bryan, no bar staff had to face redundancy and the typewriter maintained its monastic silence.

The next week, I woke up to a day with no work. As usual. But this time there was no salary and no expenses and I had to use my own telephone for calls to Australia. It was a bit like being orphaned. 'Typically Scorpio,' as my fellow Yorkshireman would have said.

I'd done it. I'd left. All the years I'd spent trekking around Britain to get here and now I'd walked out.

Me and the *Mirror*, over. And I remembered what Matt Coady had told me on the day I moved down from Manchester. 'In newspapers, Colin, nothing ever lasts.'

Including, apparently, me.

*

3

Quite a crowd had gathered round Jim Lewthwaite as he laid out his souvenirs on the desk. He'd just returned from Bangkok where he'd been sent to write a series on... now what was it? Early Siamese porcelain? Oriental calligraphy? The new spice trade?

Actually, no. This was the *Sun*. So, just for a change, it was a series on sex.

From among his mementoes, he selected a scrap of paper bearing his first name. It looked innocent enough. Just his name, Jim, in unschooled and wobbly writing. Hardly worth bringing halfway round the world. It had been written, he said, by one of the young bar-girls he'd interviewed. I said I didn't think much of her hand-writing.

'She didn't write it with her hand,' said Jim.

Let's move on quickly. We can't discuss things like this in polite company where any young innocent – Hilary Bonner or Philippa Kennedy, say – could easily stray in.

This was my introduction to life in the *Sun*. After I walked out of the *Mirror* – okay, flounced, I won't argue – I found myself in the south of France where the novelist Paul Gallico had died leaving his sequel to *The Poseidon Adventure* unfinished – a story I've just related;. I had been hired to pop in the odd full-stop and, if required, a nifty metaphor or two.

Ken Donlan, much-acclaimed and much-feared news editor, had invited me to join the *Sun* as soon as I returned. So ten weeks later I found myself walking towards St Paul's and turning right instead of left.

I won't say I had never been south of Fleet Street before, after all both the Harrow and Scribes were somewhere down there. But it felt strange. *Mirror* men weren't accustomed to too much travel.

Inside the *Sun*, that felt strange too. It was a newspaper office at odds with all the conventions of Fleet Street. Where were the leisure classes who populated the higher floors at the *Mirror*? Where were the storage rooms for writers and mistresses who had slipped from fashion? Where the corridors of the handsomely paid unemployed, some of them ennobled, that we had at Holborn?

Before I'd been there half a day it was clear that here was a completely new system. There was a curious symmetry between stories to be written, hacks to write them, space available and subs to fit them. It flew in the face of everything Fleet Street stood for.

The way the *Sun* played the newspaper game, everybody was on the field and there were no spectators. Murdoch's plan didn't seem to incorporate a holiday home for hacked-off hacks. What's more, I'd seen more reporters in the *Mirror* New York office than they had here. Six years after the launch, Larry Lamb, the editor, who was ex-*Mirror* and ex-*Mail*, had proved his point. The sexy, slim-line *Sun* – they should have got me to write their ads – was roaring away. Big momma *Mirror*, running to fat and losing her looks, was on the slide.

I must confess that once I'd got over the shock it was refreshing to work in an office that was buzzing as opposed to snoring.

This is not to say it was a fun-free zone. Oh no. Have you ever met any of the industrial reporters? I have.

If Albert Lamb, the editor, took his nickname from Larry the Lamb in the *Children's Hour* classic, then Ken Donlan should really have been called Mr Grouser (No? Ask your dad). When a new district man phoned in on his first Monday and said it was a sunny day in Birmingham, Donlan snapped: 'If I want a weather report, old man, I'll ring the Met Office.' He didn't do the light touch.

Donlan tucked Lewthwaite, who was chief reporter, and me away at the back of the building, with John Kay and Peter McHugh, their young industrial team. It was a small room, far too small to accommodate the rowdy energy from the two most exuberant hacks I'd ever met. Laughter, jokes, insults, personal abuse, pub games, laddish dares and challenges, public schoolboy Kay reading out snippets from *Wisden*, Geordie McHugh singing 'Whisht lads, ha'ad yer gobs,' – it was rather like being on a permanent stag party.

Every lunchtime and evening, they would charge over to the 'thirst' floor bar of the Cheshire Cheese, to join Bob Bedlow of the *Telegraph* and Bob Porter of the *Mail*.

By the time you added Mick Costello, who was possibly the only diplomat's son on the staff of the *Morning Star* and who spoke fluent Russian and also liked a fight, and Paul Routledge of *The Times*, the stag party had become a mobile riot. To soak up the pints Ron, the waiter, would occasionally smuggle Yorkshire puddings awash in gravy out of the kitchen.

Bedlow, who was more accurately known as Bedlam, was credited with this exceptional slice of dialogue when he went to the post office during a Blackpool conference to pick up some wired money. All you need to know is that it was after lunch.

Female counter clerk: Can I help you, sir?

Bedlow: Yes, a large gin and tonic, please.

167

Clerk: I'm afraid this is a post office, sir.

Bedlow: Good Lord. In that case, a first-class single to Euston.

The industrial boys had their own Good Samaritan system. If one of them was unable to file his story because of an unexpected attack by seven pints of Marston's, then one of the others would cover for him.

Terry Pattinson of the *Mirror* once rewrote his own story and sent it to the *Mail* to help out an incapacitated Bob Porter. Later, Pattinson got a bollocking from the night newsdesk because Bob Porter had got a better story.

Sure enough, when McHugh and Kay returned in the afternoon, bounding in like big puppies, they would, almost certainly, attempt to take someone's trousers down – if necessary, their own.

I wouldn't have been at all surprised if they'd given me an apple-pie desk. Maybe you had to be there, but it was great fun.

Amazing really how all this giddiness evaporated at the sound of the soft tread of Donlan coming down the corridor. My memory may be at fault, but I don't think they ever took Ken's trousers off.

For some years now the *Sun* has had a much-admired chief reporter called Kay, occasionally winning British press awards. The director of programmes at GMTV until recently was a McHugh. Obviously it can't be the two I remember, but it is an odd coincidence.

In Manchester, they used to say that Donlan, although a legendary news editor, was also an unpleasant bully. I didn't find this at all. Maybe he'd quietened down by this time, or maybe it was because I was supposed to be writing cheeky, giggly, and preferably naughty features. Ken knew nothing about features. Giggle? – He'd die before he'd giggle.

He used to fire people for being cheeky. And his idea of being naughty was to have a Polo mint – before noon sometimes. So he used to read my copy with a puzzled look on his face.

But he could command space. I wrote my daft bits about sex in Sweden and sex in France, interviewed Page Three girls – and Brigitte Bardot – and then wrote about sex by the seaside and sex in the office. I wrote them, Ken gave them to Larry. Larry put them in the paper. That was it.

I even got to do some serious stuff too. In Berlin, to write a piece on the Wall, I was taken round by an Army PR major, who was perhaps new to the job, and a leathery sergeant driver.

As we drove along the Wall, I asked whether soldiers from opposing armies still did their traditional exchanges and if there was a chance of getting a bit of Russian militaria for my young son. The major tore a strip off me. It was against Queen's regs. Most irregular. No soldier would ever do such a thing. Simply wouldn't happen.

Over his shoulder, the sergeant asked me what I had in mind. I said a cap badge would be good. A couple of hours later he handed me one.

What happened was that at crossing points, the British soldier would leave a copy of *Playboy* by the car and conduct a lengthy examination of the rear axle. When he came back, the magazine had gone and something would be in its place. The most prized item was a general's hat which was rumoured to be made from sable.

What, I asked the sergeant, could he get me for a pile of Page Three pictures? 'For those,' he said, thoughtfully, 'I could get you a Russian general's hat with a bleedin' Russian general inside it.'

In the passenger seat, the major choked down on his coronary.

In Magaluf, at the end of the season, I watched as the shopkeepers took down the inflatable breasts and willies and scrubbed off the boastful graffiti arithmetic (girls multiplied by times), and put out dinky little tables and chairs, with tea-for-two and an Arrowroot biscuit each. Changeover week, when the young singles – *Sun* readers every one – were replaced by Saga holidaymakers, who had once been *Mirror* readers. The future of newspapers was there for us all to see.

One Spanish hotelier told me that his countrymen believed there were two islands called Britain: one was populated by murderous teenagers, poisonously pissed all day, constantly fighting or fornicating in the gutter; the other was home to genteel elderly couples with walking sticks and squeaky deaf-aids who had very little money but perfect manners. They could not believe they came from the same country.

Oddly enough, in an office where almost everybody was writing about sex, there wasn't an awful lot of it about. It was true there was one near-editor who became entangled with a lady features person.

Chris Potter, political writer, certainly did his best to remedy this. At a Tory party conference – and this was long before he was married – he was seen escorting two women, one a little older than the other up to his room. Clearly no harm could come of this because he pointed out that they were mother and daughter. Whatever was going on up there seemed to require a non-stop flow of champagne until eventually the kitchen protested. 'I'm afraid, sir, it's interfering with the breakfast arrangements.' It wasn't long after that he died.

Even so, that was out of town and it wasn't much to show for a paper that sold on sex.

Even in Pacesetters, the women's department dedicated exclusively to writing about the female orgasm (and where, judging by the noise as you walked past, they were getting the hang of it), they were more interested in getting to the Pineapple gym than getting to men.

And the cleaners at the *Sun* never complained, as they did at the *Mirror*, that you couldn't open a door without the risk of seeing a naked editorial bottom bobbing up and down.

There was a streak of northern Puritanism at the *Sun*. Jim Lewthwaite, a brilliant newsman who came from a distinguished newspaper family in Manchester (dad, a news editor; brother on the *Baltimore Sun*), bore a quite startling resemblance to an American film star. One night when he got home late-ish (train problem, no doubt) to Clacton, he stood, swaying a little, in the bedroom doorway. 'I've just met a bird who says I look like Robert Mitchum,' he pronounced, to the unmoving mound of blankets.

All he heard was a voice in the dark. 'She must be mental.' Keeps a chap's feet on the ground.

At the time, the *Sun* had its stars. Walter Terry, the political columnist, was a real heavyweight who'd come from the *Express*. John Dodd, firmly in the first division of newspaper writers, was there. So too was Clive Taylor, prince among cricket writers.

When Clive retired, Larry Lamb challenged anyone who wanted to replace him to write a job description. At that time, for reasons I can no longer remember, it seemed a good idea to be absent from Britain's shores for as long as possible. I applied. Larry called me in. He liked it. Frank Nicklin, the sports editor, would be talking to me.

Nicklin opened the door to our office and tilted his head towards the upstairs bar of the Tip. As I followed him down the back stairs, over his shoulder he outlined his plans for a new cricket writer. 'There's two chances of me giving our cream job to some feature writer,' he called out. 'Fat and no.'

Well, he'd certainly talked to me. And anyway, I would only have missed our wonderful British seasons, wouldn't I?

In Jon Akass, I always thought they had the best columnist in Fleet Street. Whereas his rivals elsewhere whizzed off their columns almost as an afterthought to all their books and plays, Jon poured all his considerable talent into his column.

Flecked with cigarette ash – picture a speckled penguin – fuelled by carefully calculated gins, in between putting out the wastepaper bin fires which he used as central heating, he turned out a column that was rarely less than wonderful.

He avoided El Vino because he thought it attracted posers, preferring instead the shabbier boozers where he would find his friends Dodd and the TV writer Kit Kenworthy. Occasionally, in the company of his friends, Akass would come up with a piercing insight into our trade. In the Coach and Horses one night, steadily filling the ashtray while emptying the gin bottle, he said: 'Everybody I ever met in newspapers who I really rated, the ones I thought were outstandingly talented, never got anywhere. And the people I identified as no-talent toadies are all in the top jobs.'

I don't think I ever replied to that. Right then somebody came in with some news. Larry was going. We were getting a new editor. Did anyone know a Kelvin MacKenzie?

Some laughed. Some cried. Some began composing letters for jobs. One or two went home and hanged themselves. Oh boy, another new deal. Just when I was getting the hang of it.

*

Thanks to my faithful friends the snappers, they're all there in the suitcase in the attic. Photographs of my encounters with those two imposters, triumph and disaster.

Here I am, in a white suit, dancing in the style of John Travolta. This was the idea of Nick Lloyd, brilliant features editor of the *Sun* and – although I didn't suspect it at the time – clearly an even more brilliant practical joker. Actually, I look more limping pimp than a strutting stud. Come to think of it, I can still hear Tony Prime's hysterical giggles as he took the pic…

In this one, I'm sinking in terror beneath a wave of dozens of slavering bloodhounds. ('Find out how the fox feels' was the brief, I think). Why didn't photographer Dennis Hussey also get covered in hound-gob and mud and general animal crap like me? Because he was on top of a ten-foot bank shouting: 'Pretend you're screaming, Colin.'

Pretend…

What am I doing here, at the wheel of my brand-new, stylish, hideously expensive Panther Lima sports car on the hard shoulder of the M1? Are those tears running down my face? Yes. On its first trip out it broke down every half-mile. I suppose I was lucky that Roger Bamber was there to record it all. He laughed so much he nearly blew his fag out.

Come to think of it, they're all disasters, except for my one triumph – the photograph of me being sexually molested by the most desirable woman on the planet. This was the occasion when Brigitte Bardot, at the very peak of her sexual prowess, slipped a silken arm around my neck and pulled my mouth down towards her moistly opening lips…

Nurse! Nurse! I'm having that dream again!

No, this is true, I swear it. The one oasis in a career that was mostly Saharan sand, and where's the photograph? Can't find the bloody thing.

Bardot apart, the truth is that I've had rather a patchy record when it comes to interviewing celebrities, which possibly explains why I've been unemployed for the last 30 years.

I'm really not very good at it, largely because I invariably don't know who they are. After Bing Crosby, they all became a bit of a blur to me. And if there's one thing celebrities don't like, it's being a blur.

The pop group I interviewed backstage in Newcastle were, to me, just a bunch of guitar-strummers who couldn't sing *White Christmas* to save their lives. They'd certainly never co-starred with Bob Hope. I'd just watched them on stage and it was clear to me they were no-hopers. What's more, during the interview they were a touch cheeky and a scrub down with a Brillo pad wouldn't have gone amiss. So when I wrote the piece, I changed their names to Nick Stagger and the Strolling Groans – pretty funny, what-what? – and gave the readers my personal guarantee that they would never hear of them again.

To be quite fair, they did insist on signing a programme for me, together with lots of abusive and coarse comments. Now I know a chap who's a dealer in showbiz memorabilia and the other day I asked him what he could get for a programme signed by the Rolling Stones just before they were famous. He said we could probably both retire on it. Where was it, he asked, the sweat beading on his brow. I told him when last seen it was in the wastepaper bin just outside the Turk's Head Hotel where I chucked it on my way home.

That was the start of my legendary career as a talent spotter.

At times of stress, I thought, celebrities would be grateful for a light quip to cheer them up. Wrong again. When a magazine – I think it was the *Mail on Sunday YOU* magazine – sent me to see Elaine Paige, it was at a time when she was breaking up with a famous chap who I will not name. I will not name him because it was a condition of the interview that I should not, under any circumstances, mention any very tall song-writers of public school background who loved cricket and who were ever so slightly married. It was absolutely forbidden. So of course I didn't. It would have been unethical.

However, when I came to write it I did mention Trim Ice, Eric Mit, Ric Time, and Ci Mitre, for the pleasure of any anagram fans. Elaine (or El Anie, as I came to think of her) was not pleased. Another star interview I'd cocked up.

Years earlier, when I got back from interviewing my great childhood hero, I was shaking so much I could hardly type a word. He was Joe Louis, sometime boxing heavyweight champion of the world, but by now a sadly reduced figure, in Britain to do a question-and-answer session in night-clubs.

It was heart-breaking, because by this time he was a stumbling, mumbling wreck who was being humiliated by scoundrels for profit. And

– as I had learnt in my early years reporting the Ladies Happy Hour – the true journalist would never flinch from exposing wickedness, and wasn't I the boy to do it?

I shared a taxi with him afterwards, Joe's hulking shape on my right, and on my left a man with a broken nose and an East End accent and eyes that didn't blink nearly as often as they should. Although they were both big blokes, I felt there was nothing to feel nervous about: after all, they had no doubt noticed and been impressed by my own finely-tuned ten-stone of whipcord and muscle. Then the Londoner, who said he was helping Joe out, expressed the hope that whatever I wrote it wouldn't reflect poorly on his friend. I think the phrase was 'make Joe look an arsehole.' I spoke up cheerfully for the freedom of the writer to express his opinions. The Londoner looked down at his broken knuckles, sniffed and said he personally would be distressed – again, I think the actual words were 'fuckin' pissed off' – if that were so.

As I squeezed out of the taxi, he shook my hand with a grip so firm that I couldn't put my mascara on for a week. 'The name's Kray,' he said. 'But you can call me Ronnie.'

The piece I wrote was so boring it was never used. Thank God.

John Dempsie and I should've had a major hit when we were the first to dig out television chef Keith Floyd as his rise to fame was trembling for take-off. It was 10am when he opened the door of the flat over his Bristol restaurant and his face was evidence of an evening well-spent. Although I had never seen him at his best, I felt sure this wasn't it. Fresh (if that's the word) out of bed, he was wearing an old dressing-gown over his pyjamas and holding a shaky cigarette.

As we reminded him why we were there, he caught Dempsie's Motherwell accent and cheered up immediately. 'Ah, a Scot. I expect you'd like a glass of Glenfiddich…'

Oh dear, it had all been going so well until then.

Some years later I stayed with him at his pub, The Maltsters' Arms, in Devon which he renamed 'Floyd's Inn'. Misnamed, in truth: Floyd was rarely in. On this occasion he had staying with him a young woman who was described as a part-time model. She came from Blackburn. Her implants came into the room 30 seconds before the rest of her.

'Are you serious about her?' I asked Keith.

'Course I'm bloody not.'

'In that case, whenever you tip her out, the first thing she'll do is ring the *Sun*.'

'Christ, you're such a cynic, Dunne,' he said.

Well, I was wrong. She didn't ring the *Sun*. She rang the *News of the World,* and the headline was: 'Floyd's a Flop in Bed – and All He Eats Is Fish and Chips.'

When I look back on it, these brushes with fame – other people's fame, that is – have always ended in pain and failure. Does anyone remember a television show called *The Avengers*? It was centuries ago, back in the days when Callan weighed nine stone, Molloy's only card game was Happy Families, and Peter Senn had a full set of teeth. I was sent to interview the glamorous female star, Honor Blackman, who came up with a snappy answer when I asked her how she'd got the role. However, the *Yorkshire Post* didn't agree, refused to use it and gave me a bollocking.

I still think: 'Because I had the biggest tits' was a good quote.

So when Ken Donlan told me to get an interview with Bardot, I steeled myself for another humiliating farce. The occasion was, I seem to remember, her 45th birthday and, long embittered by fame, she hadn't given an interview for six years. In fact, she'd hardly been seen in six years. She'd begun to devote most of her time to animals. Over the next few weeks, I fired off several letters and phone calls. No response.

Ken Donlan insisted I should go to Paris. Again, it wasn't my idea of fun but I went. I dashed off a hand-written letter emphasising my hatred of animal cruelty, seal-bashing, fox-hunting, gerbil-stuffing (she'd know about that from Hollywood), haddock-teasing, and included a photograph of myself with my children's Airedale, Roly. I pushed it through her letter-box. Then I enlisted an English freelance called Roger who was helping me with my researches into the effect of pastis on the Anglo-Saxon brain.

The next morning I was awakened by a call from her PA. Miss Bardot would see me at 11am.

Ken had selected me for this task because he'd heard I spoke fluent French. It was quite true, I did. I spoke only 14 words of French but each one was perfectly pronounced. I took Roger with me because, as a French-based freelance, he'd help with any language problems. And although her PA had specified no pix under any circumstances, he also had a small throwaway camera.

When she came into the room, we were both speechless in several languages. In those six invisible years, she'd flowered unseen. That careless moon-blonde hair was still piled above the perfect heart-shaped face, and the eyes... well, with eyes like that no wonder she loved baby seals. When she glided into the room in a sheath of cream cashmere, it was all moving, even the bits we couldn't see. She smiled the smile of a woman who could read men's minds, and she was right.

She sat down opposite me, legs together and elegantly slanted. We exchanged pleasantries. She was charming. I tentatively moved on to one or two harmless questions. Immediately she stood up and, with a gentle sway of the hips, left the room.

What had I done, for God's sake? After six years, after all those letters, after all those phone-calls, I'd got into her house, it was all going beautifully, and now – whoosh, she'd gone. Somehow I'd blown it.

I was gathering together my recorder and note pad when she came back in. She was carrying a silver tray with three glasses and a bottle. 'For such a charming Englishman, we have champagne, yes?'

I was saved, but only for the moment. As she lifted her glass to me, she said: 'I get so tired speaking English. Now we speak in French.'

I looked at the freelance. Roger shrugged. 'Haven't got the hang of it yet,' he said. For the next 90 minutes I worked every possible permutation of my 14 words, plus some truly excellent mime. Most of my own French, I could understand. Hers... well, all I can say is that she didn't learn it at Skipton Grammar School.

She rose to her feet. Time up. All over. No, she said, Roger was not to take any pictures. Not even a photograph with me? Just for me?

Laughing, she slung herself down next to me on the sofa, wrapped her arms round my neck and turned my face to hers. It was a kiss all right. Lips indubitably met and the after-shock travelled all the way down to my desert boots. I'm the last man to besmirch a woman's reputation but I had the impression she'd done it before.

Then she was gone, and so were we, straight into the café across the road. I listened to the tape. I checked my notes. I dredged my memory for every last word.

Whether she'd actually given a good interview, I'm not so sure. But when I came to think about it, it seemed to me that she'd said some pretty good stuff. In fact, the more I thought about it, the better it got. By the time I left that café, I'd got enough for a pretty strong three-parter. If I'd stayed another hour or two, I think it would have made a five-parter.

And I think Brigitte would've been surprised at just how fascinating, how controversial, how frighteningly honest she'd been. It was one of the very few interviews that gained in translation.

I had that photo for years. I used to get it out to show colleagues. And friends. And family. And complete strangers in the street too. And now I can't find it – the record of the only successful star interview I ever did.

Actually I lie. I did once have a goodish interview with Bernard Manning. But he didn't kiss me, the big softie.

*

Bunting in Bouverie Street? No, I don't recall any bunting when Kelvin became editor. No cheering crowds, flags, brass bands, or hats-in-the-air either. What did happen – and this was perhaps more a reflection of the mood of the moment – was that a senior exec on the *Sun* summoned Tom Petrie off the news desk up to El Vino.

'Have you heard the dreadful news?' he asked. 'It's Kelvin.' And the poor chap burst into tears. Just to clear up any ambiguities here, let me make it clear that these were not tears of joy.

Kelvin. Kelvin who? Don't be silly. Although it's 30 years since he slipped into the editor's chair, he's the only Fleet Street man I can think of whose first name is identity enough. That's fame. Or something very similar.

The other day I heard him presenting a radio programme on Jack the Ripper, and I couldn't resist reflecting that if the staff of the *Sun* had been given the choice between the two of them, it would've been a close call.

Even then, I never for a moment saw his appointment as one of the principle pall-bearers at the funeral of Old Fleet Street. But it was.

We'd had the gradual demise of the old working-class, the dockers and miners and factory workers who read the *Mirror*. We'd had the arrival of television. And Larry Lamb had demonstrated how it was possible to produce a brilliant national tabloid with only a fraction of the staff.

Now we had Kelvin who was about to demolish the culture that had flourished so joyously between Ludgate Circus and the High Courts.

He hated lunch. Cor, how that man hated lunch. How he ever got to be such a little tub I'll never know because if there was one thing guaranteed to light his blue touch-paper it was the thought of people eating between noon and three.

Or, to be quite fair, drinking.

Without lunch, the Fleet Street we knew and loved could not survive. Without lunch, you'd have lines of sour-faced sobersides nibbling at egg-and-cress sandwiches over their keyboards and praying for death. And that's exactly what we got. Have you seen inside the *Indie* lately?

The trouble was that whenever Kelvin saw an empty office – or even an empty chair – he was overcome with the fear that somebody somewhere was having a good time. And it was his personal mission here on earth (as Son of Rupe) to put a stop to it.

It was what headline-writers call a blitz. Memos were fired off around the building warning that the lunch-hour was 60-minutes, or preferably less, and that staff were forbidden to return to the office the worse, or even the better, for drink.

One reporter was surprised to find a letter delivered to his home warning him about 'whiling away the hours in the Wine Press or Cheshire Cheese.' It surprised him because George Lynn, a model of restraint and decency, was a very modest drinker indeed. 'Frankly,' Kelvin wrote, 'if you don't like the tone of this letter then there is a simple solution: don't work here.'

Not only was he going to save the *Sun*, the nation itself stood in peril of Kelvin's salvation. In a memo to all feature writers and executives, he came over all Winstonian: 'Two-hour breaks do not do this newspaper, this country or yourselves a favour. It is no wonder that Britain is rapidly turning into a Third World nation.'

He was like a man possessed. He even stopped a reporter in the corridor to warn him that if he was seen with a glass in his hand anywhere within a mile of the office he'd be fired. When he found Tom Petrie next to a double Scotch in El Vino he asked 'Is that yours?' Tom said it belonged to one of those lawyer chaps.

These were the days of the Kelvin Lunch Terror. Even now, all these years later, the few survivors don't like to speak of it.

It peaked with the Happy Wok. It was, I believe, one of his very finest performances, and I was lucky enough to have a ringside seat.

Kelvin, who used to flash around the building with almost supernatural speed, shot into the features room, which was mostly empty apart from a few subs and me. Where was everybody? Lunch. He grunted in disgust and was making for the door when Jerry Homburg, I think it was, said they'd all gone to the Happy Wok.

Kelvin froze in the doorway. Slowly he turned. 'Where?' he hissed. The Happy Wok. A new Chinese. Everyone said was great.

I think it was the word Happy that did it. It wasn't a word you would use a lot around Bouverie Street in those days.

'Oh do they,' he said, at first quietly, and then building a crescendo worthy of Olivier playing Lear. 'They like the Happy Wok, do they? And they're all being happy in the Happy Wok, are they? Well, in that case, it's going to be fucking Unhappy Wok any fucking minute now. Ring the Happy Wok and tell them I want them all back in the Happy fucking Office right now.'

If Fleet Street had been run as something of a holiday camp, which it had, Kelvin was here to tell us the holiday was over. It didn't occur to any newspaper management that happy campers may produce better newspapers than a surly gang of prisoners manacled to their desks.

Many things changed with Kelvin's arrival. On the *Mirror*, when a raft of new recruits joined the paper, their predecessors just moved up a floor. The new regime on the *Sun* decreed that superfluous hacks had to go.

177

Certainly Jo Foley and Bridget Rowe (later known as Death Rowe), recent recruits from women's magazines, made off at some speed. So did Frank Nicklin, the sport editor.

For the rest, he seemed to target anyone who'd shown a glimmer of talent under the old regime – Jon Akass, probably one of the top three columnists in London, and Walter Terry, the distinguished political writer, for a start. Kelvin, it seemed, wanted to encourage them to leave without a big pay-out. He called Akass in, told him his column was crap, and chucked it in the bin. Akass, a man not easily cowed, calmly said he was paid to supply a column and that was exactly what he'd done. Walter Terry came in for a force-ten blast from the new and red-faced editor in the newsroom.

Walter picked up a paper, waved it gently up and down in front of the editor's face, and said: 'Calm down, Kelvin, you'll give yourself a heart attack.'

Walter went, with the money, and Akass decamped over the road to the more civilised atmosphere of the *Express*. Liz Prosser, a former women's editor, sat it out for months, red-eyed and unloved, before she too slipped away. Later, John Dodd and Kit Kenworthy, two writers who were admired and respected throughout Fleet Street, also moved on, unlamented by their new leader.

Anyone on the hit-list would look up and see Kelvin standing in front of them. 'You still here then?' he'd say. It didn't make for a sense of security. Is it better to turf people out *Sun*-style or preserve them in idle perpetuity like the *Mirror*? Look, I don't know anything. I'm not an editor, thank goodness. I'm a humble word-smith. If you want any help with a semi-colon, I'm your man. Man management? Forget it.

At first, it didn't look too good for Ken Donlan, the news editor. He had once described Kelvin as a loud-mouthed yob. On his return, Kelvin swept into the newsroom with the announcement: 'The loud-mouthed yob is back, Ken.'

And Jim Lewthwaite had once, in front of the newsroom and back bench, given Kelvin a full character analysis that suggested that he was some way short of perfection. Inexplicably, I believe the popular name for female reproductive equipment came into it. Yet both survived. Even in its newer, brasher form, the *Sun* would need one or two proper journalists.

By this time, all the writers – whether television, women's stuff, fashion or any of the softer disciplines – had been grouped together on the fourth floor. There was a theory that this was for economic reasons: if Kelvin shot one at the front, the bullet may well go straight through and take out a couple more.

Two or three times a day he would hurtle in, do a few cyclonic circuits of the room to make sure no-one was making restaurant reservations, say 'You still here then?' to some weeping hack, and then exit. One of our lady writers was heard to say: 'If his willie worked properly, he wouldn't need to do that.' A wicked calumny if ever I heard one.

His new team was in place now. Roy Greenslade came from the *Star* with the secrets of how to run a bingo campaign. About this time, on a visit to his doctor, John Dodd was warned that he was suffering from poor circulation. 'Are you going to give me bingo?' he asked. 'That's what we do in Fleet Street.'

In an earlier existence, Roy had been something of a union revolutionary who never saw a barricade without storming it, usually wearing an Afghan coat belonging to his wife, a *Mirror* writer. It's no reflection on him to say that it looked a great deal better on the elegant Noreen Taylor. Wendy Henry turned up as a sort of executive-in-waiting, which caused some loss of sleep for those who supposed they were executives. They were not reassured by the fact that Wendy only seemed to blink once every three days: disturbing. When I weedily muttered that I didn't care for all the bullying, she merely yawned and lisped: 'Goeth with the territory.' She became an editor. I didn't.

I came back from holiday to find myself sitting opposite the slight figure of a Scotsman with a little-boy hair-cut. Les Daly immediately regaled me with the story of his night at a fancy-dress party at a London club where the waiters wore only satin shorts and walked as though their knees had been stapled together. He had gone, he said, as a Zulu, which entailed coating himself in some black cosmetic from head to foot. Since Les weighed around eight-stone, and was the only man beside whom I looked chunky, this created an interesting picture.

'Did you find,' I asked him, 'that your make-up got smudged as the evening wore on?'

'Hey, you're wicked,' he said.

Les was what our editor called a shirt-lifter, a gay soul in every sense of the word. Even more surprisingly, Kelvin rather liked him.

This was the time when the Kelvin legends were born. One at least was mis-reported (which shouldn't be too surprising). The story was that Kelvin answered the telephone from a man who was complaining, so he banned him from reading the paper. The next day the man rang back to ask if his wife was allowed to read bits out to him.

Well, the first bit's true. I told it to my pal Peter White in East Sussex that night. And it was Peter – a world-class practical joker – who made the second call the following day.

At that time, Kelvin had nothing but contempt for those sad souls who were labelled writers. 'Don't need writers – my subs can do all that,' he said once. If anyone was in doubt, he made his disdain quite clear by awarding the Akass column to an unknown man in an anorak. The message was quite clear: anybody can write this rubbish. Unfortunately, this particular anybody couldn't and Kelvin was obliged to let him go.

For a man at the furthest and most fanciful wing of the trade like me, this wasn't terribly promising. There was another problem too. I hope you can bear with me while I try to explain it. As I understood it, reports in newspapers were an account of something that had occurred in the real world. Thus, on the *Craven Herald*, when I wrote that Mrs L. Tupman presided over the Ladies' Happy Hour on Wednesday, this meant that if you had gone to their meeting on Wednesday, you would have seen the ladies of the Happy Hour with Mrs L Tupman in presidential mode. Simple really.

However, at this time, tabloid journalism seemed to have swung off into creative writing. Some reports reflected things that hadn't actually happened in that way. Or indeed, not happened at all. Somehow, the connection between events and reports had come to be less... well, shall we say, clear. If Kelvin had known about it, I do not doubt that he would have been furious.

This was the time when the SAS went public and everybody was desperate for derring-do copy. I was told to write a piece on what SAS men do when they leave the army. Here you will perhaps forgive me if I move into the passive voice. I was told: 'Make it up – it's all *Boys' Own Paper* anyway.'

Luckily, I didn't need to. I turned in the copy with a couple of names and telephone numbers of men who were willing to be photographed. The reception was one of surprise. 'What?... You mean... they're real?'

However, it doesn't do to be too sanctimonious about these things. It's just that I'm not very good at invention, although I must confess I may have slipped in a few fake quotes when I interviewed that talking dog.

What was interesting – and, in a funny way, rather heart-warming – was the way the readers soon sensed a new relationship with the tabloids. Newspapers that had once been filled with affection and fun now seemed to contain stories that were designed to be hurtful. The public latched on to the new mood. At one time, if you telephoned a reader from the *Mirror* or the *Sun* and asked for an interview, they'd get quite excited and say: 'Course you can – as long as you bring one of them Page Three girls.' Now they sounded nervous and said they'd rather not.

It was fairly obvious that I didn't fit in to the new regime. When I told Roy I was leaving, he told Kelvin and came back with a surprising message.

Kelvin was asking me if I'd think again. I said sorry, but no. Roy went back in and came out a second later. 'In that case, he says fuck off.'

You may have spotted in this the tiny seed of a rather splendid irony which blossomed later. After we'd all gone, Kelvin decided that even the *Sun* needed one proper writer. He picked up Richard Littlejohn, an industrial reporter who was beginning to flourish as a feature writer, and who – as we all know – went on to become one of the few columnists who can write five-star fireworks.

And here's the irony. Years later, Kelvin attempted to do the same on the *Sun*. The writer-hater became a pale shadow of a famous writer, not so much a sub-Littlejohn as a Tinyjohn. You can't say he doesn't have a sense of humour.

And of course Kelvin won. When the blood-letting was over, Fleet Street never was the same again. Kelvin was father to the egg-sandwich lunch. Journalists were seen unashamedly sober in daylight. The fun faded. The carnival truly was over.

*

4

No doubt there are dozens of people who would like to fling me ten feet through the air in the hope that I would land, rather painfully, in the middle of a rhododendron bush. But, on this particular Sunday lunchtime, with a few friends gathering from drinks on their lawn in Henley, Philippa Kennedy's husband had good reason to chuck me around. John Pullinger was helping me with my research.

I was attempting to write a book, a thriller that involved a certain amount of guns-and-violence. I knew nothing about either, which is pretty amazing when you think that I was working for Kelvin MacKenzie at the time.

Philippa – *Mirror, Express*, editor of *Press Gazette* – volunteered her husband, who was then a major in the Paras, to give me an intensive education in both. And, helpful chap that he is, he did. He took me out double-tapping with a Browning 9mm (see how well I speak the language now?) on the army ranges and hurled me around the shrubbery to the great delight of their two little daughters.

I was attempting that circus leap from papers to paperback. A few had done it with spectacular success: Forsyth, Waterhouse, Taylor Bradford, Gerry Seymour – not all that many, when you think about it. Like everybody reading this, I had three coruscating chapters in my sock drawer, where they had curled up and died. Those who have been following these senile droolings will recall that I was then asked to finish a novel by a Famous Author who had, inopportunely, become a Late Famous Author. It was enough to inspire me to finish my own book.

It was based on a story I did with photographer Dennis Hussey for the *Mirror* about half-a-dozen fishermen who struggled to make a living on the Northumberland coast.

This hit the publishing world with all the impact of a used tea-bag. I was wondering what to do next, if indeed there was to be a next, when Ros Grose, one of the *Sun*'s brighter lady writers, introduced me to her husband Peter, who worked for Secker and Warburg, who introduced me in turn to the man he called the most respected editor in British publishing.

John Blackwell was indeed much sought-after. Real writers, people like David Lodge and Malcolm Bradbury, men who could employ a gerund without hesitation, queued up for his services. His skill was in assembling books; he had no equal when it came to the mechanics of what should go where and how it should all fit together. Although he seemed to have read every book that had ever been written, he insisted that he couldn't write himself.

But he liked hacks, he liked lurching around Fleet Street and when I met him he was already helping Leo Clancy, *News of the World* reporter, with a book called *Fixx*.

Blackwell was whacky. I liked him enormously. With his dark hair creamed and neatly parted and his heavy-framed specs, he looked like a librarian. Yet he never wore anything other than an old denim top – he once wore it when he was best man at a wedding – and made his way around London on an old sit-up bike that was probably a shade too slow for Miss Marple.

Secker and Warburg then was an old-fashioned publisher in a tall thin building in Poland Street filled with rickety staircases. The qualifications for working there seemed to be high intelligence, a classical education, a passion for books, and an interesting collection of eccentricities. Take out the education, and it wasn't unlike Fleet Street.

They ran on the very same fuel as Fleet Street. At any time of day, you'd find Peter Grose, of the floppy hair and unfailing smile, patrolling the steep staircases with a bottle, menacing friend and visitor alike with wine. He and his wife Ros were both Aussies and formed a sort of publishing-newspaper link. Peter liked recruiting journos to write books: 'they don't get too bloody precious,' he told me.

One of the great legends of publishing, Barley Allison, seventy-ish, stick-thin, silver hair piled on top of her head, drank huge glasses of neat vodka on the rocks. She warned me against trying to keep pace with her. 'It will only make you terribly ill,' she said. 'And then I'll feel guilty.'

They were great people, tremendous fun and, not unlike our lot, they loved their work so much they never wanted to go home. When John Blackwell handed me his notes on my first manuscript, there were over 100 suggested alterations. 'I'll have a look at them,' I said, begrudgingly.

'It's your book,' he said, 'don't do them if you think I'm wrong.' I took them home and studied them carefully. Every one was right.

Their one failing – a fatal one, unfortunately – was one I didn't notice until it was too late.

Our problem was that Blackwell was excruciatingly shy. The only way he could break the dam was to down four or five pints, which freed him up to talk. So he insisted that I should meet him at six o'clock so that we could dash to the nearest pub. The trouble with this system was that after four or five pints I couldn't even stand up, let alone take on board his advice. We compromised. I drank halves. Slowly.

This coincided with a feature I'd done for the *Sun* on retired SAS men. Someone – I really can't remember who – suggested it may be wise to show the copy to one of Murdoch's men who was involved in industrial relations in Bouverie Street. He also, it was said, had some mysterious intelligence connections.

That was how I met Bandy. That was his nickname. I think he's probably dead now. But, just in case, I'm going to stick to Bandy. He is not a man I would wish to upset. In truth, Bandy was the most frightening man I ever met.

I showed him the copy. He suggested a few changes. I rather sniffily said I might think about it – you know the deathly pride of we features creatures. He was in his early fifties, fit-looking, expensive suit, sarf London accent, ice for eyes. He chuckled. Certain people who might perhaps take exception to what I'd written could be very difficult, he said. Not for me, I chuckled: these mysterious people would hardly want that sort of publicity.

'Where you park, Colin? The arches at Ludgate Circus? You're going dahn there one night, couple of blokes jump you, kick the hell out of you, break an arm or a leg, knock your teeth out, nothing too serious. Take your wallet, watch, cash. That's just an everyday muggin', innit?'

I was suddenly struck by the penetrating intelligence of his suggested changes. I made them.

I got to know Bandy quite well. He had an interesting CV. Joined the Army as an alternative to prison after nearly killing a gypsy in a pub fight. He was in the Army prison for yet more fighting when an officer who was recruiting for a new and highly specialised regiment came to see him. 'They tell me you're a very violent man,' he said.

'Piss off before I break your fucking neck,' replied Bandy.

'You're in,' he said. He served more than 20 years with the SAS. Fighting terrorists in Malaya, he nailed one of them to a door by his scrotum as a warning to his associates. On his Army record, his personal qualities included 'Lack of compunction.'

His stories, together with Major Pullinger's back-lawn aerobics, kept me supplied with thriller material for books for the next couple of years. John Blackwell would peddle his bike down to Fleet Street to discuss them. Peter Grose published them. And I called my hero Sam Craven, as a nod to the *Craven Herald* in Yorkshire.

I once rang Bandy with a problem. My hero needed to kill a man instantly. 'What's he got? A brick? A bottle?' Nothing. So he told me. For a man with strong hands ('not you, Colin; you got ladies' hands'), a stiffened forefinger driven into the corner of the eye would hit the brain. Instant death. 'Makes a mess though – the eye jumps out.'

Seckers, who were worried what would happen if this information got into the hands of Britain's football hooligans, declined to print this detail. If this got out, the King's Road would look like the Somme after a Chelsea home game.

His nickname had nothing to do with his legs. On an operation against terrorists in Malaya, they had to make a rapid retreat leaving three or four injured colleagues behind. Nobody much fancied the job of making sure they weren't captured alive. Bandy did it. That's when 'lack of compunction' comes in. And that was also when he got his nickname. 'Short for Bandicoot. The biggest rat in the world.'

After the SAS he'd gone on one or two unofficial security jobs. This was the time when London was plagued with the Richardson torture gang, who seemed to be beyond the reach of the police. Bandy joined the gang and provided the evidence to put them in prison.

The rumour – and I'm sure there's not a word of truth in it – was that after I'd done my SAS piece, Kelvin said he'd like to meet some of these men. Bandy brought a couple into the office. After they'd gone, Kelvin, who must have been daintier than we realised, said they were no more than animals.

Then – this is the story: complete rubbish, I'm sure – my man Bandy grasped Kelvin's collar-and-tie in one hand, his trouser crotch in the other, and lifted him above his head. He then shook him gently, so that all his loose change and pens and keys clattered to the floor. He then set him gently back on his feet and told him not to insult people. If this happened, which it didn't of course, it would not be good for the public standing of the editor of a national newspaper.

Bandy, the rumour went, had resigned.

Even so, Alan Rusbridger, who was then running the *Guardian* diary, included a couple of mischievous pars on it. And when I eventually wound up back in the *Mirror* building, who did I bump into in Orbit House but Bandy? Maxwell had snapped him up when he left Murdoch. His job? To help close down the print unions. As usual, he did a good job.

This was all towards the end of my days on the *Sun*. One of these mornings provided the happiest three hours of my life. It was a Tuesday and, sitting at my desk on the fourth-floor, I was planning my farewell party from Fleet Street and my new life as a tax-exile zillionaire. Every hack's dream – that of becoming a best-selling author – was about to became reality.

I'd sent my novel about Northumbrian fishermen to David Niven – I'd done some minor writing for him in the past. To my amazement, he wrote back to say he wanted to buy the film rights; he would produce it himself; and his namesake son would put together the package. The figure he was suggesting seemed to take up most of one line of eight-point.

Forsyth, Waterhouse, Seymour, Taylor Bradford – now me.

That was why I was spending the morning planning my farewell party and the rest of my life. The Savoy, I thought, would be a bit flash. I'd be perfectly happy with the whole of the Cheshire Cheese. Who to invite? All the people I'd met on the way here. Perhaps Jack Heald would come down from the *Craven Herald*. Bill Freeman, from the Manchester *Mirror*, who'd launched me on this uncertain journey. Gordon Chester from Tyneside, Dennis Hussey and Brian Wood from Manchester features, Neville Stack from the old *Sun*, all the *Mirror* London and Lewthwaite and Kay and Dodd from Bouverie Street…

Kelvin? Why not? This was no time for pettiness. It wasn't his fault that he was wearing the skipper's cap when the tide turned.

For somewhere to live, I fancied a *grand manoir* in the French Pyrenees, with maybe a good old farmhouse in Swaledale to keep in touch with my roots. Should I change my office Escort for an Aston Martin maybe?

As I say, I was having a moment of delirious self-indulgence when the telephone rang. It was Niven. He would, he said, come straight to the point. He could spend only a limited number of days in Britain each year. That didn't leave him sufficient time to shoot the film. So, terribly sorry, old chap, can't go ahead with it.

'Don't worry,' he said, before ringing off. 'Someone else will soon snap it up.'

The snappers must have lost my home number.

There never were any other offers, of course. I don't think anybody else ever read it. The other books that followed – drawing heavily on background from Bandy and John Pullinger – were great fun to do and were much enjoyed by my few blood relatives. Some got into paperback, and some even got to America. Where they didn't get was into the bookshops, which was Secker's one weakness: they knew how to produce beautiful books, but they didn't know how to sell them.

About this time I also learnt the First Golden Rule of Writing – you'll make more money from a one-page piece in *Good Housekeeping* than you will from a novel.

Unless you happen to be called Forsyth, Waterhouse, Seymour, or Taylor Bradford.

Much as it warms my heart to see my name on the spine of a book, the calorific effect would be much greater on a big fat cheque.

Oddly enough, about this time publishing and newspapers experienced the same violent spasm. Lovely old firms like Secker and Warburg were later absorbed into the bland vastness of Random House. Characters like John Blackwell departed, with their bikes and vodka.

Back on our side of the fence Kelvin found his lunchless paradise. At Wapping, a few thousand murderous printers stood between the hacks and the nearest wine list. And somewhere out there, a couple of rough beasts called Maxwell and Montgomery were slouching towards our own little Bethlehem, waiting to be born.

For the time being at least, my future driving an Aston Martin around the Pyrenees was on hold. Writing books paid just about as well as reading them.

So, back to the hackery. Surely somewhere there must be a quiet corner where an old-fashioned boy could put his aching feet up, trot out the odd piece, take a glass from time to time, and think about life?

Have you ever heard of the *Daily Record*?

*

5

Halfway down the *Daily Mirror* newsroom in Holborn was a small pen containing half-a-dozen desks and half-a-dozen journalists. One quiet morning, a man who used to be a downtable sub in Manchester – slim, thin-rimmed specs, a pale face as expressionless as a shop dummy – hurried past, stopped, stepped back and poked his head inside.

'What exactly are you doing here?' he asked, in a honking Ulster accent.

Damn. They'd been rumbled. Worst of all, it was by David Montgomery, restless in his quest to make himself even more unloved by uncovering nests of quaking hacks to boot down the stairs. He'd done it again.

You may remember that I was feeling a little queasy in the choppy waters of the MacKenzie frenzy at the *Sun* and cast about, a little nervously, for a quiet harbour where I could drop anchor for a while. (Can we return to dry land now? Thank goodness – I felt a 'pieces of eight' simile coming on.)

Well, the *Record* London office was that sort of place.

Lesley Hall who was my old chum in the *Mirror* building – not exclusively mine, because she was just about everybody's best chum – tipped me off that the Scottish *Daily Record* was looking for a London-based writer. Like most people in England, even in newspaper offices, I'd barely heard of the *Daily Record*. To my surprise, I discovered that it was a major publishing success: massive circulation of over 700,000 – the highest market saturation outside of Japan – with about 400 hacks, pots of dosh and bouncing with self-confidence. Just the place for a shell-shocked *Sun* survivor.

It wasn't just as simple as that. Bernie Vickers, the editor, offered me the job, but would I first have a chat with his assistant editor (features), John Burrowes? I would've liked a chat with Mr Burrowes but, inexplicably, he didn't seem to want a chat with me.

A small man with large glasses, he gave me an icy reception. As I sat across his desk, he stared unsmiling at the wall beside him.

As a gesture, he asked one or two questions, like what did I know about Scotland. Since all I knew about Scotland was that it was somewhere north of Yorkshire and they didn't play cricket – I didn't actually say that – the answers didn't amount to much. He wasn't listening: it didn't matter. When I mentioned the *Mirror*, he gave a choked snort that somehow suggested limitless loathing. When I left his room, I don't think he noticed.

187

I wrote to Bernie and said much as I would like to work for him, I felt John Burrowes did not share our enthusiasm. Burrowes rang to smooth things over, and there I was, on board (oh god, we're at sea again).

On the *Sun* I had seen the future. It worked, which is more than you could say for the hacks who were de-jobbed. But when I walked back into the *Mirror* building, nothing had changed. The party was still rocking.

And my next four years were up there with the best – having my own little columnar empire on the *Evening Chron* in Newcastle, working for Freeman and Price in the *Mirror* Manchester office, and my too-short time with Larry Lamb's *Sun*. The *Record* writer was detached from the third-floor pen, which was probably just as well.

Even now I hate to admit it, but Montgomery did have a point. The precise function of the *Record* office in London was difficult to define. Liaison, it was called, and in pursuit of this somewhat blurred goal they had assembled a cast that looked like the blending of an end-of-the-pier show with a psychiatrist's waiting room.

Our leader was Jim Dalrymple – ex-*Express* – who had recently returned from running the *Mirror* training scheme in Plymouth. He had also just concluded a drinking career which included such highlights as breaking the nose of Frank Howitt as he sat at the bar in the Bell. He'd given up the booze, and – at least temporarily – given up hitting people. Instead, he was polishing his golf swing, between feeding snips of London gossip to Bernard – his major responsibility. If there wasn't any, Jim would make it up. ('The word is that Christena Appleyard's the next editor…').

Alongside him we had a smoothly sophisticated man with beautifully cut suits, a BMW, and a well-stocked wine cellar. Brian Cullinan was a smoothie with great charm. He was their London reporter, and an excellent reporter too, but since the *Mirror* had quite a number of people already doing reporting, Brian's services were rarely required. This left him free to give his full attention to his plan to trace and consume the world's supply of Rioja. He didn't miss many.

With a face that was all specs and smiles, g-and-t in one hand, ciggie in the other, Lesley Hall was possibly the best-known and best-loved woman in newspapers. Thin as an elegant rail, signature silk scarf waving, she raised cries of welcome in every establishment from Vagabonds to Scribes. Fleet Street met her every need, even down to the husky young barristers she would pluck from El Vino to help her in the hunt for the elusive G-spot. She was a one-off, our Lesley. Her job was to tell Glasgow what London were up to. It wasn't too exacting.

I always thought that Barry Tranter had something of the poltergeist about him. Whenever he came into the room, you expected pots and pans to start flying about. Some said it was the drink, but he gave that up and remained as wild-eyed as ever. He made life interesting. He once told Glasgow that Jimmy Tarbuck's wife was holding a press conference to announce her divorce. The message went to the *Record*'s hot-shot-showbiz reporter John Millar, a man so on top of his job that he immediately raised Tarbuck on the telephone.

Tarbuck was astounded and enraged: it wasn't true. It was, in fact, Mike Yarwood's wife. This was fed back down from Glasgow to London where it only briefly discomfited our Barry. 'Well I knew it was one of those comedians.'

People used to call in to our pen to admire the secretary, Jackie, a young woman of tumbling hair and pouting lips, who also had tumbling and pouting breasts. She had, it was rumoured, been a Playboy bunny girl. I believe Paul Callan had to be locked in the gents throughout her time.

The *Record* London photographer, John Dempsie, who'd earlier been with the *Mail*, was one of the few truly busy people in the building. He covered most of the big news stories, escorted the constant stream of *Record* feature writers who came down from Glasgow, and completed a double act with me. John was, I think, the best photographer I ever worked with. He had the great gift of being naturally likeable, which made his job – and mine – much easier.

The job. Ah. Actually, it was wonderful. Quite simply I had to provide a piece on whatever the big story was south of the Border. That meant colour pieces on royal weddings (Duke of York's), major happenings (Hungerford massacre), the anniversary of Aberfan, and celebrity interviews. I'd never done these before, largely because I didn't think they were very interesting people. I was right: they mostly weren't, although there was the odd surprise.

In the St James' Club, where many visiting stars liked to meet the press, Kirk Douglas sprang in from a side room quoting from a piece I'd written. He'd had his people dig it out to show how interested he was in me. Phoney, of course, but flattering. By then he'd be about 70, an actor of established reputation. So why did he bother seeing people like me? 'I'm here to sell the movie, so I have to make sure that journalists like me. And you are going to love me, you son-of-a-bitch.' He was right. That's why he never got a bad press.

In Jersey, the best-selling writer Jack Higgins came to greet us clothed from head to foot in black leather. He didn't trouble to remove his leather gloves before shaking hands.

At lunch, at an excellent Italian restaurant, he ate scrambled eggs and bacon. He didn't drink. Didn't eat much. Didn't travel because he didn't like the sun. Didn't like Jersey much.

Good to see a man enjoy the fruits of his labours.

With a new book out, Alan Whicker delivered to me a silken bollocking. My first question, he said, was answered in the book. For my second question, if I'd looked at Chapter Three... The third was also explained. 'Do you know, old chap,' he said, his smile still on full beam, 'whenever I interviewed someone about their latest book, I tried to make a point of reading it beforehand.'

'So do I,' I said. 'But your publishers failed to deliver to me last night, so I couldn't.'

There was a pause. Then he held out his hands, palms upward. 'My dear fellow, what can I say?'

'How about sorry?'

It was a great time. Eventually, Burrowes and I got on wonderfully. His opinion of the English was so low that he wouldn't even change flights at Heathrow (although, as I pointed out, he'd be most unlikely to encounter any English there) and he wasn't all that impressed with the work-rate of the *Mirror* staff. I let that one go. In the end, he resolved his problem by deciding that Yorkshire wasn't really England and my Irish father clinched it: I was okay.

He despatched me and Dempsie all over the place. In Bremen one snowy Christmas, so cold I was glad to be wearing my heavy sheepskin, we accidentally strayed into some sort of formal party in our hotel. The room fell silent. They all stared. Then one man came over and, after a bit of heel-clicking, said he would be honoured to buy us a drink. It was a Luftwaffe reunion. And my coat was a World War II flying jacket. We were lucky we didn't have to tunnel our way out.

There was also something to be said for having your boss 500 miles away. When I said I was going down to Kensington, Burrowes' deputy asked if that was an overnight. 'Probably,' I said. But then, I wouldn't have known if Perth was an overnight from Glasgow. If anybody ever comes down from the *Record* accounts department, they will be surprised to find that the Old Bailey isn't 28 miles from Holborn, as Cullinan's expenses led them to believe.

At that time, the *Record* would send down their writers every week. Some of them – Stan Shivas and Tom Brown particularly – were as good as any, and their showbiz writer John Millar would come down and knock off half-a-dozen features in three days. The Fleet Street papers – the *Mail* in particular – tried desperately to sign him up, which would have meant they could lay off four or five London writers. Millar the high-speed Scot, however, had other, better, things in mind.

About once a year, I was invited up to Glasgow to see my leaders, and to have lunch with Bernie Vickers. Bernie, who'd edited the broadsheet *Sun* in Manchester, was an extraordinary man. With his slanting, florid face, flattened hair and large glasses, he looked like a Japanese general. He did enjoy a drink. In fact, that doesn't quite cover it. Even in Scotland, he excited admiration and occasionally astonishment. Certainly he's the only lunch companion I've had who, on entry to the restaurant, held up four fingers to indicate the number of bottles of his favourite claret. One each. And that was just for openers.

He had one talent that was invaluable both professionally and socially – total recall. At conference, he could remember every story in every paper – 'page four, column two.' After a heavy night, however damaged they'd all been, he could always remember who had said what. The next morning, people didn't always want to be reminded. 'Aye, Bernie, but I didn't mean fucking useless in that way…'

Then, Maxwell and then Monty. The *Record* team broke up. All the energy that Dalrymple had directed into drink now went into work. On the Plymouth training scheme he'd had quite an array of talent pass through his hands, from Hilary Bonner and Philippa Kennedy to Matthew Symonds and Alastair Campbell. He picked up the phone and was immediately on the staff of the new *Indie*. He won Writer of the Year there and went on to the *Sunday Times* colour magazine. These days he doesn't need to write at all.

Lesley took redundancy and was always worried that her stash of money wouldn't cover her remaining years. Sadly, she ran out of years first, and the memorial service for The Naughtiest Girl in the School, in St Bride's, packed the church with every hack who could still walk. Afterwards in El Vino, her rugby team raised a glass.

Barry Tranter, I believe, retreated to the West Country to spread more confusion, no doubt. Dempsie is still snapping away south of Croydon.

John Millar, still in his beloved Scotland, spends much of his time in Hollywood organising publicity for Disney and other major film-makers. The Fleet Street daily rate wouldn't pay for his golf tees.

Bernie moved south of Guildford and briefly worked on the *Today* paper. When that ended, the local giveaway, the *Haslemere Messenger*, found they had one of the best back-bench men in Britain.

As soon as Montgomery stuck his head round the corner, Brian Cullinan knew it was over. Clever chap that he was, he took himself off to the *Northern Echo* where he worked as an unpaid sub to learn a new trade.

When he returned, he was soon recruited to the *Sunday Times* business section. One evening, in a very minor accident, he was knocked over, but suffered brain damage that meant he was never quite the same delightful man again.

Before Monty blew the whistle, I'd taken the Maxwell pay-off, which, while not enough to fund a retirement in the Bahamas, was ample for a weekend in Filey. For one. I wasn't replaced. The *Record* London Writer was no more.

For me, the next job. I'd had one or two exacting masters in newspapers, from MacKenzie to Maxwell, but now I found myself working for the nastiest, meanest, most demanding little bastard I'd ever encountered.

Have you ever been self-employed?

*

6

Look in the Oxford English Dictionary and I think you'll find it there:

> Freelance n 1 mendicant, beggar or impoverished person, euphemism for unemployed; (hence: 'poor as a northern f–'); one who hangs around bars cadging drinks; nuisance; irritant ('it's that bloody freelance on the scrounge again'); 2 unemployed person, unwanted, often homeless, one who sits beside phone that never rings; 3 v i to freelance, to lose your job, to plunge into despair, to abandon work, to leave civilised society ('he's f– ing now, poor sod').

Or perhaps this is nearer the mark:

> Freelance n 1 most successful writer, one who chooses employers, sets own hours and fixes own terms ('don't upset him – he's a top f– '); 2 rich, having abundant income for little effort, homes in Hampstead also S. of France, children at public school ('Croesus was a f– '); one who is constantly flattered by editors; v i to freelance, to accumulate vast wealth, to become powerful and important ('see that bloke in the Roller – he's a f–').

Ah, but which one? I have known plenty of the former, and maybe two of three of the latter. If I was going to freelance, and my job as the *Daily Record* London writer had gone very wobbly indeed, then those were the visions before me.

Disaster was in the air. In bars where once they'd talked of nothing but the comparative merits of the *Mail*'s intro over the *Express*'s, who'd done the best piece, who'd got the best show, who'd got herograms, and who'd been told to double his exes, now nobody cared. The talk, mostly slurred, was of cut-backs, downsizing, and possible pay-offs.

Newspaper managements, Christian gentlemen though they were, were just adjusting to the delightful discovery that, having got rid of the printers, they could now offload at least half the journalists, and they could slash the pay of the lucky survivors. Hacks who'd been to Sunday school remembered what happened after the seven fat years, and shivered in their sheepskins. Oddly enough, I'd somehow been a freelance and a staffman at the same time. This wasn't brilliant professional positioning: it was, as usual in my case, all down to carelessness.

Quite unsuspectingly, I'd run up against the First Law of Work: this states that the more you do, the more you can do, and the more you want to do. Scary, isn't it?

They ought to warn students on media courses about walking into this trap.

It happened like this. The *Record* kept me briskly busy. It also gave me an office in, to my great delight, the *Mirror* cartoonists' department. This meant I had men like Wally Fawkes and Charles Griffin for company, and Pat Whykes, our shapely sloe-eyed secretary, handing out tea and gossip. I had computers and telephones and the papers and, since I'd long since stopped lunchtime drinking, once I'd done a couple of pieces for the *Record* each week, how was I going to pass the time?

With lots of encouragement from Peter Grose at Secker and Warburg, I was still writing some of the finest unread thrillers in English literature. This meant getting up around 5.30am and hitting the keyboard before going to work. That still left me with lots of unoccupied hours at work.

I stood outside Smith's on Charing Cross station and looked at the towering bank of magazine covers. Inside, millions and millions of words, many of them correctly spelt. I could spell – well, after a fashion. So why not me?

Hesitantly at first, I began to tap out the odd piece. And I soon discovered that the style into which I'd been directed by everyone from Bill Freeman in Manchester to Nick Lloyd on the London *Sun* was... well, just about the only thing I could do. Amazingly, it was sellable.

There was a market for verbal candy-floss. All those years of racing lawnmowers and penetrating interviews with talking dogs and the fun of a night-out in Accrington – indeed, what the local Accrington reporter shrewdly identified as 'plaiting fog' – was surprisingly popular.

You may scoff, but Pilger and Edwards and McQueen were not the only ones to know the smell of cordite and fear. Sometimes we fog-plaiters put our lives on the line too. On the *Sun*, Nick Lloyd once sent me to Paris to write a piece on why the French didn't like the Brits. On the way from the airport to the city my taxi was the second in a 40-car pile-up. My driver was lying flat on his back, groaning. I was on the floor in the back. Every few seconds there was a thud as yet another car ran into the line of crashed cars. I thought the liquid dripping from my forehead was blood: it was only sweat. Somehow I dragged myself out of the wreckage, found a taxi in the next lane, and got into Paris with a chipped knee that was rapidly seizing up.

I rang Nick and told him what had happened. 'I can confirm that they don't like us because they just tried to kill me,' I said. 'But they didn't say why.'

'Sounds very funny,' said Nick. 'I'll put you on to copy.'

You see? You can die laughing – as long as you've filed first.

In the magazine market, funny was quite a good thing to be. For the women's magazines, I found myself writing quite a few 'Hey' pieces. You know the sort of stuff. The headline is always 'Hey Girls, here's ten ways to turn your feller on...' or 'Hey Girls, tell us your bedroom secrets...'

It was fun. I could fit them quite easily into the quiet afternoons in the cartoonists' department. Between thrillers, magazines and the *Record* I was writing so much that somewhere in Scandinavia there must have been a forest with my name on it.

Then it began to get tricky. I had a call from *The Times* to go and see their editor, Charlie Wilson. When he was northern news editor of the *Mail*, he and Annie Robinson (then Mrs Wilson) had been near-neighbours, although I didn't know either of them well. Would I go and see him? Who says no to the editor of *The Times*? Not me.

Now I was freelancing, he said, he'd like me to do the odd light piece for him. Yes, I know, there was an opportunity there to say I was a staff man but somehow it slipped past me. I said nothing. No, that's not quite true. I said that for a variety of reasons (all unspecified) I'd like to write under the name of Colin Duncan. Fine, he said, which was a relief. Too many Colin Dunne by-lines might attract attention. And I'd borrowed the surname from Andrew Duncan, a freelance whose stupefying success was a source of envy and admiration. Mostly envy.

And here was another echo from Manchester. Roger Collier, sometime sub in the *Mirror* features department there, turned up as features editor in London. He'd like to use some of my *Record* stuff in the *Mirror*.

Next came a phone call from my old *Sun* chum, Les Daly. Guess what his new job was? Deputy editor of the *Sunday Times* magazine. Would I be interested in doing the odd piece? It would mean giving up sleep entirely, but yes, of course I would.

At this point, they must have planted another forest in Sweden.

See how easily it can sneak up on you? For someone schooled in the *Mirror* tradition of six pieces a year, this was crazy. But I couldn't seem to stop. On one occasion, I did a piece for the *Record* that the *Mirror* also used, and rewrote it for *The Times* as Colin Duncan. Nobody noticed, which says a lot for my unforgettable prose style. Even so, it was frightening: I was a runaway writer but, unlike a horse, no-one dashed out to drag on my reins. In the pub, my fingers tapped feverishly on the bar, looking for keys to hit. This was probably how Waterhouse started (unless, of course, he had four more Waterhouses chained to computers in his cellar – which, with his output, was always a possibility).

One morning, poised between dawn thriller writing and *Record* duties, I came in early to find my office locked. So I went down to the *Mirror* newsroom to write up a freelance piece. At the far end of the room was a group of people I took to be the cleaners.

As I was tapping away, they came nearer. I looked over my shoulder to see that it was actually a party of Japanese men being escorted around by a big fat chap with hairy-slug eyebrows. 'And this,' boomed Big Bad Bob, indicating me, 'is the early bird who is catching the worm.'

If he saw the screen, would he be proud to think that Mr Murdoch was sharing his employee's time and talents? Perhaps not. Frantically I searched for the delete button. I breathed again as FOR THE TIMES vanished from the screen.

That was when I began to think about freelancing. The problem was, what sort of pay-off would I be likely to get? A couple of years earlier, lots of people had got generous pay-offs. At the *Express*, it was said, hacks had to hire pantechnicons to take away their loot. I think it was when Jim Davies was the union man that he negotiated several six-figure pay-offs which should keep a large fox from the door, if not the wolf itself.

The most enviable deal I'd come across was when Jon Akass left the *Sun* to join Jimmy Goldsmith's *NOW* magazine. With a team of the finest writers around, it had been going for a year when they asked Akass to join at £36,000 a year. Incredibly, if I remember correctly, he was paid only around £24,000 as the *Sun*'s top columnist, and Larry Lamb declined to make a better offer.

He joined *NOW* on the Monday. On Friday the magazine closed. He got a year's pay. And Lamb, kicking himself for letting Akass leave, offered him his old column back... at his new salary.

In one week he got a wage rise of £12,000 and £36,000 in the bank.

But since then, generous payments had fallen from fashion. Fresh from their triumphs over the printers, the managements now realised that you could push a hack out of the back door with enough for a round of drinks and a Cornish pastie.

It was no time to be proud. I put in a formal inquiry. The answer was about six months' pay. I took it.

When I told Andrew Duncan I was thinking of freelancing, he was most encouraging. 'Come on in, the water's lovely,' he said. But he would, wouldn't he? He's the one with houses in Hampstead and the South of France. 'Can't talk now,' he added, 'just taking Ivana to Le Caprice.'

I was just taking Bryan Rimmer to the Stab. Bryan, who had taken my old job on the *Mirror*, was less enthusiastic about my freelancing future. 'But what about job security and pensions?' he asked, with a doubtful shake of the head.

'Bryan,' I said, 'who do you work for?'

'Maxwell.'

'Quite.'

It was round about this time that the First Mrs Dunne, after many years of neglect and provocation, decided that she'd been saintly for long enough and was prepared to hand the title on to anyone brave enough to take the job. There were no offers.

The young Dunnes were not only growing up, they were coming to find me – a truly alarming thought. Daughter One, a trainee nurse at Bart's, enjoyed her visits to Fleet Street, probably because she liked to see that she had all those potential heart attacks and wrecked livers working their way towards her. The hacks loved meeting her: they didn't get to see many people from the real world.

One lunchtime I went down to *Mirror* reception to find she was waiting with her hands dripping in blood. She'd been helping someone who'd got a fractured skull after being run over at Holborn Circus.

'You silly girl,' I said. 'What on earth were you playing at?'

Clever, sensible daughter sighed. 'Dad, it's my job.'

Oh yes. Of course.

Daughter Two had taken a job on the *Eastbourne Herald*, before slipping away in civil service PR. Later, having a job from which you could never be fired with a fat pension began to look very clever indeed.

No 1 son was having girl-friend trouble. He didn't like going out with girls more intelligent than himself. This, as I pointed out, left him with only two in the whole of Sussex. Later he worked on the Haslemere freebie where Bernie Vickers finished his career, for Cassidy and Lee's agency at Hindhead, for LWT and others as a series producer... before becoming a medical student.

All this excitement going on, and there I was with an alarming new life before me. At ten o'clock on the Monday morning, I sat at my desk and wondered what to do next. I'd been freelancing for an hour and hadn't made a penny. Within minutes, the telephone rang. It was Les Daly from the *Sunday Times Magazine*.

'I know how terrifying it is, that first morning's freelancing,' he said. 'So are you free to do a job?'

Free? Well, I wouldn't say free. But I was certainly very cheap.

*

All three of them had been warned. 'You are my children whom I love above all others,' I said, in a rare burst of Kiplingese, 'and whom I will defend as the tiger does his young. But when it comes to writing a piece for the women's mags, let's face it kids, you're just so much raw material.'

Staffmen may make a principled distinction between their private and professional lives, and those with guaranteed monthly payments into their bank accounts may take a high-minded view of what is, and what is not, reportable.

If you're a freelance, believe me, you use whatever's to hand. If that means looting your own personal life, and that of those around you, then tough. The self-employed writer would not only sell his own mother, but he'd want a couple of pars in the business pages too. It's not so much if you've got it flaunt it: more if you've got it, file it.

That was one of the first lessons of my life as a freelance. Women's magazines, and indeed women's pages, are pleasantly susceptible to stories about the peaks and hollows of everyday life. Domestic humour sells.

And if you should find yourself sitting looking at an unmarked diary, next to a silent telephone, it's four o'clock and you haven't earned a penny and the clock can no longer hold down the unpaid bills, well there's a lot to be said for using what's around you.

My kids hated it.

In an operating theatre at Bart's Hospital, the nurse was about to leave the room when the surgeon lifted his head from some poor sod's intestines and said: 'Don't slam that door, please, Sarah.' Slam the door? In an operating theatre? Why on earth would she do that? Baffled, she went out. When she came back, the same surgeon said: 'Careful with that door, Sarah.' Behind their surgical masks, she could see there were broad smiles and hear the sniggers.

197

Then she saw, pinned on the wall of the operating theatre, a page from *Good Housekeeping* about Sarah, the troublesome teenager who resisted fatherly constraint by slamming doors all over the house.

Daughter Two, as related earlier, having been born during a blizzard in those *Evening Chronicle* days, had been in appearing in print since childbirth.

And when I had to write a piece on first love – you know, those wonderful semi-romantic friendships between pre-pubescent children – what more natural than a pic of son Matt, aged about eight, holding a buttercup beneath the chin of pretty little Claire, as they perched on a stile. A beautiful photo, thanks to Tony Prime, who may well have thought about this charming moment when he shared an Argentinean prison cell with Simon Winchester during the Falklands War.

All the women's mags liked this sort of stuff, and my kids were kind enough to keep me well supplied. Indeed, Pat Cairns-Roberts, editor of *Good Housekeeping*, gave me a page at the back to record all these stories, and great fun it was. For me, if not for the kids.

Some of it really struck a note with the public. I remember writing one piece about how young teenagers lie in bed until four in the afternoon; then they slowly descend, wrapped in duvets, and lie on the floor to watch television designed for five-year-olds; at seven o'clock they go back upstairs again and re-emerge at eight, dolled up, dressed up, made up, and looking about 23 years old. From the response, it seemed that every family in the land had this experience.

Similarly when I took my two daughters, when they were around 15 and 16, on holiday in Greece... In the restaurants and bars, I never had such service in my life. When I produced a cigarette, 11 lighters clicked as one as the hovering waiters moved in. The service fell off, I noticed, when the girls got changed. Some nights, by 10pm, they'd be sitting shivering in their bikinis, begging for a cardigan. Some call it pimping: we call it freelancing. I got good service and a piece for *GH*.

I was lucky. Whereas most other freelances were created overnight and had to start from scratch, I'd been practising for some time. Right from the start I loved it. I loved having breakfast (three Bensons and a cup of tea), and then walking to my desk at 9am. No tube, no pushing through the crowd, no cramming in the lift, no conversation about last night's TV. It took me one minute to get to work.

It was just so... so comfortable. Of course this can be a danger for someone who is a little careless when it comes to personal appearance. I remember once answering the door and seeing whoever it was recoil in shock. When they rang the bell, they weren't expecting to be confronted by a half-crazed unshaven figure in shabby old pyjamas and with uncombed hair. Not at 6pm they weren't. No wonder the cat kept hiding under the sofa.

At least now I could abandon my Colin Duncan by-line in *The Times* and use my own name. What I did for them mostly was the basement feature, the one at the bottom of the features page, which was usually a lightish piece. For the most part, I shared this with Liz Gill, a former *Express* feature writer who married Danny McGrory, *Express* and *Times* foreign man, now, sadly, no longer with us. I liked Liz. That is, I liked her as a lunch chum at Joe Allen's, but not so much as competition for the funny slot: she had a lovely light touch, which is not something I wish to see in a competitor. Now of course I'd be delighted to read her witty pieces, but mostly these days she does travel stuff, which is a scandalous waste of talent.

Mind you, I didn't say that when we were fighting for space.

I also did some interviews for their Media Page, one with Roy Greenslade and one with Derek Jameson. I knew Roy well, of course, from my time on the *Sun*. Anyone who could move from young revolutionary to the man who brought bingo to the tabloids, and not only manage Kelvin at his wildest on the *Sun* but execute a swift gear-change as associate editor of the *Sunday Times*, then editorship of the *Daily Mirror* and then a professorship of journalism, has to be damned clever. Roy was. And, as the *Guardian* media man commentator, still is.

When the half-page piece appeared, one word had been changed. I'd incorrectly described his Georgian house in Islington as Victorian. Roy had changed it when friends let him check the proof. He wasn't going to let that go through without running an eye over it. Clever chap, eh?

Although Jameson was in Manchester when I was there I hardly knew him. When I interviewed him about his radio career, he referred to himself in the third person, which is always rather unnerving: I kept looking over my shoulder for this mysterious other person. Of his listeners, he said: 'Millions of people feel cosy. They know that Del's here, Del will sort 'em out, Del will tell us what's going on.' Del didn't much like the piece. But Col had done his best with it.

I found myself doing tabloid-style pieces for *Woman* and *Woman's Own* that were good fun and not too much of a jump in style. They didn't take too much time either. Typically, they involved a quick ring-round. For the things your partner does that drives you mad, I rang up a few friends and that did it. I remember that Pat Wykes, the *Mirror* secretary, said her husband used to take off his shoes when watching television and rub his socked feet together: for some reason, it enraged her. Another woman told me that every time her husband needed to fill up the car, he said: 'Need some of the old Petroleum Bonaparte.' The man doesn't deserve to be alive. If, after all these years, he is.

After years of writing for the *Mirror* and *Sun*, it wasn't too difficult.

The first thing I had to learn was that time – which, as you may remember, had almost come to a halt in the slowly stirring depths of *Mirror* features – was money. With fees of up to £3,000, *Reader's Digest* paid the most, but their fact-checking procedures afterwards were so exhaustive that one piece could take weeks. It was much more profitable to write for the IPC mags at £800 a shot for a piece you could do in a day.

Although I enjoyed the pattern of work, I was more or less in a state of perpetual panic. With no monthly cheque, I felt I must work more, must work faster. Soon I was writing regularly for five or six publications, which meant I ate while moving and didn't see much daylight. After six months I told my accountant that I hadn't time for lunch because I must keep my hamster-wheel spinning.

Now I'd been with Ian Spring since my first days in London. His office was in a side-street off Hatton Garden, just above a Jewish restaurant called the Nosherie...

(Quick diversion here. Lesley Hall and I used to go to The Nosh, as it was known, for the Golden Syrup Roll, a steaming heap of cholesterol-sodden, vein-blocking, heart-bursting joy. We'd always have one each. Occasionally we'd have two. And very occasionally, when we were feeling peckish, we'd eat three. That's three each. Since our combined weight was probably about 12 stone – not much more than the Golden Syrup Roll itself – we would stuff this down under the hate-filled eyes of fat diamond-dealers as they toyed with their lettuce. Sometimes, skinny is good.)

Because he was so near to the *Mirror* Holborn office, Ian looked after several Fleet Street folk, everyone from Paul Foot to Peter Senn, and Tony Miles to Mike Taylor. He soon slowed me down. In my first six months, he told me, I'd already topped my previous annual income. Relax. Perhaps it wasn't going to be so bad after all.

I began to work on that most difficult of freelance accomplishments: learning when not to work. 'You like cricket, don't you?' said Ian. 'So if you've got a quiet day, walk up to Lord's.'

It was quite a triumph to learn how to enjoy the quiet periods. But I never beat the other freelance terror over money. It works like this. When you've sent out a few invoices, you know that you have several thousand pounds owing. You race to the post. Any cheques today? All those people owe me. Dammit, why don't they pay? I'll never eat again.

200

Then they do pay. All of them. And you realise no-one owes you anything any more. There are no more cheques on the way. Now you really never will eat again.

It's a straight choice. You can be terrified because people haven't paid you. Or terrified because they have. I never got over that one.

With some disappointment, I have to record here that there had been no rush for the vacancy for a Second Mrs Dunne. The title was less attractive than I might have thought. If I'd posted it down at the Jobs' Centre, I wouldn't have been quite sure what to say. 'Unemployed writer of intemperate habits seeks wife. Beauty and intelligence okay, but less important than ability to produce sincere laughter and enthusiastic applause to order. Familiarity with bottle-opener essential.' What was needed was a waitress who'd trained at RADA and dabbled in psychotherapy – not too much to ask surely. If you ask me, they just don't want to work these days.

And then a possible Second Mrs Dunne hove on to the horizon. I had met her briefly in Peter Evans' on Fleet Street. If she hadn't been the prettiest girl in the world (or certainly that bit of it between the Tipperary and El Vino), I probably would never have noticed her. She had tried to bribe me with a pair of boots – but she'd also sent a pair to Christopher Ward (a *Mirror* columnist in those days), the little minx. It seemed an odd way to man's heart, particularly since the boots were hideously ugly and totally indestructible: then it dawned on me – she was doing PR for Clark's Shoes.

But it wasn't until they had an unusual promotion at the *Sun* that I got to know her better. I don't like to be more specific than that. You know how people misunderstand these things. So when people at dinner parties ask how we got together, I usually say I bought her at an auction in Saudi Arabia or won her playing poker at the Press Club.

Somehow they're both better than saying we really got to know each other during Pussy Week in the *Sun*.

*

Ah yes. I suppose that could be open to all manner of misinterpretation. Careless of me, I admit. But having worked for the Fleet Street tabloids, I was completely unaware of the power of the pun. So, sorry about that.

Pussy Week in the *Sun* was – as all right-thinking people would realise – a celebration of cat-owners. This daring concept – Arthur Brittenden's, if I remember correctly – presented one problem. While the pets were pretty enough, the cat-owners themselves were mostly elderly, with wispy whiskers and occasional teeth which, in women, does not make for great pix.

And here was this young Chelsea PR girl with her lovable but difficult cat – it was incontinent, although I think we skipped round that – which made the spread.

Some years later, my son and brother-in-law made great play of dragging me, a protesting groom, up the steps of Chelsea Register Office for John Dempsie's pix. Across the road, workmen on the roof of a building watched in silence, until one shouted: 'Don't let 'em make you do it, mate.'

That led to my freelance career being based two doors away from Bob Geldof just off the King's Road. By this time, the incontinent cat had gone, probably on the piss.

Say what you like about Bob; I won't hear a word against him. He provided me with a steady supply of champagne – although he may not have been completely aware of it. In our basement we had a wonderful old Irish lady, Mary McCurrie, who'd been a parlour maid in the Cadogan estate. When the estate broke up they found bedsits for their staff and Mary was one of these. She was a classic old cat-lady, with an over-supply of hair (dyed red at the ends) and under-supply of teeth, whose appetite for life was undiminished by a badly twisted leg from a fall into a hay baler in Co. Donegal.

She was also almost completely deaf. This didn't bother her. She simply guessed at what you might've said and replied accordingly. It made for interesting conversations.

Because I worked at home, she'd come and ring the bell with any problems – or indeed just for a chat. One day she came up with a DSS form, knowing it was important to do it correctly because it affected her pensions and benefits.

Speaking loudly, I asked her the first question. 'Are you single, married, widowed or divorced?' Sharp little eyes fixed on my face, she asked me to repeat it. 'I'm none o' dose,' she said.

I tried to remember what she'd told me in the past. 'Didn't you have a husband in the British Army?'

'I did,' she said. 'The bastard buggered off in 1964 and I never saw him again – feck 'im.'

Widowed.

Then there was a whole section about disability claims, which could be important because of her leg. But the word 'disability' was not in Mary's vocabulary, so instead – and rather ingeniously, I thought – I asked her if

202

she was lame. She asked me to repeat it. I almost bellowed 'Are you lame?'

Speaking slowly, as though to a retarded child, she said: 'Mary... Ellen... McCurrie. But I don't use the Ellen.'

It was a shame she never knew she'd found fame in the pages of *Woman and Home*. I suspect she would have preferred a page lead in the Argos catalogue.

As an act of benevolence to a fellow Irish-person, after a party at his house, Geldof would send down any leftover bottles of champagne. Mary, of course, had no idea what it was. However, she did know she didn't like it. On the one occasion I opened a bottle for her, she was sipping champagne with one hand and gulping Rennies with the other. 'This stuff gets me guts,' she said.

She passed the champagne on to me, and I repaid her with old ladies' nectar, Bailey's Irish Cream. 'Jaysus, Mary and Joseph,' she said, 'now dat's what you call a feckin' drink.'

This was the eighties, when celebrity journalism arrived with a bang. My friend Dempsie, the photographer, had passed on to me a tip he'd had years before from his fellow snapper at the *Mail*, Monte Fresco. Celebrities, Monte had said: that was the future. As prophesies go, that was one of the best.

Indeed, I think that Andrew Duncan ('The Richest Freelance in London – damn him') had been one of the first with his celebrity lunches in the *Sunday Express* magazine. His exes for one lunch included £300 for a bottle of champagne. When the magazine queried it, he simply said: 'What do you expect me to give Joan Collins – Babycham?'

For the most part, I'd steered clear of star interviews. I was slightly handicapped in that I didn't know who half of them were when I took the commission and I couldn't recognise them when I got there. I remember going to interview some boy singers called Bros and I still didn't know who they were on the way home. Actually, it worked okay. I spoke to them as though I was their dad. 'Now I don't know anything about this music, if that's what it is, so you'd better tell me...' Good as gold they were. Probably afraid I'd stop their spending money.

They were a sad trio. Imprisoned by fame in the Park Lane Hilton, they were desperately unhappy. Nothing to eat. What – in a five-star hotel? 'Menu was all in frog,' one of them said. They used to dream of joining the queue at a Macdonald's for a burger. When their manager eventually did let them go, it was in a chauffeur-driven Rolls Royce and the minder had to queue while they waited in the car. Every night they looked out at hordes of screaming girls knowing they weren't allowed to get their hands on any of them. No wonder they were a bit sulky.

The real reason for my failure as a star interviewer was that when it worked, it worked brilliantly; but when it didn't... oh dear me. Not good. Tarbuck: cocky little squirt. Cilla: clever-clogs, know-all. Parkinson: deeply patronising. Bernie Winters: Snorbitz had the brains. Lenny Henry: well, he was certainly very fond of Lenny Henry.

They thought much the same of me, I don't doubt. Those interviews failed to sparkle. But others worked wonderfully.

With some, I got on if not like a house on fire, at least like a smouldering bungalow. I rang the Broadway momma Elaine Stritch to ask for an interview. Perhaps, I said, I could pop round to Claridges to see her? Long pause. 'No,' rasped that smoke-soaked voice. 'You dress yourself up real smart, you come here in a cab, and you take me to a very nice restaurant. You squire me. Then we see.'

I squired her. Well, as best I could. Certainly at Luigi's restaurant in Covent Garden, after 15 minutes of twittering into her hard-eyed silence, I gave up. I switched off the tape-recorder. It was clear she wasn't happy, so we'd abandon the interview and just have dinner.

An elegant hand landed on mine. 'No you don't, buster. Switch it on. I give all writers a half-hour. If I don't like 'em they go. You stay.'

She then talked for more than two hours. A stream of anecdotes, funny and fascinating. When she was leaving home to go to drama school in New York, her father took her to one side on the station. 'Elaine, you're a good-looking girl, so remember when you've had two martinis you're a different person.' She got on the train and had four. Brando took her back to his flat where the cat was howling. She asked what was wrong with it. He gave her his up-from-under look and said it was on heat. So why not open the window and let it cool down, she suggested.

He called her a cab. She gave up a sexy Italian guy when she saw Rock Hudson looking dazzlingly handsome in his tux. 'Boy,' she sighed, 'was that some mistake.'

By this time, the restaurant was in silence. Every waiter, like most of the diners, was leaning forward to hear. I heard it all again, about 15 years later, as her one-woman show at the Old Vic. By then she'd given up the booze, although she insisted she never had more than two glasses of wine before going on stage. 'Then I noticed I was buying the glasses in the vase department...'

That was for one of the women's magazines. So delighted were they that the next week they sent me to interview a weather girl. The interview was so boring that I fell asleep typing it. The editor thought so too. 'Why isn't it as fascinating as that piece about Elaine Stritch?'

Because the weather girl had never done anything? Because she'd never been anywhere? Because the biggest event in her personal history was changing eye-shadow colour? Because she had all the sparkling vivacity of a tortoise? Because she'd got the tits but there was a hold-up with the brain delivery?

Weather girls apart, it was great fun. The *Radio Times*, then *TV Times*, heaved me on board, and it got even better. Like every other hack, I forbore to mention that Joanna Lumley smoked: blinded by lust, we couldn't see her lighting them. Sylvester Stallone was one inch shorter than my five-eight, and that was in his built-up heels. Even shorter, Charles Bronson wouldn't leave his Winnebago while there was a photographer on the set. He didn't want to be seen next to anyone taller than him, and Charlie Drake wasn't in town.

In Masham, in the Yorkshire Dales, I watched the Two Fat Ladies, both soundly right-wing, tease their oh-so-right-on BBC producer. As they walked up the path to a Georgian vicarage, Clarissa said: 'Of course they had these homes when vicars were married with families. They're all gay and living in bed-sits now.'

Behind her, Jennifer, who liked to invent little songs as she went along, began singing:

'Gay vicars, in frilly knickers...'

Under her breath, the producer muttered: 'That's coming out.' It did too, more's the shame.

The writing of books, sad to say, had withered away. Once you begin counting your income by the word, it's difficult to write 90,000 without seeing a cheque of some sort. I let it fall away, one of my many mistakes.

But I did keep writing the silly bits of candy floss that had somehow become my mainstay ever since I was coaxed and bullied into doing them by Bill Freeman and Alan Price in Manchester, half a lifetime and about three livers ago. The only difference with magazines was the timing. Sitting at home with the hot August sun beaming through the window, I found myself writing: 'Ten Ways to Survive Christmas'. I seem to remember writing The Secret Diary of Prince Harry, Aged 8 and a half, for one of the mags. And of course, like any good father, I continued to expose the private lives of my children to the readers of the more middle-class mags. Since their friends, by and large, didn't subscribe to *Woman and Home* or *Good Housekeeping*, it wasn't too painful.

The working pattern was different too. I soon discovered that the Spring flu and the October twisted ankle, two personal holidays I had added to my annual entitlement, vanished. If you're self-employed, you are immune to all known germs and minor accidents. Smashed both hands? Type with your toes. Holidays too lost their allure. Sitting on a Greek beach with the time and money provided by a Transylvanian con-man or an Australian media emperor was more enjoyable than a holiday where you paid all the bills, plus all the money you were losing away from that keyboard.

Inevitably, I developed the freelance fear of Executive Motion. When you have spent several years assembling a splendid little team of editors (of the features, assistant, or commissioning variety), what you really don't want to hear is that one of them is moving on.

What makes it even more complicated is that you then have to fake joy. 'Marvellous! Having a baby? You must be so delighted...' or 'Opening a bistro in Northumberland? Wonderful news!' The two questions you want to ask – when will you be back and who's sitting in for you? – have to wait.

It wasn't always bad news. Sometimes the more mobile execs would take you with them. It was very good news for me when Les Daly bobbed up on the *ST* magazine and when Sally O'Sullivan opened a new magazine. *Riva* closed after three or four months. I was paid out for a one-year contract. No-one wants to see a magazine go down, but a cheque dulls the pain.

And when Brigid Callaghan jumped ship from *New Woman* to *The Times*, I carried on writing for her replacement at the magazine, and also for the paper. Leaving to have a baby... some people can be so selfish.   B

There was only one thing worse.

Two or three times in my life as a freelance, one of my commissioning employers rang me to pronounce the sentence we dreaded above all others: 'You seem to have such a wonderful life freelancing, I'm going to try it. Can you give me any good names and numbers?'

Even for the most good-natured and generous of hacks, this was a major test of character. Me? Oh I failed it every time.

As I say, the freelance life does have its drawbacks. But I realised how good it really was, and how well it suited me, after two conversations. I was on the phone to a features chief at the *Telegraph* when, without any provocation, he asked: 'Have you thought of going back to a staff job?' I think it was more in the nature of a mild inquiry rather than a job offer, but by god it frightened me. A staff job? I hadn't got a tie. I hadn't combed my hair for weeks. In any case, where was the nearest tube station?

The second was with Mary McCurrie on one of her trips upstairs from the basement. She watched me tapping away at the keyboard.

'Do you do that all day?'

'Quite often, Mary.'

She clawed at her dyed ginger hair. 'Have ye never thought of getting a job?'

That brought it home. No, I'd never thought of getting a job. Even since I joined the *Craven Herald* at the age of 16, it had never occurred to me that you could call it a job. Other people did jobs. Journalists had fun. Then they went for a jar. Then they had more fun.

It was then I realised that with no comb, no tie, no means of negotiating public transport, I had achieved the one ambition which must have been my secret driving force all these years.

I had become totally unemployable.

Bliss.

*

7

Even in today's housing market, it would sell for around £350,000. Small, certainly, but it was everybody's ideal of a dream country cottage: stone-built, about 150 years old, tucked away off the road in the lovely grey silence of the village of Giggleswick.

From the back, you could see High Fell rising above Settle on the far side of the River Ribble. At the front, only a few feet from the door, the Tems beck – Old Father Tems, as we wittily called it – tinkled prettily along.

An ageing relative who rented it asked me if there was a chance I could buy it for his peace of mind. I said I would if I could afford it.

That brought in Eddie the plumber who, for some reason that was never clear to me, masterminded property deals with the local estate. He shook his head in warning. Prices had been going mad. It was nobbut greed. A week later he was back. Bad news. 'Tha'll need to 'ang on to thi 'at, Colin lad. Tha'll nivver guess what they're asking.'

He almost gasped out the price. 'Seven hundred pound. Seven hundred! It's bloody doollaly. Tha'll nivver see thi money again.' He said he'd read about it in the papers. It was bloody Rachmanism. 'Is it t'same down London way?'

I assured him it was very similar.

Now this was about 30 years ago and even though, as Eddie had warned me, it was clear that Mr Rachman was making inroads into the property market in pothole country, foolishly I bought the cottage. It meant I could keep a toe-hold in the north.

And of course, citizenship of the Yorkshire Dales puts you on the inside track for all the celebrities who also make their homes there, which works out at around one star per thousand sheep, probably much the same as Knightsbridge.

But it did nothing to help me crack the story that might have been headlined: Inflation Battle by Topless Dales Girls.

(For you southerners, Topless Dale is just on the left past Wensleydale).

Russell Harty was the first famous face to turn up in the village. Although he was from Lancashire, a category which in those parts means you usually have to carry a bell and ring it loudly, he'd been a teacher at Giggleswick School. I once met a man who'd been to Charterhouse who asked if there really was such an establishment as Giggleswick School. At his prep school, idle students were threatened: 'Keep this up and you'll end up in Giggleswick', and he wasn't sure whether it was a school or a state of lost grace.

I was able to set his mind at rest. When I knew the village there was indeed a school and also a loony-bin: we liked to say that it wasn't always clear who was attending which. Harty taught there before joining the BBC and returned, in his glory, to live in Rose Cottage with a young gentleman friend.

There was great amusement when Princess Diana paid a visit to open an old people's home. As she was leaving for her helicopter, she asked Harty if he'd like a lift back to London. How could he possibly turn down the chance to travel with the princess? Slavering with gratitude, he hopped in. He had to pay for a taxi to bring him the 300 miles back.

So I went to interview him in some London television studio. He told me with some feeling of the humiliation of being picked for sports teams at school where the captains had alternate choices. Poor Russell was always the one left. 'Aw, no sir, not us again, we had him last week...'

Strangely, Harty still felt bitter about it. 'I don't suppose any of those footballers have got their own show on television,' he said, a little snippily.

Rather to my irritation, he did have copy approval, but when it came back only one word had been changed. What I had described as his silk track-suit was amended to satin. Silly me.

In the next village up the road, Clapham, lived the only writer I know whose words can be unfailingly recognised at a distance of three miles in thick fog. Only Alan Bennett can write like Alan Bennett. And only Alan Bennett can talk like Alan Bennett. Since he rationed his interviews to about one every three years, I was determined to get it. I approached him on behalf of the *Sunday Times* magazine. No thank you. I approached him on behalf of *YOU* magazine. No thank you. I approached him behalf of the *TV Times*. No thank you.

It was puzzling. Baffled, I tried to work out what sort of audience Bennett would enjoy. That's it – of course. Middle-aged ladies of taste and refinement, that's who he would like. I applied again under the flag of *Good Housekeeping*, and Mr Bennett replied to say he would be pleased to see me at the National Theatre at three in the afternoon. Bull's eye.

Now I admire Alan Bennett more than almost anyone else I can think of – well, if you omit Geoff Boycott – and I was anxious to make the right impression. What to wear? I changed into grey flannel trousers and a slightly shabby sports jacket.

Afternoon tea sounded to me like a very Bennett sort of event. I suggested it to the press woman at the theatre. She was completely dismissive. 'Why on earth should he want afternoon tea?' she barked.

In the foyer of the theatre I saw Bennett coming down the stairs in grey flannel trousers and a slightly shabby sport jacket. We shook hands. 'Shall we try to find some afternoon tea, Mr Dunne?' he said. 'I'm very partial to carrot cake.'

He was – need you ask – brilliantly and uniquely himself. Occasionally he would slip in a deliberate snippet of self-parody, then glance up to see if you'd spotted it. 'I don't cook, so Marks and Spencer's is a boon to men like me. I rather think it's like going to the lavatory: if I don't go once a day, I think there's something wrong.' If you saw that quote on the side of a bus, you'd know who'd written it.

Since I'd left Yorkshire, new motorways meant that the Dales had become a fashionable address for show-biz folk. There was Mike Harding in Horton and Janet Street-Porter in Dent. You know her: when she was appointed editor of a bus ticket, Kelvin said she couldn't even edit *The Independent*. Or was it the other way round?

Every village seemed to have a resident star, in the same way they had vicars. Now there's a recession on, villages probably have to share them.

Bennett lived a few yards from the then office of the finest little magazine in the world, *The Dalesman*. He even wrote the odd piece for them – 'although I have as yet to receive any payment,' he said, with no surprise. When in the north, I used to see Bill Mitchell, editor, writer and the beating heart of the magazine. Bill, who also lived in Giggleswick, had started on the *Craven Herald* even before me, Bill Freeman, or Don Mosey. He was the only journalist I ever met who never smoked a cigarette, tasted alcohol or swore. I didn't think it was possible to write even your name without at least two of those professional supports in place, but it never bothered Bill. Annoyingly, he seemed none the worse for these shortcomings.

I envied him. While the rest of us had dashed off to Leeds, Manchester, and that place even further south –London, that's it – he'd moved 15 miles north. He was fond of telling the story how on his first day on *The Dalesman* the editor, Harry Scott, greeted him with the cry: 'Hail to thee, blithe spirit!' I seem to recall Ken Donlan welcoming me in exactly the same way. Or was it Maurice Wigglesworth?

Bill hadn't so much pursued a career as strolled leisurely in that direction. He'd spent a lifetime producing a charming magazine in the quiet of the Dales.

'Oh it's not as peaceful as you think,' he said. That's when he told me to be grateful with my lot because 'in London you don't find yourself trapped behind a herd of cows at milking time. That can put you back five minutes or more.'

Talking to Bill gave me the idea for my next career: simultaneously the best and worst idea I ever had. Later, later…

As soon as I heard about the Fifty Pee Topless Girls, I knew this was a news story that was well out of my league. I passed it on to the *News of the World*, and even their team couldn't crack it.

What had happened was that a late-night drinker, crossing the road as he left a pub outside Settle, was knocked over. At the hospital in Skipton, looking for identification, the nurses were surprised to find in his pocket two or three photographs of women. They were what I think you'd call comely. From waist to chin, they were naked. Topless as we say now, but then not only was it truly shocking, we didn't even have a word for it. Pre-Page Three. They were also young: too young. And the photos were clearly the work of amateurs – talented amateurs, but amateurs.

Who took them? Who were the girls? What was going on here exactly?

Those were the very questions the police asked the next day. The answer was that the pub was staging DIY photo-calls in an upstairs room. Local chaps took in their cameras. Local girls took off their tops. Some (the girls) were under 16. The fee, apparently, was a flat 50p, although flat was not a word you would want to use in this context. The landlord seemed strangely unworried, even when the police inspector himself confronted him.

'When they see this lot at the Assizes, you won't be laughing,' the inspector, said, grimly. 'You could go down for this.'

'Nay, it'll not get that far,' said the landlord, with a confident grin.

'How d'you reckon that?'

'Because tha hasn't seen this 'un yet,' he replied. On the counter, he laid a beautiful black-and-white picture of yet another splendidly over-developed teenager.

'Is that our Edith?' the inspector yelped.

'Aye. Right grand pair she's got, an't she? She'll be doing 'er CSEs soon, eh?'

The landlord was right. It never reached the Assizes. It never reached the pages of the *NoW* either.

In the bar of the Black Horse, where they offered no late-night photography facilities, it was agreed that it was doubtful morally. 'But at fifty pee,' said Tommy, 'you've got to admit it's a blow against inflation.'

I trailed my Lad o' t'Dales identity around with me for years even though, along with the rest of the world, I'd changed. I realised this identity was no longer a snug fit when I pulled up at traffic lights in Soho beside a bunch of young tourists who were, at a guess, on their 15th pint. In a second I recognised their accents as the soothing cadences of the broad acres. With waving arms, I greeted them in their own strange tongue: lots of ayups and whister-barns and quite possibly a mention of the foot of our stairs.

As one man they turned and threw their pints over me.

What I should have explained was that I was in an open-top blue Morgan sports car and I was giving a lift to Jill Evans, Fleet Street's most glamorous lady, on her way to beguile another celebrity. What they saw was not a fellow exile, but a poncey little bugger in a flash motor with a fit red-headed bint who was taking the piss out of their accents. What else could they do?

This was a time of great turbulence in newspapers as managements everywhere followed Kelvin and pledged themselves to stop hacks from drinking, laughing, smiling and telling disgusting jokes. They pretty much succeeded. Dozens of reporters and writers transformed themselves into freelances, went to the Bell, the Harrow, the Punch or the Stab, and carried on as before, a short-lived strategy if you have neither salary nor exes.

Some, of course, were successful. With talented writers like John Dodd, Kit Kenworthy, Bryan Rimmer, Paul Callan and Philippa Kennedy offering themselves, frankly, I was very thankful that I'd got a few years start. The rackety freelance life didn't suit everyone. I bumped into Philippa with her husband John Pullinger in the King's Road one morning. She was going in to the *Express* to see the new editor, Nick Lloyd. 'All this uncertainty, freelancing isn't for me,' she said. Sure enough, Nick took her on board, and Callan swiftly followed her.

The stormy waves that were rocking newspapers even splashed on freelance shores. *The Times*, which had been paying £200 for the funny piece at the foot of their main feature page – which could usually be written in half a day – dropped it to £150. When it fell again to £100, I dropped out.

The world was still full of magazines, magazines were full of advertising, and the freelances' doors were still relatively wolf-free. Still, it was always nice to run across an old friend...

Sainsbury's had a high-quality publication which, although it sold only in their stores, was one of the best-sellers in the country. Mainly a food magazine, it also usually carried two or three standard feature pieces, and any writer would be delighted to linger in its pages. One of their young lady assistants – Fiona? I expect so; they were all called Fiona – rang for a chat. She wondered about my qualifications. What had I done exactly? I pointed out that if I started with my O-levels, this conversation was going to take a long time.

'Oh,' she said, only momentarily disconcerted. 'Perhaps you should speak to the editor, Mr Molloy, then.'

'Ah. Not... not Mike Molloy?'

'Yes,' she said, astonished. 'Do you know him?'

'A little. Would you put me through?'

And some people say there is no God.

The cottage in Giggleswick? Eventually I did sell it, of course. I wasn't too greedy about it. At that time there was a three-level price system in the Dales. Top price for southerners (from Leeds). Middle price for those up from Skipton. Low price for real locals. I sold it to a local. So, for once Eddie was wrong. I did see my money again. And a tiny bit more.

*

Time, I think, for a little philosophy. A career in journalism is like a funnel. You start off at the narrow end, on, say, a weekly paper in the Yorkshire Dales. As you move off, through Darlington, Halifax, Manchester, the funnel widens; every place is different, packed with new and exciting people.

Then, at some point unknown to you, some clever sod turns the funnel round. You find yourself going back into the narrow end. You keep meeting the same people you met before. In El Vino, you see Roy Stockdill, last spotted in the Bull in Halifax. In the Stab, you see Alastair McQueen, famed in Manchester for his regular plunge into the typists' pool. Tom Petrie, who looked like an unmade bed in Huddersfield and Newcastle, still looks like one but now he's on the *Sun* news desk.

So I shouldn't have been surprised when, ten years after I'd left the *Mirror*, the telephone went and there was the pleasing light tenor of Mike Molloy, or that bloody Molloy, as I may have called him.

Let me explain. There are only two sorts of editor. There are the ones who use your copy: they are excellent editors. Then there are the ones who don't use your copy: they are – you'll be amazed to learn – crap editors.

When Mike was editing the *Daily Mirror* the paper had enough room for about four or five writers. It also had about 50 writers. I was among the 45 left in the features catacomb. Several had been there so long that if you touched them they turned to dust. When I left, I must admit that I did so with a flounce that would have embarrassed Violet Elizabeth Bott. If I did speak unkindly of Molloy from time to time, it was only because under the hacks' Law of Simmering Resentment, the editor is always guilty.

Yet that one telephone call moved him, in a second, into the league of journalist of genius. Editor, designer, writer, cartoonist, novelist, wit and, more to the point, at that moment the editor of *Sainsbury's Magazine*, which had loads of space. Pages of it. Acres, possibly. Enough to run a small herd of Ayrshires with room for a couple of rows of potatoes.

And Mike Molloy, fine fellow if ever I saw one, chose the writers.

A man of impeccable taste and refined judgement... have I mentioned this already? Only the best would do for Molloy, oh yes. And here he was ringing me, and I didn't even have to sleep with him (although I had my winceyettes in my briefcase, just in case).

As briefings go, this one was exactly that. Brief. 'Two thousand words,' said Mike Molloy. 'On happiness.'

Pencil poised, I said that was fine. 'What sort of piece?' I inquired.

'Whatever you fancy,' he said, quite calmly. 'See what you can do with it.'

After years of knocking out eight-par page leads for the tabloids and comical bits for the magazines (which always began 'Hey girls, here's ten ways...') this was... well, freedom. Like taking somebody off a seaside beach donkey, and putting him on a Derby winner in the middle of Salisbury Plain – oh yes, and without a saddle.

Terrifying and exhilarating in equal measure, and when I typed the last full-stop, completely satisfying.

With Molloy in charge and lots of space, this was getting close to heaven.

I went down to see him at his offices on the South Bank. He'd teamed up with an old friend, publisher Michael Wynn-Jones, with whom he'd run *Mirror Magazine* years earlier, when they had employed MW-J's girl-friend Delia as a cookery writer. He later married her. But she kept her professional name, although I always thought Delia Wynn-Jones sounded better than Smith. No wonder she never got anywhere.

Molloy was as slim and dapper as ever. The only change wrought by years of success was that he appeared to have stepped out of a Zhivagoan winter, with hair and moustache gleaming white. And now that he was employing me he was somehow… well, just better.

Sainsbury's Magazine was unusual, possibly unique, in that they sold it through their stores for the then price of £1 (now about £1.40, I believe) and they cleared well over 300,000. Since they had no wholesalers, no distributors, no newsagents to pay off – and that lot take more than half the cover-price – this meant they kept exactly 100p in every £.

Who needs W H Smith with a deal like that? This was the mag that put profit in profiteroles…

(Sorry about that.)

The magazine itself was high-quality since it was aimed at Sainsbury's shoppers who were, mostly, people whose lips remained still as they read. It was a handsome production all round and at £850 a shot, most writers were happy to take their calls. True, most of their features were food-based, but writers were encouraged to broaden them out to make general-interest pieces. And some, like Happiness, had nothing to do with food at all.

Every job I did for Mike-with-space was pure joy. I did quite a few for a series called Anatomy of an Ingredient. The first was the almond. An eye-shaped nut. Does that sound exciting? Perhaps not. Let me add this, then. To do it, I had to visit the almond orchards of California, and to get there I had to fly Virgin as the guest of the Almond Growers' Association, who I believe were put on this earth to make hacks smile.

I had to fly Upper Class. That was the deal, like it or not. To get to the airport, I had the hideous embarrassment of having a white stretch Merc arrive at the front door with a uniformed chap to take me. At Heathrow, I was fast-tracked through so as to avoid the risk of brushing sleeves with Lower Class people. The PR team were a little nearer the tail, probably in Upper Middle Class, and worrying whether they were holding their knives correctly.

In Virgin Upper Class in those days, the practice was to hold the passengers down while voluptuous stewardesses forced gourmet delights and champagne between your lips. As you sleep, they stuff your pockets with wads of dollars and naked women are specially commissioned to frolic through your dreams.

The only complaint I had was that I was left to work my own lungs. Room for improvement there, I think.

For those who believe in the power of nature, it was a great story to write. In the San Joaquin Valley, 7,000 growers occupy 400,000 acres to supply 80 per cent of the world's almonds. It is the heart of a highly sophisticated intensely mechanised global marketing system. Tiny robot trolleys trundle round shaking the almonds off the trees. Huge vacuum machines sweep them up.

But nothing was happening.

Beekeepers had been handsomely paid to bring in their hives. Here and there, a bee would saunter out, have a look around, go back in. It wasn't warm enough for them. If conditions aren't right, bees stay home. No bees, no pollination, no nuts. So the whole international industry – delivery trucks, salesmen, supermarkets – had to wait. The man from the almond growers glared at the hives with a murderous look. 'One day,' he hissed,' we'll invent a self-pollinating tree – and these little sons-of-bitches can starve.'

To Western eyes, Pete Yamamoto and his wife, almond farmers, had those Japanese faces that are completely unreadable. When I asked them to stroll together beneath the blossom for a photograph he said, a little stiffly, that it was quite impossible. Desperately, I tried to scramble back from whatever gaffe I'd made. Had I unknowingly hit a nerve?

'My wife,' he carried on, 'has to defer to me at all times, which means she has to walk two yards behind me. It is our culture.'

As I stumbled out an apology, his wife gazed up at him adoringly as her rosebud mouth framed her reply: 'In your dreams, sunshine.'

Then they both burst out laughing. As second-generation immigrants, on the outside they look Japanese, but inside they were pure American.

Working for Sainsbury's had many benefits, the most obvious of which was food, glorious food. Wherever I went in the world, I was dealing with foodies. They were determined not to let me die of starvation. Ordeal by Food, I called it.

In Aguilas in Southern Spain, I was there to study the caper – those little green chaps you find sitting on top of your pizza. Aguilas was a lovely town of fishing boats and shady squares. Those civilising teams of missionaries from Britain, the package holidaymakers, had yet to get there with their inflatable breasts, their unquenchable desire for cerveza, and endless renditions of *Una Paloma Blanca*.

In the absence of the Great British Belly-buster Breakfast, I had to eat Spanish. 'A quick snack,' said my guide Manolo. It took three hours, but it was still quick. To get through ham with olive oil, peeled prawns with red pepper on bread spread with garlic mayonnaise, tuna with tomato and red pepper sauce, grilled roe of tuna, and grilled pork steaks in three hours, you had to get a move on. Which meant I had to skip some of the capers on slices of brie, caper berries on anchovies with red peppers, and squares of bread laden with cheese, pineapple, tomato, pate and red peppers – with a sprinkling of capers on each one, of course.

But then, we Sainsbury guys knew the value of restraint.

Oddly enough, we did have difficulties getting pix of the peasants picking capers. I suspect this was because most of the picking is done in Morocco because the Spanish are too busy picking young British tourists off the floor.

In Jamaica, I almost lost a photographer. Now I know this is a risk of our trade, and I wouldn't be the first to lose a snapper to drink or to lust, or, more likely to a combination of the two. At least they come back later (if it's lust, about five minutes' later). But in Jamaica I nearly lost the lovely Debbie Rowe to marriage. They didn't even ask me to be best man.

This was another of those enviable Sainsbury missions, this time to study the pimento, or all-spice, in the Caribbean. At that time, worldwide demand for the pimento far outran supply, which you would think would be good news for places like Jamaica where it grows. Not so. Wages for picking pimentos off the trees can't compete with wages in tourism, so they stay on the trees. The pimentos.

On his 200-acre estate high above the blue-green Caribbean, Hugh Lyon watched as the birds and the thieves stole the berries from tens of thousands of trees on his estate. His family – French, English and Irish – had been there for ten generations. His face was white, but his accent was pure black Jamaican. At one time, visitors' cars crunched on the circular drive outside his cedarwood mansion; servants brought Earl Grey out to those playing tennis, and everyone took cocktails on the verandah.

All gone. What was left was the shuttered doors and windows because it had been burgled so often; the jungle had reclaimed the tennis courts and drive; and 72-year-old Hugh was left looking after his 93-year-old mum in a bungalow where once a servant lived. Fending off the jungle and thieves, one night he snatched up a machete to chase a gunman down the hill.

Looking at poor old Hugh and the place, you'd say it was a battle lost. At the sight of our Debbie, however, he perked up remarkably. That was exactly what he needed, he said: a young wife, an energetic and hard-working woman who could help him restore the estate to its old glory. He was a tottery old guy who didn't look like a man who got to meet lots of what I believe are called hot chicks. Debbie, then around 30, I suppose, was hotter and chickier than anything he'd seen in a long time, and his damp blue gaze rested on her without blinking. 'With a woman like that,' he said, 'I could soon get this place in shape.'

With a woman like that, I thought, he'd be in intensive care by lunchtime. We shall never know because the lissom Debbie showed no interest in restoring his fortune and his estate. He wanted her hand. The only thing she gave him was F8 at 15ft.

I bet Arthur Edwards would've taken his arm off.

I even enjoyed spending three weeks touring Britain in search of the finest fish-and-chips. I visited O Sole Mio, The Right Plaice, and any number of Fryeries and Batteries, and emerged smiling and three-stone heavier. Near Glasgow, I did find the classic Scottish fish supper supplier where they deep-fried Mars bars. And black puddings. And steak and kidney pies. And pizzas. In fact, they deep-fried everything. As the proprietor explained: 'This is the heart attack capital of western Europe and we're proud of it.'

The best, I seem to remember, were fried by a Mr Patel in Blackpool. When it came to food, that was where Blackpool's gourmet reputation rested. Later, another magazine sent me back to the town to gauge how the north was keeping up with the increasing sophistication of the southerners. 'See if they know about sun-dried tomatoes,' was the somewhat patronising brief. Somewhat accurate too.

When I asked for sun-dried tomatoes in a busy shop at the back of the Tower, the young girl asked me to repeat it, and then turned uncertainly to an older man. 'Dad,' she stage-whispered, 'there's a feller 'ere who's asking for some dried tomatoes...'

'Tell 'im we only do fresh,' he said.

All in all, I was delighted to welcome Molloy back into my life again. But I'm a bit worried about that theory of mine about the funnel effect. If it's true, I could end up back on the *Craven Herald* with Mr Waterhouse warning me yet again about wasting pencils through excessive sharpening.

*

Before we start, one stipulation if you please. Do not ask about Penny Perrick. We don't talk about Penny Perrick. The guilt is too much. Okay? Now let's carry on...

When abroad, it's up to the gallant British hack to set an example to lesser breeds. I'm sure you'd agree. Certainly that was the view Alan Hamilton and I took in a smart Georgetown bar in Washington when we asked how to get to a hotel where we were to witness a major sporting championship.

'Three minutes in a cab,' was the answer.

'And on foot?'

217

It was worth saying it just to see the reaction. Barmen and customers, all pleasingly aghast, weighed in with that American tough-talk – 'Hey, you fellers, you don't walk in this town.' I mean, you'd never say in-this-town if you were in Stockport, would you? So we rather enjoyed the fuss; lambs being saved from the slaughter, and then, naturally, we felt obliged to do it. Walk, that is.

'It's a nice evening for a stroll,' we said, and left them open-mouthed.

Alan was – and no doubt still is – one of the few Fleet Street writers who is as funny in the flesh as he is on the page. He had that Scottish humour that is always described as dry, although there was nothing dry about this evening. We had consumed a number of what Alan referred to as Dr Bell's Patent Brain Fuddlers, which possibly explains what followed.

As we stepped out into the soupy evening air, we did wonder for a moment. The streets were empty. Brains fuddled, fearlessly we set off. Not a soul, not a sound. We both nearly leapt out of our skins when a police car, siren howling, swept up alongside us, screeched to a halt in the middle of the road, and two cops – as I believe they call them over there – jumped out. One ran round behind us, the other ran in front. They were holding out their arms. They seemed to have things in their hands. They were pointing them at us. Were they offering us their sandwiches?

Good Lord no, they looked like guns.

And one of them, I believe, actually shouted: 'Freeze!'

Reassured by our less-than-menacing appearance, they moved in on us. What the hell, they wanted to know, were we doing?

I thought I'd make it easy for them. 'We are muggees,' I said. 'And we're looking for muggers.'

'You two guys sure are gonna find them,' said one of them, as they put away their guns. At least they didn't call us weak-assed nigga bitches, but then they probably hadn't seen *The Wire* at that time. Indeed, they couldn't have been kinder. They put us in their car and delivered us to the hotel. They were still laughing as they drove off, and, as Alan said, it's always a pleasure to bring happiness to the people.

The evening finished much as it began. The championship being contested here was for Monopoly and this too seemed to involve clinking glasses. The winner got so excited that he put the dice in his gin-and-tonic and tried to shake it. Even better, he was Irish.

I tell this story to illustrate that the journalist life – or certainly this journalist's life – did not always go smoothly. From earlier pieces, it may sound as though the entire sequence of commission-write-cheque is as simple as it sounds.

Sometimes it did go like that. Sometimes it didn't. Since I occupy a personal chaos zone of organisational disasters – not ideal if you're trying to run a freelance business – I frequently found myself at home to Mr. Cock-up.

That is why I hope never to see Penny Perrick again. I can't stand the shame. Just don't ask me, that's all.

The Washington Muggees night could easily have ended in disaster, and hospital. I had another lucky escape when I was going to New York with the long and languorous Geoff Wilkinson (the happiest of snappers and a treat to work with) on an assignment so important and so top-secret that even now I cannot reveal what it was. (Okay: I've forgotten.)

In the Heathrow business lounge, half-an-hour before boarding, Geoff, who was familiar with my forward-planning skills, suggested a last-minute run-through on all the paperwork. No probs: tickets, hotel booking, taxis, schedule of who to see and places to go. 'Passport?' said Geoff, as he picked up his bag.

At that moment, I could see my passport quite clearly. It was where I'd left it, in the drawer of my desk which was a 90-minute taxi drive away.

'In that case,' said Geoff, dropping his bag, 'no-one's going anywhere.'

The next 15 minutes were a bit of a blur. I whizzed down to the post office where a young Asian man, who clearly had not absorbed the public servant ethos traditional to the British culture of letting the customers rot, decided to save me. He rang the Home Office who confirmed I had a passport. He then made out a holiday passport for 14 days, while I shot off to find a photo-booth. We just made it.

If we hadn't, that would have been one less employer for me.

(No. Don't ask about Penny Perrick.)

One morning I was summoned by a young woman who had been commissioned by IPC to try to put together a dummy magazine. Delightful young girl, strongest Lancashire accent I'd heard since George Formby, an amazing sheaf of carrot-coloured hair, she was clearly a keen young amateur. She could offer only £50 for a piece but if it worked out...

Yeah, yeah, yeah. Always glad to help out a youngster, me. Bit of a saint like that. I did it.

A few weeks later she rang again. It had worked out fine. She was editing a new mag and was offering me columns and pieces and lots of space, together with lots of money. Yeah, yeah, yeah, I said, not listening. I was pretty busy, maybe another time, glad she was okay.

That was how I turned down the legendary Glenda Bailey, *Marie Claire* magazine, and no doubt thousands and thousands of pounds. Yet another shrewd move by the master freelance.

Incidentally, the carrot-coloured sheaf of hair must've been a wig. I saw it on Rebekah Wade later.

At least it wasn't as embarrassing as Penny... Oh you know about that, I suppose.

Mistakes, I've made a few. A few thousand actually. In Sweden, I found a local fixer, a young man who spoke American English and who provided a couple of pretty young models for Dennis Hussey to use in his pix. You know how difficult it is to assess people when you don't speak their language? There was something that made me a little uneasy about these two. As we drove along with the young women in the back, I began to worry. Could he perhaps tell me exactly what sort of young women these were? How would he describe them?

He took the cigarette from his mouth to speak as he drove one-handed. 'Chickenshit,' he said.

I tell you, for most of my time as a hack I made failure my friend. Almost my live-in companion too.

In Prague, soon after The Wall came down, I found a university lecturer to act as my interpreter and general guide. Under the communist regime, he had been made to work as a street cleaner because he wasn't a party member and, excellent bloke though he was, it had left its scars. Everywhere we went, if anyone was less than slavishly helpful, he would start hissing: 'He is communist svine, I know it!' There were an awful lot of communist svine about, but I'm not sure his candour helped ease things along.

I know I was fairly young when I interviewed the singer Kathy Kirby for the Tyneside evening. Even so, I'm sure I could've done better. She was about 20, as famous a young singer as Britain had at the time, and startlingly glamorous too. Her manager was an old dance-band leader called Bert Ambrose, sixty-plus and portly with it. As I went into the Turk's Head Hotel (or the Tork's Heed, as Gordon Chester taught me to say), the woman on reception told me that although singer and manager had adjoining rooms, only one bed was slept in. Throughout the interview, Ambrose sat with his fat hand resting on her thigh and answered all the questions himself, telling me to run them as Kathy's. She didn't speak a word.

I did what he said. Why? I was young. I knew no better.

When *Punch* was relaunched in the nineties by Mohammed Fayed with Mike Molloy and Peter McKay in charge, to my delight, they asked me to write for them. In retrospect, I do recall that the magazine was so fat and frequent that I suspect anyone who could join up letters was also asked. Printing nearly half-a-million, and sending out thousands of free copies to every mailing list he could find, Fayed swiftly established the old Jewish saying: if it costs nothing, it's worth nothing. It failed.

But before we got to that, I was commissioned to go up to the North-East to write a piece about Tony Blair's constituency. To my surprise his agent, John Burton, not only saw me, but escorted me around, introduced me to everyone, maintained a steady flow of pints, and even insisted that I stayed at his house. 'I checked you out with Alastair Campbell,' he said. 'He says you're a friend so you can have anything you want.'

You can't ask much more than that, can you? What I didn't ask for was the discovery, when I got back to London, that the editorial team had been replaced and no-one remembered me, my commission, or wanted to read the result.

Do we really have to do the Penny Perrick story? Okay, let's get it out of the way.

As a self-employed freelance, my method of organisation was to scribble things on the corners of newspapers and hope to find them later. As a system, it had its weaknesses.

When Penny Perrick called, I was pleased to hear from her. She had, of course, one of the most famous names in Fleet Street (daughter of Eve Perrick, of the *Express*) and no mean reputation herself. I'd known her on the *Sun*. Here she was now, features editor of some magazine, and calling me to commission a humorous piece.

'Delighted, Penny,' I said, making a note of the brief and the date for delivery. So far, it was all under control.

Exactly where I wrote that note – the back of my latest divorce papers, a parking ticket, a beer mat – I have no idea. Possibly it was stolen by a jealous rival freelance (Andrew Duncan springs to mind) or even, perhaps, thieved by a passing magpie. But it went. I never saw it again. The memory of it was struck from my mind until a couple of weeks later when Penny Perrick rang.

Had I finished the piece?

What piece?

The piece she'd commissioned.

Oh. Ah. Slowly the memory came back. I've a nasty feeling that for the next couple of minutes I told more lies than I had in the last ten years. I waffled. I ducked. I dived. Recalling days of missing homework, I may well have said the dog ate it. As a performance of dismal dishonesty, it would take some beating.

When she realised what I was saying – that I was letting her down for no good reason – Penny Perrick reduced me to the size of wriggling worm and rang off. The awful thing is that she was right. My behaviour was as disgraceful as it was unprofessional. I've never been so ashamed in my life.

I never heard from her again. I never saw her again.

But then, it's only lately that I've dared to leave the house in daylight.

There. I've confessed all. Well, most. Because next came one of those golden patches that happen rarely. I found myself working for a magazine that employed the best, demanded the best, and paid the best.

What I was doing there, I will never know. But I didn't complain.

*

8

After having my first two pieces accepted by the best magazine in the land, I was desperately eager to ease my way into their cast of regular writers and not to put a foot, or even a toenail, wrong. So my heart sank when I heard his opening words on the telephone:

'I'm afraid, young Dunne' – one of Jonathan Bouquet's favourite phrases as opposed to an accurate chronological assessment – 'that we're far from happy with your invoice.'

Panic. What was wrong with it? I'd charged £650, the same as the two earlier ones and, in point of fact, not overly generous. Yet just when I was trying to insinuate myself into their favours and their accounts system, I'd clearly upset a senior commissioning editor.

'Not happy at all,' he went on. 'We've had a talk about it here and we've decided to change it. I'm afraid you're going to have to take £900. Is that acceptable?'

Hacks' Heaven. After all these years, all those evenings and mornings, all those scruffy newsmen and elegant magazine ladies, all those on-the-day funnies and portraits of a town I'd only driven through, all those young men in a hurry and old men clinging to the wreckage, after all that I'd finally found a place where they jacked up your pay by 50pc...

Whether you liked it or not.

Unilaterally.

It's the sort of tyranny I can live with.

At that time, the late eighties, there were two sorts of writers in Britain. Those who worked for *YOU* magazine. And those who wished they worked for *YOU* magazine. When I say it was the best mag in the country, I mean it was the one with the most space, the highest standards, and the fattest cheque book. Most freelances would settle for those three. Actually, most freelances would settle for just one.

So not only was I through the door, but I was being bombarded with dosh. I knew then I was going to like it there.

Can we take a small slice of history here? The launch of the *Mail on Sunday* in 1982 was one of the great Fleet Street cock-ups. It was saved by *YOU* magazine, which doubled the circulation immediately and let instant sunshine into the dull world of colour supplements. It was the creation of two men: Dennis Hackett (ex-editor of *Queen, Nova,* and *Today*) and John Leese, an old Associated hand. They were both admired and respected by journalists who don't usually go in much for either admiration or respect.

They thought that colour supps were pompous and boring, packed with what they called 'Brazilian rain forest features'. Instead, Hackett and Leese returned to that old journalistic rule of telling stories through people. It was a runaway success. Some weeks it was 150 pages, advertisers fought to get into it... and so did writers.

It hit its peak when Nick Gordon, who was being groomed to succeed David English at the *Mail*, was given the editorship with Felicity Hawkins, who'd been one of Jim Dalrymple's trainees at the Mirror Plymouth scheme, as deputy. What they wanted was ripping yarns and spiffing wheezes.

They liked extraordinary people doing ordinary things (Mrs Thatcher making Sunday lunch) and ordinary people doing extraordinary things (mouse-racing in an Irish pub).

There were rumours of a budget. Everyone ignored it. All that mattered was getting superb copy and stunning pictures. The cost was immaterial. A time of magic in our penny-pinched trade.

It's not often you get to read a paragraph like that, is it?

Amazingly, for several years I was part of it. They were, of course, the best years of my life, and it came about, like most things in my life and quite possibly yours, by accident.

With every other freelance trying to elbow his way to the front, how did you get on board? I decided to try to write a *YOU* piece. The story I picked was the 50th anniversary of *The Dalesman*, the delightful little magazine that I'd known all my life in Yorkshire. The story was that the pocket-sized mag outsold *Country Life* and was thought to have a quarter of a million readers throughout the world. You wouldn't have thought it to look at it. Their most popular running photo-feature, their equivalent of Page 3, was one on Yorkshire Letterboxes, Surely it must make a fortune? The managing director, amused that anyone would ask such a silly question, simply replied: 'Let's say we make a living – now that's a good Yorkshire expression, isn't it?'

So, you see, it was a quirky piece. *YOU* liked quirky. I liked doing quirky. But what clinched it – and how about this for luck – was that it landed on Felicity Hawkins' desk.

Astonishingly, Felicity recognised my name from a piece I'd had in the *Mirror* (on taking a pet rock for a walk) when she was at school. She liked it. I was in.

The smile stayed on my face for several years.

For one thing, I found myself surrounded by my heroes. Val Hennessey, who persuaded Pavarotti to do an interview by giving him an encyclopaedia of pasta. John Sandilands, who when told by an editor that he enjoyed his copy more when reading it a second time, replied: 'Can't you read it a second time, first?' He was so plagued by writers' block that Felicity used to shout into his answersphone: 'I know you're there, John, come out from under the bed.' Stan Gebler Davies, a wild Irish writer who would announce his arrival by saying: 'I'm an alcoholic – have you any whisky in the house?' Rod Tyler, ex-*Mail* and ex-*NoW*, would spend six weeks each year knocking off features from the five-star Mansion on Turtle Creek in Dallas. Angela Levin, ex-*Observer* magazine, did the celebrity interviews, Lee Wilson and Alasdair Riley did the light-touch pieces. Pearson Phillips, an elegant writer who did the grander stuff, had enjoyed an earlier Golden Age on the *Telegraph* magazine under John Anstey.

Doug Thompson in LA could get any star, no matter how big. He and photographer Paul Harris once knocked on Glenn Close's door in New York and persuaded her to do an interview and photo-shoot – just like that. Tom Hibbert, a charmingly eccentric interviewer who I once saw playing cricket in his socks...

Then there was Dermot Purgavie in New York, who could do anything better than anybody else, with the possible exception of his old friend, John Sandilands.

You wouldn't find a more engaging bunch of oddities, some of them certifiable, outside The Priory. Come to think of it, if you'd carpeted *YOU* magazine's offices you could have closed The Priory down.

As editor, Nick Gordon was brilliantly gifted and, I'm delighted to say, was never tempted to attempt the role of restraining influence. If anything, he led the charge. Sometimes the stories took wackiness right up to the border with lunatic. When the England rugby team had an impending game with Fiji, he sent Sandilands and photographer Phillip Dunn to the South Seas with a wax model of the head of Will Carling, the English captain. The photograph showed the head suspended over a cannibal-style cooking pot while locals in grass skirts danced around it.

Good story? Oh yes. Good taste? I'll get back to you on that.

Nick's one – or possibly major – weakness was African wildlife. With the power of popularity and circulation, *YOU* could get to anyone, from Nelson Mandela to Imelda Marcos. Once they set up an interview and pix with a particularly difficult Hollywood star (Warren Beatty perhaps) who agreed to do it only on the basis that he was the cover pic. At the last minute, Nick decided to substitute a photo of a baby gorilla together with a save-the-gorillas appeal. Felicity Hawkins was out of the office when she got the call to rush back. 'The fucking monkey's died...'

Lee Wilson was dressed up in a superman outfit and sent back to his home town to right any wrongs he could find. Sandilands went to the West Indies on a banana boat. Some poor sod was smuggled into Somalia in a tanker.

With Patric Walker, also ex-*Mirror*, doing the stars column, every time it was promoted the circulation went up by another 100,000. Midas never had it this good.

However difficult they were – and here I'm thinking about the team of three who were arrested in Wales when enquiring into coal-smuggling, or the snapper and writer who, on their way to New Zealand, had a fight before they reached Gatwick – all was forgiven if the copy and pix were of diamond quality.

Ideally, to control and conduct this band of random talent you'd need someone with a chair and whip. Instead, they had a team of commissioning editors who wouldn't have lasted half an hour on *The Lady*. Somehow, John Koski contrived to look perpetually worried, yet he was so quick-witted he could analyse a piece while you were reading the menu. The wine list took a little longer. He came via York papers and a marketing weekly. The name comes from Finland. Jonathan Bouquet, a man of elegance and style, had edited a glossy girly mag when he was about 20, which probably explained his smiling air of contentment. The name is Huguenot, which may explain his penchant for silk ties. Large, amiable, and deceptively innocent, Joe Houlihan was South London Irish: one of the few South London Irish who can speak passable Russian.

Together with Aussie John Chenery, twice a week they would go off to Il Barbino, an Italian restaurant on Kensington Church Street, for a four-bottle lunch followed by grappa. By the end, the Finn, the Huguenot, the Mick and the Aussie, who were not after all starring in a rude joke, had invariably tidied up two or three features that needed attention and come up with another two or three workable ideas.

Possibly this explained the reaction of Dee Nolan when she became editor. 'You treat this place like a gentleman's club,' she said to Bouquet, as he drifted in around 3 45pm trailing expensive cigar smoke.

'The funny thing is,' Bouquet reported later, 'that she said it as though it was a criticism.' That was later.

I worked for all of them during my time with the mag. Knowing what delicate little creatures we writers are, they liked to take the pain out of it. The commission came over the phone. Then came the DR with the package, which contained a full brief, copies of all the essential cuttings, air tickets (usually business class), a schedule of people, times and places, and a fat wodge of the local currency.

I imagine they would've come round with a sharpened pencil if you'd asked. They liked writers. They liked to look after their writers, which is more than most writers' wives can say.

It was quite easy: in return all they wanted was excellence. With pieces of 2,000 or even up to 3,000 words, the story had to be spelt out clearly, the backing facts and quotes all in place, a summary of the history, full colour and description of places and people, and – oh yes – it had to be assembled and written with a clearly defined voice.

Wry, detached, ironic, amusing, emotional even: but every piece had to be held together by the style of the writer, all the way through.

Koski, Bouquet, Houlihan and Chenery could read and dissect copy as quickly as a milkman reads a housewife's note. They were more like publishing editors than subs in that they were concerned with the shape of the piece and that everything was in the right place.

A little less of this, a little more of that, perhaps move page seven up to page two, writers who thought they'd done their best found they could do better. It was very demanding. I knew a number of newspaper features men – all highly-regarded, one a Writer of the Year – who attempted it, and found they couldn't do it.

For those who could, there was the satisfaction of being in there with the best. And if the international quartet of Finn, Huguenot, Mick and Aussie liked it, from time to time they would impose a completely unsought fee increase on you. I never quite caught up with Rod Tyler on his £2,000, but I wasn't grumbling.

It was the highest concentration of journalistic talent I'd ever seen in one office. Or, more commonly, one restaurant. Which was convenient, because when the business was done, there was really only one question... white or red?

It was never this good before.

It was never this good again.

Where is Andrew Morton these days? Anybody know? Soaking up the Caribbean sun on the deck of his yacht somewhere, I suppose, or ski-ing down his own private mountain. I've heard it said that he won't look at a woman these days unless she's won three Oscars, is still under 22, and has been marinated in Dom Perignon. Even his NUJ card is in a Louis Vuitton crocodile-skin wallet.

Makes you sick, doesn't it? Makes me sick, I can tell you. That should have been mine, all mine. At least you'd think Morton would offer to split it with me, but no, I've not heard a word from him.

As soon as the tears stop splashing on my keyboard, I'll tell you about it.

At the time, I was doing a piece for the *YOU* mag on William Bartholomew, the man who organised parties for those who live at the junction of society and show-biz. When Prince Charles wanted a party, he rang Will. So did Tina Turner, Diana Ross, and Prince Edward. I did too, but that's a slightly different story.

He was a lovely chap, a sort of 16-stone schoolboy with floppy hair and a shy smile. When I chanced to mention (chanced – do you like that?) that in a few weeks' time I was proposing to undergo a form of marriage myself, he offered to do the catering. I pointed out that I couldn't possibly afford him, to which he replied: 'I'll make it so you can.' He did. People have been begging me to get married again ever since.

At one of his parties he'd posed as a waiter so he could take a glass of champagne to the beautiful young woman who later became his wife. That was Carolyn. She used to share a flat with the woman who later married the man who one day – if he should live long enough – will become king. She didn't live long enough, of course.

About this time, Carolyn and a handful of Diana's other best friends decided to spill the beans over the royal marriage. Casting about for a suitable scribe, they picked out a chap who wrote about such nonsense for the *Star*. Why Andrew Morton? Although he certainly wasn't One Of Them, he did sound most of his aitches and occasionally gave his shoes a polish. So, no doubt to his astonishment, they chose him, and he found himself sitting on a Matterhorn of cash. Four million has been mentioned.

A few weeks after this story broke, I met Will in the King's Road. When they decided to make Diana's story public, didn't my name cross his mind? 'No,' he reassured me. 'I knew you wouldn't want to be mixed up in that sort of gossipy trash.'

Ah. I thought of saying he'd be surprised how trashy I could get for four million, but the moment, and the money, had gone.

Writing for *YOU* magazine took you to some interesting places and interesting people. There was always a slightly harum-scarum air about the magazine right from the start. The first issue was due to have an exclusive about Princess Grace of Monaco, but she featured in a road accident that was an eerie prequel to Diana's, and Julio Iglesias took over the cover.

Since it was the magazine that carried the newspaper, the staff were sometimes a little short of respect. At one Christmas party, Stewart Steven took one look at the magazine team and asked: 'Who the fuck are all these punks?' A researcher then asked him who he was to which, with some irritation, he replied: 'Just tell this bitch I'm the editor.'

'So you say,' quipped a jovial commissioning editor. To his surprise, Jonathan Bouquet was still a jovial commissioning editor the next morning.

So it was one of those offices where fun played a major part. For their first Christmas party, they presented an Oscar for the best-dressed woman to Bubbles Rothermere, blithely ignoring the soiled knee bandage.

Since the magazine was created as a reaction to all those colour supplements with their profiles of unknown Romanian ballet-dancers, it wasn't surprising that fun was also an essential ingredient in most of their pieces.

Which made it all the more surprising when Nick Gordon, the brilliant if slightly capricious editor, told Bouquet that a piece I'd done was too bloody whimsical. Bouquet amputated all signs of whimsy. 'This is a boring piece,' Nick said; 'tell Dunne to rewrite it.' Bouquet resubmitted the original and the editor beamed with pleasure. 'Brilliant,' he said, 'I knew you could get it out of him.' But then, we all know about editors.

What made this all the more remarkable was that, while there were a handful of sturdy vessels like *YOU* magazine, buoyantly bouncing in the waves, the rest of the fleet was in trouble. Those two bold captains, Murdoch and Maxwell, were prodding many of my fellow mariners down the plank and the rest were jumping overboard.

This was not a happy time. Older chaps who were within reach of the pension were okay, but for the rest, hard times beckoned. Men who dated their dreams back to the days of fat pay-offs that would buy a small thatched pub somewhere west of Exeter, discovered it would cover a farewell piss-up in the Bell and a taxi home. And you could bet the cabbie would offer you a fistful of blank bills when you could no longer use them. London suddenly acquired several dozen reluctant new freelances.

Yet here we were, beavering away for a publication where cost was a vulgar incidental... and excellence was the only criterion. This wasn't the first golden age, or so I am assured by older writers like Andrew Duncan.

(Older? Make that aged – and wizened). In the sixties, John Anstey's *Telegraph Magazine* operated a similar open-handed policy. There was then a sort of aristocracy of writers: Andrew, Geoffrey Wansell, Bron Waugh, Pearson Phillips and Tim Heald were the benefactors at that time. The *Telegraph* always described them as 'leading writers' so they formed a satirical club called Leading Writers of Great Britain and conned the *Evening Standard* diary into carrying a piece.

These men are indestructible. In the *Telegraph* days, Phillips, between divorces, was said to be living in an E-type Jag outside the Savoy, which shows a certain amount of style. But since the 'was said' came from Andrew Duncan, it may simply be the creative mind at work. Anyway, Phillips emerged 20 years later to be a big name on *YOU*. Even now, you can still find Wansell's by-line in the *Mail*, and Duncan's in *Radio Times*, and Tim Heald's on various books. I'm not at all sure they haven't made more money than Andrew Morton. They've certainly made more than me, which is in itself very annoying.

The story we freelances all tell and re-tell in dark days when hope flags is that of Gordon Burns. He was a great operator who, sadly, died recently. When Associated started yet another magazine, called *Night and Day*, which was about as long as it lasted, they asked him to write a piece for a generous £2,000. He turned it down. He was writing a book that he couldn't leave. The commissioning editor came back after a few minutes to make it £3,000. His answer was the same. Eventually, when it reached £5,000, he gave in and did it. When times are hard, it's good to remember Gordon.

It's also good to remember a time when editors were prepared to spend money to back their own judgment, confident they could produce a better publication than their rivals. Later, less sure-footed editors only competed to see who could pay the least and save the most. We freelances do not care for such people.

Back to those *YOU* days which were the closest I got to writer's delight. I spent several nights trotting up and down Park Lane sampling dinners in the taller hotels. I was conducting a personal poll on who was the best after-dinner speaker, at the behest – I think – of John Koski. There are worse ways to spend an evening, and some of the speakers were excellent.

Brian Johnston – Jonners, the ebullient cricket commentator – had an excellent story about a visit with his wife to Bangkok. While she went off to do some shopping he fell into conversation with a pretty little thing in a doorway. Her price was £100. Jonners was aghast. He thought probably a fiver would be the local price. He met his wife for lunch and as they were walking back they passed the same girl. 'See what you get for a fiver,' she said. We all thought this was very funny. So, to my surprise, did Mrs Johnston.

No wonder Jonners laughed so much when Botham couldn't get his leg over.

Peter Moloney, ex-teacher, ex-paratrooper, ex-Trappist monk, had some good lines about the Kerryman who broke both ankles trying to make coconut wine, the Welshman who took his car in for its first service and crashed into the pulpit, and the Scotsman who called the undertaker when his wife was ill because he didn't like paying middlemen.

Our only famous woman cricketer, Rachel Heyhoe Flint, told us some frisky female jokes. Women cricketers, she said, used coconut shells for protection when batting. 'Two if you're shy, three if you're nervous.' She'd heard a male commentator say that a Dutch woman hockey player had 47 caps. 'That probably accounts for the way she's walking...'

The funniest of all, however, was a young barrister who I found addressing a dinner for motor manufacturers. You wouldn't have heard of Graham Davies then, and you probably haven't now. He keeps away from television cameras which can kill your act in minutes.

He had a way with hecklers. 'Thank you, but when I do a ventriloquist act, I bring my own dummy.' Or, even more dismissively, 'See what happens when cousins marry?' He went to a school where rugby and homosexuality were compulsory and where the bullies would beat you up and make you stand barefoot on the hot radiators... 'but that's nuns for you.'

When I'd written it, Koski asked me to score them so we had a winner. Although he was the least known – perhaps because he *was* the least known – I picked Graham Davies. A couple of days after it appeared he rang me to say that his fee had just about doubled and his phone had never stopped ringing. He sent me a bottle of champagne and coached me through a father-of-the-bride speech I was dreading. 'You can borrow some of my jokes,' he said. And I've just borrowed them again.

The most surprising people turned out to be good fun. Instructed to accompany Sister Wendy to Rome for a preview of her television arts programme, my main concern was whether I could conduct a conversation which excluded drink and sex. I needn't have worried. She seemed to know quite a lot about both.

At lunch with photographer John Rogers and me, she walloped back a fair amount of wine without showing any signs of tearing off her wimple and dancing on the table. In – I think – the Galleria Borghese, she stood in front of a sculpture of the Rape of the Sabine Women which she then analysed in astonishing detail. She pointed out the men's fingers sinking into the women's flesh, and how one woman, even as she tried to flee, was looking back almost with yearning.

For a consecrated virgin who lived a solitary life in the grounds of a Carmelite monastery in Norfolk, she seemed to have a more sensitive grasp of the reality of sex than, say, Kent Gavin. Yet was it a subject of which she knew nothing? She smiled and patted my hand. 'I haven't climbed Everest but I know quite a lot about it. I read books, you see.'

I drove her around the city and when we came to one of the bridges over the Tiber, I couldn't resist a bit of showing-off. Dragged from the half-remembered but mostly forgotten remains of my education, I quoted the opening lines from *How Hadrian Kept the Bridge*.

'Lars Porsena of Closium by the nine gods he swore, that the great house of Tarquin should suffer wrong no more…'

She then ran through the next 30 verses, which served me right.

On one of the seven hills, she pointed out to us how the city had remained much the same for 2,000 years. 'Yeah,' said Rogers, a London boy, rather begrudgingly, 'but just think what it must've looked like when it was new.' Sister Wendy looked puzzled.

Back we went, back down into the city to find a delightful pavement restaurant near the bottom of the Spanish steps, where we ate and drank, and our consecrated virgin was the most entertaining company.

Unlike poor old Andrew Morton. He was probably at home counting my money, the sick bastard.

*

9

This life-story is taking longer to write than it did to live.

Most of those who were here at the start, about 100,000 words ago, will have been driven by boredom to get the single ticket to Dignitas (or, for *Mirror* pensioners, the cheaper option at Beachy Head). Those who are still clinging to the wreckage may remember that, in those early days, I rather resented being sent to interview talking dogs and running in lawnmower races. This, I felt, was poor preparation for my career as one of those big-time foreign corrs of the here-in-blazing-Beirut school.

As it turned out, I was much more at home with dogs and lawnmowers than with war and pestilence. My only skill, and a pretty slender one at that, was for plaiting fog: writing stories with as few facts as possible; occasionally – in moments of true inspiration – with none at all. It took me a little while to settle to the idea that I was essentially a writer of candy-floss crap.

I had found my natural home.

So, inevitably, one of the first things *YOU* magazine did was to send me to Blackpool. Editors and their assistants usually come up with the Blackpool idea round about the fourth bottle over a languid Langan's lunch, largely, I suspect, because they don't believe there is such a place. So when writers and snappers come back with stories of smelly donkeys and clattering trams it's as near as they wish to get to the real world. Since I was thought to speak the language, I was sent there several times.

But since *YOU* was the best ideas factory I ever came across, it was with a brief of delightful brevity: Find the original Gypsy Rose Lee. Now anyone who has ever fooled around in the shallow end of our trade will know that the best ideas are both simple and silly. What you don't want is an idea that comes with a list of people to interview and questions to ask them. As we all know, it's much better just to go along and see what happens. Find Gypsy Rose Lee? You couldn't get much simpler, could you? Or much sillier.

Practically the first thing I saw on the promenade was a sign outside a gypsy fortune-teller's booth that yelled: 'Read what Colin Dunne Wrote about Me in the Daily Mirror.' That was from an earlier visit. What I had said about her was that when it came to second-sight, she was in serious need of bifocals, but somehow that bit seemed to have been omitted from the cutting.

Where the soothsayers were spot on was that they saw a skinny Yorkshireman with a fat wallet heading their way, and soon it would be stripped bare. If you really want to get rid of your money quickly, this was on a par with playing poker with Sid Williams.

Nowhere could I see Gypsy Rose Lee. On Blackpool prom, they were all called Petulengro, which apparently is the Romany version of Smith, and they were all accustomed to dealing with the world's leading glitterati. Outside their booths, beneath photos of famous faces, they assured Bruce Willis that he'd got a TV biggie coming up, that Liz Taylor had health problems, and Warren Beatty was restless. What's more, these stars of that time hadn't even had to extend their palms. These were free samples. For me, they weren't quite so free. The crystal ball was £50 even then, and that was without broadband.

A five got me a quick palm-reading and my future was laid before me. Money, success, health and happiness were heading my way in embarrassing profusion, so were grandchildren – nine at least – and I would be going over water. Not bad, eh? And that was long before we even knew about Ryanair. So far I've got only five grandchildren, but I've had a word with my kids about it and they're going to try again.

The gypsies predicted a long life with good health which, as they said, was better than a long life with poor health. And better still than having perfect health when you're dead.

Would this be in the magazine, they wanted to know. Yes, I assured them; you can buy it at W H Petulengro's.

I continued the search at Epsom on Derby Day where the racecourse was lined with Lees: Harriet Lee, Maria Lee, Nancy Lee, Betsy Lee, and probably a Robert E, if you looked hard enough. According to their posters, they'd made some astonishing predictions. They'd told the former Prince of Wales that he'd be crowned but would never be king. They'd told John Lennon what fate awaited him. They'd told Grace Kelly she would be a princess. Of course since this was all after the event, it was predicting the future with hindsight, which certainly makes for greater accuracy.

It was then I learnt the secret rallying call of the ancient Romanies. Wave a wallet in the air and they're all around you in less time than it takes to bake a hedgehog. They all gazed into my eyes and said I was clearly a gen'l'man who was generous with money. Like their sisters in Blackpool, they too had had all the stars in. 'Like that Judith Chandler.' Did she perhaps mean Raymond Chalmers, the well-known thriller writer and TV presenter?

But the best, the one who was real value for Rothermere money, was old Betsy, who crooned: 'Many's the sorrowful hour you've had and many's the crooked road you've travelled.' She must have been with a touring company production of Macbeth. Or reading my expenses.

As I was picking my way through the line of shining Mercedes behind the caravans, a shirtless man who was no bigger than a furniture van beckoned me over and said he earnestly hoped I wouldn't be writing anything unfavourable about the fortune-tellers.

As he said this, he ran a plastic comb through his chest hair, a surprisingly intimidating gesture.

I looked around for Bradshaw, my fearless photographic companion, and saw he was moving away rather faster than the nag I'd backed in the 2.30. He'd seen the future and he didn't think much of it.

Whenever you hear those occupying lower ranks of journalism presume to rate their officer class, you must remember that there is an unseen influence at work here. It's not so much about the intelligence, creativity and flair rating of the editors: it really comes down to whether or not they used my stuff. So when I say that Peter Stephens on the *Evening Chronicle* in Newcastle, the Freeman-Price team at the Manchester *Mirror*, or Larry Lamb and Nick Lloyd at the *Sun*, were of the journo-genius class, you've got to allow for the fact that they put me in the paper day after day. If I rave less about the Molloy-Hagerty and Kelvin-Greenslade double-acts at the *Mirror* and *Sun* respectively, I am possibly influenced by the memory that they were able to survive for weeks without reading my by-line. Inexplicable, I know.

Even so, when I repeatedly say that the team that produced *YOU* magazine was the best I ever encountered in half-a-century of non-stop typing, you've got to bear in mind that they commissioned me almost every week, sent me on the sort of stories I dreamed about, and then kept stuffing fat cheques through my letterbox.

That's all true. Equally it's true that newsagents reported their customers were stealing the magazine out of the *Mail on Sunday* and slipping it between the pages of the *Sunday Times*. So it wasn't just my vanity. Well, not completely.

With Nick Gordon and Felicity Hawkins running it, and Jonathan Bouquet, John Koski and John Chenery doing the commissioning, *YOU* mag was simply the wittiest and most original editorial team I ever met.

Their idea was that if it's fun to write, it's fun to read, which beats *Honi Soit* as a motto, hands down.

Bradshaw didn't always escape quite so easily. When we went to spend a little time with Katy Cropper in Wensleydale, he was left – okay, we were both left – in need of intensive care. Raucous, warm-hearted, riotously funny and startlingly pretty, Katy had won television's *One Man and His Dog* and toured the country shows with her travelling circus of dogs, ducks, sheep and pony. When we found her in the Moorcock Inn at Garsdale Head, she picked up a large gin and warned both of us: 'Don't try to drink with me.'

With my three-drink capacity, I thought then I must careful. Bradshaw, always the macho smoothie, gave the forgiving smile of man who's been around a bit (everywhere from El Vino to Vagabonds, not to mention the Florida bars of the *Enquirer*) but doesn't like to boast. He certainly wasn't unduly alarmed by... ahem, a shepherdess. That was his first mistake. His second was promising to help her round up her animals for tomorrow's show at 5.30am.

I'd like to say that I'll never forget that evening. The truth is that I can hardly remember any of it.

There were gins. There were tonics. Large ones. Again and again. There was Katy tossing those black curls back as she belted out *Old Shep*. There were glasses of wine, well more like buckets really, in her cottage, once you'd fought your way through the letters, old bills, muddy wellies, silver cups, and designer clothes – this was a woman who had her hair cut by Toni and Guy in London or did it herself with sheep shears when at home. 'Shut up you daft buggers,' she shouted, as her dogs start barking. Then, another crisis: 'Bloody 'ell, I've got to clip me sheep's bottoms.'

Back in the pub, with her dog Trim sitting beside her, paw on bar, she declared she would never have children. 'You haven't seen what sheep go through,' she said. Then she began to tell us, and Bradshaw and I begged her to sing *Old Shep* – yet again.

In a dark Dales dawn the next morning, I was praying for death. Staggering with exhaustion, face a sick yellow, coughing piteously, Bradshaw, to his great credit, helped to round up her eight dogs, 19 ducks, five sheep (including a black one called Fergie and its lamb, Beatrice), and one pony in her truck and trailer. Bradshaw never did say whether he'd helped clip the sheep's bottoms, and I never liked to ask.

YOU magazine liked what Felicity called 'ripping yarns', and there were few more ripping than the aristocratic German family who, threatened by the advancing Russians in 1945, buried the family silver in a field near their mansion in Magdeburg and fled west. After the Wall came down, they went back to try to find it.

With Bradshaw yet again, I went to Bremen where, our stringer had assured us, they were expecting us and would relate the whole story. They did. Unfortunately they related it in German. They were the only Germans I have ever met who spoke no English. When Bradshaw and I walked in, Herr Shroeder and his wife sat at the table smiling, with an Anglo-German dictionary in front of them. It took all that day and most of the next to get the story: but it was good stuff.

Herr Shroeder was about six when the war ended and he could remember helping to wrap the silver in newspapers and put the goodies in a huge chest before dragging it down the field to bury. He knew exactly where: right next to the wooden stables. Unfortunately, when they got there the stables had long gone.

By chance, he managed to find an ancient parlour maid who could remember where the stables used to be. Sure enough, they unearthed dozens of huge silver cups and plates.

YOU also liked fly-on-the-wall pieces, which I always enjoyed doing. Real reporters like being up at the front, asking questions and demanding answers. Delicate little features creatures like me are better employed lurking and skulking on the fringes, which is the way to do wall-fly pieces.

At Al's car auction in South London, I lurked while Al himself sat behind barred windows. Experience had taught him to keep a little distance between himself and any disappointed customers. Although he was merely a middleman who took the entrance fee and commission, he had ended up in hospital with broken bones. There was the Austin Princess that was down at the front and had been levelled up by filling the boot with ready-mix concrete. The buyer had to get it out with a road drill.

The auctioneer's patter said it all. A battered Lada had lots of extras... 'pump-up tyres, see-through windows, opening doors.'

About once a fortnight, I'd be summoned to the Wodka restaurant just behind the *Mail* office, where Koski, Bouquet, Houlihan and Chenery would suggest a final polish to the last piece, hand out the brief for the next one, wave up the red wine and the hunters' stew, and – every once in a while – inflict a unilateral fee increase on me. It beat coal-face work.

It worked because they all knew exactly what the magazine wanted. Each idea was carefully worked out, and they matched stories to writers with infinite care. With a dream set-up like this, it seemed to me impossible for any writer to fail...

That's not quite true. Out of the scores of pieces I wrote over the years for them, only one failed to make it. I was paid for it, of course.

Do you think anyone would notice if I tried to flog it again? Once a freelance...

*

It was one of those dream jobs: a few days in the West Indies and a cracking story.

But you know how it is. You start thinking about the air fare and the huge hotel bill and all those daiquiris, and you know that there's no room for slip-ups here. Yours has got to be the best piece.

That was just going through my mind when, in the hotel reception – I hadn't even reached my room – I saw the very last thing you want to see under these circumstances.

Bill Greaves.

Don't get me wrong. Fine fellow, Bill. Excellent company, amusing chap, likes a glass. But he's one of that small group of hacks who's a fine reporter and a lovely writer. You could send him into the coal cellar wearing a blindfold and dark glasses and he'd come out with a superb colour piece. When it comes to writing, I don't even want to be in the same country as Bill, let alone on the same island.

This was Jamaica, where the *Antiques Road Show* was paying a visit. Frankly, it would have cheered me enormously to know that Bill was safely snuggling up to a pint in the Old Bell.

But he wasn't. He was here for *Radio Times*. I was there for *YOU* mag.

It certainly was a great story. Why the BBC had decided to go to a country where there are no antiques, there are no antique shops and no-one even knows what the word means was never satisfactorily explained. The one thing you can be sure of is that Auntie Beeb certainly wouldn't go halfway round the world just to give their guys a free jolly at the licence-payers' expense.

When the Beeb's experts set up their stalls for giving valuations, the queue stretched two miles down the road. The first problem was that the Jamaicans interpreted antique to mean anything over about three years old. And I mean anything. It looked like the left-overs from a church jumble sale. Pots, pans, kettles, hats, clothes, shoes, records, tables and chairs, more chipped than Chippendale.

One man plonked down a pair of shabby trainers. 'They're old,' he said, 'but they don't leak.'

Another said he'd like a valuation on his three-piece suite. 'We can't do home visits,' said the expert. 'No, man, I got it here,' he replied, pointing to the furniture loaded in the back of a wagon. The expert was struggling to put a price on 1960s uncut moquette but, anxious not to appear impolite, suggested it could be worth £100. The owner clapped in delight and held out his hand. 'I take it, man,' he said. He thought a valuation was an offer.

Simon Bull, the watch expert, had certainly attracted a huge haul of timepieces. 'I seem to have founded the Jamaican Museum of Broken Fold-up Alarm Clocks,' he said. It was a situation that called for a high level of diplomacy when Ian Pickford, the silver expert, was invited to value Captain Morgan's Treasure – the Jamaican equivalent of the Crown Jewels. Ian encountered a tricky problem. As the Jamaican army stood guard over the heaps of silver, shining yellow in the hot sun, he shook his head. Captain Morgan, the buccaneer who was said to have seized the silver, had died well before the German silversmith who made it was born. Crisis time.

With all eyes on him, Ian Pickford delivered a short but brilliant speech on the importance of the silver in their national history. 'What's the value, man?' several of them called out. He never hesitated. 'It's priceless,' he said, and their cheers swayed the coconuts in the trees.

This was paradise for we features folk. We were knee-deep in snappy quotes and humorous happenings, even in the evening in the hotel. Henry Wyndham, then the show's art expert, was leaning his six-foot-five frame against the bar to get down to my level to tell me about a conversation he'd had with one of the professional ladies in the hotel foyer. What they wore, which wasn't much, was short, tight, and designed to display rather than cover. Henry had asked one of the girls what she charged. One hundred. 'Is that US dollars or pounds?' he asked. US, she said. 'I am in the business of buying and selling,' he said, 'and that is a very serious over-valuation.'

I asked him if I could use the story. Thinking about possible embarrassment with wives and mothers, he asked me not to. Then, the next morning, he called me over to say that if I found it amusing I could use it. He later became chairman of Sotheby's, I believe.

That evening the High Commissioner had invited us all for dinner in the garden. We all buckled on our stiff shirts, wrestled with our hand-tied bows, and donned our travel-crumpled dinner jackets. By the light of lanterns, waiters dressed like 18th century bombardiers ferried in the wines and food and somewhere under the palm trees a small orchestra played. Henry Wyndham came in a blazer and – I'll swear I'm not mistaken – jeans and trainers. He offered no apology or explanation. The effect was immediate. We all felt ludicrously over-dressed. Eton... It never fails, does it?

One problem I have found is that when I slip into my memories like this of the *Mail on Sunday YOU* magazine, within about 20 seconds the room empties. I often wonder if there is some sort of connection.

Indeed, my golfing friend Russell Twisk, former editor of *Radio Times* and *Reader's Digest*, once paused on the 14th at Petersfield after hitting a particularly fine chip shot up the hill to the green. 'When you say Glory Days,' he asked, innocently, 'do you mean the days when they used your stuff?'

Why I play golf with a man capable of such demonic cruelty is quite beyond me.

I was still writing for the other magazines as well. Indeed one of them asked me to write about two of my most distinguished colleagues, James Whitaker and Harry Arnold, then royal reporters for the *Mirror* and the *Sun*.

It was a lovely piece to do. First, there was the contrast. James, never Jim, Harry, never Harold. With his tweed caps and sleeveless jackets, green wellies and country coats apparently fashioned from linoleum, the booming James was more royal than the royals. Son of a Kent greengrocer, five-foot six, slick-haired and dapper, Harry was more the cocky corporal, the cheeky chappie.

There was only one thing you needed to know about these two. Never stand between them and a story. You'd be trampled to death.

The peak of their careers came when James traced Charles and the pregnant Diana to an island retreat in the Bahamas. By diligent probing, he found out where they sunbathed. After measuring the distance along the coastline, he then crossed to another island and measured out the same distance.

At dawn the next morning he fought his way through the jungle to the spot he knew would give him a clear view of the royal couple. Jagged thorns and thick foliage ripped at his designer shirt until, dripping blood, he stepped into a clearing. In the sweltering gloom of the jungle, there was just enough light to make out a figure sitting on a log, smoking a cigarette. 'Morning James', said Harry Arnold. 'One egg or two for breakfast?' In the history of the tabloids, this was Stanley and Livingstone.

They'd both found the right place, and sure enough Charles and Di came out on to the beach. So who won?

'Harry wasn't to know,' said James, 'but I'd got a charter plane waiting to take me to Nassau. We beat him by two editions. Poor Harry.'

'James didn't realise,' said Harry, 'but I found a wire machine on the island and we wired our stuff back. Beat him by two editions. Poor James.'

They were, of course, both right. I'm not at all sure that it's not the perfect Fleet Street story.

In newspapers and magazines, there was a sense of an era coming to an end. The newspapers had moved to Docklands. Fleet Street was left to the bankers. In the Old Bell there was no Jim Davies or Harry Dempster, no Ed Vale or Tom Tullett in El Vino, no Charlie Catchpole or Roy Stockdill in the Wine Press. They'd all gone. Some to Docklands, some a little further. The trade-tested staff men, their substantial salaries bulked up by weekly injections of expenses, no longer packed the bars and restaurants. Instead, young men brought from the provinces on wages you wouldn't pay to a Filipina cleaner nibbled egg sandwiches at their desks.

One celebrity magazine paid what looked like recent school-leavers fifty quid a shot to do interviews, and then paid a real writer £200 to come in for a day and rewrite the lot. So they got 15 or 20 pieces for next to nothing.

Entirely by luck, for the moment, I was okay. Three or four magazines had enough work to keep me ticking over nicely, although I couldn't ignore the crash of falling circulations and the non-stop shrieks from the farewell parties.

With money left over from a crashed marriage, I had bought a small weekend cottage in a village in West Sussex, which had been pointed out to me by John Dodd. It was visiting the South Downs that gave me my next brilliant idea.

In all these years in journalism, I'd never been an editor. I'd never been a publisher. I'd never hired writers and artists. I'd never dealt with advertising and circulation. This was my chance to experience them all. I would open my own magazine. I would show them how it was done.

I'd never been simultaneously on the edge of bankruptcy and a nervous breakdown either...

Ah yes, that story in Jamaica with Bill Greaves. Who wrote the better piece? I'm afraid that question represents an intrusion into private grief. Push off.

*

10

Okay, we're nearly there. *The Life and Hard Times of a Happy Hack* is nearing the last lap. After all this time, I couldn't tell you how delighted I am to report that I have finally detected some sort of pattern in my working life ('career' would be pitching it a bit high, I think) which I think may also explain the meaning of the universe.

My personal journalistic journey, which took me more than 40 years, went from Waterhouse to Waterhouse.

That is, from Waterhouse, R, known only as Mr Waterhouse to me, first name unused, deputy editor, chief reporter, and sub of the *Craven Herald* in the Yorkshire Dales, where I first laid my fingers on a two-cwt Underwood...

To Waterhouse, Keith, who bought me my first drink in the Stab, the *Mirror* pub in London; one half of bitter.

It's neat, isn't it? Two more contrasting bookends to a working life you could hardly imagine. The first Waterhouse went on his way some years back, and now Keith has also left us, which sort of takes it full circle.

Can we just for a moment rewind back to the young Dunne, the skinny spotty one, working for the first Waterhouse? Like most of us starting out, he had no idea where he would end up, but he wasn't short of role models.

Should he follow the tall and charming Ron Evans, who I remember eating a daffodil sandwich at the cricket club dinner. Why? He was bored.

Drunk? Possibly, but it doesn't do to be censorious. Or how about Bill Freeman, who drove his new Ford Popular for 50 yards on the Draughton Road? What's so special about that? Well, the car was upside down at the time, thus founding the Holy Rollers Club. And what about Don Mosey who had the nerve to marry a girl called Josephine (Josie Mosey?).

Heroic figures all, men of daring and imagination to a 16-year-old school-leaver like me. They showed me the way, too. Just to prove my admiration was not misplaced, they all went on to even greater triumphs. Via the *Telegraph and Argus* in Huddersfield and the *Sunday Times* in London, Ron became boss of Harlech Television. Via the *Yorkshire Post* and the *Sunday Express*, Bill became editor of the *Sunday Mirror* in Manchester. Via the *Yorkshire Evening Post* and the *Daily Express* in Manchester, Don became a commentator with the BBC's celebrated *Test Match Special* team. He was the only man I ever knew who was brave enough to call Fred Trueman by his middle name – Seward.

But of course the one I should've been watching was Bill Mitchell, the quietly smiling chap who moved a few miles up the road to join *The Dalesman* magazine. Why did I miss him? Perhaps because he didn't smoke, didn't drink, and – to the best of my knowledge – never smuggled a girl out of the Town Hall dance and across the road into the office to get his face slapped.

Bill was also a Methodist, which – and here I speak as the owner of the most slapped face in the Dales – was not one of my ambitions. And, let's face it, *The Dalesman*, quaint and cosy as I saw it, didn't fit the snap-brim, poker-playing, bourbon-drinking image I was hoping for.

Yet 40 years later, standing amid the smoking ruins of old Fleet Street, it was Bill Mitchell who came to mind. After all the politics, manoeuvring and back-stabbing of the nationals, what could be better than life on a cosy little countryside magazine? From my weekend cottage in West Sussex, I looked out towards the South Downs.

Inspired by *The Dalesman*, I would start my own magazine right here.

I hadn't been so excited since Mr Waterhouse first put my initials on a review of Settle Amateur Operatics' appalling production of *The Desert Song*.

This was a wonderful time, dreaming up my magazine, planning the content and the style – everyday stuff to the Molloys, the MacKenzies and the Lambs, but new to me. It would be defined by all the things it wasn't: no politics, no celebrities, no crime, no glossy gossip, and none of the bubbling malice of the tabloids. Like *The Dalesman*, it would be A5, pocket-sized. A traditional country magazine. Diaries from farmers and countrywomen, history, natural history, lots of humour, with a strong dash of nostalgia. Real people; real life. Readers would wallow in its warm affection. *Downs Country* – that's what I'd call it.

Oddly enough, the *Mail on Sunday YOU* magazine, which liked my words almost as much as I liked their cheques, was still flourishing. What I didn't realise at the time was that my future, and that of several other innocents, was decided on the putting green at the Northcliffe Golfing Society tournament. A tall, blonde, athletic Australian woman sank a brilliant putt to win the cup for Lord Rothermere's team. Next thing, Nick Gordon, editor of *YOU* had gone, and Dee Nolan was in the chair. Lesson for young journos: forget Pitman's, get out and practise on the putting green.

Her first job for me, via John Koski, was to interview Anne Robinson. Now I'd known Annie as a near-neighbour in Derbyshire when she was married to Charlie Wilson. I'd known her partner-manager-husband, John Penrose, when he was a young reporter on the *Daily Mirror*. At that time, I was living near Tunbridge Wells and John used to visit the town occasionally to see a female freelance who made a living writing for *Forum* (and occasionally the *Mail*) about surgical enhancements to her body and their effects on her social life. Penrose, I understood, was helping her tighten up her prose.

By this time, Penrose and Robinson were halfway up Celebrity Mountain, I'd interviewed her before for magazines, so it should be no problem. Exactly John's phrase when I rang him. So I was astonished when he rang back later to say Annie wouldn't do it. For me? No, I wasn't the problem. She wouldn't do it for Dee. I breathed in deeply and reached for a pen. I'd need a note of this. Why exactly was she refusing an interview for Dee?

Apparently Annie had somehow formed the impression that when Dee and Penrose were colleagues on the *Mirror* they had worked so closely together they had momentarily merged. A ridiculous idea. Complete nonsense. Penrose was a man of legendary celibacy, a man who had never shown the slightest interest in tall blondes and wouldn't dream of sullying his desk with one.

And Dee too. Although her grip on the putter had attracted some admiration, she was a woman of impeccable reputation.

There I was, stuck in the middle. The weakest link. It's a wonder nobody thought of turning it into a television quiz show. I told Koski. He said: 'Bloody hell, I can't tell Dee that,' but I never did discover what he did tell her.

242

So there's the truth. If, even at this late date, I can help to save the reputations of two fine journalists and bring peace to the tortured mind of a telly presenter, then these jottings have not been in vain.

Meanwhile, *Downs Country* was coming on apace. I placed ads in several local papers looking for writers and illustrators. An avalanche of mail hit my Sussex cottage. I set off driving around the south to assemble my talented team who were going to fill my magazine at ten quid a go. Slowly it built up. A farmer to write a diary… a naturalist to do notes…a dainty lady dealer for the antiques page… a designer for an international pharmaceutical firm who loved drawing old country gates… a young man who could compile a crossword full of local references… an historian who could bring country houses to life…

Local enquiries steered me towards a man who used to sell ads for the local papers. He'd look after that for me.

What had been the dining room in my cottage near Midhurst became the office. One second-hand desk £10. One boot-sale chair £5. One rickety filing-cabinet £2.

So far so good. But it struck me that for all this flying around and the adrenalin rush of putting the magazine together, I had no idea how to get it to the shops. Apparently what I needed was a distributor. I approached one, and to my amazement discovered that I had to audition in front of them and make out a case for my magazine. If I convinced them, they'd take it around the wholesalers; if I didn't, they wouldn't.

After some hesitation, they decided to accept it. But they didn't like the pocket size because it wouldn't slot in with the others on the shelves and could easily get lost. Because it was so much against the tide of celeb and glam mags, they weren't totally convinced it would sell. But, no matter, they took it on.

Partners came and went. Originally, I'd planned it with Joe Houlihan, one of *YOU*'s commissioning editors. He backed out when he was offered a tempting job at LWT. It was the start of a distinguished career in television where he is to this day. After Joe left, an accountant came in, then backed out. One or two others showed an interest, then backed off. By this time I had become so obsessed with the idea that I think I was incapable of sharing it with anyone.

It was my baby. It was also my £10,000 backing it.

What was the problem? *The Dalesman* sold 70,000, most on subscription (which meant they kept all the money) and it was stuffed with ads. If it worked in Yorkshire then surely my magazine, tailored exactly to the more sophisticated and wealthy audience in Sussex, couldn't fail.

Could it?

Feeling a little guilty, I explained to my eager contributors, most of whom had never been published before, that I could pay only £5 for a one-page piece, £10 for two pages. But I'd signed an awful lot of cheques by the time the first issue was ready to go. A good friend put me on to Sue Miller, a designer who'd worked on major titles like *Good Housekeeping*, and who would do the design and put it on disk for £1,200. A not-quite-so-good friend put me on to a printer – that was going to cost around £5,000.

My £10,000 was already slimming like a weight-watcher. No matter. We'd soon be up to 70,000 sales, the ads would flood in. Oh yes; the books... Diana, friend, neighbour and book-keeper, agreed to do a day a week to keep an eye on the accounts and the post when I was up in London.

'Tell me,' said my accountant Ian Spring, 'I'm interested in your earnings pattern. At the moment you come up the A3 to earn money, then go back down to lose it all again.' He had a point.

This was the early 1990s. Around that time, Dee Nolan made the big announcement. *YOU* would cease to be the best general magazine since *Picture Post*; it was to be a women's magazine.

Newspapers were now encroaching on the colour ads that had been the exclusive province of the colour supplements. *YOU* would be left with the ads for elasticated trousers, nylon sheets, and pendants with astrological signs which would then drive away the glossy upmarket ads. Downward spiral... closure. There was a personal factor too. The rumour was that Nick, much admired as an editor with the golden touch, didn't have many friends close to the throne at Associated.

Even since that winning putt, Dee had been working quietly with David English on producing a new woman's mag while Felicity Hawkins kept the old *YOU* going. Felicity left to become deputy editor of the *Sunday Mirror* with oversight of their magazine. And *YOU* did indeed become a woman's mag, which guaranteed its survival.

Sadly, it didn't guarantee mine. Writers who'd enjoyed fees of up to £2,000 for several years were informed the fee was now £650.

It really was all over. The revolution that had swept the offices down to Docklands or out to Kensington and whisked scores of stunned hacks off to early retirement, redundancy, or a job driving taxis in Tonbridge, had caught up with me at last. After two weeklies, three regional dailies, two national staff jobs and writing for everyone from *The Times* to *Women's Own* as a freelance, four decades of arranging and re-arranging the 26 letters of the alphabet into interesting shapes, I'd hit the buffers.

Luckily, I had my own magazine...

*

Did I really say that? 'Luckily, I had my own magazine'? Hand me the tissues while I dry my streaming cheeks – half laughter, half grief. 'Luckily', indeed.

Although, I suppose, that was the way it felt when I saw the van chugging round the village green to deliver the first copies. My West Sussex cottage is just off the green, so I had to push my wheelbarrow down the lane to take delivery of them. I expect Rupert Murdoch does much the same.

In the kitchen, I was fizzing with excitement as I broke open the first box.

There it was, smiling up at me, the first issue of my own magazine: *Downs Country*, masthead above a charming cartoon illustration of a village. Then, as I flicked through the pages, delight turned to despair. The print was so faint some pages were quite difficult to read. The pictures were grey. The entire magazine looked as though it had been printed with dirty bath water.

After all my efforts, this was shattering. I would've wept then if I hadn't been afraid of washing the print away with my tears.

After all that effort, driving hundreds of miles to find contributors, coaxing and encouraging writers and artists, then all the endless hours of writing and re-writing, chopping to length and headlines, all with the thrill of seeing it come together...

For this disaster. Only the cat's speedy reflexes and years of practice saved it from my boot.

By the time I'd got to bed I'd decided I would have to abandon the whole enterprise.

The next morning I was having breakfast, wondering what I was going to do with three boxes of magazines that appeared to have been printed in invisible ink, when the telephone rang. It was a woman. She'd got the magazine. She'd read it (she must have had the eyesight of a sniper). She liked it. In fact, she loved it. So did the next 20 or so calls, who all wanted to know when the next one was out and how they could subscribe.

The next day the letters started coming. Again, they all thought it was wonderful. They spoke of its gentle charm and intelligent wit and what a change it was from everything else on the news stands.

I realised what had happened. Normal readers don't care about the production values: all that matters to them is the content, and they were more than happy with that.

From wrist-slitting despair to open-the-champers joy in half-a-day. Come to think of it, that describes how the next six years went. I'd look with pride at my little magazine slowly moving upwards. Then I'd look at my bank balance, rapidly moving downwards. The Agony and the Ecstasy: My Life in Publishing.

Guess which one won in the end. No, don't. Let me tell you.

In the meantime, there was the second issue to put together.

Encouraged by the response, I set about it with great enthusiasm. I found the cartoonist to do the cover behind the bar of the Elsted Inn, just up the road. Malcolm was an architect in West London who had a great gift for *Beano*-style cartoons. Anthony Howard I found at the Meridian Television studios where his *Country Ways* series was a lovely piece of lyrical filming. His brother Phillip was well-known for his column in *The Times* and their father, Peter, had been assistant editor of the *Daily Express* half a century earlier – he was also the captain and scrum-half of the England rugby team.

An intelligent and cultured man, Anthony had developed a distaste for modern media, so of course he loved *Downs Country*. For the next six years he wrote a column for me for which he would never accept a fee.

Given the cynical nature of our trade, I was surprised by the way several hacks sprang to my aid. Kit Kenworthy and John Dodd, both former *Sun* writers, pitched in with excellent pieces. So too did John Koski, still with *YOU* mag. Charles Lyte, former gardening columnist for the *Mirror*, came up with an off-beat page. He could justify it financially with the thought that the fee, pitiful though it was, could be seen as a decent bottle of wine. Liz Gill, ex-*Express*, ex-*Times*, came up with one of her superb light pieces.

My days with *YOU* magazine were coming to an end. Of all my old chums, only John Koski remained. Jonathan Bouquet had moved to the *Observer*, Joe Houlihan was rocketing up the ladder in television, and John Chenery (ex-husband of Amanda Platell: and whatever happened to her?) ended up in Canada.

One of my last jobs for them was to interview Neil Lyndon, a gifted writer and columnist. He had published a book that calmly made the argument that – with early pensions and longer lives – modern women were perhaps not so savagely persecuted as we'd been told. He was buried by a howling mob of testicle-tearing feminists. Oddly, *YOU* magazine, now edited by Dee Nolan, didn't use the piece.

Neil was fascinated by my attempt at publishing. He had once bought a weekly newspaper in Suffolk, a venture that ended in disaster. Seeing my struggle, he would sometimes turn up on the doorstep at breakfast, having travelled all the way from Suffolk, to help. That, I thought, was true generosity. Even better, he wrote a series about his younger days living in mid-Sussex. It immediately created a mystery. He mentioned all his fellow pupils at village schools around Cowfold. Several of them contacted me to say that, although his stories were all true, they had no memory of a Lyndon. Tentatively, I asked Neil about this. 'You'll see,' he said. 'The explanation will be in the last word of the last piece.'

It slowly unrolled. His father was a successful show-biz agent in London, who became embroiled in a funny-money scandal and he went to jail. His wife, Neil and his brother, had to do a midnight flit and took her maiden name of Lyndon. Until then – the last sentence read – he had been called Neil Barnacle.

It was a wonderful series. We published it as a small book and at the launch in the pub in Cowfold all his childhood friends turned up. 'Good to see you, Barney,' they said, a nickname he hadn't heard for more than 40 years.

Neil's only fee for this entire profitless endeavour was the occasional pint. But the only writing he had ever done unpaid became quite seriously rewarded when the *Daily Telegraph* ran a large chunk from his book and paid him a large chunk in return. Which proves something (I'm not quite sure what) quite conclusively.

I wrote the Editor's Notebook, a light piece at the front. More often than not, I wrote most of the letters' pages, frequently picking fights with myself. I would usually have to do a couple of interview pieces. Several of the contributors' columns had to be re-written or at least given a final polish, then the whole lot had to be put on disk ready for the designer. One way or another, I tapped in more than 20,000 words for each issue.

I managed to dig out an excellent advertising man for the eastern area. For the rest, I had a series: three thieves who made off with the cash, two drug addicts who converted it into something injectible, a whole raft of incurable liars, one agoraphobic who tried to sell without leaving home, and one man who went potty. He rang me from the psychiatric ward to say he was still on top of the job.

The trade – that is distributors, retailers and advertisers – said quarterly mags didn't work: no continuity. So I upped it to six times a year. They still shook their heads. Up again to 10 issues a year. Yet somehow it wasn't making an impact in the newsagents.

It was a mystery. Some would take two or three copies, often stuffed away in a corner beneath the Benson and Hedges. Yet whenever I tried to discuss it with them they fled into the back room.

I even offered them a plastic stand so they could put the magazine on the counter. They weren't interested.

Gradually, I found that the only way forward was to promote *Downs Country* myself. With my little plastic display stands, I persuaded all sorts of outlets, from pubs to antique shops, to sell it. Soon I had dozens of outlets. The only snag was that I had to race round re-supplying them and collecting the cash. The other good news was that, right from the start, subscriptions had arrived in a steady flow. Scores became hundreds, hundreds became thousands, and Diana, my neighbour/friend/bookkeeper had to set up a database to service them all.

What we needed was more promotion. I dragged myself off around the Women's Institutes with a jokey little talk about how a hopeless businessman like me tried to start a magazine. At the first meeting, a hearty lady asked me about my fee for the talk. I said I didn't know there was a fee. 'Hmm,' she said. 'You're not much of a businessman, are you?'

So a couple of nights a week I would be rushing around the south coast talking about *Downs Country*, and selling a few at the same time.

At least, as a hack myself, I was able to drum up some publicity. I slipped pieces into most of the local papers, bobbed up on local radio, and even on regional television when Mike Vestey did a couple of pieces.

To my great delight, the *Daily Telegraph* did a full page piece. It was written – beautifully, of course – by the talented Elizabeth Dunn, who came down with her husband Peter, who'd written for several of the broadsheets. I remembered him from the *Yorkshire Post*, a lifetime earlier. They liked the idea so much that they launched a similar mag in Dorset.

It was heady stuff. Between the writing and the re-writing, the in-putting and the rounding up of material, I was in a whirlwind of non-stop action. At the keyboard by 6am, often I'd still be rushing around at 10pm.

Another possible partner arrived. Jim Dalrymple, my former colleague from *Mirror-Record* days, came down to see the operation. This, he said, was exactly what he'd always wanted. Something to call his own. What was I doing that day? I showed him. I was writing, then running off, 140 letters to send out with the magazine to pubs and hotels, suggesting they should take out subscriptions for their customers' enjoyment. Then I had to sign them all. Then I had to address the envelopes. Then I had to take them to the post office.

Jim went grey. 'Haven't you got someone to do things like that?' Yes, I told him: me.

Jim, who'd recently won the Writer of the Year award and who'd just written a much-praised piece on Mike Tyson for the *Sunday Times* colour supplement, slipped quietly away. Wise man.

By this time, my old world seemed like a half-forgotten foreign land. Whereas once I might've been worrying whether I could remember the Turkish for blank bill, now I found my problems were getting a crossword with local clues and someone to compile a country quiz. Restaurant bills lay in front of me unclaimed.

I met Timothy Benn, originally one of the Benn Brothers publishing company in Kent. He'd taken over *The Dalesman*, so now we had a man who lived in Tonbridge running a magazine in the Dales, and a Dalesman running a magazine in the Downs. How about a swap? He thought not.

Every day there were new subscribers. To my surprise I found I had branched out into a tea-shop. From studying the illustration of the cottage on the contents page, readers would track me down. 'We've come to the home of *Downs Country*,' they would announce. They were mostly ladies in their middle years, with sun-hats and West Highland Whites. I learnt to stock up on the Earl Grey.

What wasn't quite such great fun was the way the money I pumped into the magazine slowly drained away. Although my round of private sales was flourishing, in the newsagents it was static. Slowly, I began to see why.

Some magazines you see everywhere: some, like mine, hardly at all. Eventually I got to know a man who knew that side of the business. How could I ensure that *Downs Country* got into all the shops and supermarkets?

'For that to happen,' he told me, 'money has to change hands.' Voice trembling, I asked how much. 'More than you've got.'

I sat in my office that night and read through the file of letters from readers saying how much they loved *Downs Country*. I looked at the list of 2,500 subscribers. Without someone to sell ads and without a real presence in the shops, it didn't mean a thing.

I was beaten. After six years of 18-hour days and seven-day weeks I was exhausted, I'd lost a stone in weight (for me, about a quarter of the total) and more money than I ever want to think about. It was all over – the course I'd set out on, nearly 50 years earlier. That was the day I saw Bill Freeman come into the Carla Beck Milk Bar in Skipton, his riding mac swirling, on a break from covering the magistrates court for the *Craven Herald*. I thought then what a great job that was. And now I'd reached the end.

After 32 issues, *Downs Country* was done. Only one copy had made a profit: £32.24. We broke open the tap water that night, I can tell you. I was done too. Call me daft – you wouldn't be the first – but I never for a minute regretted it.

In a trade where we all become very familiar with the Two Imposters, this was undeniably a Disaster. That's the odd thing. It still feels like a Triumph to me.

In a rare moment of insight, I was right that morning in the milk bar. It was a wonderful job. What I didn't know, however, was that I'd just slipped under the net. I'd caught the last 50 years of newspapers at their best, and Old Fleet Street at its finest and funniest. That was my great good fortune.

I wasn't exactly a pioneer. From country weekly to EC4 was a well-trodden path at that time. Most of the sophisticated wits in El Vino could, if pushed, type out a wedding form or do a couple of pars on a lost dog. They'd be less enthusiastic about standing outside a church in the rain, gathering names of funeral mourners – but they'd know how.

It will never happen again. Someone really ought to put it all down on paper, you know. Unless, of course, that's what I've just done.

As for me, I have only one real regret. If I'd followed my sister's other boy-friend (the one with the café) 50 years ago, by now I'd probably be the world's best cheese-on-toast chef.

Now there's a real book. And after all, books about food sell better than books about journalism.

###

The Best Of Vincent Mulchrone

A lifetime of wit and observation of the folly and splendour of his fellow humans by the Daily Mail's finest reporter.

ISBN: 978-0-9558238-1-7

Cassandra

At His Finest And Funniest

By William Neil Connor

ISBN: 978-0-9558238-2-4

Forgive Us Our Press Passes

By Ian Skidmore

Revised and expanded, 2008

ISBN: 978-0-9558238-0-0

 Revel Barker Publishing

www.booksaboutjournalism.com

Lightning Source UK Ltd.
Milton Keynes UK
22 October 2010

MATHS

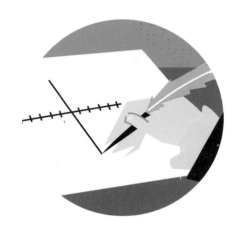

A CRASH COURSE

MATHS

BRIAN CLEGG & DR. PEET MORRIS

IVY PRESS

First published in the UK in 2019 by
Ivy Press
An imprint of The Quarto Group
The Old Brewery, 6 Blundell Street
London N7 9BH, United Kingdom
T (0)20 7700 6700 **F** (0)20 7700 8066
www.QuartoKnows.com

British Library Cataloguing-in-Publication Data
A catalogue record for this book is available
from the British Library

ISBN: 978-1-78240-863-5

This book was conceived, designed and produced by
Ivy Press
58 West Street, Brighton BN1 2RA, United Kingdom

Publisher Susan Kelly
Editorial Director Tom Kitch
Art Director James Lawrence
Project Editor Angela Koo
Design JC Lanaway
Illustrator Beady Eyes
Design Manager Anna Stevens
Visual Concepts Paul Carslake
Series Concept Design Michael Whitehead

Printed in China

10 9 8 7 6 5 4 3 2 1

INTRODUCTION

We don't know how the basics of math were first devised, as it predates written language and history. The simple ability to be aware that there is a difference between, say, one object and two is likely to have been innate in human ancestors long before *Homo sapiens* emerged around 200,000 years ago. We can say this because it has been shown that dogs have this kind of awareness. When a trick is performed on a dog so that it thinks that two items of food have been put in its bowl, but in reality there is only one, it does the canine equivalent of a double take.

Such an awareness of numbers without any concept of counting, then, seems to have been with us for a long time. However, it is likely to have been when humans began to have assets, to trade, and to build, that a more concrete form of math became necessary. The specific trigger was likely the formation of early cities and the development of writing—without notation, math could only ever be trivial.

The earliest mathematics

The oldest example we have of math being written down is 6,000 years ago, in the city-state of Uruk, in present-day Iraq. Uruk was at the center of the Sumerian civilization, and with unprecedented numbers of people living together, the need to keep track of foodstuffs and other tradable goods was key. And as buildings became more sophisticated, measurements were needed for their construction. However, the people of Uruk were yet to equate abstract numbers with collections of objects. Today, we can deal with a concept like "four" as a number and apply it equally to anything from the Four Horsemen of the Apocalypse to the four legs on a dog. But in Uruk, the inhabitants considered some objects to be so different that they needed alternative representation. So, while they used the same numbers to count live animals and dried fish, they used a different set for cheese, grain, and fresh fish.

As civilizations became more established, new concepts arose that were increasingly removed from reality, notably in Greece, India, and China. Later, this sophisticated form of math would move via the Arabic-speaking countries to Europe, and eventually the US. Only with the step back from pragmatic application to thinking about what was actually happening in the math itself was it possible for math in the modern sense to be born. The Sumerians knew, for example, that a right (or right-angled) triangle—so useful when surveying a piece of land—had a ratio of sides such that if one of the shorter sides was three units and another four, then the longest side would be five units. They knew this from observation, but proofs that this was exactly the case for all right triangles came much later.

Building the mathematical toolkit

For many uses, the math developed over 2,000 years ago largely serves today. No one needs topology to deal with the basics of everyday life. But from the sixteenth century onward, the possibilities for applying math blossomed, becoming applicable not just to reality, but to what might be—"probability," the mathematics of chance, for instance, would transform our ability to think about the future.

Early mathematicians had dealt only with futures where there were distinct rules. Given, say, a known rate of interest, it was possible to calculate exactly how much money you might have in a bank account in a year's time (if nothing was added or removed). These were very artificial conditions. The real world was full of unknowns. But, as US defense secretary Donald Rumsfeld would famously observe, there are both known unknowns and unknown unknowns. Probability would prove an ideal mechanism for dealing with known unknowns. We don't know what will come up when we toss a coin, but we do know that, with a fair coin, there's a 50 percent chance of a head and a 50 percent chance of a tail.

Sometimes a new field of math opens up when there is a clear application. In the seventeenth century, Isaac Newton and Gottfried Leibniz devised the techniques now collectively known as "calculus" in order to deal with specific problems—how to work out, for example, the distance traveled when a moving body is accelerating. However, in many cases, mathematicians were simply happy exploring their mathematical universe without any thought of an application. Yet surprisingly often, such apparently pointless work would later have major practical applications.

All manner of mathematical oddities have eventually proved useful. "Imaginary numbers"—the square root of negative numbers—were devised long before applying them; the sixteenth-century Italian mathematician Girolamo Cardano commented that an imaginary number was "as subtle as it is useless." Yet by the nineteenth century they were widely employed by both physicists and down-to-earth electrical engineers, and continue to be used today.

Another example is the importance of math in the history of computing. Originally, computers were people. Up to the 1940s, the term largely applied to individuals who performed manual calculations with pencil and paper. The potential advantages of mechanizing the work of a computer were clear for centuries, and there were early attempts with mechanical calculators, but electronic computers—first developed in the 1940s—took the mathematical content to a whole new level.

Math and the digital era

Three huge mathematical leaps were required to develop the electronic infrastructure at the heart of the modern world. The first was using binary digits: no longer working with everything from 0 to 9, but simply with 0s and 1s. Humans could, of course, have always done their mathematics this way—but it would have been tedious in the extreme. However, for a computer there is no disadvantage, and a huge positive. The values 0 and 1 can be represented very easily by physical things. A switch that is on or off. A device that either has an electrical charge or no charge. Either/or situations are easily represented by electronic components.

Secondly, computers are designed around mathematical logic. Those same 0 or 1 values can also be considered as false or true. And in the nineteenth century, a mathematical approach to logic had already been developed. This would underpin the architecture of the innards of computers: they are, in essence, huge logic engines, connecting together vast numbers of very simple logic "gates"— mechanisms for making logical combinations or transformations of those 0s and 1s.

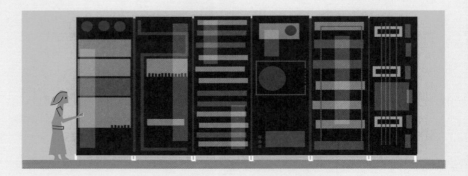

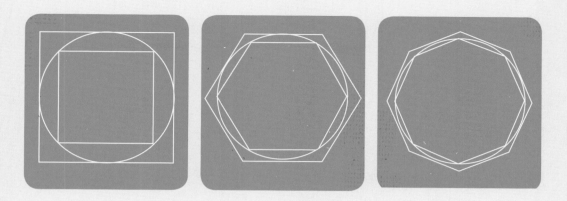

The final mathematical component came when electronics moved from vacuum tubes to solid-state devices such as transistors. The design of such devices required an understanding of quantum mechanics, the physics of the very small particles that, for example, make up matter. And quantum mechanics, like most modern physics, is extremely mathematical. Not only did solid-state design require an understanding of the tools of higher mathematics, quantum physics has probability at its heart. Without a profound understanding of mathematics, the modern computer could never have been constructed.

The unreasonable effectiveness of math

It's a sad truth that math has the reputation of being "difficult." Part of the problem is that many of us simply don't speak the language. To a mathematician, an equation is a compact, efficient way to put across a relationship that would be far less comprehensible in words. But to many of us, the merest sign of x's, y's, and other symbols is an impenetrable mess that our eyes bounce off.

There is a story that the physicist Eugene Wigner told in a paper exploring the "unreasonable effectiveness of mathematics in the natural sciences." Wigner describes two school friends, meeting for the first time after leaving school. One works in mathematics and shows his friend a paper he has written on population change. The mathematician tries to explain what all his strange symbols mean in this document containing very few words.

His friend is doubtful. How can such a bunch of squiggles bear any resemblance to what actual people do in the real world? The mathematician, trying to reassure his friend, points to a π symbol in the equations. "That's pi. You know what that is? The ratio of the circumference of a circle to its diameter." The friend shakes his head. "Now I know you're messing with me. What has the population got to do with the circumference of a circle?"

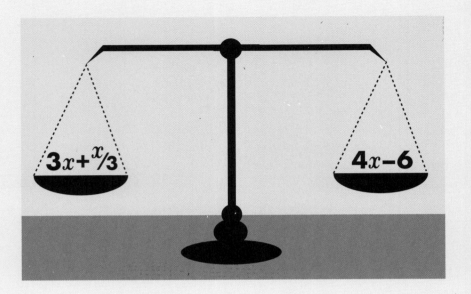

Math is, in the end, an abstract discipline operating in its own world. Although it may have started with a degree of one-to-one correspondence between, say, numbers and physical objects, it soon set off on its own path with the introduction of concepts like negative numbers, which it's harder to envisage as real objects, or irrational numbers, such as the square root of 2. An irrational number is one that can't be represented by a ratio of any two whole "real" numbers, making it much harder to link directly to reality in the mind.

In math, anything goes, as long as it is consistent. Mathematicians can decide that 1 +1 = 3 or that there are 27,319 dimensions of space. However, as Wigner points out, despite its arbitrary nature, mathematics has an apparently unreasonable ability to be supremely useful in a real world where we can't make up our own rules.

It would be impossible to overstress how important mathematics is to the modern, technology-driven world. Of course, that's obviously the case when we buy something or do our banking, but it's far more. Physics, the science behind most technology, became utterly dependent on mathematics in the nineteenth century, and is now often nearly indistinguishable from pure mathematics. And, as we have seen, the information and computing technology at the heart of today's modern economy and life is entirely driven by mathematics. We see the physical computer or cell phone—but inside the digital technology it is the manipulation of numbers and logic that makes everything happen. Living in a digital world inherently means living in a mathematical world.

The biggest problem we have with math is the way that it's taught in school. Once we've learned the basics that we'll need for the everyday handling of money and measurements, we go on to study the kind of math that will be useful if we subsequently work in the sciences or engineering. But for the vast majority, this will never be the case—giving the impression that higher math is a waste of time. If we were provided with an engaging overview of what math is and what it can do, without having to solve simultaneous equations or prove geometric theorems, then far more of us might get the point of it. That's exactly what this book is designed to do.

This book is divided into four chapters, each covering a major developmental route in the topic, and containing 13 short articles. That's an article a week for a year—but feel free to consume them at your own speed. However you chose to look at it, though, this book takes a subject that can seem intimidating and makes it approachable. So let's get started with Chapter number 1 . . .

How to use this book

This book distills the world of mathematics into 52 manageable chunks, allowing you to skim-read or delve in a bit deeper. There are four chapters, each containing 13 topics, prefaced by biographies of key figures, alongside a timeline of significant milestones. The introduction to each chapter gives an overview of the key concepts you might need to navigate.

Each topic has three paragraphs.

The Main Concept provides a theory overview.

TRIGONOMETRY

THE MAIN CONCEPT | The relationship between angles and the length of sides of triangles is a natural extension of geometry, called "trigonometry," meaning "triangle measurement." Thinking of one of the angles in a right triangle, the "sine" of that angle is the ratio of the length of the opposite side to that of the hypotenuse (longest side). The "cosine" is the same measure but using the ratio of the third side to the hypotenuse. And the "tangent" is the ratio of the opposite side to the third side (you may be familiar with the "SOH CAH TOA" method of remembering this). These simple "functions" have proved useful in surveying, navigation (the example, with sextants), and astronomy. Trigonometry also enables triangulation—deducing distances by measuring the angles of triangles between known positions and a new point, which proved transformational for accurate map-making. However, the triangular definition of the trigonometric functions was limiting as it could only deal with angles up to 90 degrees. An extended definition imagines the triangle drawn in a circle with the right angle at the center. The hypotenuse is the radius and can be swept around the circle, giving values that oscillate periodically. This approach produces an alternative unit of angle, the "radian." Trigonometry was also extended out of the plane, using a sphere rather than a circle as the base.

DRILL DOWN | Once trigonometric functions were measured using a circle, it became possible to think of the size of an angle as the amount by which the hypotenuse of the triangle has swept around the circumference of a circle. Based on a circle with a radius of 1, the circumference is 2π—so a rotation of 360 degrees is considered 2π radians, the name given to this new unit. This approach proved invaluable when trigonometry was combined with calculus, as using the radian measure produced simpler results. It is also a more mathematically rigorous unit than the culturally influenced degree. Radians are now the standard scientific unit for the measurement of angles.

FOCUS | In many countries, high points in the landscape are marked with different styles of concrete pillars, usually topped with a metal plate, known as "triangulation stations" in the US and "trig points" in the UK; these are mounts for theodolites, optical instruments used to enable trigonometric measurements. They have largely been made redundant by GPS satellite navigation systems.

The Drill Down functions as a critique of the main concept, or looks at one element of the main concept in more detail, to give another angle or enhance understanding.

The Focus provides a counterargument or an alternative viewpoint from a key player in the field, or a key event subsequent to the initial theory.

"Mathematics attempts to establish order and simplicity in human thought."

EDWARD TELLER,
THE PURSUIT OF SIMPLICITY (1981)

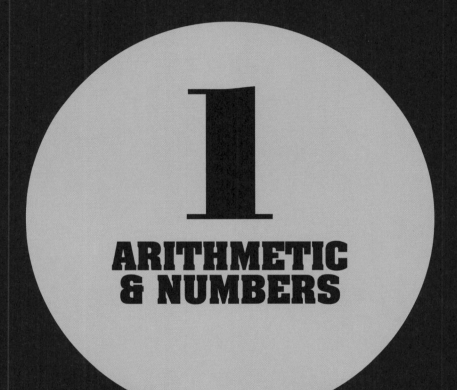

1
ARITHMETIC
& NUMBERS

INTRODUCTION

Counting is likely to have begun with fingers and thumbs. This accounts for both the familiar decimal approach, with one number per digit (hence the use of the term for numbers as well as parts of the anatomy) and the use of "base 60" by the Sumerian and Babylonian civilizations. Where decimal (base 10) numbers run from 0 to 9 before starting a new column, base 60 numbers run from 0 to 59 before restarting. Counting to 60 on two hands may seem a stretch, but it has been suggested that this was done by touching a thumb to each of the 12 finger joints on one hand in turn, while using the other hand to count off 5 lots of 12. (Of course, the same approach could have been used for base 144, counting 12 on each hand, but thankfully no one seems to have thought of this.)

The birth of numbers

Soon, hands would have been supplemented by markers—tally marks carved on bones or wood, or groups of stones—which would eventually transmute into that powerful early calculating device, the abacus. But the step that took us from counting to arithmetic was the introduction of numbers—symbols and words representing these finger positions or tally mark combinations. Initially this may have just been a convenience—it's easier to say "five" than to show someone a hand with the fingers all in the right position—but with the advent of writing, numbers became essential.

Once numbers were regarded as things in their own right, it became clear that they fell into different categories. There were even numbers, which could be split into two equal amounts, and odd numbers that couldn't be so divided. As we will see in Chapter 2, early mathematicians were very interested in shapes because of the importance of being able to divide up land and design buildings. It was also noticed that some numbers seemed to correspond to shapes. So, for example, 6 was a triangular number: envisage a set of pebbles arranged in rows of 1, 2, and 3 beneath each other; it can easily be made into a triangle. Other numbers made squares: 4, 9, and 16, for example.

Working with numbers

With numbers given names and symbols it also became easier to consider mechanisms for manipulating those numbers—combining them and interacting with them, just as it was possible to manipulate physical objects. Sometimes discoveries would be made that had no practical application but were nonetheless entertaining. The members of the Pythagorean School of ancient Greece, for example, were aware of linked pairs of numbers known as "amicable" numbers.

Understanding amicable numbers required another arithmetical concept—the factor. The factors of a number are the values it can be divided by and still leave a whole number. So, for instance, the significant factors of 12 are 1, 2, 3, 4, and 6; 5 isn't a factor because $^{12}\!/_5$ isn't a whole number, and anything bigger than 6 can't be a factor as it would produce a result smaller than 2. (Strictly, the number itself is a factor, but this is considered trivial.) Amicable numbers are those where the factors of one number add up to the other, and vice versa. The best known are 220 and 284: add the factors of 220 and you get 284, and those of 284 give 220.

Once the concept of factors was understood, another strange set of numbers emerged—the primes. These are numbers that only have 1 and themselves as factors. Primes would repeatedly prove valuable in the development of higher mathematics, yet even today the way they are distributed cannot be predicted. With time, other interesting types of numbers were discovered, too. Division implied ratios, but there also seemed to be non-whole numbers that weren't ratios, or fractions—the so-called irrational numbers, of which pi is the best-known example. With each extra feature, the power of numbers seemed to increase. What had once been little more than a way of checking nothing had been lost or stolen was transformed into a parallel world of numbers and their manipulation, which could be sent on wild journeys of its own. Mathematics was taking off.

TIMELINE

SUMERIAN NUMBERS
The Sumerian numeral system, later taken over and developed by the Babylonians, is introduced. It is base 60, rather than the now-familiar base 10—and uses notations positioned in columns to indicate multiples of 60. We still use base 60 to measure time in for minutes and seconds.

BINARY NUMBERS
The Indian mathematician Pingala makes the first known reference to binary, or base 2, numbers. He also refers to Pascal's triangle (a triangular arrangement of numbers starting with three 1s, then producing numbers below by adding adjacent numbers above) and the Fibonacci series, all to explain the meter of Sanskrit writings.

At least 35,000 BCE — **c. 3000 BCE** — **c. 530 BCE** — **c. 200 BCE**

TALLY STICKS
The Lebombo bone—a carved bone from a baboon's leg—is the oldest near-certain tally stick, featuring 29 notches. It is found in the Lembombo Mountains bordering South Africa and Swaziland. Some date it to even further back—around 41,000 BCE.

THE PYTHAGOREANS
The School of Pythagoras is founded in Croton, southern Italy. With an obsession with whole numbers, including a belief that the whole universe is based on whole numbers and ratios, the Pythagoreans take numbers from a simple tally mechanism to a separate concept that can be operated in its own right.

NEW NUMBER SYSTEMS

Fibonacci (a nickname meaning "son of Bonacci") writes *Liber Abaci* ("Book of Calculation"), which introduces both zero and Indian/Arabic numbers to Europe. The new numbers are resisted at first, in part because accounts can be fiddled by changing 0 to 6 or 9.

LOGARITHMS

John Napier publishes *Mirifici Logarithmorum Canonis Descriptio* ("Description of the Wonderful Rule of Logarithms"), which makes use of logarithms, simplifying multiplication and division by using the exponents that can be added or subtracted. They become the standard vehicle for calculation before mechanical and electronic devices take over.

628 CE — **1202** — **1545** — **1614**

TRUE ZERO

The Indian mathematician Brahmagupta makes the first known use of "true" zero (the value of a number taken away from itself). Zeroes used as placeholders to keep numbers in columns in a positional system date back much earlier to the Babylonians, who started to use \\ for an empty space around 1,200 years before Brahmagupta's work.

NEGATIVE NUMBERS

Publication of Girolamo Cardano's book *Ars Magna* ("The Great Art"). Cardano is the first to explicitly manipulate negative numbers and to consider (if partially and inaccurately) the implications of having the square root of a negative number, now known as an imaginary number.

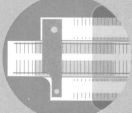

BIOGRAPHIES

PYTHAGORAS (c. 570–c. 495 BCE)

For most of us, the ancient Greek philosopher Pythagoras is only associated with the geometrical theorem about the square on the hypotenuse. In fact, though, this predates him. It's difficult to pin down biographical details, or to separate his work from the wider school he founded, but Pythagoras was born on the island of Samos, and around the age of 40 founded a school at Croton in the south of Italy. The Pythagorean School believed that the universe was driven by whole numbers; the school is said to have had the words "All is number" carved on its door lintel. Where basic use of numbers in counting probably originated in everyday transactions, intimately linked to physical objects, the Pythagoreans made numbers an abstract ideal. Arguably it was they who broke mathematics away from its direct link to reality, making it more independent. Whole numbers were given particular attributes, and patterns of numbers were studied in everything from the stars to musical notes. According to legend, when one of the followers of Pythagoras, Hippasus, threatened to reveal to the world that the square root of 2 could not be made with any ratio of whole numbers, he was drowned.

GIROLAMO CARDANO (1501–1576)

The Italian mathematician Girolamo (or Gerolamo) Cardano, often known by the French version of his name, Jérôme Cardan, was born in Pavia. He studied medicine at the University of Pavia and went on to practice (without a license) in the town of Saccolongo. From there he moved to Milan, where he continued with medicine but also taught mathematics. Cardano stretched the boundaries of the concept of numbers, working with negative numbers and even touching on imaginary numbers. He was also one of the first to seriously study the basics of probability, though his book on the subject, *Liber de Ludo Aleae* (*Book of Games of Chance*), was not published until long after his death. It seems that anything so closely associated with gambling was considered unsuitable for publication. Despite being dated, the book helped kickstart the study of probability. Cardano later moved to Bologna, where he was arrested by the Inquisition in 1570. Several months later he was freed and moved to Rome, where, in contrast, the Pope gave him a lifetime annuity. He remained in Rome for the rest of his life, continuing to practice medicine and writing on philosophy.

CARL FRIEDRICH GAUSS (1777–1855)

Though not a familiar name outside math and physics, the German mathematician Carl Friedrich Gauss was one of the greatest pre-nineteenth-century mathematicians. Born in Brunswick to a poor family, Gauss showed mathematical skills from an early age. According to legend, aged 8 he amazed his school teacher by adding up every number from 1 to 100 in seconds (he realized that the series was just 50 pairs of 101). By the time Gauss was at university—sponsored by the Duke of Brunswick, who had been made aware of Gauss's mathematical ability—he was already breaking new ground. He toyed with a career in philology, but the appeal of making new proofs and discoveries won him over to math. Gauss's contributions to mathematics fit into every chapter of this book. For this chapter he contributed to number theory, and particularly modular arithmetic. He was one of the first to think about non-Euclidean geometry and topology. He proved what became known as the "fundamental theorem of algebra," and he developed applications of mathematics in astronomy, optics, and the study of magnetism.

GEORG FRIEDRICH BERNHARD RIEMANN (1826–1866)

Although German mathematician Georg Friedrich Bernhard Riemann made a wide range of contributions to mathematics, he is best remembered for something he failed to prove. Riemann studied theology at the University of Göttingen, but there his ability in mathematics blossomed, and he transferred to the mathematically oriented University of Berlin. One of his earliest developments was Riemannian geometry, which applied calculus to smoothly varying multidimensional surfaces (Einstein had great trouble understanding this sophisticated mathematics in relation to the curvature of space-time when developing his masterpiece, the general theory of relativity). Riemann contributed to the detail of calculus and Fourier series. But it was work on the prime counting function, approximating the number of prime numbers in a range, that led to the Riemann hypothesis. This is a complex mathematical conjecture related to the distribution of prime numbers that, were it true, automatically generates a whole range of proofs in number theory. One of the most significant unsolved mathematical problems, a $1 million prize awaits its solution.

TALLIES

THE MAIN CONCEPT | The tally is almost certainly the oldest known application of mathematics, with the purpose of keeping track of objects, or things that have happened. For a tally, a mark is made—for example, on a piece of wood, stone, or bone—corresponding to each of the items or events being monitored. The very earliest precursors of tallies probably involved using either fingers, or simple objects that could be used as markers, such as sticks or pebbles. However, the problem with these was that they were ephemeral. You only have to make use of your hands for something else, or move the tally objects, and the record is lost. By carving the tally into a durable substance, a tally could be kept indefinitely; later they would frequently take the form of marks made with a stylus in clay, which could be baked hard. A tally might be used to keep score in a game, or to record the number of livestock or provisions in someone's possession. Tallies are also invaluable for recording trades—marks can be added to or removed from a tally when items are loaned to someone else or traded for other goods and services. All of these activities can be carried without ever introducing the concept of numbers.

DRILL DOWN | Though it is unlikely to have occurred to to its early users, the concept of a tally can be expressed in terms of what modern mathematicians call set theory (see page 106). Two sets of items (just collections of things) are the same size if the items can be put in one-to-one correspondence, pairing off an item from one set with an item from the other until all are used up. So, for example, imagine a set of major compass directions and a set of seasons. You could pair off north with spring, east with summer, south with fall, and west with winter. In each case, all the items would be used up, so you would know the sets were the same size without ever knowing how big they were.

FOCUS | *Although the short-lived tallies of fingers or pebbles are long gone, some very ancient markings have been found that are almost certainly tallies. The Lebombo bone (see page 16) is the oldest known tally. A clearer example, with more intricate groupings of notches, is the Ishango bone, from around 20,000 BCE.*

NUMBERS

THE MAIN CONCEPT | Numbers started as a useful shorthand. In verbal communication, having a word for, say, "five" is much easier than saying "Here's a bag of corn, and another, and another, and another, and another." Once written records were used, numbers also made bookkeeping simpler, capable of keeping track of a collection of values that changed with time. The method of representing numbers emerged from tally marks (see page 20), and many numeral systems still use I to represent one, corresponding to a single mark. However, tally marks quickly become unwieldly, so extra symbols were introduced across the world. The crudest approach was the Roman system. Reflecting the fingers, it introduced just two symbols between 1 and 10—V for 5 (one hand), and X for 10 (two hands). Like a tally, there was no significance to the position of the symbols. And yet the Romans did not lack precedents in this respect. The Sumerians and Babylonians had used a sophisticated system where the position of the symbol indicated the size of the number (see page 24), just as we do today. Similarly, Chinese and Indian cultures used positional systems, with the Indian form, modified in translation via Arabic, forming the basis for our present system.

DRILL DOWN | In formal mathematics, numbers correspond to sets of items. The number 0 is an empty set. The number 1 is a set containing the empty set—it has one thing in it (the empty set); 2 is the set containing the previous set . . . and so on. We can then can match real objects with members of the set to assign numbers to them. So, if I have some apples and can pair one of them with the first member of the number 2 set and one with the next member of the number 2 set and there are no more apples or members of the set, there are two apples.

FOCUS | *"Arabic" numerals came to Europe in the thirteenth century, in a book by Italian mathematician Fibonacci, but they could have arrived sooner. Bishop Severus of Syria noted in 662 BCE that Indians had remarkable abilities of calculation and excelled at astronomy. He noted that their approach "surpasses description," and that "this computation is done by means of nine signs" (before the widespread use of zero).*

Brahmi		—	=	≡	+	Ν	ⓔ	ๆ	Ƽ	?
Hindu	o	၃	२	३	४	५	६	७	८	९
Arabic	٠	١	٢	٣	٤	٥	٦	٧	٨	٩
Medieval	O	I	2	3	୧	৭	6	ᚠ	8	9
Modern	0	1	2	3	4	5	6	7	8	9

NUMBER BASES

THE MAIN CONCEPT | We use a positional system of numbers in base 10 (where the column a number is placed in is significant). When we write out a number such as 6923, the position of each number indicates how many 10s it should be multiplied by. In this case, the 3 is multiplied by 1 (or 10^0), the 2 by 10 (10^1), the 9 by 100 (10^2), and the 6 by 1000 (10^3). Base 10 is a natural choice as it reflects the digits on our hands, but it is not the only option. Ancient Sumerians and Babylonians used base 60 (shown opposite). In this system the rightmost column was for numbers up to 59, the next left for multiples of 60, the next left for multiples of 3600, and so on. We now only use base 60 for seconds and minutes. We also make wide use of binary, or base 2, numbers. These are far easier for computers to handle, both logically and physically with electronic circuits, which can be either electrically charged or not (written 1 or 0). Logical values of true or false can be handled by treating, for example, 1 as true and 0 as false. Binary is often translated to other bases for human consumption—programmers often use base 16 (hexadecimal) and, less frequently now, base 8 (octal), as explained opposite.

1	11	21	31	41	51
2	12	22	32	42	52
3	13	23	33	43	53
4	14	24	34	44	54
5	15	25	35	45	55
6	16	26	36	46	56
7	17	27	37	47	57
8	18	28	38	48	58
9	19	29	39	49	59
10	20	30	40	50	

DRILL DOWN | Binary numbers, used by computers, rapidly become unwieldy (it takes a while to realize that 11111100010 is 2018), so programmers translate binary to octal or hexadecimal. The now-outmoded octal system takes bits in groups of 3 and replaces them with 0 to 7. So 11111100010 or 11-111-100-010 becomes 3742. Hexadecimal is trickier as it requires 16 digits, but we only have 10 numerals, so the letters A to F are added, where A is 10, B 11, and so on. For this, a binary number is divided into blocks of four bits: 11111100010 or 111-1110-0010 is 7E2. Hexadecimal is common as modern computers split data into chunks of 16, 32, or 64 bits—easier to divide into 4s than 3s.

FOCUS | *Most number systems have positive integer (whole number) bases, but this is not essential. For example, with a base of −10, there is no need for the "−" sign. As a negative multiplied by a negative is a positive, as with $(-10^2) = +100$, and where $(-10^3) = -1000$, alternate columns indicate positive and negative values. In base −10, 174 is the equivalent of $1 \times 100 - 7 \times 10 + 4 = 34$.*

NUMBERS
Page 22

**BASIC ARITHMETIC;
NEGATIVE NUMBERS**
Page 26

POWERS, ROOTS & LOGARITHMS
Page 34

BASIC ARITHMETIC: NEGATIVE NUMBERS

THE MAIN CONCEPT | Arithmetic provides simple ways to manipulate numbers. Even with tallies there were two of the basics of arithmetic: addition increased the items on a tally; subtraction removed them—corresponding to, for example, storing and removing bags of grain at a granary. The third operation, division, was also a natural concept, particularly when food had to be divided up. Although easier to perform, multiplication (the reverse of division) is the most sophisticated of the four operations. It may have begun as repeated addition, though it would also have been useful when calculating the area of a piece of land. Division also provides the concept of a fraction— the result of dividing a whole number by another. However not all numbers between the integers are such ratios—irrational numbers, for example, like the square root of 2, could only be represented numerically once decimal fractions were introduced. Early arithmetic involved positive numbers, but the action of removing objects from a collection produces a negative inverse. If we start with 7 apples and end with 2, then there are 5 apples removed, usefully indicated as −5, to distinguish it from apples added. The result was a continuum of numbers from negative to positive, known as the "number line."

DRILL DOWN | As it has only been relatively recently taught in schools, the concept of the number line can seem modern, but it's not. A kind of number line, for example, was involved in the BCE/CE dating system (dating forward and backward from the birth of Christ) popularized by the Venerable Bede in the eighth century. Addition and subtraction become simply moving up and down an imaginary line showing all the numbers in order. Negative numbers helped complete the number line by providing a mirror image of the positive side. If the number line is thought of as a ruler, with the integers providing the marked "notches," fractions fill in the gaps between them.

FOCUS | *The ancient Greeks struggled with fractions. They conceived of fractions as the parts that made up a whole, and considered all fractions, with the exception of $2/3$, as $1/n$ (if necessary, multiple copies were added together), where n is a whole number. A fraction was represented by a letter with a mark to indicate that it was a fraction, making manipulation of them difficult.*

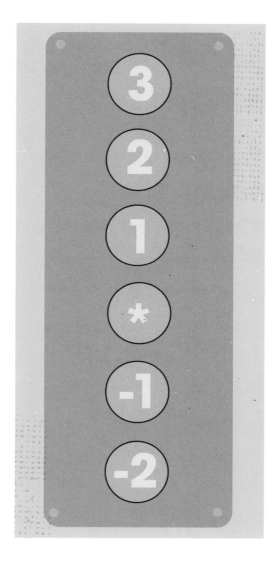

PRIME NUMBERS

THE MAIN CONCEPT | Not all whole numbers behave the same way. There is the distinction between even numbers (divisible by 2) and odd numbers (not divisible by 2). But as numbers get bigger, they can have factors— smaller numbers up to half their value that they can be exactly divided by. (Apart from its own value, a number can't be divisible by a number bigger than half its value.) But some numbers can't be exactly divided by anything other than 1 or themselves—these are prime numbers. So, for example, 2, 3, 5, 7, 11, 13, 17, and 19 are prime, whereas 4, 6, 8, 9, 10, 12, 14, 15, 16, 18, and 20 are not— the second list can all be divided by another whole number. The number 1 seems prime, but we don't count it as one because it breaks the "fundamental theorem of arithmetic," stating that any number can be written as the product (multiplication) of a unique set of other primes. For example, 12 can be written as $2 \times 2 \times 3$. If we allowed 1 in, we could get to 12 using $1 \times 2 \times 2 \times 3$ or $1 \times 1 \times 2 \times 2 \times 3$, or $1 \times 1 \times 1 \times 2 \times 2 \times 3$. As we need a unique set of primes, 1 was ejected. Prime numbers are interesting because of the way that they jump around— there is nothing neatly regular about the sequence as there is in, say, the odd and even numbers. Of the primes, 2 is the only even value, so is also something of a special case. If not a prime itself, a number is called a "composite," for example, $20 = 2 \times 2 \times 5$.

0 1 2 3 4 5 6 7 8 9 10 11 12 13 14 15 16 17 18
19 20 21 22 23 24 25 26 27 28 29 30 31 32
33 34 35 36 37 38 39 40 41 42 43 44 45 46
47 48 49 50 51 52 53 54 55 56 57 58 59 60
61 62 63 64 65 66 67 68 69 70 71 72 73 74
75 76 77 78 79 80 81 82 83 84 85 86 87 88
89 90 91 92 93 94 95 96 97 98 99 100

DRILL DOWN | Prime numbers appear less and less frequently as values get bigger. However, more than 2,300 years ago the ancient Greek mathematician Euclid proved with some simple logic that there is an infinite set of prime numbers. He first imagined multiplying together every prime you can think of to produce a value N, then added 1 to that value. Either the new number created ($N+1$) is a prime, or it is made up by multiplying together primes that weren't in the original list, as dividing $N + 1$ by any of the original primes would leave a remainder of 1. So however long your list of primes, there will always be at least one extra.

NUMBERS
Page 22
BASIC ARITHMETIC;
NEGATIVE NUMBERS
Page 26
INFINITY
Page 94

FOCUS | *Prime numbers may seem only of interest to mathematical geeks but are essential to keep us safe on the Internet. When we use a secure connection, generating the encryption key typically involves multiplying together two huge prime numbers. It's easy to multiply them, but almost impossible to deduce the primes from the answer: this hard-to-reverse process is at the heart of one of the most commonly used encryption methods.*

AXIOMS & PROOFS

THE MAIN CONCEPT | We are used to mathematics being very formal and structured, however, very early math was far more pragmatic—more like a cook's recipe. From practical experience, a certain combination of things worked and if they did, they would be repeated and used again. Long before the formal proof of what we now know as the Pythagorean theorem, the Babylonians and other early cultures knew from experience that triangles with a right angle had sides that were in the proportions of 3:4:5. These triangles were very useful in measuring plots of land and designing buildings. It was only after more than 1,000 years of using such "recipe-based" math that the idea of a formal proof began to be used by the ancient Greeks. The idea was to start with a set of axioms (a word that means "that which is self-evident"). These were assumptions that were so obvious that no proof was needed, such as any two points can be joined by a straight line. Proofs were then built up, using logical steps, from the axioms. In the case of the Pythagorean theorem, the Greeks went from simply observing the 3:4:5 ratio to proving that the square of the length of the longest side (the hypotenuse) is equal to the sum of the squares of the other two sides.

DRILL DOWN | So far we've talked about one kind of proof—the kind where, starting with a handful of axioms, mathematicians produced more and more sophisticated theorems, each a collection of arguments that proves a relationship based on axioms and simpler theorems. However, even in ancient Greek times other mechanisms were used for proofs, such as logical arguments or "proof by contradiction." The latter was employed in the proof that the square root of 2 is not a rational fraction. The method involves assuming the result required *is* true—in this case, that there is a rational fraction that equals the square root of 2— and showing that this produces an impossible outcome.

FOCUS | *Many mathematicians dislike proof by exhaustion: trying out every possibility and checking that they behave as expected. However, the four-color theorem, which says that it only takes four colors to make a map where no country has the same color as an adjacent one, was proved this way, working through 1,936 options (later reduced to 1,476) using a computer—the first major theorem of its kind to be proved with this method.*

SERIES

THE MAIN CONCEPT | A series gives the sum of an infinite set of values, where each value is generated from the previous one using a rule. The infinite nature is indicated by stating the first few entries, followed by an ellipsis (...). Many series have an infinite sum, for example 1, 1, 1, 1 ... or even 1, $1/2$, $1/3$, $1/4$ ... However, some series tend to a finite value. So, for example, the sum of 1, $1/2$, $1/4$, $1/8$ ... would be 2 for an infinite set. The idea that an infinite series can have a finite sum is challenging: ancient Greek philosopher Zeno illustrated this with the story of Achilles and the tortoise. Achilles runs faster than the tortoise, so gives it a headstart. Achilles soon reaches where the tortoise was when he started, but by then, the tortoise has moved on. This repeats over and over: according to Zeno, Achilles will never catch the tortoise. In practice, though, the distance between them is like the series 1, $1/2$, $1/4$, $1/8$ ...; there's a finite sum of distances, which Achilles soon passes. Not all series are so simple. The rule can vary, for example, by oscillating—for example, 1, 2, 0, 2, −2, 1, −5 ... Series proved valuable in the development of calculus (see Chapter 3) and in the calculation of constants.

DRILL DOWN | The familiar constant pi (π), the ratio of a circle's circumference to its diameter, is an example of a constant that can be calculated using a range of series. The more entries in the series that are added, the closer it gets to the exact value of pi, though some series converge on the value faster than others. For example, pi can be calculated using the sum of the series $4/1$, $-4/3$, $4/5$, $-4/7$ ... or $\pi-3$ results from the sum of the series $4/(2\times3\times4)$, $-4/(4\times5\times6)$, $4/(6\times7\times8)$, $-4/(8\times9\times10)$ ... Pi can also be calculated by a different type of infinite sequence where the operation is not addition, such as $\pi/2 = (2/1) \times (2/3) \times (4/3) \times (4/5)$ ...

NUMBERS
Page 22
PI
Page 58
INTEGRAL CALCULUS
Page 100

FOCUS | *Because a series is made up of an infinite set of entries it is susceptible to the paradoxes that arise from infinite calculations. Take the sum of the series 1, −1, 1, −1, 1 ... By bracketing pairs, the sum is 0: (1 − 1) + (1 − 1) ... but it also gives a total of 1 if the brackets are shifted: 1 + (−1 + 1) + (−1 + 1) ...*

POWERS, ROOTS & LOGARITHMS

THE MAIN CONCEPT | Raising a number to a power (called "exponentiation," as the size of the power is the "exponent") is a staple of mathematics. A positive whole number power represents multiplying a number by itself that many times. So, for example, 3^2 is 3×3, while 3^3 is $3 \times 3 \times 3$. Powers turn multiplication into addition. If we multiply 3^2 by 3^4, we add the exponents to get 3^6. This shows that 3^1 is just 3—when we multiply 3^4 by 3 we get 3^5, adding 1 to the exponent. Similarly, dividing involves taking exponents away. So, 3^5 divided by 3^2 is 3^3. But powers are not limited to positive integers. Dividing 3^1 by 3^1, which must give 1, produces 3^0 by subtracting exponents—any number raised to the power 0 gives 1. If we divide 3^0 by 3^1 we get 3^{-1}. This is $1/3$, so 3^{-1} is the inverse of 3^1, and so on for other negative powers. Fractional powers produce "roots." As $3^{1/2} \times 3^{1/2}$ is $3^{1/2+1/2}$, we get 3^1—so $3^{1/2}$ is the square root of 3. Roots have the same hierarchy as powers, with cube roots and so forth. Logarithms, devised in the seventeenth century, came from the observation of the behavior of powers—the way that they can be added and subtracted. Tables of powers were provided to make multiplication and division simpler.

DRILL DOWN | In a logarithm, often shortened to "log," a fixed value (the "base" of the logarithm) is raised to a power to represent a number—the power required to represent a number is its logarithm to that base. So, for example, the log to base 10 of 100 is 2 because $100 = 10^2$. Although base 10 is easiest to get our head around, natural logarithms (shortened to *ln*) are widely used in science, where the base is *e*, a constant of nature with a value around 2.718. This is because natural logarithms make it easy to calculate the way that changing values grow with time. Similarly, logs to base 2 are valuable in computing because of its basis of binary arithmetic.

FOCUS | *The most famous bit of math involving powers is Fermat's Last Theorem, which says you can't have three whole numbers—say* x, y, *and* z—*where* $x^n + y^n = z^n$ *for any integer powers other than 1 or 2. French mathematician Pierre de Fermat claimed to have proved this in 1637, but if he actually did, he never wrote it down. It was proved conclusively by the English mathematician Andrew Wiles in 1994 (see page 75).*

ZERO

THE MAIN CONCEPT | Arguably, one of the biggest steps forward in mathematics involved nothing at all—the introduction of zero. Some early number lines (see page 26) skipped directly from −1 to 1 with nothing in between. We can see that still in our year dating system, which goes directly from 1 BCE to 1 CE. However, the idea of a number representing nothing would change all this. Zeros began as placeholders. When the Sumerians and Babylonians first used their positional numbering system, where the column identified whether a number just meant what it said or was to be multiplied by 60 (60^1), 3600 (60^2), and so on (see page 24), a column that was not in use was just left as a space. This meant that the symbols for, say, 63 and 3603, similar to y yyy and y yyy respectively, were only distinguished by a slightly wider gap between numbers. Eventually it was realized that it would be a good idea to mark an empty column. Now 63 would be y yyy, but 3603 was y \\ yyy. Such placeholder use occurred off and on for centuries. But the big breakthrough came when it was realized that zero could be both a placeholder and the answer to the question "What is (say) 3 − 3?"—the center point on the number line.

DRILL DOWN | Pinning down the arithmetic behavior of zero took some time. It behaves consistently, if oddly, with addition, subtraction, and with multiplication. Adding and subtracting a zero does nothing at all, while multiplying by zero reduces anything else to nothing. But there was confusion over division. The smaller the thing you divide by, the bigger the result. At the extreme of zero, it would seem the result is infinite. And things get even stranger when dividing zero by zero. Some early mathematicians thought the result was zero, others infinite. It is now considered indeterminate—it doesn't have a value, so don't try it (if you see a result of "NaN" on a calculator, it means "not a number").

FOCUS | *Along with Indian/Arabic numerals, the fully functional zero was brought to the West by Fibonacci in his* Liber Abaci. *He referred to it as "zephirum," which seems to have been an attempt to render the Arabic word* sifr *(which also became "cipher"), a special, egg-shaped empty number. The assumption is that this reached the Arab world from India. Zephirum became zero.*

FIBONACCI NUMBERS

THE MAIN CONCEPT | Just as we separate some whole numbers off as odd or even or prime, there is another subset of the whole positive numbers known as the Fibonacci numbers. These are the numbers in the sequence 1, 1, 2, 3, 5, 8, 13 ... where each number is the sum of the previous two numbers in the sequence (the sequence can also be started with a 0). The name comes from Leonardo of Pisa, the thirteenth-century mathematician better known as Fibonacci. He described the sequence in his book *Liber Abaci*, which also introduced Arabic numerals to Europe. However, these numbers were known up to 1,400 years before in Indian mathematics. Fibonacci showed how the numbers described the way a population of rabbits might increase, but they came to have a wide number of applications. Though the rabbits provided a very artificial example, flowers often average a Fibonacci number of petals, and the numbers are also sometimes reflected in layouts of seed heads and tree branches, simply as a result of the way the structure of a plant builds up. If the numbers are used to create a set of squares with these widths, the result is the spiral shown opposite. And if you divide each number in the sequence by the previous one, it homes in on the "golden ratio" of around 1.618, which many think is artistically and architecturally pleasing (though nobody knows why).

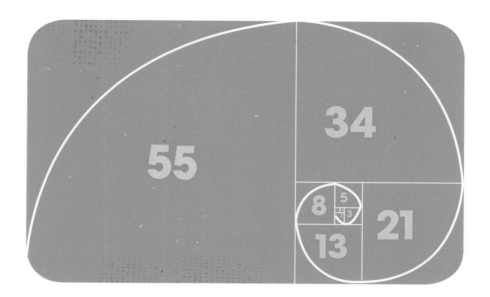

DRILL DOWN | The *Liber Abaci* used Fibonacci numbers to show the number of rabbits in a highly simplified population model. The picture starts with a breeding pair. It takes a month to produce baby rabbits, who are always born in pairs, one male, one female. It also takes a baby rabbit a month to be ready to breed. So, after one month there's still one pair. After two months there's a second pair. After three months the original pair produce a new litter. After four months the first and second pairs produce a litter each. And so on. The result is 1, 1, 2, 3, 5, 8, 13 . . . pairs of rabbits.

FOCUS | *It might appear that the Fibonacci numbers are a very well-explored and simple aspect of number theory, but mathematicians would beg to differ. Ever since 1963, a group known as the Fibonacci Association has published a journal,* Fibonacci Quarterly, *dedicated to the Fibonacci series and associated aspects of mathematics. So far, they haven't run out of things to say.*

NUMBERS
Page 22

BASIC ARITHMETIC; NEGATIVE NUMBERS
Page 26

SERIES
Page 32

IMAGINARY NUMBERS

THE MAIN CONCEPT | One of the most interesting aspects of negative numbers is that when you multiply a negative number by another negative number you get a positive one. So, for example, $-2 \times -3 = 6$. But what, multiplied by itself, makes a negative number? What is a negative number's square root? There is no natural answer, so a purely hypothetical concept, which the philosopher Descartes sarcastically labeled an "imaginary number," was dreamed up. The value i is assigned to the square root of -1. As a result, the square root of any negative number is a multiple of i. For example, the square root of -4 is $2i$ (-2 is approximately $1.41i$, and -3 is $1.73i$). Of itself, an imaginary number might have been an amusing mathematical oddity without any real significance. But such numbers proved extremely useful. When combined with a real number, an imaginary number provides a valuable mechanism for representing points on a two-dimensional plane—and that makes such a "complex number" perfect for dealing with the mathematics of anything with a wavelike behavior, which crops up repeatedly in both physics and engineering. A complex number is represented as, for example, $6 + 2i$, combining the real number 6 and the imaginary number $2i$, and can undergo all the usual operations applied to a number.

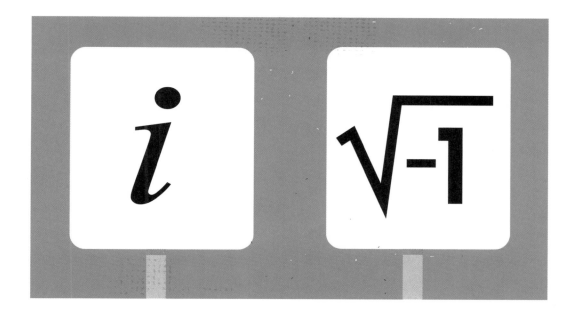

DRILL DOWN | The concept of the number line (see page 26) is central to applying complex numbers to coordinates on a plane. If we imagine a pair of axes, the horizontal axis is the number line of real numbers, centered on zero, with negative numbers to the left of this and positive numbers to the right. The vertical axis is the number line of imaginary numbers, again with zero at the center, positive imaginary numbers above zero, and negative imaginary numbers below zero. Then, for example, the point $3 + 5i$ sits in the top right quadrant of the plane, while $-4 - 6i$ is in the bottom left quadrant. Equations describing the progress of a wave are represented using changing real and imaginary components.

FOCUS | *In the nineteenth century, Irish mathematician William Hamilton introduced a supercharged complex number called a "quaternion." Instead of having a single imaginary element, it had three different imaginary elements. This was designed to handle something that was changing in three dimensions at once, but was largely superseded by a branch of maths known as "vector analysis."*

NUMBERS
Page 22

**BASIC ARITHMETIC;
NEGATIVE NUMBERS**
Page 26

VECTOR ALGEBRA & CALCULUS
Page 104

MODULAR ARITHMETIC

THE MAIN CONCEPT | When small children are asked to divide 13 by 5, they might say "2, remainder 3," because 5 divides into 13 twice, with 3 left over. As adults we tend to think of division in terms of fractions or decimals—so 13 divided by 5 becomes $^{13}/_5$ or 2.6. However, the child's approach makes sense when dealing with physical objects that can't be split. If we divide 13 pens between 5 people, for example, we can give them 2 each, with 3 left over. Underlying this is modular arithmetic. In modular arithmetic, which only deals with integers, the value cycles back to the start after a maximum, known as the "modulus." So, for example, if the modulus is 5, we count 1, 2, 3, 4, 5, 1, 2, 3, 4, 5, 1, 2, 3 . . . Working with a modulus of 12, for instance, we identify a position on the cycle as, say, 3 modulo 12, or 9 modulo 12 (often shorted to 9 mod 12). Modular arithmetic crops up in everything from clocks to music to ciphers, or codes, all representing cyclical processes. In computing, it's a handy way to test if an integer value is odd or even. If n mod 2 yields a remainder (it will be 1 if it does), then n was odd.

DRILL DOWN | If it's 9 o'clock, 5 hours later it will be 2 o'clock. Normal clock times are modulo 12. Modular arithmetic usually starts at 1 or 0. On the 24-hour clock, 0 and 24 are congruent—they mean the same thing. Similarly, ciphers are often modular. They often use a key, a secret word creating the enciphered text when the number values of each key letter are added to the original text using modular arithmetic. Enciphering DOG with the key CAT we add 3, 1, and 20 to the number values in DOG. This gives GPA. The final letter is G + T or 7 + 20. But the answer is to modulo 26 with 26 letters, so we get 1 or A.

NUMBERS
Page 22

BASIC ARITHMETIC;
NEGATIVE NUMBERS
Page 26

SET THEORY
Page 106

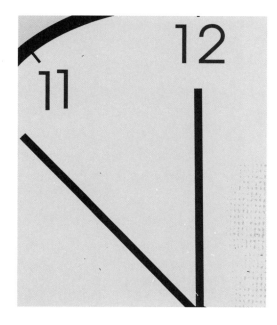

FOCUS | *Modular arithmetic crops up in checksums, where a digit is added to strings of numbers to force a modular result. ISBNs, used to identify books, end with a check digit calculated this way. The old 10-digit ISBNs used modulo 11 arithmetic, using X to represent 10; this has been dropped, but the modulo 10 approach in the new ISBN lets some errors through.*

MATHEMATICAL LOGIC

THE MAIN CONCEPT | Logic began in ancient Greek times as a mechanism for exploring reasoning, used to deduce new information from existing relationships. So, for example, if it is true that all dogs have four legs and we know that a particular person has two legs, we can deduce that that person is not a dog. Later, mathematicians devised an approach to logic using the tools of mathematics. This would be turned on its head to define the basic workings of mathematics based on logical premises—building from simple starting points such as set theory (see page 106), and using step-by-step logical processes. The best-known aspect of mathematical logic is Boolean algebra, named after English mathematician George Boole. This uses operators, mathematical tools, to work on the logical values "true" and "false." The simplest operator NOT turns "true" into "false" and "false" into "true." Other operators combine pairs of values. So, for example, AND returns "true" if both inputs are true, and "false" otherwise. Similarly, OR returns "true" if either input is true, and "false" otherwise. These relationships are often portrayed in Venn diagrams. For a long time regarded as interesting but without practical application, Boolean algebra came into its own in the computer, where it is used to manipulate bits—binary digits—substituting 1 for "true" and 0 for "false."

DRILL DOWN | It is easy to spot mathematical logic at play in computers when we try to reduce a large number of items to the relevant ones, particularly in a search. If, for example, I wanted to find a red car, but didn't want a diesel engine, I would be looking for "car AND red AND NOT diesel." However, this logic is also at play at a more fundamental level in all the circuitry that handles data within the computer. This is made up of small parts—originally separate physical components—that are called "logic gates," which carry out Boolean operations on data bits. These gates are now combined by the billion on processor chips.

NUMBER BASES
Page 24

AXIOMS & PROOFS
Page 30

SET THEORY
Page 106

FOCUS | *The most complete attempt to derive the core of mathematics from logic came in the three-volume* Principia Mathematica *by Alfred North Whitehead and Bertrand Russell. Published between 1910 and 1913, it famously took several hundred pages to get to 1 + 1 = 2. The approach took a battering when it was proved by the 25-year-old Austrian mathematician Kurt Gödel that a complete system of mathematics can never be built up this way.*

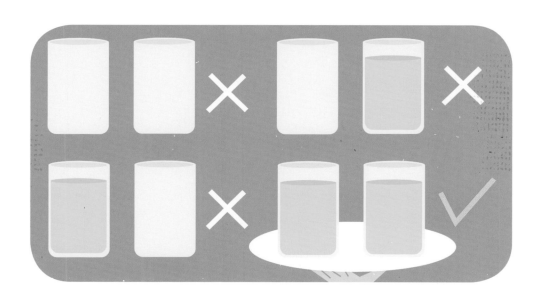

"[The book of the universe] is written in the language of mathematics, and its characters are triangles, circles, and other geometric figures, without which it is humanly impossible to understand a single word of it."

GALILEO GALILEI, *THE ASSAYER* (1623),
TRANSLATED BY STILLMAN DRAKE,
DISCOVERIES AND OPINIONS OF GALILEO (1957)

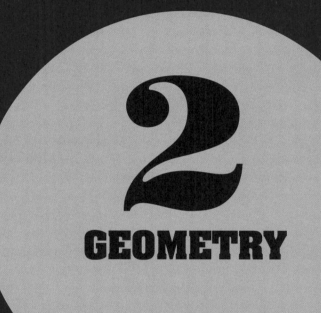

2

GEOMETRY

INTRODUCTION

The word *geometry* means "earth measurement." It is the mathematics of shapes—originally those that could be drawn on a flat surface, but then extended to take in three-dimensional forms and more. Those of us who were taught traditional geometry at school will be familiar with a tedious sequence of theorems, ending in the obligatory QED. (The original Greeks wrote *OEΔ*, the initials for an equivalent term: QED comes from the Latin *quod erat demonstrandum*, meaning "what was to be shown.") But it's a shame that geometry has a boring image, as it is so much more than rote learning. Originally concerned with land measurements, geometry expanded from two-dimensional surfaces to as many dimensions as you would care to consider, and also to related fields such as topology and knot theory.

Euclidean geometry

Going back to basics, the ancient Greek enthusiasm for geometry reflected their visual approach to mathematics—very different from our modern fondness for equations. Instead of manipulating symbols, the Greeks thought in shapes and areas. Even fractions were visual. Rather than say "a quarter," they would use "the fourth part," visualizing four separate parts of the size needed to make up a whole.

Traditional geometry—or "Euclidean geometry," after the fabled ancient Greek mathematician Euclid—begins with a set of axioms (assumptions considered so obvious there is no need to prove them), in turn leading to a set of theorems, which are proved step by step. The best known of all the theorems, the Pythagorean theorem, describes the relationship of side lengths that must exist in a right triangle. The technology might have changed, but even now surveyors make use of Euclidean geometry to deduce distances and angles. But geometry and related subjects, as we've seen, have gone much further. It's strange that the Greeks limited most of their work to the geometry of flat surfaces as so few natural surfaces are flat—the Earth itself, of course, is spherical. It was only in the nineteenth century that the geometry of shapes on curved three-dimensional surfaces became widely studied.

Beyond Euclid

Once the surface a shape is inscribed upon is no longer flat, things get interesting. For example, parallel lines can meet (contradicting Euclid's claim that "two lines are parallel if they only meet at infinity"). If you start from two points on the Equator and head for the North Pole, those lines are parallel at the Equator. But by the time you reach the North Pole, they meet each other. Draw a triangle on the surface of the Earth and Euclid's theorem that the angles of a triangle add up to 180 degrees goes out of the window—the angles add up to more than 180 degrees, while on an indented curved surface, they sum to less than 180 degrees (consider drawing on the inside of a sphere).

Working in three dimensions (four, if you allow for time) is as far as we can sensibly get in the physical world, but despite the difficulty of imagining what is meant by, say, "ten-dimensional space," mathematicians were able to take geometry into the behavior of curves and manifolds. Manifolds belong to a linked branch of geometry known as topology, which concerns the behavior of shapes in multiple dimensions that can be stretched but aren't allowed to be cut or glued. If these seem arbitrary distinctions, all mathematical systems are based on sets of arbitrary rules. (Even Euclidean geometry has its own restrictions separating it from reality.) As far as a topologist is concerned, a ring donut and a teacup with a handle are the same shape—each has a single hole totally surrounded by matter, and the rest is just down to stretching and deforming the one into the other.

Although in physics Einstein's use of non-Euclidean geometry in general relativity and all sorts of manifolds occurring in later physics take the geometric limelight, the biggest impact has been with the concept of fields—aspects of nature that have a value that can change from point to point in space and time—and which have come to dominate physics. And geometry has also found intriguing spinoffs in the nature-reflecting crinkliness and self-similarity of fractals and the oddities of knot theory. This is far more than just triangles.

TIMELINE

EUCLID'S LEGACY
Euclid writes his *Elements of Geometry*, which provides the foundations of both modern geometry and the wider structure of robust mathematical proofs based on a small number of pre-identified axioms. It is used as a textbook for more than 2,000 years.

DESCARTES
René Descartes, French philosopher and scientist, publishes *La Géométrie*, as an appendix to his book on the scientific method containing the phrase "I think, therefore I am." In this, far more valuable, appendix, Descartes links geometry and algebra to show the relationship between equations and curves.

c. 2000–1500 BCE   **c. 300 BCE**   **c. 1420 CE**   **1637**

EARLY GEOMETRY
The earliest surviving examples of geometrical working, such as Babylonian clay tablets and the Egyptian Rhind Papyrus, are produced. Evidence of geometric considerations—basic information on triangles and relationships between shapes and areas—goes back around 1,000 years further.

PERSPECTIVE
Italian architect Filippo Brunelleschi makes the first geometric analysis of perspective (though he did not publish details, which would come 20 years later in a book by Leon Battista Alberti). Brunelleschi constructs a reflecting device to enable viewers to compare a view with a perspective painting.

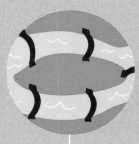

FIELDS
English scientist Michael Faraday coins the term "field" to describe what he has previously referred to as "lines of force"—a mathematical entity with a value at every point in time and space that can be used to describe the influence of electromagnetism: much of modern physics is based on fields.

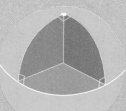

FRACTALS
French mathematician Benoit Mandelbrot publishes "How Long Is the Coast of Britain?," which pulls together thinking on what he will later describe as "fractals" and will lead in 1979 to the introduction of the Mandelbrot set.

1736   **1845**   **1854**   **1967**

GRAPH THEORY
The Swiss mathematician Leonhard Euler publishes what is arguably the first application of "graph theory," applied to the "Seven Bridges of Königsberg" problem—devising a walk across each of the city's bridges without ever crossing any given bridge twice.

NON-EUCLIDEAN GEOMETRY
In the early nineteenth century, Carl Friedrich Gauss, Johann Bolyai, and Nikolai Lobachevsky experiment with versions of geometry where parallel lines meet, moving away from flat surfaces (non-Euclidean geometry). By 1854, Bernhard Riemann has taken an alternative approach to the subject in relation to smooth surfaces.

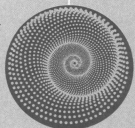

BIOGRAPHIES

EUCLID (c. 325 BCE–c. 265 BCE)

Euclid was a Greek mathematician who pulled together the scattered work on geometry undertaken in the ancient world and turned it into a refined, structured whole, starting with simple assumptions and building up increasingly complex proofs. Very little is known about him biographically; details about his life, such as his being born in Tyre, seem to be fictional additions by later authors. It has even been suggested that Euclid did not exist as an individual, but rather that his output was that of a group of philosophers making use of a fake name. (This certainly happened in the twentieth century, when a group of mathematicians wrote under the pseudonym Nicolas Bourbaki.) If this was the case, it's likely that Euclid was named for the earlier philosopher Euclid of Megara. Many ancient Greek authors simply referred to "the author of *The Elements*," the 13-volume book on geometry (with a bit of other mathematics) that was Euclid's famous work. It appears to have been written in Alexandria, and he is sometimes referred to as Euclid of Alexandria accordingly.

GASPARD MONGE (1746–1818)

Born in Beaune in Eastern France, Gaspard Monge would make significant contributions to two areas of geometry. After mathematical and physics training at the Collège de la Trinité in Lyon, he became a draftsman at a military engineering school in Charleville-Mézières. He went on to become a professor of mathematics there. Monge became a significant academic figure in the French Revolution. Before he became more of an administrator, his experience as a draftsman stood him in good stead in developing what is now known as "descriptive geometry"—the mathematical procedures needed to project three-dimensional objects onto two dimensions to enable engineering drawings and other plans to be drawn up. He started to develop this while still working as a draftsman, when asked to produce the plan for a fortification that made it impossible for an enemy to see or fire at a military position. Monge's more sophisticated contribution to geometry was the branch known as "differential geometry." Again, he was dealing with three-dimensional shapes, but here it was the use of calculus and algebra to describe the behavior of curves and shapes in a three-dimensional environment. Monge died in Paris, aged 72.

HERMANN MINKOWSKI
(1864–1909)

Born in Aleksotas (then in Russia, now in
Lithuania), Hermann Minkowski moved with
his family to Königsberg (then in Germany, now
Kaliningrad in Russia) when he was a child, so he
is usually regarded as a German mathematician.
Specifically, he was the mathematician who
persuaded Albert Einstein to accept a more
geometrical view of the world in thinking of
space and time as a unified entity: space-time.
Minkowski lectured at a number of universities,
including the ETH in Zurich, where Einstein
was one of his students. However, it was after
Minkowski moved on to Göttingen that he
worked on the mathematics of space-time and
devised the Minkowski diagram, still the main
method of representing space-time events.
Geometrically his most significant work was on
the geometric properties of multidimensional
space, including the four-dimensional space-
time, and the "geometry of numbers," which links
number theory and multidimensional spaces.
Göttingen was Minkowski's final teaching post,
where he worked with the greatest German
mathematician of that period, David Hilbert.
Sadly, Minkowski was only 44 when he died
of a ruptured appendix.

CHRISTIAN FELIX KLEIN
(1849–1925)

Christian Felix Klein was born in Düsseldorf
in Germany. He studied at Bonn, originally
intending to work in physics, but became
fascinated by mathematics, which would take
him as lecturer and then professor to Erlangen,
Munich, Leipzig (where his chair was explicitly
in geometry), and Göttingen. One of his most
significant achievements in the field was not
directly in mathematics, but as editor of the
journal *Mathematische Annalen*, which had
been very much in the shadow of *Crelle's Journal*,
but became a leading mathematical publication.
Klein's dissertation was on the geometry of lines
in a plane, and geometry would continue to
be the central focus of his output. He carried
forward work on non-Euclidean geometry, and, in
his so-called Erlangen Program, linked geometry
to "group theory" and aspects of symmetry that
would become important in twentieth-century
physics. He also worked in complex analysis—
calculus for complex numbers. To lovers of
recreational math, he is best known as the
creator of the Klein bottle, a bottle that, like a
Möbius strip, has only one side—though it can
only be made in three dimensions as a projection
of a four-dimensional object.

EUCLIDEAN GEOMETRY

THE MAIN CONCEPT | Euclidean geometry primarily deals with shapes on a flat plane. The mechanism Euclid used in his *Elements* was to start with five simple axioms ("postulates")—statements assumed to be self-evident about lines, angles, and circles—and build a series of proofs on these. These are: a straight line can be drawn between any two points; any straight line can be extended indefinitely; a circle can be defined by its center point and its radius; all right angles are equal; and a fifth, the "parallel postulate," which states that if the angle between two lines is less than 180 degrees they will meet (often phrased as "two lines are parallel if they only meet at infinity"). With the axioms established, Euclid proved a series of theorems—each a statement about the behavior of geometric shapes. The theorems of Euclidean geometry build on one another to prove, for example, that the angles of a triangle add up to 180 degrees, or that if each of two sides on a pair of triangles are of equal length and the angle between them is the same, the triangles are identical, known to geometers as "congruent." Other triangles can be proved to be "similar" to one another, where the same triangle is scaled up or down. The best known of all the theorems, the "Pythagorean theorem," describes the relationship of side lengths that must exist in a right triangle.

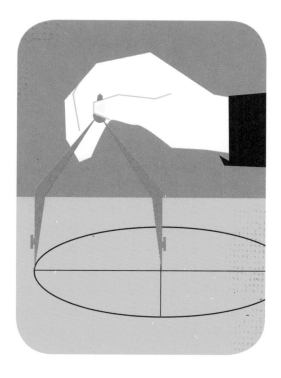

DRILL DOWN | Although classical geometry is sometimes thought of as being all about shapes on a flat, two-dimensional surface, Euclid did give some consideration to three dimensions. One topic of considerable interest in early times was the Platonic solids—three-dimensional shapes that could be made from sides of identical regular flat shapes. There were only five of these: the tetrahedron, octahedron, and icosahedron with 4, 8, and 20 triangular faces; the cube with 6 square faces; and the dodecahedron with 12 pentagonal faces. There is something appealing about the regularity of these solids and some ancient Greeks considered them linked to the five elements of earth, air, fire, water, and the quintessence, or ether.

FOCUS | *Seventeenth-century German astronomer Johannes Kepler believed that there was a relationship between the five Platonic solids and the six known planets: Mercury, Venus, Earth, Mars, Jupiter, and Saturn. He envisaged a structure of spheres, separated by the Platonic solids, producing the scale of the solar system. The concept had no scientific basis: it was an early theory based on "beauty," a concept physicists still pursue.*

TRIGONOMETRY

THE MAIN CONCEPT | The relationship between angles and the length of sides of triangles is a natural extension of geometry, called "trigonometry," meaning "triangle measurement." Thinking of one of the angles in a right triangle, the "sine" of that angle is the ratio of the length of the opposite side to that of the hypotenuse (longest side). The "cosine" is the same measure but using the ratio of the third side to the hypotenuse. And the "tangent" is the ratio of the opposite side to the third side (you may be familiar with the "SOH CAH TOA" method of remembering this). These simple "functions" have proved useful in surveying, navigation (for example, with sextants), and astronomy. Trigonometry also enables triangulation— deducing distances by measuring the angles of triangles between known positions and a new point, which proved transformational for accurate map making. However, the triangular definition of the trigonometric functions was limiting as it could only deal with angles up to 90 degrees. An extended definition imagines the triangle drawn in a circle with the right angle at the center. The hypotenuse is the radius and can be swept around the circle, giving values that oscillate periodically. This approach produces an alternative unit of angle, the "radian." Trigonometry was also extended out of the plane, using a sphere rather than a circle as the base.

DRILL DOWN | Once trigonometric functions were measured using a circle, it became possible to think of the size of an angle as the amount by which the hypotenuse of the triangle has swept around the circumference of a circle. Based on a circle with a radius of 1, the circumference is 2π—so a rotation of 360 degrees is considered 2π radians, the name given to this new unit. This approach proved invaluable when trigonometry was combined with calculus, as using the radian measure produced simpler results. It is also a more mathematically rigorous unit than the culturally influenced degrees. Radians are now the standard scientific unit for the measurement of angles.

FOCUS | *In many countries, high points in the landscape are marked with different styles of concrete pillars, usually topped with a metal plate. Known as "triangulation stations" in the US and "trig points" in the UK, these are mounts for theodolites, optical instruments used to enable trigonometric measurements. They have largely been made redundant by GPS satellite navigation systems.*

PI

THE MAIN CONCEPT | A handful of universal constants are familiar to most of us—and leading the pack is pi (π), the ratio of a circle's circumference to its diameter, named using the first letter of the Greek word for circumference. Approximate values of pi were known at least 4,000 years ago. Later, the ancient Greek mathematician Archimedes came up with a clever mechanism for setting limits on pi—he drew a regular polygon that just surrounded a circle and a smaller similar polygon that just fitted inside the circle. The length of the circle's circumference had to be in between the perimeters of the two polygons. The more sides the polygons had, the more accurate the calculation (as in the illustration opposite). Archimedes used a pair of 96-sided polygons to show that pi lay between $223/71$ and $22/7$ (3.1408 and 3.1429). The number is both "irrational" and "transcendental," meaning effectively that it can't be calculated exactly by a finite mechanism. Far more decimal places were pinned down later by calculating parts of infinite series that sum to pi. It has now been calculated to quadrillions of decimal places. Pi obviously has a use in geometry, but it also turns up in many aspects of physics, from vibrating strings to the uncertainty principle, in the normal distribution of statistics, and in many more places.

DRILL DOWN | Pi appears where it's least expected. Because of its occurrence in probability distributions, a cocktail stick and a set of parallel lines (floorboards will often do) can be used to calculate an approximate value of pi. Repeatedly drop the stick onto an area divided up with lines that are farther apart than the length of the stick. An approximate value for pi is $2ln/wx$, where l is the length of the stick, n the number of drops, w the width of the line gaps, and x the number of sticks that cross a line. The greater the number of drops, the closer the value will get to pi.

FOCUS | *Ever since ancient times, geometers have tried to "square the circle"— devise a way to produce a square with the same area as a circle using only the geometry tools of a straightedge and compasses. The ancient Greeks even had a name for people who tried to do this:* tetragonidzeins. *Sadly, because pi is transcendental, squaring the circle is impossible.*

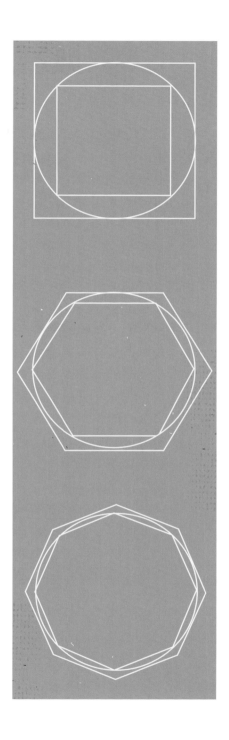

CONIC SECTIONS

THE MAIN CONCEPT | Conic sections, which have been studied *ad nauseam* through mathematical history, are simply the shapes obtained by cutting a slice from a cone. Although an arbitrary-sounding concept (why not sausage sections or Gummy bear–shaped sections, say?), it proves valuable because the cone is unique in the range of useful shapes produced this way. Slice it parallel to its base and you get a circle. Cut it across the cone at an angle to the base but staying within the cone and you get an ellipse. Make the same cut but slicing through the base gives you a parabola. And making a similar cut but with all of the slice on one side of the vertex gives a hyperbola. (Strictly you need two cones, point to point, to get both pieces of this "bipartite" curve.) When it comes to applications, all the sections have metaphorical uses—we speak of a circular argument and an elliptical expression, parables are parabolic, and when we come up with hyperbole it is excessive, just as the hyperbola exceeds the bounds of the cone. More practically, all the conic sections turn up in astronomy, and most are relevant in areas of physics and engineering, from mirror shapes to the design of gears.

DRILL DOWN | The topic where conic sections probably have the broadest application is in orbits. For a long time, planetary orbits were assumed to be circles—the "perfect" shape—and many orbits are in fact nearly circular. But German astronomer Johannes Kepler showed observationally that planets follow elliptical orbits, while Isaac Newton proved mathematically that a gravitational inverse square law—where the attraction falls off with the square of the distance between the bodies—produces an ellipse. Not every object stays in continuous orbit, though—some comets, for example, dip into the solar system and fly out again. Depending on whether or not they go around the Sun, their orbits follow either a parabola or a hyperbola.

FOCUS | *The practical applications of conic sections tend to be of particular value to specialists, but a treatise on them gave us an iconic symbol. In his 1655* Tract on Conic Sections, *Oxford mathematician John Wallis wrote, "let the symbol ∞ represent Infinity." He never said why he chose this distinctive shape, though some have suggested it's the next simplest continuous loop after 0.*

POWERS, ROOTS & LOGARITHMS
Page 34
EUCLIDEAN GEOMETRY
Page 54
GEOMETRY & ASTRONOMY
Page 62

GEOMETRY & ASTRONOMY

THE MAIN CONCEPT | Astronomy and mathematics have gone hand in hand since humans began studying the heavens—so much so that astronomy was counted part of mathematics rather than the natural sciences until well into the nineteenth century. Keeping track of the motion of the planets was difficult, and sometimes even weird, particularly in pre-Copernican days—before Nicolaus Copernicus proposed that the Sun, not the Earth, sat motionless at the center of the universe, with the planets orbiting around it. Sometimes outer planets appeared to reverse their direction of travel. We now know this is because the Earth's orbit means we see, for example, Mars's orbit from a changing viewpoint. But when it was thought that everything traveled round the Earth, complex geometric patterns known as "epicycles," where smaller circular motions traveled around larger orbits, were required. Although Newton used calculus to work on his gravitational theory, his masterpiece on gravity and forces, the *Principia*, almost entirely employs geometry and the properties of conic sections in its arguments. Geometry would also be used to calculate astronomical distances, from Archimedes's early attempt to calculate the size of the universe to modern-day parallax methods. It is also required in telescope design.

DRILL DOWN | Hold a finger in front of your face, then open and close each eye in turn. The finger appears to move from side to side. Do so with an object farther away, and it seems to move less. This is parallax. By measuring how much the object appears to move, and knowing the distance between our eyes, we can use simple trigonometry to work out the distance to the object. Astronomers often use separate telescopes this way, but a more powerful parallax technique uses the same view six months apart, when the Earth will be on the opposite side of its orbit—the equivalent of using eyes separated by 190,000,000 miles (300,000,000 kilometers).

FOCUS | *The strangest book Archimedes wrote was called* The Sand Reckoner. *In it, he estimated the number of grains of sand it would take to fill the universe. His intention was to show how the limited Greek number system could be indefinitely extended. But to do so he had to employ several geometric techniques to estimate the size of the universe before considering filling it.*

PERSPECTIVE & PROJECTION

THE MAIN CONCEPT | Very old paintings have a strange, flat appearance—there is no depth because the painter has not taken into account the geometric effect of perspective. Put simply, the farther away things are, the smaller they appear to be. To get an image correctly in perspective involves drawing (literally or mentally) a series of perspective lines from the viewer's position into the distance. Parallel lines in the actual world converge at distant points known as "vanishing points." The idea of perspective was so novel when architect and artist Filippo Brunelleschi demonstrated it in the early fifteenth century that he needed a visual aid. This was a mirror image of the Florence Baptistery, painted with perspective on the back of a board, with a hole through the vanishing point; as a nice detail, Brunelleschi made the sky of polished silver, so it reflected the clouds. Viewers looked at the real baptistery through the hole on the reverse side of the board, then a mirror was used to switch their view to the painted version. Perspective views are part of graphical projection, where a three-dimensional object is projected onto a two-dimensional surface. The shape of a cube, for example, alters significantly when drawn from different viewpoints. Projection is essential both for providing maps of the Earth on flat paper and in technical and architectural drawings.

DRILL DOWN | We are so used to projected maps of the Earth that it is easy to forget that what is seen cannot be 100 percent accurate. Something has to be lost in going from a spherical surface to a flat map. The familiar map of the world is a variant of cartographer Gerardus Mercator's 1569 "Mercator projection," which projected the features of the Earth onto a cylinder surrounding the equator and was then unfurled. The result is beneficial for nautical navigation but provides a distorted view of the areas of countries: areas are magnified as you move away from the equator. For example, Greenland looks much bigger than India; in reality, they are very similar in area.

FOCUS | *One effect of perspective is that the farther away an illuminated object is, the dimmer it appears to be. This effect is used by astronomers to estimate distances using "standard candles." These are particular types of astronomical object that appear to have consistent brightness. The first standard candles were stars known as Cepheid variables—identified in 1912 by astronomer Henrietta Swan Leavitt as having a regular cycle of brightness.*

GEOMETRY & ASTRONOMY
Page 62
GRAPH THEORY
Page 68
NON-EUCLIDEAN GEOMETRY
Page 70

CARTESIAN COORDINATES

THE MAIN CONCEPT | In the early days, geometry was considered totally different from arithmetic—as different as art and music are to each other. It wasn't just that there was no obvious way of connecting them, they were simply considered totally different things. By the seventeenth century, though, French philosopher and mathematician René Descartes was the first to widely publish a link between the two, although others—notably French mathematicians Pierre de Fermat and Nicole Oresme—achieved similar results. The essential step was what became known as "Cartesian coordinates," after Descartes. The system used today (incorporating a refinement made to Descartes's original, see opposite) involves using a pair of number lines, one horizontal and one vertical, crossing at zero. By convention, the horizontal line is the "x axis," and the vertical line the "y axis." Then a point on a two-dimensional plane, for example, 1 unit to the right on the x axis, and 2 units up the y axis, can represent variables x and y with the values 1 and 2 respectively. In principle, there can be more axes at right angles to the existing pair—dealing with as many dimensions as a mathematician wants to play with. The real power of the system is that an algebraic equation, such as $y = x^2 + 3x + 2$ now became simply a curve, mapped out with Cartesian coordinates (a parabola in this case).

DRILL DOWN | The ability to relate equations and curves meant that Cartesian coordinates were far more than simply a way to give an identifier to a position on the plane. It made possible what would become known as "analytic geometry," where the results of different equations could be derived from curves (or later, multidimensional shapes). When Newton and Leibniz came up with calculus, this relationship between equations and curves or shapes would be fundamental to the development of what proved to be one of the most versatile and powerful tools of mathematics. Arguably, the introduction of Cartesian coordinates was the point at which mathematics became the essential tool for physics.

FOCUS | *Although Descartes is credited with inventing the Cartesian coordinate system, unlike the one we use today, his original version had only a single number line, the x axis. The other value was simply represented by a measurement away from it in the up or down direction, rather than having a second axis. This would be added a decade or so later by other mathematicians, making Descartes's concept complete.*

LINEAR ALGEBRA
Page 92

DIFFERENTIAL CALCULUS
Page 98

INTEGRAL CALCULUS
Page 100

GRAPH THEORY

THE MAIN CONCEPT | Topology (see page 72) involves reducing shapes to flexible equivalents, but a subset of topology takes things even further, leaving the bare skeleton of the original object. Where most of us think of a "graph" as an alternative term for a chart, to mathematicians it is a visual representation of this cutdown form. Graph theory converts more complex objects—both physical or virtual—into dots (known as "nodes" or "vertices") connected with "lines" (or "edges"). Such graphs can refer to shapes, corresponding to the vertices and edges of that shape, but are also used to study networks of relationships. Although not formally identified as such, graph theory is generally said to have originated with German mathematician Leonhard Euler's 1736 analysis of the "Seven Bridges of Königsberg" problem (see opposite), though it was not formally established until the late nineteenth century. Examples of graph theory include the types of family tree that feature each person as a node, with the lines representing familial links. Similarly, the trees and cladistic diagrams of biology are graphs. Sociologists use graphs to describe social networks, while in computing they are widely used both to analyze a communications network—the Internet, for example—and the organization of data. Graph theory has proved useful wherever there is a structure that involves linkages between data points.

DRILL DOWN | The Seven Bridges of Königsberg problem (below) involved finding a route across each of that city's seven bridges without crossing a bridge twice. Leonhard Euler approached the challenge by effectively introducing graph theory—ignoring geography and turning land masses into nodes, and bridges into lines. Leaving aside the first and last node, every other node had to have an even number of attached lines. This was because a line could only be used once, so these nodes needed the same number of entrance and exit lines, otherwise the route would end at that node. But in Königsberg, each actual land mass had an odd number of bridges leading to it; the route didn't exist.

EUCLIDEAN GEOMETRY
Page 54
KNOT THEORY
Page 76
SET THEORY
Page 106

FOCUS | *A popular concept derived from graph theory is six degrees of separation— the idea that everyone in the world is a maximum of six contacts away from everyone else. The number six is not rigorously scientific, emerging from a piece of 1920s fiction and ad hoc experiments involving forwarding letters in the 1960s, but we do live in a strongly connected world.*

NON-EUCLIDEAN GEOMETRY

THE MAIN CONCEPT | Although the ancient Greeks extended geometry beyond a flat plane to take in simple three-dimensional forms such as a sphere, cone, and Platonic solids (see page 55), it does not seem to have occurred to them to extend the theorems of geometry, such as the sum of the angles of a triangle, to deal with the familiar three-dimensional space that we occupy. It's perfectly possible to do geometry on a curved space in three dimensions, for example, such as the surface of the Earth. Here angles of a triangle add up to more than 180 degrees, while the shortest distance between two points, a straight line on a flat surface, becomes a "great circle"—a line connecting the two points that follows a circumference of the sphere. Simple non-Euclidean geometries are either elliptical—where the surface curves as an ellipse (including the special case of a sphere)—or hyperbolic, where the surface is the interior of the curves of a hyperbola and triangles have angles that add up to less than 180 degrees. This is only the start though— there is no reason mathematically to be limited to three dimensions. And more sophisticated geometries exist, such as Riemannian geometry, which allows for non-regular surfaces, and where the main requirement on the curved space is that it does not vary discontinuously.

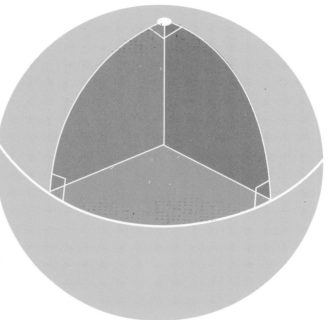

DRILL DOWN | The use of three dimensions in geometry seems perfectly natural because we are familiar with orientation and measurement in three-dimensional space. But what about further dimensions? Even the natural world demands we consider four dimensions—with time as the fourth—while mathematicians deal with imagined spaces containing thousands of dimensions. No one can visualize what a more-than-three-dimensional object looks like, but there are some commonly used four-dimensional shapes, such as the tesseract, or hypercube, which has a total of eight cubic sides. In practice, though the mathematics may be working in many dimensions, illustrations are projected onto two or three dimensions, often by selecting the most relevant to observe.

FOCUS | *The most famous application of non-Euclidean geometry is Einstein's general theory of relativity, which is our best theory of gravitation. It was nearly Hilbert's general relativity. Einstein was struggling with the mathematics of curved space and mathematician David Hilbert set out to produce his own equations. They were ready to be published before Einstein's, but the last-minute discovery of an error held Hilbert up.*

TOPOLOGY

THE MAIN CONCEPT | The word "topology" literally means the "science of place." It's the mathematics of surfaces and objects that has total disregard for size and shape—it is just concerned with how a substance (real or imagined) is either continuous or broken. Two shapes are topologically identical if one can be deformed into the other without tearing it, just stretching it or compressing it as required; it has sometimes been described as "qualitative geometry." So, for example, thinking of pasta shapes, spiral fusilli are topologically identical to spaghetti—neither has any openings—while penne and cannelloni are topologically identical, with a single hole. Topology is also concerned with concepts such as surfaces and edges. So, for example, a ribbon that makes a circular loop has two sides and edges (being a perfect, mathematical object with no thickness), while a looped ribbon with a twist in it—a so-called Möbius strip—has just one side and one edge. There is no way to transform one into the other by simply stretching it. Topology has also been extended to include the equivalent properties of sets. Apart from its mathematical interest, topology is relevant in physics and engineering where surfaces and manifolds are involved, while the linked area of topology known as knot theory (see page 76) is useful both in physics and biology.

DRILL DOWN | Although it's possible to get an overview of topology by thinking of what can be manipulated in a sheet of infinitely stretchable and squashable rubber, there are some definitions required. Most notably there is a divide on whether it is possible to so compress a part that sticks out until it is no longer there. Topology that assumes this is possible is known as "homotopic." This approach regards, for example, the letters O, D, and R to be identical, as the legs of the R could be squashed to nothing. If the assumption is that there will always be some residual bumpiness, the approach is "homeomorphic." Here O and D are identical, but R isn't.

FOCUS | *Topology was a relative latecomer as a mathematical discipline, with the term "topologie" first used in German in 1847 by the mathematician Johann Listing, and not gaining its English form until the 1880s. We perhaps should call the familiar Möbius strip a Möbius-Listing strip as Listing came up with the concept in the same year as August Möbius, and went on to study more complex twisted structures.*

GRAPH THEORY
Page 68

KNOT THEORY
Page 76

SET THEORY
Page 106

ALGEBRAIC GEOMETRY & FIELDS

THE MAIN CONCEPT | "Algebraic geometry" sounds like another term for the links between algebra and geometry formalized by Descartes (see page 66)—and its starting point is a subset of that, focusing on the points at which a polynomial (what we'd think of as one side of an equation, with a mix of constants and variables) hits zeroes. But algebraic geometry leads on to the more general study of the way the solutions of sets of polynomials vary in a geometric fashion. This has become a major area of study in mathematics, whether for abstract mathematical benefit—the proof of Fermat's Last Theorem made use of algebraic geometry techniques (see opposite)—through to modern physics, which since the nineteenth century has been increasingly dependent on such solutions, especially since Einstein's general theory of relativity, and continuing with concepts such as string theory. The fundamental change in physics was the idea of a "field," originated by Michael Faraday and made mathematical by Scottish physicist James Clerk Maxwell. At its simplest, a field is just a number space—it's a mathematical construct that has a value at points in space and time. So, for example, the altitude of every point on the surface of the Earth is a field. Farady used lines to show the strength of a field, such as the Earth's magnetic field, where the field is stronger the closer the lines are together.

DRILL DOWN | Fields were first used on electricity and magnetism, but have been extended to everything from gravity to the Higgs field, which gives fundamental particles their mass. Maxwell took fields from a qualitative idea to a quantitative mechanism, forging a bridge between maths and physics. An essential contribution was the realization that the values at points in the field could represent "vectors"—values with both a size and direction—as well as "scalars" (just numbers) and the development of mathematics to deal with their changes. Some physicists consider the entire universe, sometimes referred to as "the bulk," to be a collection of interacting fields. Working with fields in this way has strong parallels with algebraic geometry.

FOCUS | *Pierre de Fermat's proof of his "last theorem" amounted to a few words scribbled in a margin, claiming there wasn't room to write it there. He was unaware of the mathematics that Andrew Wiles would use between 1993 and 1995 in a pair of papers totaling 129 pages in length, and making use of number theory and the algebraic geometry of elliptic curves to crack the 350-year-old problem.*

POWERS, ROOTS & LOGARITHMS
Page 34
CARTESIAN COORDINATES
Page 66
NON-EUCLIDEAN GEOMETRY
Page 70

KNOT THEORY

THE MAIN CONCEPT | Mathematicians have long been fascinated by knots—though being mathematicians, their version of a knot bears limited resemblance to the real thing: one of the requirements for a mathematical knot is that the "string" the knot is in must have no ends. Also, like the lines of classical geometry, these strings are strictly one-dimensional, having no thickness. Knot theory is an important part of topology (see page 72), and as always in topology, two examples are considered identical if it's possible to transform one into the other without tearing—in this case, without cutting that continuous loop. There is a hierarchy of knots, starting with the open loop (entertainingly known as the "unknot") and adding in more and more loops—so the next form up, for example, is the "trefoil," where the string overlaps at three points to produce three lobes. The mathematical study of knots may seem abstract, but like so many areas of pure math it has proved to have value. Knots, like molecules, can have chirality (handedness) and symmetry, and the parallels between knot theory and, for example, the structure of DNA and the folding of proteins has proved valuable. Similarly, physicists have found the mathematics needed to deal with transforming knot structures useful in both statistical mechanics and quantum computing.

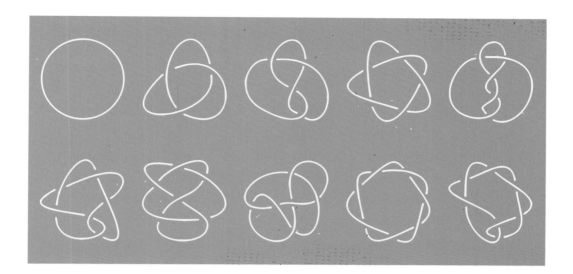

DRILL DOWN | When knots were first studied in the nineteenth century, a leading proponent was Peter Guthrie Tait, a lifetime friend of James Clerk Maxwell (see page 74). Tait was inspired by an (incorrect) theory by William Thomson, later Lord Kelvin, suggesting that atoms were knots in the ether—the rarefied substance assumed to fill all of space, and which light waves passed through. Tait compiled a table of "prime" (non-compound) knots with up to ten crossings, of which there proved to be 165. Tables have now reached at least 16 crossings, producing an impressive 1,388,705 different knots. Though knot theory became part of topology, its origins were therefore, in part, a failed physical theory.

FOCUS | *An unlikely sounding feature of knots is their "writhe," a measure of how coiled up the string is. The writhe is, loosely, the number of positive crossings in the knot minus the number of negative, where a positive crossing is one where the string under the crossing goes from right to left. It's possible to change writhe without changing the topology by twisting the string.*

PERSPECTIVE AND PROJECTION
Page 64

GRAPH THEORY
Page 68

TOPOLOGY
Page 72

FRACTALS

THE MAIN CONCEPT | Traditional geometry has largely focused on regular, smoothly shaped objects—but the natural world is crinkly. Fractals are mathematical forms more like real-world shapes. This often involves having structures that naturally scale up in a consistent way. If you zoom into a part of a fractal, it will look similar to the whole—a concept known as being self-similar. Again, this is a common feature of the natural world where, for example, the branch of a tree often resembles a scaled-down version of the whole tree. Fractals often display interesting behavior. Arguably the earliest example, the Koch snowflake, has an infinite perimeter yet can be enclosed in a finite area. It was soon followed by the Sierpinski triangle (or gasket, illustrated opposite), an intricate pattern that manages to have no area at all. The best-known exponent of fractals was French mathematician Benoit Mandelbrot, who gave them their name in 1975 and popularized fractals as graphic art with computer-generated images such as the Mandebrot set, based on iteratively evolving, relatively simple mathematical formulae. As well as being used to generate CGI landscapes, an early hope for fractal technology was highly compressed images. This was extremely effective, but was overtaken by hardware developments. However, fractal methods are used to structure data in a number of analytical methods.

DRILL DOWN | By the late 1980s, computers were handling increasingly large images with expanding color palettes—images were growing faster than the disk technology to store them. The English mathematician Michael Barnsley devised a method using fractal compression that looked for fractal style similarities, so was particularly good on natural images. The compression was effective, but by the early 1990s the simpler JPEG compression standard was available and disk storage grew fast enough to cope with most requirements. Although fractal compression could render some images far smaller than JPEG (an image could be compressed into an "equation"), it was much more processor intensive. There were applications of the technology, from Microsoft's *Encarta* encyclopedia to some video games, but fractal compression has yet to become a mainstream approach.

FOCUS | *Mandelbrot's breakthrough 1967 paper "How Long is the Coast of Britain? Statistical Self-Similarity and Fractional Dimension" analyzed the coastline paradox—an oddity not noted until the twentieth century. It's impossible to say how long a coastline is, as the shorter the units you measure it in, the more you can dip into crinkles, giving a longer result. The value for Britain varies by hundreds of miles, depending on the measure.*

"The study of mathematics, like the Nile, begins in minuteness, but ends in magnificence."

CHARLES COLTON,
*LACON: OR MANY THINGS IN FEW WORDS;
ADDRESSED TO THOSE WHO THINK* (1820)

3

ALGEBRA & CALCULUS

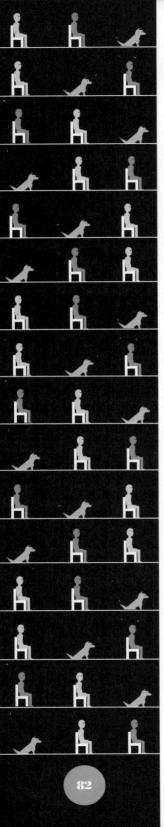

INTRODUCTION

There's an infamous student's complaint, "When will I ever need to use algebra?" Leaving aside the many jobs where it can be directly useful, learning algebra teaches us far more than a way of determining the value of the mysterious x; it's about understanding how to manipulate data in a logical way—something that is beneficial to everyone. Algebra provides a wonderful mechanism for generalization. Where arithmetic deals with explicit numbers, algebra provides us with "variables" such as x and y, which act as containers into which we can plug a whole range of numbers to get a new result. In effect, an "algebraic equation" is a simple kind of algorithm for manipulating data. Yet it didn't start in such a sophisticated form.

The development of algebra

Algebra arguably began with the third-century Greek philosopher Diophantus. He worked with algebraic expressions, though lacking the symbols for operators, he would have rendered, say, $5x^4 + 2x^3 - 4x^2 + 3x - 9$ as something like SS5 C2 x3 M S4 u9. (Of course his version would have been in Greek letters, but this example uses S for square, C for cube, x for unknown, M for minus, and u for unit). However, all of his work was one-off—he didn't generalize the way modern algebra does.

The book that brought algebra to medieval Europe, Al-Khwarizmi's *Hisab al-jabr wa'l muqābalah*, was even less like modern algebra in that it only presented the problems to be dealt with, and the workings, in word form. It wasn't until the sixteenth century that symbols like +, −, and = began to be introduced and algebraic equations could be relatively easily manipulated. But Al-Khwarizmi did show the all-important generalization of solutions. His simple equations were just the start of taking mathematics to the next level, and few contributions to mathematics have proved as powerful as one of the next major developments, calculus.

Calculus

Calculus makes it possible to calculate the outcome from constantly changing values, to work out the areas and volumes of interestingly shaped objects, and far more. Predecessors to calculus date back to the ancient Greeks, who, for example, calculated the area of a circle by dividing it up into more and more triangular-shaped segments. But the full mathematical approach was devised seemingly independently by Isaac Newton and Gottfried Leibniz in the seventeenth century.

Although the seventeenth-century version of calculus made some dubious assumptions that had to be ironed out later to be made mathematically precise, it worked wonderfully in analyzing the mathematics of change and space (it is now more often refered to as "analysis"). Much scientific calculation, particularly in physics, depends to a great extent on the use of calculus.

Sets, groups, and infinity

Equally important to the ability to use mathematics and understand its nature was the introduction of "sets." These crop up as the basis of arithmetic, and took on a whole new level of capability when their definition was expanded to include a special type of set known as a "group," which has a mechanism for generating members of the group from other members. Some groups would prove of particular importance to dealing with symmetry, a mathematical concept central to understanding nature. The use of symmetry in science began with one of the greatest female mathematicians of history, Emmy Noether, who discovered that there was a direct relationship between symmetry and the conservation laws in physics—one was not possible without the other.

Sets also cropped up in the study of the most mind-boggling aspect of mathematics, infinity. Ancient Greek philosophers had contemplated what happens as we count to greater and greater numbers. However, the Greek word for infinity, *apeiron*, has connotations of chaos and disorder. It was not thought of as anything that could have real mathematical significance, but rather something that could be envisaged without ever actually existing.

This was the version of infinity that powered calculus, which involves manipulating an infinite set of infinitely small entities. But at the end of the nineteenth century, German mathematician Georg Cantor combined the ideas that Galileo had first considered with set theory, to examine some of the properties of "real" infinity, including the discovery that one infinity can be bigger than another. In this chapter, the topics go large.

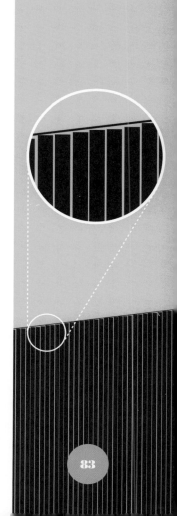

TIMELINE

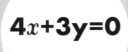

AL-KHWARIZMI
The Persian philosopher Al-Khwarizmi writes the *Hisab al-jabr w'al-muqabala* (*Compendious Book on Calculation by Completion and Balancing*), which will be translated into Latin as *Liber Algebræ et Almucabola* by the English scholar Robert of Chester in 1145.

NEWTON AND CALCULUS
Mathematician and natural philosopher Isaac Newton is forced to spend two years at home in Lincolnshire when Cambridge University is shut down due to the plague. During this time, Newton develops his first ideas on calculus.

c. 240 –270 · c. 820 · 1557 · 1665

EARLY ALGEBRA
Greek philosopher Diophantus produces 13 books of *Arithmetica*, containing a series of algebraic problems. The six surviving books will help shape the development of algebra in Europe—and it is in the margin of a copy of *Arithmetica* that Fermat will write his "last theorem" claim.

PLUS AND MINUS
Welsh mathematician Robert Recorde introduces the = sign saying "I will sette a paire of paralleles . . . because no 2 things can be moare equalle." He also introduced the + and – signs to Great Britain, though they were already in use in Germany.

INFINITY

Bohemian priest and philosopher Bernard Bolzano's work on infinity, including infinite sets and series, is published posthumously. In his book *Paradoxien des Unendlichen* (Paradoxes of the Infinite), Bolzano builds on Galileo's early observations, laying the ground for Georg Cantor's groundbreaking work on infinity.

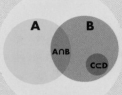

NOETHER'S FIRST THEOREM

German mathematician Emmy Noether proves her "first theorem," which demonstrates the relationship between symmetry and conservation laws. Published in 1918, this will become one of the most important papers in the establishment of particle physics and the unification of physical forces.

1684 · **1848** · **1874** · **1915**

LEIBNIZ VS. NEWTON

German mathematician Gottfried Wilhelm von Leibniz publishes his own version of calculus after meeting with Isaac Newton. Despite little evidence, 24 years later Leibniz is accused by the Royal Society of plagiarism. Leibniz's notation becomes the standard, as does his name for it—calculus.

SET THEORY

German mathematician Georg Cantor publishes the first of a series of papers that establish set theory, which will be used both as the basis for his later work on infinity and as the most basic building blocks for number-based mathematics.

BIOGRAPHIES

AL-KHWARIZMI (c. 780–c. 850)

There are few certain biographical details of Muhammad ibn Musa al-Khwarizmi who was possibly born in Baghdad. He was a scholar in the House of Wisdom there, an academy established by the caliph Al-Mamun, to whom Al-Khwarizmi's manuscript on algebra *Hisab al-jabr w'al-muqabala* (from which the word "algebra" originates) was dedicated. His interest in algebra was at least in part driven by the complexity of Islamic inheritance laws; Al-Khwarizmi stated that its applications included "inheritance, legacies, partition, lawsuits, and trade." The two terms in the title refer to simplifying equations by combining identical powers (*al-jabr*, or "completion") and by combining numbers (*al-muqabala*, or "balancing"). The book used both algebraic and geometric methods, perhaps inspired by Euclid's *Elements*. Other influences were Hebrew and Indian mathematical writing. Al-Khwarizmi also wrote on astronomy and geography. However, his other best-known book was translated as *Algoritmi de Numero Indorum* in Latin. Although it was Fibonacci's *Liber Abaci* that established "Arabic" numerals in Europe (see pages 38–39), Al-Khwarizmi's book also explained them, and the Latinized version of his name gave us the word "algorithm."

ISAAC NEWTON (1643–1727*)

Now regarded as a physicist, in his time Isaac Newton was considered primarily a mathematician. Born in Lincolnshire, he went to Cambridge in 1661, but soon after he graduated, the university closed due to an outbreak of the plague. During time spent at home, Newton claimed he came up with many of the ideas that made him famous, including calculus. After returning to Cambridge, he became Lucasian Professor of Mathematics in 1669 (as did Stephen Hawking in 1979). Two years later he was elected a Fellow of the Royal Society. After falling out with the Society's demonstrator, Robert Hooke, Newton withdrew from the scientific mainstream until the 1680s, when astronomer Edmond Halley persuaded him to consider the motion of the planets. Later, Halley paid to have Newton's mathematical masterpiece on motion and gravity published—*Philosophiae Naturalis Principia Mathematica*. In 1696, Newton became Warden of the Royal Mint and engaged little further in science, apart from publishing *Opticks* in 1704, based on work from decades earlier.

* Newton's birthdate is often given as Christmas Day 1642, and his death year as 1726, but that is old-style dating.

EMMY NOETHER (1882–1935)

Although born Amalie, in Bavaria, Germany, Emmy Noether always preferred Emmy. Unusually for someone who became a leading mathematician, she showed no interest in math at school, and initially trained to teach languages. But by 1903 she was studying mathematics at the University of Erlangen and was awarded a PhD in 1907. By 1915, the German mathematician David Hilbert had put her forward for habilitation, the German academic requirement for professorship, barred to women—Hilbert petitioned the government to make a special exception. The work that put Noether among the mathematical greats was her theorem linking symmetry and the conservation laws of physics. She proved that each of these laws, such as conservation of energy, could be derived directly from assuming a symmetry of nature—if, for example, a system continued to act exactly the same way when rotated, then angular momentum, the "oomph" of rotation, was conserved. Noether's theorem would become absolutely central to developments in twentieth-century physics. In 1933, Noether's Jewish ancestry and support for communism led to her losing her position under the Nazi regime. She moved to America, where she died two years later.

GEORG CANTOR (1845–1918)

Born in St. Petersburg, Russia, of a Swedish father and a Russian mother, Georg Cantor moved with his family to Germany when he was 11. In 1862, he started a course at the ETH in Zurich, but when his father died a year later, he moved to the University of Berlin. Two years after receiving his doctorate in 1867, he took a position at the University of Halle. At the time, Halle was famous for music—but not for math. Undoubtedly Cantor saw this as a stepping stone to return in triumph to Berlin, or another university highly regarded for its mathematics, but the response to his ideas would prevent this happening. Cantor's first major discovery was that it was possible to pair off the infinite points on a line with those on a plane, or multidimensional space—something he himself struggled to accept. He went on to develop the hugely influential mathematics of set theory and, expanding on his work on infinite sets of points, the concept of transfinite numbers. His work was considered outrageous by some, notably the German mathematician Leopold Kronecker who went out of his way to damage Cantor's career. Cantor suffered from depression and in later years spent increasing amounts of time being treated in sanatoria.

EQUATIONS

THE MAIN CONCEPT | If numbers and arithmetic got mathematics started, equations made it soar. The principle is simple—an equation tells us that two things are equal. Typically, an equation will be algebraic, having a combination of variable and fixed quantities, though this isn't necessary. Equations are often compared to old-fashioned weighing scales that work as a balance. When the balance is level, we know that the weight on one side equals the weight on the other, even though, say, one side contains apples and the other, metal weights. Equations can also appear in geometry, as became apparent once Descartes had brought geometry and algebra together with Cartesian coordinates (see page 66). Many shapes can be represented by equations—a simple circle, for example, can be represented as $x^2 + y^2 = r^2$, where r is the radius. Similarly, an equation can feature trigonometric functions, such as $x = sin(y)$. Equations are solved when conditions force one or more of the variables (x and y in the examples above) to have particular values. Depending on the application, solving equations can be used to do anything, from working out the interest in a bank account to the path of a spaceship. Often this involves "simultaneous" equations, where two or more equations are combined to fix the values of the variables (see opposite).

DRILL DOWN | Simultaneous equations bring together multiple equations to provide a solution, using one equation per unknown variable. If we have a single variable, one equation suffices. It's easy to work out x in $2x = 4$ by dividing both sides of the equation by 2. But $2x + y = 5$, has an infinite set of values for x and y. For example, x could be 2 if y was 1, or x could be 1 if y was 3. However, if we also know that $x + y = 3$, then we can replace y in the first equation with $3 - x$ and the only possible values for x and y are 2 and 1 respectively.

BASIC ARITHMETIC; NEGATIVE NUMBERS
Page 26

CARTESIAN COORDINATES
Page 66

BASIC ALGEBRA
Page 90

FOCUS | *The ancient Greeks focused their mathematical expertise on the visual and spatial in geometry. It's not surprising that they didn't develop the concept of equations—not only did they lack the symbols to produce something like A + B = C + D, they would have written them without any spacing. Their equivalent would be* theaandthebtakentogetherare equaltothecanddtakentogether.

BASIC ALGEBRA

THE MAIN CONCEPT | Basic algebra consists of simple algebraic equations, such as $3x + 4 = 0$, or quadratic equations, such as $3x^2 + 8x + 4 = 0$, as well as equations containing multiple variables, such as $4x + 3y = 0$ or $4xy = 0$. Algebraic equations are used to work out the outcome of a process represented by the equation by finding solutions for the variables. For equations with a single variable, the number of solutions depends on the "order" of the equation—the highest exponent of the variable indicates the maximum number of solutions. So $3x + 4 = 0$ is order 1 (as $3x$ is the same as $3x^1$) and has a single solution, easily worked out by taking 4 from both sides of the equals sign, giving $3x = -4$, then dividing both sides by 3 to give $x = -4/3$. Quadratic equations, such as $3x^2 + 8x + 4 = 0$, have two solutions. These can often be worked out as a pair of multiplied mini-equations—in this case $(3x + 2)(x + 2) = 0$. If we give x the value $-2/3$ in the first bracket or -2 in the second it makes the value 0, so these are the solutions of the equation. Usually, a formula is used to work out the solution.

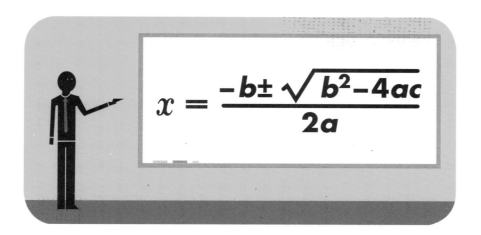

$$x = \frac{-b \pm \sqrt{b^2 - 4ac}}{2a}$$

DRILL DOWN | Although the quadratic equation features heavily in school math it has relatively few applications—it's best seen as training wheels to become familiar with algebra. Even so, when in 2003, the UK's National Union of Teachers suggested teaching the equation was cruel to schoolchildren, mathematicians leapt to its defense. They pointed out that it had been used to calculate crop yields, and that the irrational square root of 2 (which is, for example, the ratio of the sides in the European A paper sizes) is the solution to the simple quadratic equation $x^2 = 2$. On a larger scale, the inverse square laws governing both gravity and electromagnetism are governed by quadratic equations.

FOCUS | *Although problems that involved quadratic equations, such as working out the lengths of the sides of a rectangle, given its area and perimeter, date back around 4,000 years, the first explicit formula for one solution to a quadratic equation was given by Indian mathematician Brahmagupta in 628 CE, while Persian mathematician Al-Khwarizmi correctly identified the familiar formula for both possible solutions in the ninth century.*

POWERS, ROOTS & LOGARITHMS
Page 34

EQUATIONS
Page 88

LINEAR ALGEBRA
Page 92

LINEAR ALGEBRA

THE MAIN CONCEPT | Linear algebra sounds as if it should be the simplest and least useful form of algebra, as it involves only adding component parts together with no powers involved. At its simplest, this could be something like $3x = 6$, though a more likely equation would be $3x + 4y - 7z = 0$. In practice, though, linear algebra underlies many important mathematical methods, including the manipulation of "vector spaces"— collections of mathematical quantities that have both size and direction—and the mathematics of matrices, which are rectangular arrays of numbers that are treated as entities in their own right and have their own system of arithmetic. Both vectors and matrices are widely used in modern physics. For example, vectors are used in field theory and to represent forces, while matrices are important in both the symmetries underlying particle physics and in quantum theory, particularly in components known as eigenvalues and eigenvectors. Eigenvectors are special single-column matrices that transform a matrix in a linear fashion, producing a result that is a multiple of the eigenvector: that multiplier is the eigenvalue. And in the modern approach to geometry, objects involving straight lines, such as lines, planes, and rotations, are defined in terms of linear algebra.

DRILL DOWN | Eigenvalues and eigenvectors are common in quantum physics, but also turn up in Google's PageRank algorithm, used to set the order of its search results. PageRank (allegedly named after Google founder Larry Page) weights pages depending on how many pages point to them and how well ranked those pages are in turn. For example, if CNN's trusted website links to your site, that link is more valued than a link from a blog. But to get CNN's rank, we have to already have ranked every website pointing to it. The algorithm sets up a matrix of rankings: a complex task. The eigenvector of the matrix with eigenvalue 1 turns out to be a score for the page rank of each page.

FOCUS | Eigen *is a German word meaning "proper," "peculiar," or "characteristic." Its use in the strange cross-language words "eigenvalue" and "eigenvector" is probably the closest mathematics and physics come to the way that "-gate" is now applied following Watergate. As well as these two there are also eigenfunctions, eigenloads, eigenperiods, eigensolutions, eigenstates, eigentones, and eigenvibrations.*

INFINITY

THE MAIN CONCEPT | Infinity can be regarded in two ways: as a limit that is never reached, or as the size of an infinite set—a set with no last member. Aristotle argued that infinity was like the Olympic Games. The Olympic Games certainly exist—but unless they are on here and now, I can't show them to you; they are a potential thing. Aristotle argued that infinity was similarly a potential entity. It exists. For example, there's no end to the integers. If there were a biggest integer, then we could simply add 1 to it to get an even bigger one. Yet we can't directly observe infinity. It was this potential infinity that formed the limit in calculus and that is represented by the leminscate ∞. However, in his physics masterpiece, *Two New Sciences* (1638), Galileo spends a little time thinking about infinity, and he describes the real thing. Galileo points out some of the strange behavior of infinity. Add 1 to infinity—and you get the same value. Double infinity … and it's still infinity. Galileo also pointed out that you can have infinite collections of things that seemed simultaneously the same size and different sizes. For example, the infinite set of squares is the same size as the infinite set of integers—every single integer has a corresponding square—even though there are plenty of integers that aren't squares, such as 2, 3, 5, 6, 7, 8, 10, and so on.

DRILL DOWN | The strange arithmetical behavior of infinity is illustrated by "Hilbert's Hotel," named after German mathematician David Hilbert. Imagine a hotel with an infinite set of rooms. (Note that though an infinite set is fine, we shouldn't refer to an infinite number of rooms: infinity is not a number.) The hotel is full. But this isn't a problem. Just move the person in room 1 to room 2. The person in room 2 goes to room 3, and so on throughout the hotel. Everyone is accommodated and there's a room spare. Then an infinite coachload turns up. No problem. Just move everyone into even numbered rooms. The infinite set of odd numbered rooms are now free.

FOCUS | *German mathematician Georg Cantor, who both developed set theory and explored Galileo's "real" infinity, introduced two new symbols for true infinity to distinguish it from potential infinity. An aleph (ℵ), the first letter of the Hebrew alphabet, represents the cardinal (counting) infinity, while the small omega (ω) represents the ordinal (ordering) infinity— the limit of the series first, second, third . . .*

FACTORIALS & PERMUTATIONS

THE MAIN CONCEPT | Much algebraic work makes use of simple arithmetic operations, but some extras have proved particularly valuable. The factorial is a shorthand for a particular repeated operation. Designated using an exclamation mark, it involves multiplying a positive integer by each smaller integer until 1 is reached. (By convention, 0! is 1.) As mathematical symbols go, this is a modern one, introduced in 1808. So, for example, 5! (pronounced "five factorial") is 5 × 4 × 3 × 2 × 1 = 120. Factorials rapidly explode in size. By the time we get to 10! the value is already 3,628,800. The most versatile application of the factorial is in permutations—the different ways that a set of objects can be arranged. For example, if we have three objects, A, B, and C, they can be arranged as: ABC, ACB, BAC, BCA, CAB, and CBA. That's 6—or 3! ways. Similarly, A, B, C, and D can be arranged 4!—24—ways, and so on. Factorials also often crop up as a divisor when calculating combinations—which are subsets of items selected from a longer list, in which we don't care about the order of the items (a "combination lock" should be called a "permutation lock"). There are non-integer equivalents to factorials, but they require calculus to function and are rarely used.

DRILL DOWN | We often want to find how many combinations of, say, three items it's possible to make from a longer list, but don't care about their order. If we've got L items and want to pick s of them, we ignore the rest by using $L! / (L-s)!$—but this counts each possible order of s items. To ignore the duplicates, we divide by $s!$ When picking 3 items from a list of 6, the total options are $6!/3! = 120$, and ignoring order we divide by $3!$ to get 20. This is written mathematically as:

$$\binom{n}{k} = \binom{6}{3} = \frac{n!}{k!(n-k)!} = \frac{6!}{3!(6-3)!} = 20$$

If you set n to 59 and k to 6, the answer is 45,057,474—the chance of winning the jackpot in a lottery with 6 numbers drawn from 59.

NUMBERS
Page 22

SET THEORY
Page 106

PROBABILITY
Page 124

FOCUS | *The exclamation mark (known to programmers as a "shriek") was not universally popular. English mathematician Augustus De Morgan complained: "Among the worst of barbarisms is that of introducing symbols which are quite new in mathematical, but perfectly understood in common, language … the abbreviation n! … gives their pages the appearance of expressing admiration that 2, 3, 4, etc. should be found in mathematical results."*

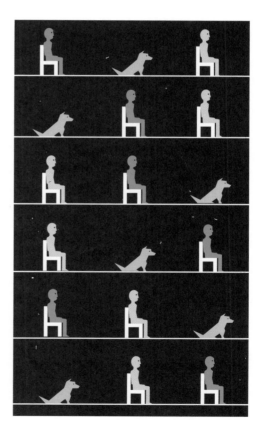

DIFFERENTIAL CALCULUS

THE MAIN CONCEPT | Isaac Newton's masterpiece, *The Principia*, which gives us his three laws of motion and his work on gravitation, is full of geometry—but to get his results Newton used a new approach he called the "method of fluxions," now called calculus, the name given to it by Newton's competitor, Gottfried Leibniz. The "differential" part distinguishes it from integral calculus (see page 100): the two approaches to calculus are inverses of each other. Differential calculus is used to work out the rate of change of one variable with respect to another. For example, imagine you are trying to work out the acceleration of a car. If the car's speed increases steadily, a plot of the speed against time is a straight line, and the acceleration is just the slope of that line—the change in speed divided by the change in time. But what if, for example, the speed increases with the square of the time? Now, the plot is curved. But imagine zooming in to a very tiny part of the curve—it's almost a straight line, and you can use the slope as before. Differential calculus takes smaller and small segments which, at the "limit," are infinitesimally small; at that point the actual value drops out. This is extremely powerful whenever one value (here, speed)—varies with another (here, time).

DRILL DOWN | In his method of fluxions, Newton used "pricked notation," where the rate of change was represented by a dot over the symbol for the thing changing. This was difficult to read and many equations in calculus don't involve time. In Leibniz's notation, still used today, the way x changes with time is shown as dx/dt, while the way that x varies with y is dx/dy. Both methods involved having a small change (represented as δx by Leibniz and o by Newton) that disappears, and could be worked using simple rules. So, for example, if $y = 2x^3$, differentiating it we get $dy/dx = 6x^2$—multiplying by the exponent and reducing the exponent by 1.

FOCUS | *When one of Newton's associates, John Keill, published a paper accusing Gottfried Leibniz, the co-discoverer of calculus, of plagiarism, Leibniz was dismayed and asked the Royal Society to establish the truth. The Royal Society set up an 11-man committee, which came down on Newton's side. Not surprising, as the report's author was the President of the Royal Society—Isaac Newton.*

INTEGRAL CALCULUS

THE MAIN CONCEPT | Where differential calculus uses disappearingly tiny changes to see how one variable changes with respect to another, integral calculus divides a shape up into disappearingly narrow segments to calculate the overall area (or equivalent in more dimensions). So, for example, to find the area of a circle, it can be divided up into slices. If more and more slices are used, the curves at the top and bottom of the slice become closer and closer to straight lines: in the "limit" of taking an infinite set of infinitely thin slices, the exact value is obtained. Approximating this way with narrow rectangles was used in ancient times before the idea of taking it to infinitesimal limits was introduced. Integral calculus is the inverse of differential calculus. As this "integration" involves adding up slices, it is represented by an *S* for "sum"—but that *S* is stretched to form a kind of bracket $\int$, which is usually annotated with small numbers top and bottom showing the range over which the variable value is being considered. Integrals are used both in finding areas and volumes, but also widely in physics to reverse the kind of operation resulting from differential calculus—so, for example, given the varying velocity of a moving body, integration will give you how far it has traveled.

DRILL DOWN | When Newton and Leibniz first introduced calculus, the philosopher Bishop George Berkeley pointed out that there were serious problems with the approach as it often involved dividing a value by another value, each of which were allowed to become zero—and zero divided by zero is meaningless. At the time, this was mostly swept under the carpet, as calculus worked and was extremely useful. Mathematicians Augustin-Louis Cauchy and Karl Weierstrass would each refine the approach until the problem was removed because instead of calculating a final result it was seen as the limit of a process which made the disappearing quantity closer and closer to zero without ever actually reaching it.

FOCUS | *Integrating often involves a range that runs to infinity, which can result in interesting results. The shape made by plotting a graph of 1/x for every x bigger than 1, rotated around the axis to make a long, pointed object known as Gabriel's Horn, has the odd property of having a finite volume, but an infinite surface area.*

FUNCTIONS

THE MAIN CONCEPT | Given its modern notation by Swiss mathematician Leonhard Euler, a function is a powerful mathematical concept that applies a "black box" operation to a number or more complex mathematical structure. A function involving the variable x is written $f(x)$—pronounced "f of x." The function's internal workings can contain any mathematical structure that uses x. That might be very simple—for example, it could be $2x$. In that case, whatever value x has, $f(x)$ has twice that value. But it could also be a 1,000-line-long piece of mathematics. We replace that mathematics with $f(x)$, and to get the result, we plug the desired value for x into that mathematical structure. Functions are like maps linking inputs (the domain) and outputs (the range). Functions occur all the time in mathematics and physics and have analogs in the physical world. So, for example, on a toaster with a dial that has positions corresponding to different amount of browning of toast, the degree of browning is a function of the position of the dial. Functions are also the main structural unit of computer programming languages. Closely related to functions are operators. Effectively, an operator is a mechanism for applying something like a function to a whole collection of variables or places in a space or field at once.

DRILL DOWN | Computer programs are usually written in a programming language. This is an intermediary between the human programmer and the manipulation of 0s and 1s that goes on within the computer's processor. It was soon realized that it would be useful to break up the code for a program into separate chunks that handled specific aspects of the job as a whole. These could then be used many times within the program and also had the added benefit of being reusable in other programs. Most such subroutines are functions, acting like a mathematical function. They produce a result and have settings determined by variables that are fed into the function, just as the x is fed into $f(x)$.

FOCUS | *The word "function" is one that non-mathematicians think of as "what something does." Mathematics makes use of a very specific aspect of this definition—executing a task. It was first used mathematically by Gottfried Leibniz to describe the relationship of a straight line to a curve (e.g., tangents), but the mathematician Johann Bernoulli expanded its use to its present form.*

VECTOR ALGEBRA & CALCULUS

THE MAIN CONCEPT | Standard algebra and calculus deal with "scalar" values—just numbers—and the way they change. However, many natural quantities are vectors—they have both size and direction. It was realized in the nineteenth century that the mathematics that worked so well with scalars could be extended to vectors. Basic vector algebra is linked to linear algebra, while vector calculus typically applies to changes in a field, each point of which has a vector value. The simplest aspect of vector algebra is addition—as vectors have both size and direction, this addition is visualized by placing two arrows on a chart, the second starting at the point of the first—the result, produced by drawing an arrow from the tail of the first arrow to the point of the second, is the result of the sum. Vector calculus has three main operations: grad (gradient), div (divergence), and curl. The gradient is the equivalent of differentiation, but applied to every point in a field of scalar values simultaneously. Divergence produces a scalar field based on the source of each point in a vector field, while curl measures the amount of rotation at each point in a vector field. Vector calculus is essential for calculating everything from heat flow to the effects of electromagnetism.

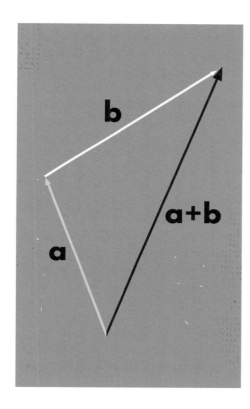

DRILL DOWN | The symbol used for the vector calculus operator ∇ is called "del"—it's an upside down Greek capital delta. (The symbol is also sometimes called "nabla," as it resembles the shape of an ancient Greek harp of that name.) The basic symbol is used directly to represent grad (∇f); with a dot to indicate the process is a "dot product" producing a scalar result for div (∇ · F); and with a cross, called a "cross product," producing a vector result as curl (∇ × F). Just as standard differentiation has an inverse in integration, each of the vector calculus operations has an integrating inverse.

FOCUS | *The terms gradient, divergence (or, to be precise, its opposite, convergence), and curl were devised by James Clerk Maxwell while he was working on a predecessor to vector calculus called "quaternions." Maxwell originally wanted to call curl "twirl" (also considering whirl, twist, and turn) but settled on curl because he thought mathematicians might consider twirl "too dynamic."*

SET THEORY

THE MAIN CONCEPT | Despite being developed much later than arithmetic, set theory is the fundamental theory on which mathematics is built. A set is a collection of items known as members or elements—they can be anything from physical objects (the set of all elephants, for example), to sets in their own right. The integers are defined using sets. Zero is an empty set—a set with nothing at all in it—represented by Ø; 1 is a set containing the empty set: {Ø}; 2 is a set containing the empty set and the set containing the empty set: {Ø, {Ø} } . . . and so on. A term from set theory has escaped into common usage: the "subset." A subset consists of some, but not all, of the elements of a larger set. So, for example, the even numbers form a subset of the integers. As with mathematical logic, sets and subsets can be represented using Venn diagrams, where ∩ indicates an intersection, and ⊂ indicates a subset. Although set theory is constructed logically, one of the axioms it is built on, the axiom of choice, is difficult to justify, and the ability to make a set a member of itself causes significant paradoxes. Nonetheless it is generally agreed that set theory provides our best fundamental theory to build mathematics on.

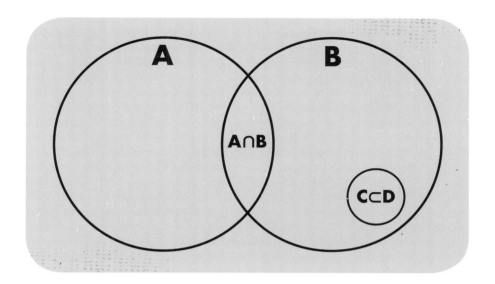

DRILL DOWN | Philosopher Bertrand Russell demonstrated the paradoxical difficulty of set theory by envisaging the set of "all sets that are not members of themselves." Sets can be members of themselves. For example, the set "cars" is not a member of itself—the set is not a car—but the set "things that aren't cars" is a member of itself, as long as we're happy that a set is a thing. The question is whether "all sets that are not members of themselves" is a member of itself. If it is, then it isn't. And if it isn't, then it must be. It's a bit like interpreting "This is a lie."

FOCUS | *The inability to properly fix the problem with the axioms of set theory does not show that set theory is a failure as the foundation of mathematics. The mathematician Kurt Gödel proved in his "incompleteness theorem" that for a non-trivial system of mathematics no consistent system of axioms is capable of proving everything required—there will always be gaps.*

NUMBERS
Page 22
MATHEMATICAL LOGIC
Page 44
GROUPS
Page 112

TRANSFINITE VALUES

THE MAIN CONCEPT | It might seem that by definition there can be nothing bigger than infinity, but Georg Cantor showed otherwise. The size of a set is its cardinality, determined by pairing off members of one set with members of another. If we can go through the whole set and do this, with none left over, the sets have the same cardinality. Starting with the infinity of the integers, Cantor showed that the infinity of every rational fraction had the same cardinality. He did this by imagining a table including every rational fraction and finding a route that, step by step, led through the table—one possible route is shown by the arrows in the diagram opposite. Then each item in the table could be paired off with the integers. Cantor called their shared cardinality $\aleph_0$ (aleph null). He then found a way to attempt the same with, for example, all numbers between 0 and 1. If we can produce a list of such numbers, we can pair it off with the integers. Cantor imagined scrambling the list (for easier visualization). He then took the first digit of the first number, the second digit of the second number, and so on, and added 1 to each digit. The new number created this way was not in the list, demonstrating that it's impossible to pair off every number between 0 and 1 with the integers. This "transfinite" cardinality is $\aleph_c$—where "c" stands for continuum.

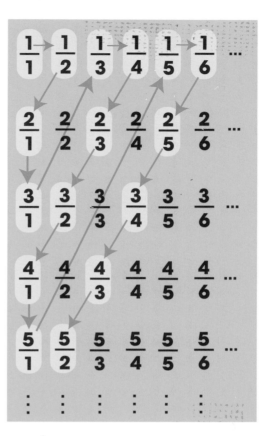

DRILL DOWN | Cantor struggled for years attempting to determine whether or not $\aleph_c$ was the same as $\aleph_1$—the next infinity up from $\aleph_0$. He showed that $\aleph_c$ was the power set of $\aleph_0$. A power set is the set of all the subsets of a set, which has cardinality 2^n, where n is the cardinality of the set. But Cantor could not prove $\aleph_c$ was the next biggest infinity, something that combined with vehement opposition from mathematician Leopold Kronecker seems to have made worse his mental problems. What Cantor would never know is that the mathematician Kurt Gödel would demonstrate that it was impossible to prove whether or not Cantor's so-called continuum hypothesis was true.

FOCUS | *Ordinal transfinite values have their own, different structure; when considering order, a one-to-one correspondence is harder to establish. Where both {a1, a2, a3...} and {a2, a3...} have ordinal value ω, {a2, a3... a1} has ordinal value ω + 1. Cantor established a whole hierarchy of the ordinals, including ω raised to the ω repeated ω times, which was called ε0, and so on.*

SYMMETRY

THE MAIN CONCEPT | In ordinary English usage, "symmetry" means mirror symmetry, where one side of a view is the mirror image of the other. Letters such as A and T are mirror symmetric, whereas R and G, for example, aren't. But in mathematics, symmetry has a wider definition. Something has symmetry if it stays the same when it undergoes *any* transformation. So, for instance, there is rotational symmetry—where something still looks the same if you rotate it. A circle has full rotational symmetry as it can be rotated by any angle on a plane and it stays the same, whereas a square only has rotational symmetry for rotations of 90 degrees. Another example is translational symmetry, where you shift your viewpoint sideways and the result looks the same. A repeated pattern, for example, has translational symmetry where a random pattern doesn't. In a theorem linked to a field of mathematics known as the "calculus of variations," the German mathematician Emmy Noether showed mathematically that if such symmetries could be applied to a system, then within that system there must be conservation of a physical property. For example, if there is translational symmetry through space, momentum must be conserved, while with translational symmetry through time, energy is conserved.

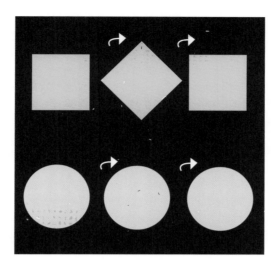

DRILL DOWN | Noether's theorem for symmetry uses the calculus of variations, which is often used to find maximum and minimum values and is important in the principle of least action, which is central to much of physics. Newton's laws of motion, for example, can be formulated from a version of the principle that says a moving object will take the path where the kinetic energy minus the potential energy integrated along the path is minimized. The related "principle of least time" says that light will take the path that minimizes its journey time, which is why it bends when passing, say, from air into water, spending less time in the medium where it is slower.

FOCUS | *Thanks to Noether's work, symmetry and symmetry breaking would become one of the great drivers of twentieth-century physics. It was symmetry considerations, for example, that led to the idea that particles previously considered to be fundamental, such as protons, had subcomponents. Symmetry was also at the heart of the unification of the electromagnetic and weak nuclear forces in so-called electroweak theory.*

PERSPECTIVE & PROJECTION
Page 64
INTEGRAL CALCULUS
Page 100
GROUPS
Page 112

GROUPS

THE MAIN CONCEPT | There's no real distinction in the English language between a set and a group, but mathematicians like to be precise, and they use "group" to mean a particular type of set—a set where there is an operation that will allow you to take any two members of the group and produce a third (with a few other technical restrictions). The integers are a group because using an addition operation on two integers will always produce an integer. Another simple group is any set of integers used in modular arithmetic. Groups form a bridge between the concepts of sets and symmetry. When an object is symmetrical (using the mathematical definition), there will be a group called a "symmetry group," which is a group of matrices that define the different ways the object can be transformed without changing it. There is a standard notation describing the different symmetry groups. So, for example, the symmetry group for the rotations of a sphere is called SU(3). Symmetry groups are particularly important in physics. For example, one type of symmetry group, called a Lie group, which deals with continuous symmetries (like that of a sphere, rather than, say, a mirror symmetry) is widely used in particle physics.

DRILL DOWN | The concept of quarks, the fundamental particles making up protons, neutrons, and particles called "mesons," emerged from applying a symmetry group. Physicists had identified a symmetry in particles which were ascribed to two properties known as strangeness and isospin. The particles were distributed on diagrams in groups of eight, which the originator of the quark concept, Murray Gell-Mann, referred to as the "eightfold way" in a reference to a Buddhist concept. Mathematically, these patterns were suggestive of the symmetry group SU(3). Gell-Mann suggested that the group comprised three "flavors" of underlying particles which he called quarks (pronounced "kworks")—up, down, and strange. A second generation of quarks—charm, top, and bottom were added later.

FOCUS | *An early developer of group theory was the tragic French mathematician Évariste Galois, who gave groups their name and devised the Galois group, which links groups and fields. He no doubt would have done much more, but he died aged only 20 as a result of a duel, probably on behalf of a young woman called Stéphanie-Félicie Poterin du Motel.*

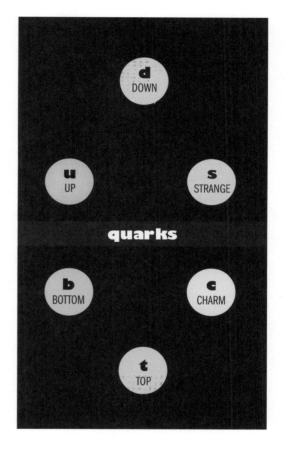

"**If you want to be a physicist, you must do three things—first, study mathematics, second, study more mathematics, and third, do the same.**"

ARNOLD SOMMERFELD IN AN INTERVIEW WITH
PAUL KIRKPATRICK, QUOTED IN DANIEL KEVLES,
THE PHYSICISTS (1978)

4

APPLIED MATHEMATICS

INTRODUCTION

It is perfectly possible to construct a system of mathematics that bears no resemblance to the real world. Although the origins of math may have been as a reflection of familiar objects, mathematics has long since become detached from the physical realm. As long as a mathematical system is self-consistent, not breaking its own rules, you can do what you like. If you want to make 2 + 2 = 5, that's fine, provided this does not conflict with the rest of your mathematics.

An unreal universe

We have already seen a number of aspects of unreal math. There is no square root of a negative number in the physical world—even a negative number requires a degree of interpretation. There are only four physical dimensions, yet mathematicians are happy to work in thousands. It's debatable whether infinity has any real-world equivalent. So, many mathematicians spend their time working in what appears to be an isolated mathematical universe with no consequence other than its intellectual challenge. As Wigner observed, "Most more advanced mathematical concepts ... were so devised that they are apt subjects on which the mathematician can demonstrate his ingenuity and sense of formal beauty." And yet, as he also said, mathematics is "unreasonably effective in the natural sciences." For something mostly built on highly theoretical foundations, it has proved remarkably useful.

It should be no surprise that the late Stephen Hawking worked not in the physics laboratory at Cambridge but in the Department of Applied Mathematics and Theoretical Physics. Modern physics is driven by math to the extent that it seems many physicists are indistinguishable from pure mathematicians, dreaming up toy universes of black hole firewalls and superstrings for which there is no evidence as yet from science, only mathematical challenges. Similarly, the information and computing architecture that underlies our modern world has math at its heart.

Math for the real world

In this book, physics and computer science are often used as examples of the use of math, but as we will see in this chapter, there are also more mundane ways that math makes its presence felt in everyday life. Whether it's the bookie calculating odds for the next horse race, an actuary setting insurance premiums (or, these days, providing an input to the algorithms that will do so), or a weather forecaster putting together tomorrow's outlook, math is central to the job.

Even the "soft" sciences such as economics, sociology, and psychology make regular use of mathematics to model the economy or reflect human behavior. This was not really possible before the emergence of probability and statistics, which as well as helping bookies and insurance workers has been central to applying numbers to the general field of human activity. Less well known is the field of operations research, developed for military purposes during World War II and expanded since to do everything from working out the best queuing systems to scheduling airlines.

All these applications would originally have made use of the mathematician's traditional tools of paper and pencil. However, since the end of the war, applied mathematics has increasingly involved computers to perform analyses and calculations that would be beyond manipulation by hand. Famously, Charles Babbage, the inventor of early mechanical computers, was said to have been inspired by helping a friend, John Herschel, to laboriously construct tables of numbers. Babbage is said to have cried out, "My God, Herschel, how I wish these calculations could be executed by steam!"

It's worth noting, though, that computers are not just the main work tools of applied mathematicians—they are themselves entirely dependent on mathematics. An electronic computer's universe is a sea of 0s and 1s, undergoing constant mathematical processes. The computer (or the smartphone in your pocket) is the embodiment of applied math, transformed from manipulation of numbers and logic into the bewildering array of applications that modern technology delivers.

In this chapter we will see math that encroaches on human behavior and the ways in which pure mathematicians' wild flights of fancy have been tamed, but also the situations where raw mathematical power seems able to overcome the ordered world we expect, whether it is in the unmasked randomness of probability-driven quantum theory or the wild power of chaos, unleashed in the theory that explains the behavior of everything from the stock market to the weather. To a pure mathematician, applied mathematics may seem a touch grubby and mundane, but to the rest of us it is where math gets its hands dirty and gets the job done.

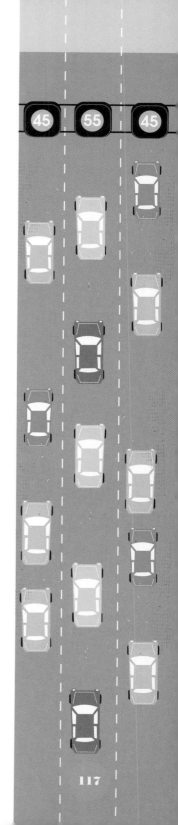

TIMELINE

FOURIER SERIES

French mathematician Jean-Baptiste Joseph Fourier introduces what will become known as Fourier series in his *Théorie Analytique de la Chaleur* ("The Analytical Theory of Heat"), showing that complex and discontinuous waveforms can be broken down to constituent simple waves in a so-called Fourier transform.

THE MATRIX

English mathematician James Joseph Sylvester coins the term "matrix" (Latin for "womb") for a two-dimensional array of numbers. Such arrays had been in use for around 200 years, but become a major tool of mathematics around this time.

| 1663 | 1822 | 1822 | 1850 |

PROBABILITY

Giralamo Cardano's book *Liber de Ludo Aleae* ("Book on Games of Chance") is published around 100 years after it was written and 87 years after his death. It is the first proper analysis of probability, but is initially ignored because it deals with betting odds and cheating.

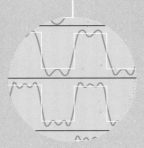

EARLY COMPUTERS

British inventor Charles Babbage completes a model of his Difference Engine, a mechanical calculator for the production of astronomical tables. He is funded to build a complete engine, but engineering limits and distraction by designing his (never begun) programmable computer, the Analytical Engine, mean that he never finishes.

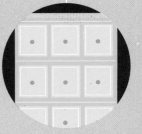

OPERATIONS RESEARCH

British physicist and radar pioneer Albert Rowe, working on radar development at the Bawdsey Research Station (Suffolk, England), introduces the formal concept of operations research (OR), although basic OR principles date back to the 1840s in work on mail sorting and the safety of railway wagons.

CHAOS THEORY

American mathematician Edward Norton Lorenz is inspired to develop chaos theory when he inputs the starting values for a weather-forecasting model on his LGP-30 computer and finds a small rounding error produces a totally different forecast.

1928   **1937**   **1944**   **c. 1960**

GAME THEORY

Hungarian-American mathematician John von Neumann publishes his paper *On the Theory of Parlor Games*, which begins the field of game theory, describing human interactions based on strategies for playing simple games. These will be employed in the development of the nuclear "mutual assured destruction" strategy.

CODE-BREAKING

Colossus, the world's first programmable electronic digital computer, goes into operation at the British Bletchley Park code-breaking center. The device and its successors are destroyed after the war on Churchill's orders, and their pioneering work not revealed until the 1970s.

BIOGRAPHIES

JACOB BERNOULLI (1655–1705)

The oldest of the great Bernoulli mathematical dynasty, also including two Nicolauses, three Johanns, and a Daniel, Jacob (also known as Jacques) was born in the Swiss town of Basel. He studied theology at the University of Basel and was ordained, but by his early twenties he was convinced that mathematics was the most important thing in his life. After several years touring Europe, he returned to Basel where he taught mechanics and began to work in mathematics. By 1687, Jacob had become a professor of mathematics. He worked together with his brother Johann for a number of years, but after a decade their mutual support had turned to bitter rivalry. Like a number of his relations, Jacob made significant contributions to probability theory, most notably in his book *Ars Conjectandi*, published eight years after his death. The book established much of the basics on permutations and combinations, as well as significant aspects of probability, such as an early version of the "law of large numbers," which says that the more times an experiment is run (provided it is fair), the closer the average outcome will be to the expected value.

ABRAHAM DE MOIVRE (1667–1754)

Born in France, Abraham de Moivre first studied logic at college in Saumur, which gave him an interest in mathematics, after which he moved to Paris to study physics. This was a time of increasing persecution of Protestants in France—by the time he was 20, de Moivre had moved with his brother to London. Here, while employed as a private math tutor to the sons of wealthy families, he came across Newton's recent *Principia* and would come to know both Newton and his supporter Edmond Halley. After some early work extending some of the math in the *Principia*, de Moivre became a Fellow of the Royal Society, but he remained an under-funded private tutor throughout his career. His biggest contributions to mathematics were in the new field of probability theory. He was instrumental in the introduction of two of the most commonly used distributions in probability—the normal distribution and the Poisson distribution (which he worked on before Siméon Denis Poisson). These explain the way randomly varying characteristics are distributed for continuous options or those coming in integer chunks respectively, helping do everything from check errors to forecast behavior.

PATRICK MAYNARD STUART BLACKETT (1897–1974)

Born in London, Blackett was technically a physicist, doing significant work on cloud chamber research, but his biggest contribution was in applied mathematics. While serving in the British navy in World War I, Blackett noticed the poor use of artillery and was inspired to take an interest in physics and math. Given an opportunity to study at Cambridge, he became an experimental physicist, working with Ernest Rutherford. From there he went on to Birkbeck College, London, and Manchester University in physics professor roles. However, he did not forget his interest in mathematics and by 1935 had joined the Aeronautical Research Committee, steering the development of radar. He worked at the Royal Aircraft Establishment in Farnborough before helping develop a new field of applied mathematics known as operations research. This involved using mathematical methods to improve the effectiveness of military operations, including the best way to structure convoys to minimize the risk of sinking and devising the optimal distribution of armor plating for aircraft. Blackett was elected to the Royal Society and became a life peer in 1969.

JOHN VON NEUMANN (1903–1957)

Born in Budapest, Hungary, as János, John von Neumann was a leading figure in the Manhattan Project to develop the atomic bomb, was central to the US development of electronic computers, and worked widely in mathematics, from topology to game theory. Von Neumann was a child prodigy, already using calculus at the age of 8; by 23 he had simultaneously achieved a doctorate in mathematics from Pázmány Péter University in Budapest and a degree in chemical engineering (a fallback subject at his father's instance) from the ETH in Zurich. He was soon lecturing in mathematics in Berlin, but by 1929 had moved to Princeton in the US, the university that was his home for the rest of his career. Mathematically, Von Neumann was influential in set theory and in the use of operators in quantum mechanics. Just one of his many achievements was the establishment of game theory as a part of mathematics. This finds strategies in games where typically two players can each make a choice that influences the outcome of the game—it would be used extensively to model the interaction between the US and the USSR during the Cold War.

ENCRYPTION

THE MAIN CONCEPT | Keeping sensitive information secure has been a concern as long as there has been writing. This can be achieved by physical concealment, codes (which replace a whole message with words or symbols; FISH could mean "Attack tomorrow at 9am"), and ciphers (which use mathematical manipulation to modify a message). For a long time, such encryption was the business of spies, but now, whenever a secure link is established on the Internet, encryption comes into play. If a website uses HTTPS: (indicated by a padlock symbol in the browser), or we use a secure messaging service, the software employs a mathematical process to make the information unreadable to an eavesdropper. Encryption usually relies on a key. At its simplest, this is a word or phrase, the letter values of which (position in the alphabet) are added to the message. So, for example, HELLO encrypted using the key APPLE adds A to H (1 to 8) giving I (9), P to E, and so on, producing IUBXT. Internet encryption, such as RSA, has dual keys—a public one that anyone can use to encrypt information and a private one that only the owner can use. The result is like a mailbox anyone can post into, but only the owner can open.

DRILL DOWN | It's easy for a computer to multiply huge prime numbers together (say with 32 digits each), but hard to work out the original numbers from the result. In a public key/private key encryption system, the multiplied number is used as a modulus in mathematical manipulations producing the keys. The public key is made freely available; data is encrypted by raising a numerical version of the data to the power of the public key and the result given with a modulus of the multiplied primes. To decrypt, a similar process is used, but raising the encrypted message to the power of the private key. Systems such as Whatsapp employ several public and private keys on each message.

BASIC ARITHMETIC;
NEGATIVE NUMBERS
Page 26

POWERS, ROOTS & LOGARITHMS
Page 34

MODULAR ARITHMETIC
Page 42

FOCUS | *RSA was the first significant public key/private key system, and is the best known. Its name references Ron Rivest, Adi Shamir, and Leonard Adleman, the American and Israeli mathematicians who developed it in 1978. It wasn't realized at the time, but the RSA system had already been invented in 1973 by British mathematician Clifford Cocks. Cocks had been working at GCHQ, the British intelligence encryption facility, so his idea had not been publicized.*

PROBABILITY

THE MAIN CONCEPT | Applying mathematics to games of chance provided the first opportunity to consider probability, a mathematical analysis of chance, which initially gave it a bad reputation. It doesn't help that probabilities can seem unnatural. For example, if a coin comes up heads ten times in a row, it's almost impossible not to feel that the next toss is more likely to be tails. In fact, the coin has no memory; there is a 50:50 chance of heads or tails, whatever was thrown before. In the sixteenth century, Girolamo Cardano extended the simple probability of a single event to take in multiple occurrences. Probability is usually stated as a value between 0 (no chance) and 1 (will definitely happen). For example, if there's a 1 in 6 (or $1/6$) chance of throwing a 5, with a die, the chance of throwing two 5s in a row is $1/6 \times 1/6 = 1/36$. The chance of throwing a 4 or a 5 on a single throw is $1/6 + 1/6 = 2/6$, or $1/3$. Probability theory was expanded to take in distributions of probability and more sophisticated aspects of random events, and would be crucial to the development of quantum physics, where the behavior of quantum particles is directly controlled by probability.

DRILL DOWN | Cardano's greatest discovery in probability was the chance of throwing, say, a 6 with *either* of two dice. Naively, this could be $\frac{1}{6} + \frac{1}{6}$. But that would mean with six dice you would have $6 \times \frac{1}{6} = 1$; in other words, you would definitely get a 6 if you threw six dice. Cardano realized that he knew the probability of *not* throwing a six with *both* of two dice. The chance of not throwing a six with one die is $\frac{5}{6}$, so the chance of doing this twice is $\frac{5}{6} \times \frac{5}{6} = \frac{25}{36}$. What was left—$1 - \frac{25}{36}$ (or $\frac{11}{36}$)—was the chance of getting a 6 with either die.

FOCUS | *Probability can even mislead mathematicians. When in 1990 Marilyn vos Savant, writing for* Parade *magazine, posed the so-called Monty Hall problem (see page 139), she was deluged with mail from mathematicians and scientists telling her she was wrong. She wasn't. Perhaps the best letter said: "You're wrong, but look on the positive side. If all those PhDs were wrong, the country would be in very serious trouble."*

STATISTICS

THE MAIN CONCEPT | The term "statistics" used to apply to a collection of data about a state—a country—the kind of thing you might find in the CIA World Factbook. However, by the seventeenth century, thanks to the work of an English button maker called John Graunt, statistics took on a new form. Graunt used data from "Bills of Mortality" in London, plus any information he could gather about births, to help understand the ebb and flow of the city's population and the spread of disease. Statistics takes data from a collection of individuals and produces collective information, often extrapolating from what is known to make predictions. One of Graunt's early efforts was to try to work out life expectancies for different groups of people, which would become the foundation of the insurance business. Statistics is not limited to human subjects, but has proved a powerful tool for assessing the behavior of any large mass of similar objects. In the nineteenth century, "statistical mechanics" was used to understand the behavior of collections of gas molecules, explaining phenomena such as gas pressure and viscosity. By this time, basic collection and collation of statistics (as, for example, in a census) had been combined with probability (see page 124) to make predictions on the future behavior of everything from stocks and shares to voters in an election.

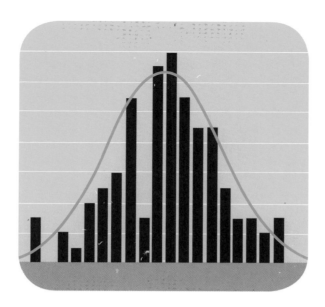

DRILL DOWN | The basic collection of statistics is not controversial, but when it is used to make predictions, a statistical approach can be misleading. Weather forecasting is a good example, where the system is so complex that it behaves in a way that mathematicians describe as "chaotic," making any prediction prone to error. Similarly, the forecasts that businesses use in their budgets often result in long postmortems as to why a company has not behaved as forecast—in practice, the real question should be the accuracy of the forecast. Statistical forecasting is very valuable, but we rarely have enough information on potential errors to make most effective use of the data.

FOCUS | *There is some confusion over who first produced the most famous quote on statistics (and one of the most famous in all of mathematics): "There are three kinds of lies: lies, damned lies, and statistics." It is often attributed to British prime minister Benjamin Disraeli. He claimed to be quoting Mark Twain, but the remark does not appear in Twain's writing.*

FACTORIALS & PERMUTATIONS
Page 96
PROBABILITY
Page 124
OPERATIONS RESEARCH
Page 140

LOGARITHMS & THE SLIDE RULE

THE MAIN CONCEPT | We are so used to computers that it is difficult to remember the long period in history when calculations that did not need to be exactly worked out by hand were undertaken using logarithms or with the mechanical device for logarithm manipulation, the slide rule. The slide rule, sometimes called a "slipstick," was an analog computer—one that used physical values rather than digital ones. Basic slide rules could multiply and divide, while more sophisticated devices had features such as roots, sines, and cosines. The standard slide-rule design had a pair of rulerlike sections, which were fixed parallel to each other, with a third sliding section positioned between them. The sliding section was moved until a pointer lined up with one value for the calculation on the top section, then the answer would be read off from one of the fixed sections. The final part of the slide rule was the cursor, a transparent part that was slid along above the three sections. This had a line running top to bottom that made it possible to read off values on nonadjacent scales. Because the scales were logarithmic—instead of being marked off regularly as on a ruler, values came closer and closer together—they produced multiplication or division by what was effectively addition or subtraction.

DRILL DOWN | A simple slide rule operation might be to multiply 2.5 by 2.8. The center rule would be slid along until the 1 marker on one of its scales lined up with 2.5 on the scale of the rule above it. The user would then move the cursor until it lined up with 2.8 on the center rule's scale and would read off the answer from the upper rule's scale, which would be positioned over 7. This worked because the center rule was moved along by a distance of log 2.5 and then a distance of log 2.8 was added on. Because with a logarithm $log(n) + log(m) = log(nm)$, the value read off was the correct answer.

NUMBER BASES
Page 24
POWERS, ROOTS & LOGARITHMS
Page 34
CALCULATING MACHINES
Page 130

FOCUS | *The first slide rules were developed in the 1620s by William Oughtred, an English mathematician. He took two existing rulers with logarithmic markings and slid them along each other to perform calculations. He then published a design for a circular slide rule (an approach that was never as popular as straight rules), but the modern style would not be introduced until the 1850s.*

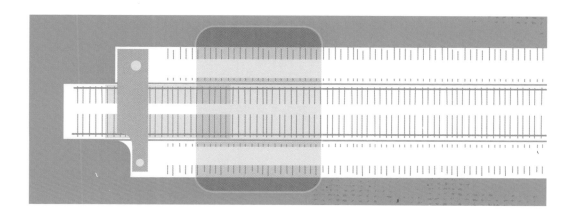

CALCULATING MACHINES

THE MAIN CONCEPT | Calculations using stones as markers were common in ancient times (hence, for example, "calculus," which means "small stone" in Latin). But when those stones were transformed into beads on wires or rods, they became what is arguably the prototypical calculating machine, the abacus. In effect, an abacus simulates the columns of position-based arithmetic, allowing a user to rapidly add and subtract, with techniques available to enable multiplication and division. But the idea of using gearing to undertake mathematical functions seems to have emerged alongside the improvement of clocks in the seventeenth century. There is some dispute over who got there first, but French mathematician Blaise Pascal produced a mechanical calculator in 1642 when he was just 19—dozens were made, but they were clumsy and prone to error. The first mechanical calculator in large-scale use was French inventor Charles Thomas's arithmometer, which became a standard from the 1850s: it was reliable and capable of true multiplication rather than repeated addition. This came after English mathematician Charles Babbage's incomplete designs for a more sophisticated calculator (the Difference Engine) and programmable computer (Analytical Engine). Mechanical calculators remained in use until replaced by electronic calculators in the 1970s.

DRILL DOWN | The Difference Engine, a small part of which was demonstrated by Babbage in 1822, was designed to work on up to seven numbers at a time and was intended to help with the automation of production of mathematical, astronomical, and navigational tables, which required tedious repeated manual calculation. Babbage lost interest in it when he put together his concept of the Analytical Engine in 1837, which would have been a programmable mechanical computer incorporating the components of modern computers in mechanical form, with data input on punched cards originally designed to control mechanical looms. Mathematician Ada Lovelace devised potential programs for the Analytical Engine in her notes on it.

FOCUS | *The oldest known calculating machine is the Antikythera Mechanism. Discovered in an ancient Greek shipwreck off the island of Antikythera in 1901, the mechanism was not properly investigated until the 1970s, when it was examined with X-rays and gamma rays and shown to be an analog mechanical astronomical calculator with at least 30 gears, and around 2,200 years old.*

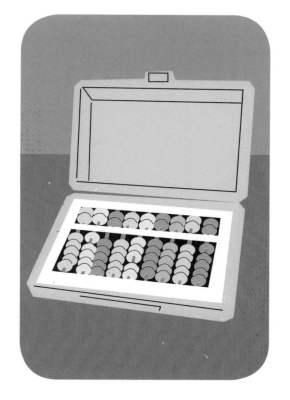

BASIC ARITHMETIC; NEGATIVE NUMBERS
Page 26

LOGARITHMS & THE SLIDE RULE
Page 128

COMPUTERS
Page 142

FOURIER TRANSFORMS

THE MAIN CONCEPT | Few techniques in applied mathematics are as impressive in their power as Fourier transforms. Named after French mathematician Joseph Fourier (1768–1830), the Fourier transform is, in essence, a powerful technique for breaking a complex mathematical structure down into a collection of simple ones. Strictly speaking, there are three Fourier entities. The Fourier series is a potentially infinite set of simple sine waves that can be combined to make up a more complex mathematical function, provided that function is continuous, rather than having sudden, discontinuous leaps. For example, in the diagram opposite, sine waves are being combined to come increasingly closer to the very different-looking square wave. The various kinds of Fourier transform are mechanisms for decomposing a function into its components, and Fourier analysis is the broader application of these kinds of techniques. One widely used variant, the fast Fourier transform, is particularly flexible as it works on a sample of the data. Although the most obvious application of Fourier transforms is in sound—for example, building up different sounds in a synthesizer by combining simple sine waves— Fourier analysis has found use everywhere from physics to the software for digital cameras to stock markets and the analysis of the structure of proteins.

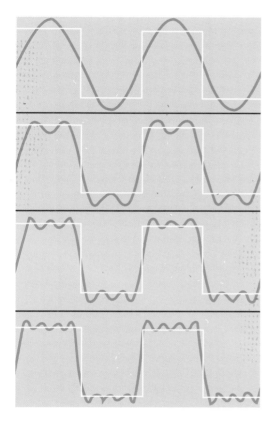

DRILL DOWN | When German mathematician Carl Gauss was working on the orbits of asteroids in the early 1800s, using relatively small samples of data, he developed a technique that would only be rediscovered in full in the 1960s. The fast Fourier transform is, as the name suggests, a fast algorithm for calculating a discrete Fourier transform—one that works on a limited set of samples of data, each taken at the same interval, dividing each sample into its separate frequency components. Most of us regularly use the output of fast Fourier transforms, as they are involved in the compression algorithms in JPEG images and MP3 sound files.

FOCUS | *Physicist Max Tegmark and astrophysicist Matias Zaldarriaga have suggested it would be possible to be build a radio telescope using an array of detectors, each performing fast Fourier transforms on the data, which would give it the flexibility of a single dish telescope but the ability to cover a wide field of view, like the much more expensive interferometer observatories featuring multiple telescopes.*

MATRIX MANIPULATION

THE MAIN CONCEPT | Matrices (or matrixes—both plurals of "matrix" are used) are two-dimensional rectangular arrays. They can be thought of as a mathematical chest of drawers that can either have several drawers in a single row, several drawers in a single column, or both rows and columns of drawers. Each row must have the same number of drawers. Similarly, columns are each the same size. At its simplest, each drawer can contain a number, but it can also hold functions. The power of a matrix is that it allows mathematical operations to be applied to a whole collection of values all at once. Matrix addition requires the two matrices to be the same shape, adding each element of one to the equivalent element of the other. Matrix multiplication is more interesting. It requires the first matrix to have the same number of columns as the second matrix has rows. This is because each value in the resultant matrix is calculated by adding together the result of multiplying the elements in the equivalent row of the first matrix by the elements in the equivalent column of the second matrix. If both matrixes are the same shape, it's possible to get two different results depending on the order of multiplication.

DRILL DOWN | In simple arithmetic, multiplication is commutative. This means that $A \times B = B \times A$. This seems perfectly natural—so much so that it's hard to see that this isn't always going to be the case. Even in basic arithmetic, though, other operations, such as subtraction, are not commutative. $A - B \neq B - A$. In general, multiplication also need not be commutative—as is the case for matrices. Only square matrices can be multiplied in both directions, because of the need for rows and columns to be equivalent. But unless the matrices are suitably symmetric, reversing the order in which the matrices are multiplied produces different answers.

FOCUS | *One of the strangest computer-programming languages ever, APL (standing for "A Programming Language") was developed in the late 1950s and early 1960s. Most programming languages consist of a series of English-like statements, but APL uses matrix manipulation to handle whole matrices at a time, producing very compact, mathematics-like code. The entire program to generate all the prime numbers up to N, for example, would be $(\sim N \in N \circ . \times N)/N \leftarrow 1 \downarrow \iota N$.*

GAME THEORY

THE MAIN CONCEPT | Game theory sounds like the rules of football, but uses simple decision-based games to explore human behavior. The games often involve two players, with opportunities to cooperate or to try to get one over on the other player, often with no knowledge of the other player's decision. Such games are frequently used by economists and psychologists. John von Neumann introduced the discipline in 1928 with his paper *On the Theory of Parlor Games*, while American mathematician John Nash—featured in the movie *A Beautiful Mind*—developed the field significantly. The most studied games are the Prisoner's Dilemma and the Ultimatum Game. The latter demonstrates how humans will sacrifice themselves to punish someone else. The Prisoner's Dilemma was the basis of "mutual assured destruction" in the Cold War. It imagines two prisoners, each of whom, without communicating, can either support the other or betray them. If only one betrays, he or she is let free and the other gets a long sentence. If both support, they each get a short sentence. And if both betray, each gets a mid-length sentence. The combined benefit is highest if both support, but an individual benefits by betraying, as long as the other doesn't. It's logical for an individual to betray—but if both follow that logic, they suffer.

DRILL DOWN | The widely used Ultimatum Game distributes a sum of money between two people. The first person decides how to split the money, while the second either accepts the split or refuses it, in which case neither gets anything. Players from Western cultures usually turn down offers less than about 35 percent. Economically this is illogical—it's refusing to take free money—but psychologically it puts a price on punishing the other player for being greedy. What is rarely observed is that with a large reward (the game is usually played for amounts in the $1–10 range), this percentage split no longer holds, as players will accept a much smaller percentage.

FOCUS | *A game theory term in wide use is "zero-sum game." This is a game in which the losses of some players are canceled out by the winnings of the other players: adding gains and losses gives zero. It rules out the possibility of win-win. If you are sharing candies, for instance, and give someone too many, someone else gets too few.*

MATHEMATICAL LOGIC
Page 44

GRAPH THEORY
Page 68

FACTORIALS & PERMUTATIONS
Page 96

MONTE CARLO METHODS

THE MAIN CONCEPT | Although probability has largely moved out of the shadow of gambling, it can't escape its origins entirely: fair games of chance are the simplest examples of probability in action. Nowhere is this more obvious than in "Monte Carlo methods," unashamedly named after the Mediterranean casino. However, despite the name, Monte Carlo methods, or simulations, are not about the best way to win at roulette, but rather a mechanism for mathematically simulating a small part of reality. The approach involves harnessing the power of randomness to make predictions. "Monte Carlo" was used as a codeword for the technique when it was developed by Stanislaw Ulam and John von Neumann, working on the Manhattan Project to develop nuclear weapons during World War II. The first application was to work out requirements for radiation shielding to stop neutrons. Because the interactions of particles is probabilistic, by repeatedly using a random selection of parameters that fit the behavior of the neutron, a picture of possible outcomes was built up. Monte Carlo simulations are often used in fields from finance to physics, in situations where the environment is too complex to develop an effective deterministic model (one that has definite values), but where it is possible to apply probabilities and statistical data to the variables.

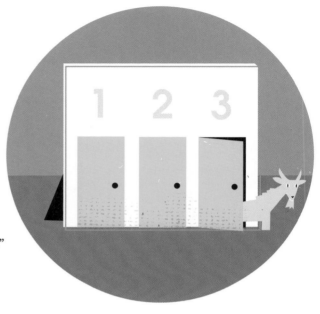

DRILL DOWN | A simple Monte Carlo simulation has been used to prove the outcome in the "Monty Hall problem." This involves a game where a contestant chooses between three doors and wins what is behind the chosen door—two doors have goats behind them, while the other conceals a car. After the contestant makes a choice, the host opens one of the other doors to reveal a goat. The question is, should the contestant stick with their choice or shift to the other unopened door? The counterintuitive reality is that they are twice as likely to win if they switch. This seems so unlikely it was often simulated by repeatedly running the game for the "stick" and "switch" options, proving the result.

FOCUS | *Monte Carlo methods need random numbers, which aren't easy to generate. True random values can be produced using quantum devices, but typical computer "random" values use a pseudo-random series. A simple example takes the previous value (the first value is "seeded" using, say, the time), multiplies it by a large constant, adds another large constant, and takes the modulus to the base of a third large number.*

OPERATIONS RESEARCH

THE MAIN CONCEPT | Also known as operational research, this is a discipline that was developed in the lead-up to World War II to apply mathematical methods to solving military operational problems, from the most effective deployment of depth charges to the best routes to take on a multi-leg journey. As well as using standard statistical techniques and Monte Carlo methods (see page 138), operations research incorporates methods such as queuing theory, which is used to minimize the time customers (or things) spend in a queue; linear programming, which maximizes a value, such as the profit of a transaction, given a range of constraints; and dynamic programming, which breaks down a problem into smaller components that can be dealt with using recursion (see opposite). Operations research is now also used in business, to deal with large, complex problems that don't easily fit simple mathematical solutions. Operations research was originally a purely mathematical discipline, but it was an early adopter of computers and now it is highly dependent on computing software, from spreadsheets to intricate visual simulations. The term "optimization," implying finding the best possible outcome, is often associated with operations research, although in practice because of the messy nature of the problems they are applied to, many techniques produce near-optimization.

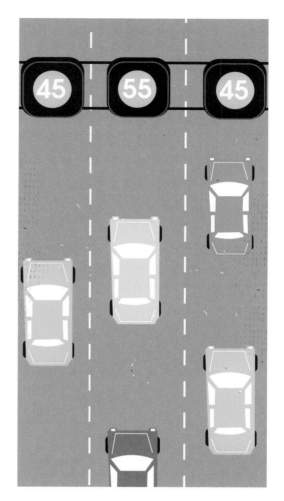

DRILL DOWN | Recursion frequently occurs in mathematics and computing and is a powerful tool in some of the algorithms that are employed in operations research. Recursion requires a starting and stopping point along with a rule that allows the next instance to be generated. Crucially, recursive algorithms are defined in terms of themselves, which enables them to be compact for the work they do. For example, the factorial of n is "n multiplied by the factorial of $n-1$." Which in turn is "$n-1$ multiplied by the factorial of $n-1-1$," etc. Recursion enables a simple rule to build up a significant outcome, and a set of recursive rules can produce complex behavior.

FOCUS | *Operations research can help make the best choice in hiring someone (or marrying someone). This kind of problem, known as an "optimal stopping problem," involves choosing something from a sequence without being able to see the whole sequence. With a total of* n *candidates, you should reject the first* √n *people and choose the next person better than any of those.*

COMPUTERS

THE MAIN CONCEPT | The electronic programmable computer transformed both the ability to perform arithmetic and much more sophisticated mathematical calculations. In effect, computers divided mathematics into two, with some mathematicians still using paper and pencil, and others adopting computer methods. The early electronic computers were based on thermionic valves, also known as vacuum tubes. The first programmable computer is now accepted to be the Colossus, built at Bletchley Park in the UK as part of the effort to decipher German military communications. Colossus went live at the start of 1944, but its role was not originally recognized, as the Colossus devices were destroyed after the war due to an unfortunate idea of military security. The more flexible ENIAC computer in the US went into use a year after Colossus and became the model for early developments. Such early computers were room-sized and used as much electricity as a modern office building. Programming was initially done with switches on the device, then punched paper tapes and cards, before moving to teletypes and display screens. Although such "mainframe" computers became much more powerful and relatively compact for that power, they remained corporate in scale until the introduction of personal computers in the 1980s. Now, a smartphone has far more computing power than the early mainframes.

DRILL DOWN | The valves (now transistors) in electronic computers are arranged in logic circuits called "gates." Each gate provides a single operator from Boolean algebra, such as NOT, OR, and AND. In the gate, the principle electronic components act as switches that control one signal with another. If the signal is active it is treated as 1, or 0 if it is not active. So, for instance, a NOT gate, which switches 0 to 1 and 1 to 0, will output a signal if there is no input signal, but won't output anything if there is an input signal. All the other gates apart from NOT have two inputs controlling a single output.

MATHEMATICAL LOGIC
Page 44

LOGARITHMS & THE SLIDE RULE
Page 128

CALCULATING MACHINES
Page 130

FOCUS | *It is sometimes claimed that the first bug in a computer was in one of the electromechanical predecessors of electronic computers, recorded by US computer scientist Grace Hopper, who in 1947 attached a moth found in the computer to the computer's log book. However, the term "bug" for a technical problem had been used in engineering since the 1870s.*

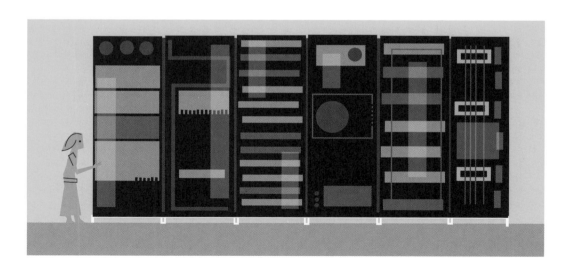

CHAOS THEORY

THE MAIN CONCEPT | Chaos sounds like a totally random concept, but mathematically speaking, a chaotic system is one that obeys clear rules—there's nothing random—but the system is either sufficiently complex or strongly interacting that very small changes can powerfully influence the outcome, meaning that it can be very difficult to predict what is going to happen next. Chaotic systems can be surprisingly simple. A pendulum consisting of two rods, one hinged on the bottom of the other, behaves impressively chaotically. Perhaps the best-known chaotic system is the weather—here it is the interaction of a whole range of weather systems that produces chaos. It was when mathematician Edward Lorenz was attempting an early computerized weather forecast that he made the first steps in chaos theory. He had printed off the numbers he needed to input into his computer program partway through the run—it took a long time and he wanted to be able to restart it at this point. But when he did so, the forecast was totally different. He realized that the printout used fewer decimal places than the program; just a tiny fraction of a difference in the values transformed the forecast. In addition to the weather, chaos turns up in everything from stock market behavior to engineering.

DRILL DOWN | Chaos and randomness each produce unpredictable behavior, but in different ways. A chaotic system is in theory entirely predictable, but is so sensitive to slight changes in the setup that in practice it behaves in a wild fashion. This gets amplified with time so, for example, weather forecasts are impossible to extend for more than about seven days. Random behavior is inherently unpredictable at the level of individual changes, but can often be predicted statistically, as many random actions have known probabilities. Some chaotic systems interact in such a way that they naturally tend toward certain possible values. When this occurs, the values the system tends toward are known as "strange attractors."

FOCUS | *The originator of chaos theory, Edward Lorenz was also responsible for the most dramatic image attached to the theory when he wrote the paper "Does the flap of a butterfly's wings in Brazil set off a tornado in Texas?" This "butterfly effect" became widely known, even though Lorenz's conclusion was, "No, it doesn't."*

FRACTALS
Page 78

PROBABILITY
Page 124

COMPLEXITY THEORY
Page 146

COMPLEXITY THEORY

THE MAIN CONCEPT | In general use, "complexity" simply means having a structure with lots of parts, or that is particularly intricate. But in mathematics and computation, complexity describes a system with multiple interacting subsystems that results in "emergent" properties: the whole is greater than the sum of the parts. A living organism is complex in this sense. It is made up of individual cells, none of which are capable of the abilities of the whole. Often the behavior of a complex system will be nonlinear—having sudden, unexpected changes—and can be chaotic (see page 144). Complexity is probably most studied in computational mathematics, but it is also used in fields such as economics, biology, and network theory. One complexity mechanism is the "feedback loop." This is where a property of a system can make direct changes to the behavior of that system. Feedback can either run away (positive feedback) or dampen down behavior (negative feedback). The most familiar positive feedback is the squeal of a sound system when a microphone is too close to a loudspeaker, so that background noise is picked up, amplified, picked up even louder, and so on. Negative feedback was first studied in the mechanism of governors for steam engines. These mechanical devices are driven by the pressure in the engine. If they rotate too fast, they release steam, automatically reducing the pressure.

DRILL DOWN | In computing, complexity describes the difficulty of solving a problem. One that can be solved in polynomial time (when the maximum time taken is proportional to a power of the number of components in the problem—say, n^2 time units, where n things are involved) is called class "P." By contrast, an "NP" problem's solution can only be verified in polynomial time. It is thought (though not proved) that solving a third class of problem, "NP-hard," in polynomial time is impossible. Such a problem takes exponential time— say, 2^n time units—to solve. Usually, such problems only have approximate solutions. A typical NP-hard problem is the traveling salesman problem, finding the best route between a number of cities.

FOCUS | *Spontaneous order, or "self-organization," is a characteristic of complexity. A layer of wax on a board can demonstrate such complexity. Pour hot water down the angled sheet of wax and initially rivulets will run all over it. But as the water melts channels, more water will run down the channels, which will get wider still. The pattern formed is self-organizing.*

GLOSSARY

ALGORITHM—a series of instructions and rules used to carry out a task in a systematic fashion. Commonly applied to the logical structure of a computer program.

ARABIC NUMERAL—the worldwide standard for representing numbers (0123456789). Of Indian origin, but often called "Arabic" as they came to Europe via the Middle East.

AXIOM—a mathematical assumption that is so obvious that it need not be proved.

BASE—the number of values that can appear in a column when writing out a number. We usually work to base 10, with values 0 to 9 in the first column before starting a new one.

BINARY—numbers written to base 2, used by computers. The number 37 is binary 100101.

BOOLEAN [ALGEBRA]—a symbolic approach to logic. It combines values of "true" or "false" using the terms AND, OR, and NOT.

CALCULUS—the mathematics of change. Calculus comes in two forms—differential calculus (which describes how one variable changes with another) and integral calculus (which combines changing values to, for example, work out areas of shapes). The two forms are inverses of each other.

CARDINALITY—the size of a set. Two sets have the same cardinality if each member of one set can be paired off with a member of the other set with no members of either left over.

CHECKSUM—a digit used to check that values in a number have been typed correctly. The last digit of a credit card number is calculated from the other numbers, providing a checksum.

COMPOSITE NUMBER—a positive integer that is made by multiplying two smaller positive integers. It can be divided by one, itself, and at least one other positive integer.

CONGRUENT—geometrical shapes that have the same size and shape.

CONSTANT—a value in an equation or expression that is a fixed number. E.g., in the equation $3x + 5 = 0$, the value 5 is a constant.

COSINE—the cosine of an angle is the ratio in a right-angled triangle of the length of the side adjacent to the angle (other than the hypotenuse) to the hypotenuse.

ELLIPSE—the shape produced by drawing around two focal points such that the sum of the distances of a point on the circumference from the two focal points is constant, or one of the shapes produced by slicing through a cone. A circle is a special case of an ellipse where the focal points overlap.

ENCRYPTION—the mechanism for concealing values (numbers or letters) by a mathematical process to keep those values secret. The reverse process, uncovering the values, is "decryption."

EQUATION—a mathematical structure with two parts, where the value of one part is equal to the other. Each part may contain any combination of mathematical terms.

EXPONENT—when a variable or number is raised to a power, the number representing that power is the exponent. For example, in the equation $E=mc^2$, the number 2 is the exponent of c.

EXPRESSION—a combination of constants, variables, functions, and so on, with symbols showing their relationships.

FACTOR—any one of a set of numbers that are multiplied together to make another number.

FACTORIAL—a sequence of decreasing sized integers multiplied together, represented by ! For example, 5! is $5 \times 4 \times 3 \times 2 \times 1$.

FIELD—a property that has a defined value for each point in space and time.

FRACTION—a part of an integer. Rational fractions can be represented as a ratio of integers, such as $1/2$ and $37/159$, or decimals such as 0.5 and 0.2327044 . . . Irrational fractions can only be represented as decimals.

FUNCTION—a shorthand way to write out a mathematical calculation that can be applied to any value. So $f(x)$ applies the function f—anything from "multiply by 2" to a complex formula—to whatever x is.

GATE—a logical building block of a computer, which switches electrical currents according to a Boolean operator such as AND, OR, or NOT.

GOLDEN RATIO—a ratio where the ratio of the larger number to the smaller value is the same as the ratio of the sum of the two numbers to the larger value. This appears in nature and has been used by many artists, who believe it produces visually pleasing arrangements.

GROUP—a set with a mechanism for combining any two elements of the set to produce a third. For example, the integers form a group with addition as the mechanism.

HYPERBOLA—a mathematical curve like a pair of letter U shapes (with the two arms heading away from each other on each U) and with their points facing each other. One of the shapes produced by slicing through a pair of cones, placed point to point.

HYPOTENUSE—the side of a right triangle that is opposite the right angle.

INTEGER—a whole number such as −3, 1, or 55.

IRRATIONAL NUMBER—a number that cannot be made up of a ratio of two whole numbers. The square root of 2 is irrational.

LOGIC GATE—*see* gate.

MAINFRAME—a large central computer, usually requiring special environmental conditions and often shared between many simultaneous users.

MANIFOLD—a multidimensional geometric structure locally analogous to traditional "flat" Euclidian geometry. The surface of a 3D object such as a sphere, for example, is a 2D manifold

because any small part of it resembles a flat plane.

MATRIX—a rectangular collection of numbers in columns and rows.

MODULUS—when we use a system of numbers that reaches a value and goes back to the start, the modulus is the maximum value. For example, on a 12-hour clock the modulus is 12—after counting up to 12, the next value is 1.

NUMBER LINE—an imaginary line that is like an infinite ruler running from −∞ at one end to ∞ at the other with zero in the middle.

OPERATOR—a mechanism that is used to apply a function or change to one or more variables simultaneously. Simple operators include the Boolean operators AND, OR, and NOT, but operators can also apply complex formulae.

PARABOLA—a mathematical curve shaped like a U but with the arms heading away from each other. One of the shapes produced by slicing through a cone.

PI—a mathematical constant, pi (π) is the circumference of a circle divided by its diameter. The number begins 3.14159 . . .

POLYNOMIAL—an expression that only contains constants and variables, which can only be added, subtracted, or multiplied.

PRIME NUMBER—a positive integer that is bigger than 1, divisible only by 1 and itself.

PROOF—a collection of logical steps starting from axioms and making a step-by-step progression to a conclusion.

QUADRATIC EQUATION—an equation in the form $ax^2 + bx + c = 0$.

RADIAN—a unit used for measuring an angle or amount of rotation; an alternative to degrees—360 degrees is 2π radians.

RATIO—a ratio describes the relative size of two numbers. For example, 3:1, a ratio of 3 to 1, indicates that the first number is three times bigger than the second. Similar to a rational fraction, where a:b is equivalent to a/b.

SCALAR—a value described by a simple number. For example, speed is a scalar.

SET—a collection of numbers, objects, or concepts. Sets provide the foundation of arithmetic, and much of mathematics can be built from them.

SIMULTANEOUS EQUATIONS—two or more equations that can be combined to provide information about the behavior of multiple variables.

SINE—the sine of an angle is the ratio in a right triangle of the length of the side opposite the angle to the hypotenuse.

SQUARE ROOT—the number that, multiplied by itself, produces the value of which it is a square root. The square root of 9 is 3, as $3 \times 3 = 9$.

TANGENT—a straight line drawn just touching a curve, and which has the same slope as the curve at that point.

THEOREM—a statement that has been proven with a formal mathematical proof.

TRANSCENDENTAL—a number, such as π, that cannot be calculated by a finite formula.

VARIABLE—a value in an equation or expression that can be changed to any value. For example, in the equation $3x + 5 = 0$, the value x is a variable.

VECTOR—a value that has both size and direction. For example, velocity is a vector as it combines a speed with the direction of that speed.

VENN DIAGRAM—a diagram devised by mathematician John Venn to show the logical relationships between different sets.

VERTEX—a point where the edges of a shape meet.

FURTHER READING

Books

Acheson, David. *1089 and All That.* Oxford: Oxford University Press, 2010.

A refreshing exploration of the joy of mathematics, from chaos theory to the Indian rope trick.

Aczel, Amir. *Finding Zero.* New York: St. Martin's Press, 2015.

A personal odyssey to discover the origins of zero.

Bellos, Alex. *Alex's Adventures in Numberland.* London: Bloomsbury, 2011.

A confection of mathematical experiences, stretching from casinos to the world's fastest mental calculators.

Blastland, Michael, and Andrew Dilnot. *The Tiger that Isn't.* London: Profile Books, 2007.

A wonderful exploration of how statistics and numbers in general have been used to mislead.

Cheng, Eugenia. *Cakes, Custard and Category Theory.* London: Profile Books, 2015.

A journey through the mind of the mathematician, incorporating Cheng's specialty, category theory.

Christian, Brian, and Tom Griffiths. *Algorithms to Live By.* William Collins, 2016.

Takes the concept of algorithms and shows how the math can be used in real life.

Clegg, Brian. *Are Numbers Real?* New York: St. Martin's Press, 2016.

A history of mathematics, showing how it has gradually become more detached from reality.

Clegg, Brian. *A Brief History of Infinity.* London: Constable and Robinson, 2003.

A history of the most mind-boggling aspect of mathematics, through the people involved in developing the concept.

Clegg, Brian. *Dice World.* London: Icon Books, 2013.

The influence of randomness and probability on our world and lives.

Clegg, Brian, and Oliver Pugh. *Introducing Infinity.* London: Icon Books, 2012.

An entertaining graphic guide to the concept of infinity.

Du Sautoy, Marcus. *The Number Mysteries*. London: Fourth Estate, 2011.

Balances five of the great unsolved mathematical mysteries with the practical applications of math in real life.

Gardner, Martin. *Mathematical Puzzles and Diversions*. Chicago: University of Chicago Press, 1961.

The classic book of recreational mathematics and its follow-up titles—including the latest, *My Best Mathematical and Logic Puzzles* (2016)—are still superbly entertaining.

Gessen, Masha. *Perfect Rigour: A Genius and the Mathematical Breathrough of the Century*. London: Icon Books, 2011.

The story of Russian mathematician Grigori Perelman, who solved one of the great mathematical challenges, the Poincaré conjecture, only to drop out of mathematics altogether and turn down a $1 million prize.

Gleick, James. *Chaos: Making a New Science*. London: Vintage, 1988.

A very journalistic and readable book on the development of chaos theory.

Hayes, Brian. *Foolproof*. Cambridge, Massachusetts: MIT Press, 2017.

A range of articles on fascinating math topics, from random walks to the story of the mathematician Gauss's feat of adding 100 numbers instantly.

Hofstadter, Douglas. *Gödel, Escher, Bach*. New York: Basic Books, 1979.

Classic, and to many mystifying, book on the essence of mathematics and cognition, but if it works for you, superb.

Livio, Mario. *The Equation that Couldn't Be Solved*. New York: Simon and Schuster, 2005.

A surprisingly engaging history of algebra and the development of group theory.

MacCormick, John. *Nine Algorithms that Changed the Future*. Princeton: Princeton University Press, 2012.

An exploration of some of the key algorithms that shape our online world, from Google's PageRank to the cryptography that keeps data safe.

Mackenzie, Dana. *The Story of Mathematics in 24 Equations*. London: Modern Books, 2018.

Uses 24 important equations through history to show how mathematics has developed.

Nicholson, Matt. *When Computing Got Personal*. Bristol, UK: Matt Publishing, 2014.

An excellent history of personal computing.

Parker, Matt. *Things to Do and Make in the Fourth Dimension*. London: Penguin, 2015.

Stand-up mathematician Parker presents a range of recreational math, from interesting ways to divide pizza to the importance of the 196,883rd dimension.

Petzold, Charles. *Code*. Redmond, Washington: Microsoft Press, 2000.

Using familiar aspects of language, this Windows expert uncovers the inner workings of computer programs for the general reader.

Scheinerman, Edward. *The Mathematics Lover's Companion*. Newhaven, Connecticut: Yale University Press, 2017.

Takes on 23 of the more interesting subjects of mathematics, from prime numbers to infinity, in some depth but still readable.

Singh, Simon. *Fermat's Last Theorem*. London: Fourth Estate, 1997.

The remarkable story of how a mathematical puzzle posed in the seventeenth century dominated the life of a twentieth-century mathematician.

Stewart, Ian. *The Great Mathematical Problems*. London: Profile Books, 2013.

A collection of some of the greatest challenges to face mathematicians through history.

Stewart, Ian. *Professor Stewart's Cabinet of Mathematical Curiosities*. London: Profile Books, 2010.

The best of mathematician Stewart's compendia of puzzles, odd mathematical facts, and more.

Stewart, Ian. *Significant Figures*. London: Profile Books, 2017.

The lives of many great mathematicians.

Stipp, David. *A Most Elegant Equation*. New York: Basic Books, 2018.

Introduces Euler's remarkable equation $ei\pi + 1 = 0$ and explains why each of its main components is so important.

Watson, Ian. *The Universal Machine*. New York: Copernicus Books, 2012.

Pulls together the whole history of computing in an approachable form.

Websites

MacTutor History of Mathematics

Old-fashioned style but a huge number of biographies and history of mathematics topics

www-history.mcs.st-and.ac.uk

Mathigon

Well-designed, engaging tutorials in mathematics

mathigon.org

The Prime Pages

Everything and anything on prime numbers

primes.utm.edu

Quanta Magazine: Mathematics

Wide-ranging articles on the latest developments in mathematics

quantamagazine.org/tag/mathematics/

The Top 10 Martin Gardner Scientific American Articles

Great math writing from the king of recreational mathematics

blogs.scientificamerican.com/guest-blog/the-top-10-martin-gardner-scientific-american-articles/

Wolfram MathWorld

Wide-ranging mathematical resources from the leading mathematical software company

mathworld.wolfram.com

INDEX

ABOUT THE AUTHORS

Brian Clegg
With MAs in Natural Sciences from Cambridge University and Operational Research from Lancaster University in the UK, Brian Clegg (www.brianclegg.net) worked at British Airways for 17 years before setting up his own creativity-training company. He now is a full-time science writer with over 30 titles published, from *A Brief History of Infinity* to *The Quantum Age*, and writes for publications from the *Wall Street Journal* to *BBC Focus* magazine. He lives in Wiltshire, England.

Dr. Peet Morris
Peet Morris is a lecturer and researcher at the University of Oxford, and also an Oxford alumnus (Keble and Wolfson Colleges). He works in various fields, including Computational Linguistics (artificial intelligence), Software Engineering, Statistics, and also Experimental Psychology.

ACKNOWLEDGMENTS

Brian: For Gillian, Rebecca, and Chelsea.
Peet: For Harriet, and also my mathematical nephew, Ben.

With thanks to Tom Kitch and Angela Koo for setting this interesting challenge and helping bring it into being. A special thanks to Martin Gardner for his *Mathematical Puzzles and Diversions*, which showed that math could be fun.

Picture credits

The publisher would like to thank the following for permission to reproduce copyright material:

Alamy: photographer unknown 19 (right); Granger, NYC 121 (left)

LANL: 119 (top left), 121 (right). Unless otherwise indicated, this information has been authored by an employee or employees of the Los Alamos National Security, LLC (LANS), operator of the Los Alamos National Laboratory under Contract No. DE-AC52-06NA25396 with the U.S. Department of Energy. The U.S. Government has rights to use, reproduce, and distribute this information. The public may copy and use this information without charge, provided that this Notice and any statement of authorship are reproduced on all copies. Neither the Government nor LANS makes any warranty, express or implied, or assumes any liability or responsibility for the use of this information.

Shutterstock: Ron Dale 16 (top left); Tupungato 16 (top right), 18 (left); Peter Hermes Furian 16 (bottom right); Prachaya Roekdeethaweesab 19 (left); Georgios Kollidas 50 (bottom right); Nicku 51 (bottom left); Zita 51 (bottom right); Chiakto 84 (bottom left), 86 (left); Nicku 84 (bottom right), 86 (right); Rozilynn Mitchell 118 (top right); Bobb Klissourski 119 (bottom left)

Wellcome Collection (both CC BY 4.0): 17 (top right), 18 (right)

Wikimedia: Mark A. Wilson (Wilson44691, Department of Geology, the College of Wooster) (CC BY-SA 4.0) 52 (left)

All reasonable efforts have been made to trace copyright holders and to obtain their permission for the use of copyright material. The publisher apologizes for any errors or omissions in the list above and will gratefully incorporate any corrections in future reprints if notified.